In Mind of Johnson

For Jane
and
For Sian

In Mind of Johnson

A Study of Johnson The Rambler

PHILIP DAVIS

The University of Georgia Press
Athens

Published in the United States of America
in 1989 by the University of Georgia Press,
Athens, Georgia 30602

First published in Great Britain in 1989
by The Athlone Press Ltd, 44 Bedford Row, London WC1R 4LY

Printed in Great Britain

Library of Congress Cataloging in Publication Data

Davis, Philip (Philip Maurice)
    In mind of Johnson: a study of Johnson the rambler / Philip Davis.
        p.   cm.
    Bibliography: p.
    Includes index.
    ISBN 0-8203-1054-9
    1. Johnson, Samuel, 1709–1784—Criticism and interpretation.
    2. Rambler (London, England: 1750)   I. Title.
    PR3534.D34 1989   88-4811
    828'.609—dc19   CIP

Contents

Acknowledgements   vii

Introduction   1

Chapter One   The Life of the Author and his Writings   4

I Dubin's Life of Johnson   4
II 'Almost every man... will be found to have enlisted
    under some leader'   10
III Discoursing like an angel, living like a man   21
IV Concluding: 'The System of Life'   42

Chapter Two   'You Tossed and Gored Several Persons'   44

I Johnson the Old Bear...   44
II 'Suffering is no duty'   60
III 'Lest we should think ourselves too soon entitled to
    the mournful privileges of irresistible misery'   76

Chapter Three   On the Strength of Limitation (1):
                      Johnson's Realism   97
I Boswell's Dilemma   97
II Johnson's fallen 'angelick counsel'   104
III Conclusion: On settling down – the life of limitation   123

Chapter Four   On the Strength of Limitation (2):
                     Johnson's Practical Art   130

I Practical Reasoning   130
II *Rasselas:* in memory of *The Rambler*   148

Chapter Five   An Anglican Saint?   172

I 'The right path... at an equal distance between the
    extremes of error'   172
II A Thought-Experiment   181
III Johnson's Anglicanism (i): of prayers and silence   198
IV Johnson's Anglicanism (ii): when Johnson said 'No' –
Beyond Negative Capability   208

V Johnson's Anglicanism (iii): The ordinary mystery of the
  Church of England 217
VI Conclusion: A Religious Writer – his limits and endings 228

Chapter Six 'In which Nothing is Concluded'? 243
I 'He runs the great circle, and is still at home'? 243
II 'What about religious people?' – Johnson and the *Essay
  on Man* 252
III Transmutations: not Pope but Butler 265
IV *King Lear* and after 280
V Conclusion 296

Endnotes 303

Index 315

Source Acknowledgements

The author and the publishers are grateful to the following for
permission to include copyright material:

Yale University Press for extracts from *The Yale Edition of the Works
of Samuel Johnson* and from Sir Joshua Reynolds, *Discourses on Art*,
edited by R.R. Wark; Oxford University Press for extracts from
Boswell's *Life of Johnson*, edited by R.W. Chapman and revised by
J.D. Fleeman, Hester Lynch Piozzi, *Anecdotes of the Late Samuel
Johnson* printed with William Shaw's *Memoirs of Dr Johnson*, edited
by A. Sherbo in the Oxford English Memoirs and Travels series,
Johnson's *Lives of the Poets* in The World's Classics edition, and
Adam Smith, *Theory of Moral Sentiments*, edited by D.D. Raphael
and A.L. Macfie; J.M. Dent and Sons for extracts from John Wain's
translation of Johnson's Latin poem 'Know Thyself' in his *Johnson on
Johnson*.

Acknowledgements

The expression of thanks is the only piece of writing in this book which is to me simply a pleasure. It is good to be able to record in print the names of people who have helped and befriended me, and I must first mention Louise Coley, Sarah Coley, Tim Langley, Dorothy Pearl, Laurence Pearl, Isobel Rivers, Jon Silkin and *Stand Magazine*. I hope that Stanley Middleton, J.H. Prynne and Wil Sanders will recognize their very different influences and not be sorry for their part in all this. At Liverpool Professors Philip Edwards and Kenneth Muir have given me much appreciated support. I have been extremely fortunate to have Bernard Beatty and Brian Nellist not only as valued colleagues but also as personal friends: they would be jewels in the forehead of any university. I am very grateful to Brian Southam of Athlone for his loyal and committed concern for my work. If this book is of any interest to the serious common reader, the sort of person I would have liked to please is my father-in-law Bryan Mooney. Stephen Gill has given me more morale-sustaining encouragement than he knows, which is why I thank him – and all these people – now.

As I have been rereading this book in proof I see that its autobiographical subject matter is really what I have rather roughly called the second stage of life. In that stage I owe everything to my wife Jane and daughter Sian. Some personal words of Stanley Middleton's come back to my mind and apply now to my own case: I was lucky to marry the right woman. This book is dedicated to Jane and Sian Davis, with love. On becoming a parent myself, I have increasingly begun to realize even more powerfully how much my own parents, Sheila and Sid Davis, have done for me during the long first stage of life and for all my family since: as my wife has said to me, what I have done best has been due to them.

Philip Davis
Liverpool

Introduction

The title of this book is taken from the words of Gerald Hamilton, quoted by Boswell, on the effect that the death of Johnson had upon those who had known and needed him as a living presence: 'He has made a chasm, which not only nothing can fill up, but which nothing has a tendency to fill up. Johnson is dead. Let us go to the next best: – there is nobody; no man can be said to put you in mind of Johnson.' I have written this book in order to try to be truly 'in mind of Johnson'.

Within that task I have also had three general purposes, which I shall merely summarize.

1. Literature and Personality

I started this work wanting to know what, in his life and writings, Samuel Johnson stood for as a human being. Matthew Arnold wrote that literature 'humanizes knowledge', but humanizing also involved disinterestedness and (as Eliot was to put it) impersonality. In this book I defend interestedness and personality as the truly humanizing forces. I take one of literature's largest and most robust personalities, Samuel Johnson – not least because in Johnson the recognized inadequacy of human knowledge necessitates the employment of other human resources, beyond or beneath pure knowledge, for the continuance of both living and writing. I thought I could recover a sense of the meaning of the man from his written words. For I do believe that we treat literature too professionally, too idolatrously and too alienatedly if we consider it as a set of autonomous, coded texts transcending the existence of their own authors and readers alike. Johnson is above all a writer who still insists on his presence as an ordinary man. He is also, of course, an extraordinary individual precisely in being committed to speaking against mere individualism as such. Chapter One, 'The Life of the Author and his Writings', is an argument for a complicated but real relationship between Johnson's writing and Johnson's life, for all his distaste for autobiographical confessions.

Under this heading I am also concerned to personalize Arnold's ideas about the use and purpose of 'culture'. To put it quite simply, I have concentrated on Johnson's moral essays in *The Rambler* not merely because they have not really received prolonged critical attention but also because I am interested in the idea of writing as a form of practical advice about how to live. In Chapter One I show how Johnson's method functions at the level of 'reminding': his general style situates itself between his own memory and that of his readers, proceeding out of the first and seeking to reawaken the second. Chapter Two is an introduction to the difficulties of recovering an eighteenth-century man and also a consideration of what lost arts of being Johnson may serve to remind us of. I ask throughout this book: What is the point of *The Rambler*, what help can it give, what help did Johnson expect it to provide?

2. Literature and 'Letters'

Chapter Two is also part of my second purpose: namely, to revalue the values of some nineteenth-century thinkers, such as Arnold and Keats, who have indirectly caused Johnson's importance to become obscured. I am particularly concerned to challenge the narrow, transcendent account (offered by some post-Romantics) of what 'literature' is . I prefer the older term 'letters' in order to allow back into the mainstream of writing the tradition of discursive prose such as *The Rambler* itself exemplifies. Nowadays such prose has become split off into literary criticism or philosophy as ventures technically separate from 'literature itself'. Again, all this has obvious relation to the idea of writing having a practical bearing upon the conduct of ordinary, non-specialist existence. In Chapters Three and Four there is a close consideration of what is at stake in that neglected form of writing we call discursive prose, and all the chapters in this book include comparisons with prose-writing in novels.

3. Literature and Belief

Above all, as I have said, I have been seeking to discover what Johnson stood for: what explicit and implicit beliefs and forms of knowledge were embodied in him. I take Johnson to be the very opposite of all Keats meant by 'Negative Capability': the Hebraic struggle of positive incapability, as it were, is what Johnson undertakes, prizing truth of belief above intimation of imagination. And yet in Chapter Five I also judge Johnson's Anglicanism to be a rare form of mature balance – between struggle and accommodation, between using and enjoying the world. Because of Johnson's belief, I oppose Samuel Johnson to, say, Samuel Beckett; although Beckett said: 'It's Johnson, always Johnson, who is with me. And if I follow any tradition, it is his', it is not his. On the contrary, it is Johnson's resistence to Beckett-like things within him (scepticism, ennui, a sense of nothing) that constitutes the value of his tradition. In the final chapter I try to show how we, plagued by modernism and its discontents, can still 'take' Johnson as a form of help, not least because of his ability to translate religion into ordinary living.

'Johnson is always profound,' wrote Arthur Murphy in 1792, 'and of course gives the fatigue of thinking.' Boswell says of Johnson: 'He delighted to express familiar thoughts in philosophical language; being in this the reverse of Socrates, who, it was said, reduced philosophy to the simplicity of common life.' Johnson himself, speaking of the difficulty of consecutive reasoning, puts the following question: 'When the radical idea branches out into parallel ramifications, how can a consecutive series be formed of senses in their nature collateral?' He also says, in defence against the charge of using difficult words, 'He that thinks with more extent than another will want words of larger meaning; he that thinks with more subtilty will seek for terms of more nice discrimination.' None of this makes Johnson, or thinking about Johnson, easy. Yet he is, I believe, vital to an understanding of ordinary life, for he not only brings seriousness down to the ordinary world, but also raises ordinary living to the utmost seriousness. Johnson needs his common readers, and we need him.

CHAPTER ONE

The Life of the Author and his Writings

I *Dubin's Life of Johnson*

Every morning, as he shaved, he would mutter to himself in the mirror, making noises and gestures from unhappy memory. This showing of loose ends upset his wife, who could hear him from the bedroom. He would sometimes realize, remember her distress at it, and shut up:

> though he had more than once reminded her that Montaigne himself used to groan 'Confounded fool' in the morning mirror. And Dr. Samuel Johnson was a noisy beehive of crackpot mannerisms.
>
> 'I'm not married to them.'
>
> 'Montaigne's motto was "What do I know?" He was a wise man. And Johnson – "winking and blinking," Blake described him – though he looked like a mad hatter, inspired men to reason and courage. He had learned from life.'
>
> 'It's your voice I hear, not theirs.'

This, at once comic and serious, comes from a novel: *Dubin's Lives* by Bernard Malamud. Dubin, the man who shaves, mutters and quotes, is a professional biographer, and just the sort of man to wonder about Yeats's saying that the Poet is utterly different from the man he is when he sits down to breakfast. This day as he shaves, Dubin knows he has to write the opening sentence to his new life of D.H. Lawrence. He already hears what the critics will say: 'Who needs another life of David Herbert Lawrence?'. For Lawrence

> was so vastly written about – someone had said second to Shakespeare; or if not second, third, Samuel Johnson intervening – therefore who needs more by William Dubin?

Why bother? With what justification?

This present work is neither novel nor biography, but it is another book about Samuel Johnson. I would like to be no more specific than this: it is a book about what I think it meant to be Johnson or about what being Johnson stood for. For I do think people stand for things – for ways which if they cannot be made explicit may be made incarnate.

But this book on Johnson is written at a time when many professional Johnson scholars are complaining at the damage done by an over-concentration on Johnson's personality at the expense of his sheer literary achievement. They call this Boswell's hijack of Johnson's reputation: the biographer making Johnson into a mere 'character'. Likewise, too many writers on Johnson, they complain, hijack Johnson by presuming that *they* are like him. More scholarly ways are called for to combat that emotional promiscuity which blurs so many important distinctions.

However, I favour blurring. I would like to feel only as free as does Malamud when he thinks about Dubin – or thinks, through Dubin, about what literary people are doing with their lives. But – it will be objected – Dubin is Malamud's own creation, while Johnson is not mine — or should not be. To miss the distinction is to judge everything to be equally fictional – Boswell's Johnson as much as Malamud's Dubin or Dubin's Lawrence. Yet actually I do not think that – that everything is equally fictional. On the contrary, I think that powers currently associated with novelists are not quite as fictional as we now suppose; that certain powers of thought, intuition and imaginative memory, at present protected by being within novels, could be further freed by being less defensively categorized. We could risk using the novelist's powers in situations which, though analogous to situations in novels, are not themselves fictional. For I guess that Malamud himself did not get Dubin from fiction, did not simply invent him, but found him from his own experience of life. Is it only novelists who are free to move in thought from one realm to another?

For example: I think Malamud would have his biographer interested in *why* Johnson suffered from convulsive tics, 'a noisy beehive of crackpot mannerisms'. For Johnson would mutter to himself even in company, nervously touch posts and keep count as he walked along, perform strange ritualistic movements with his hands and feet:

Sometimes he would make the back part of his heels to touch, sometimes the extremity of his toes, as if endeavouring to form a triangle, or some geometrical figure, and as for his gestures with his hands, they were equally as strange; sometimes he would hold them up with some of his fingers bent, as if he had been seized with the cramp, and sometimes at his Breast in motion like those of a jockey on full speed; and often would he lift them up as high as he could stretch over his head, for some minutes.[1]

This great man, we might remind ourselves, looked like an idiot. We *might* remind ourselves, but we do not often in conventional studies of books and writers – though Johnson has always tempted people to wicked 'extra-literary' speculation: perhaps because of Boswell, but also perhaps because he has always seemed so much more than just a writer. None the less, for the most part, when an author is dead and has become a safe classic, all the thoughts and doubts and amazement that people had about him while he was alive and his work in progress die too, become lost as a way of thinking, or at best anthologized and settled down into so-called proper historical perspective. We might try to recover what it might be like to be with Johnson and read Johnson while he was alive and real and strong and weak; but we do not, and I think that we should – at least try.

Johnson's twitching, then. Boswell diagnosed St Vitus's dance, but he also thought that in talking to himself Johnson was often muttering prayers. Bishop Percy thought, or wanted to think, that this last was nonsense: Johnson's short-sightedness prompted him to compose sentences in his head; his muttering was his writing practice.[2] But I think Dubin would have seized upon Sir Joshua Reynolds's explanation, which Boswell also printed:

> Those motions or tricks of Dr Johnson are improperly called convulsions. He could sit motionless, when he was told to do so, as well as any other man; my opinion is that it proceeded from a habit which he had indulged himself in, of accompanying his thoughts with certain untoward actions, and those actions always appeared to me as if they were meant to reprobate some part of his past conduct.[3]

The twitching was that mind's unwitting revelation of its own loose ends, as though unable entirely to contain itself. That is a sort of psychological interpretation, though there were also, as we have just noted, interpretations in physiological, religious and literary terms. Of course, instead of thinking about the relative claims of these different categories in life, we could simply erect another category and call all this just a matter of biography, nothing to do with Johnson's work. But I do not think that will do, and I think Reynolds's anecdote suggests why it will not. In an individual as powerful as Johnson was, everything seems to hang together even in his divisions and compartments. And what Reynolds's almost novelistic piece of biography suggests is this: a man of mind so powerful as to render unstable within itself the very boundaries between inside and outside, as well as between past and present. Hence the redoubled need of that mind to establish categories all the more securely on second thought; hence Johnson's own angry reaction to people who acted oddly in public. But at some deep level Johnson did not know where he was, and perhaps this is characteristic of a deep thinker. For the mind does not experience itself or its thoughts as simply, safely taking place within itself. Words form and get blurted out, necessarily.

Johnson, said Dubin, 'had learned from life'. It seems a poor cliché. But what Malamud is thinking is: 'Has Dubin learned from life? Has Dubin learned from the lives of others? And what is the relation between the two?' That is the idea which the novelist embodies in a character and a story. And, in that, perhaps the novelist could have remembered what the biographer also must have feared – Johnson's own warnings in *The Rambler* against living life at second hand in merely self-justifying circles:

> The great fault of men of learning is still, that they offend against this rule, and appear willing to study any thing rather than themselves. (*The Rambler*, 24)

> A student may easily exhaust his life in comparing divines and moralists, without any practical regard to morality or religion; he may be learning not to live, but to reason. (*The Rambler*, 87)

> Many who compare the actions, and ascertain the characters of ancient heroes, let their own days glide away without examination. (*The Rambler*, 180)

'Their *own* days' lay under their very noses yet were not the subject of their eyes' attention: 'any thing' instead. So they 'let their own days glide away', not knowing that those *days* were their *lives*, unowned; days so easy to lose with imperceptible gradualness, that the lack of fear is itself frightening. Words such as 'glide away' hit home as they

pass. Before, in Reynolds's eyes, Johnson's thoughts found
themselves inadvertently blurted out as words that others noticed;
here the words are deliberately blurted out as thoughts that others
have neglected or repressed and must now own. Others such as even
Dubin or Malamud.

What happens in *The Rambler* through sheer language occurs in
Dubin's Lives through language made into character. So much of the
power of the *Rambler* essays seems to be in memory of specific fears
behind them and in imagination of readers' fears before them. Their
generalizing weight presses for a particular context, a specific use in
which they may be taken. Where they come from in Johnson and how
we use them in ourselves may be the realization of their fullest
meaning. The essays are short, bitten-off pieces, concentrated
catalysts; that is why we need a novelist's mind to do justice to the
meaning of their received expansion back within the life out of which
they have been distilled. For Malamud is testing *himself*, as realist
novelist, through Dubin, by analogy: What happens to your own life
as you write about lives? What is literature for? What is the point of
having literary heroes? How does writing stand to living, to the reality
of its own subject matter? Indeed, is even to ask these questions of
writing in writing to describe a vicious circle equivalent to Dubin's
own? These seem to me to be questions that Johnson throws up too.
What the novelist does is enable the thinking to be felt immediately in
humanly embodied terms, giving us, as it were, the imagined human
biography of an idea.

Let us borrow this novelist's attitude for a while, if only to be less
adamant than professional men of learning sometimes are about
compartments: about necessarily keeping separate the realms of
'fiction', 'biography', 'literary criticism', 'autobiography', 'language',
'real experience', and so on. For otherwise, in Johnson's own words,
we 'may be learning not to live, but to reason'. I propose that we do
not worry too much initially about daring to blur the boundaries
between life and art. Johnson will always make us worry about them
later.

So, for example: Samuel Johnson was a deeply religious man and
an irregular attender at church. Like the biographer, the novelist
would be interested in that characteristic, apparent contradiction; the
way it is both surprising and unsurprising. Here, like a sub-text to a
Rambler essay, is Johnson's own private account of it to a friend:

> I am convinced I ought to be present at divine service more
> frequently than I am; but the *provocations* given by ignorant

and affected preachers too often disturb the mental calm which otherwise would succeed to prayer. I am apt to whisper to myself on such occasions – How can this illiterate fellow dream of fixing attention, after we have been listening to the sublimest truths, conveyed in the most chaste and exalted language.

But this time the guilty pressure behind the blurting out is rationally converted in front of it:

> *Take notice, however –* though I make this confession respecting *myself,* I do not mean to *recommend the fastidiousness* that led me to exchange congregational for solitary worship.

So here, in contrition, he exchanges solitary confession for social re-evaluation: 'I do not mean to recommend . . . '. Too learned to go to church: you can feel Johnson wincing in the mirror; you can imagine Malamud's Dubin thinking of Tolstoy giving up writing the *Anna Karenina*s to write simple religious fables for peasants instead. Here is what one of Johnson's latest biographers has to say of the passage:

> The word 'fastidiousness' is typical. For of course he is trying to remind himself – as a part of him never ceases to do in other contexts – of the futility of the attenuated tastes and of gestures of disdain ('elegance refined into impatience') of intellectuals who forget, for the moment, how completely and helplessly they share the collective 'doom of man' ('Nor think the doom of man reversed for thee,' as he tells the young scholar in *The Vanity of Human Wishes*).[4]

I am sure that, like Johnson *and* like Dubin, Walter Jackson Bate there is thinking of himself. Johnson's words have stuck in his mind and activated memories there ('intellectuals who forget . . . '). And I think that is the reality of reading about which professional critics, although they write so much so technically, are almost always silent. In someone's *life* the questions – What is the use of learning? What is the distinction between learning to reason and learning to live? What is the propriety of identification? – become more real *and* more blurred than writers about books commonly allow. As George Eliot puts it, there is a roar on the other side of silence. Johnson, I believe, encourages us to hear that silent inner roar and try to speak back to it.

*

II   *'Almost every man... will be found to have enlisted himself under some leader' (The Rambler, 164)*

I want to attempt two things, now, in this section. First, to imagine, through the person of Sir Joshua Reynolds, what it is really like to learn from, and identify with, the thinking of a great man. Second, to show Johnson himself supporting sympathetic identification in reading and writing, as well as in living.

Sir Joshua Reynolds, thinking about Johnson's influence on himself, concluded that Johnson had formed his mind for him and that this, although in one sense extraordinary, was also so far from shameful as to be normal:

> In reality, indeed, it appears to me, that a man must begin by the study of others. Thus Bacon became a great thinker, by entering into and making himself master of the thoughts of other men.[5]

Study, thought Reynolds, is the art of using other men's minds – just as this present work, for example, is an attempt to get to know Johnson's. Reynolds concluded that he had used Johnson's mind, in a general rather than a particular way, in order to write his own *Discourses on Art:* 'The observations which he made on poetry, on life, and on every thing about us, I applied to our art; with what success, others must judge'; 'Those very people whom he has brought to think rightly will occasionally criticize the opinions of their master when he nods. But we should always recollect that it is he himself who taught us and enabled us to do it.'[6] For not only did Reynolds learn from Johnson, he also made that process of learning from another the very subject matter of his *Discourses* to the students of his newly formed Royal Academy:

> Invention is one of the great marks of genius; but if we consult experience, we shall find, that it is by being conversant with the inventions of others, that we learn to invent; as by reading the thoughts of others we learn to think.
>
> Whoever has so far formed his taste, as to be able to relish and feel the beauties of the great masters, has gone a great way in his study; for, merely from a consciousness of this relish of the right, the mind swells with an inward pride, and is almost as powerfully affected, as if it had itself produced what it admires... What is learned in this manner from the works of others becomes really our own.[7]

Boswell reports Johnson's admiration for Reynolds's *Discourses:* 'He observed one day of a passage in them, "I think I might as well have said this myself.'[8] We do not know the passage, and there are many candidates. My own guess would be that in which Reynolds attacks the idea of art as 'gift' or 'magic' of the imagination, in much the same spirit as Johnson himself attacked wonder as the mere effect of ignorance.[9] But I also offer the Reynolds passage above for showing what such aggression against the extraordinary was really in defence of: a tradition of common human identification from artist to recipient and back again.

Reynolds's sixth discourse, from which our passage is taken, was delivered in December 1774; Boswell refers to Johnson's remarks on Reynolds as being made in June 1784. Between the two dates Johnson set down in his *Lives of the Poets* critical touchstones which had obviously been forming themselves in his mind for years beforehand. Thus on some lines from Congreve:

> He who reads those lines enjoys for a moment the powers of a poet; he feels what he remembers to have felt before, but he feels it with great increase of sensibility; he recognizes a familiar image, but meets it again amplified and expanded, embellished with beauty, and enlarged with majesty.

The lines are most especially these:

> 'Tis dreadful
> How reverend is the face of this tall pile;
> Whose ancient pillars rear their marble heads,
> To bear aloft its arch'd and ponderous roof,
> By its own weight made stedfast and immoveable;
> Looking tranquillity! It strikes an awe
> And terror on my aching sight; the tombs
> And monumental caves of death look cold,
> And shoot a chillness to my trembling heart.[10]

The architecture of Johnson's own mind must have felt to him as if it were like that: the powerful solidity of its yet precarious form ('Looking tranquillity') raised still to contain beneath and within it thoughts of its own mortality and weakness. In 1749 Johnson had written in *The Vanity of Human Wishes*:

> For why did Wolsey near the steeps of fate,
> On weak foundations raise th' enormous weight?
> Why but to sink beneath misfortune's blow,
> With louder ruin to the gulfs below?   (125–8)

How could that mind, which could hardly contain itself, raise itself to express itself? By the security of leaning on, borrowing, 'familiar images' which themselves then internally expressed their own precariousness of formation. Human beings need support, even borrowed from themselves; that is why Johnson praised Gray's *Elegy* just as he had Congreve:

> The *Churchyard* abounds with images which find a mirrour in every mind, and with sentiments to which every bosom returns an echo. The four stanzas beginning *Yet even these bones,* are to me original: I have never seen the notions in any other place; yet he that reads them here, persuades himself that he has always felt them.[11]

It is the very praise that Reynolds gives Raphael:

> it is from his having taken so many models, that he became himself a model for all succeeding painters; always imitating and always original.[12]

As the artist has learnt from art and from his predecessors in art, so in turn we may learn from him. For he not only learns from his predecessors, he also learns about the act of learning. He implicitly acknowledges that process of learning as humanly essential by making his own art likewise a thing to be learnt from. Reynolds called Raphael's genius 'conformable', 'analogous'; his figures, unlike Michelangelo's, 'remind us of their belonging to our own species'.[13] To understand what is at stake here, imagine how Reynolds felt when he said he had learnt from Johnson even to criticize Johnson; then translate that to a more impersonal level, for it is only by such translations – which nowadays novels often perform for us – that most of us begin to learn at all. Just as Reynolds learned from Johnson, then, so the artist, in Reynolds's view, learns from the pre-existing form of human expression. For sometimes, an exceptional human being such as Johnson has to stand as representative in the personal of what is more than personal, and so it was that for Reynolds Johnson was the representative of human tradition itself.

Reynolds's artist *learned* from others how to become himself, and through his art, he now in turn *feels for* others, his readers or viewers, that they may also find the support of feeling like him. For we are the creatures who have the freedom to learn from each other and ourselves; whose nature it is to acquire more than we are simply given by nature in the first place. The artist is the prime example of the human being as sharer, 'always imitating and always original' – preserving in himself that balance of sameness and difference, as well as the balance between art and nature. In such a view we are all a mixture of ourselves and others at much the same time, learning afresh from our predecessors, yet learning even in the same sort of way as they themselves did. The handing on of such a human tradition constitutes 'something', as Reynolds called it, 'steady, substantial, and durable, on which the mind can lean as it were, and rest with safety'.[14] For in such a tradition we feel at once secure and flexible as human beings, at once basically the same and potentially different:

> Every man, says Tully, has two characters; one which he partakes with all mankind, and by which he is distinguished from brute animals; another which discriminates him from the rest of his species, and impresses on him a manner and temper peculiar to himself; this particular character, if it be not repugnant to the laws of general humanity, it is always his business to cultivate and preserve. (*The Rambler*, 179)

As we shall see, it was Johnson's main – but difficult – 'business' to try to keep these two characters of general and particular in one, in him.

One of Johnson's most wonderful remarks to Boswell, made merely in passing, shows something of the life of this whole idea:

> There is not so poor a book in the world that would not be a prodigious effort were it wrought out entirely by a single mind, without the aid of prior investigators.[15]

The remark is wonderful, I think, because it is also already dimly known, familiar, every time we read or write; so simply basic is it to the background of memory we find bequeathed in re-performing any human act. Practically no one has ever written, ever could have written, a single book on his or her own – not even in a lifetime. Even a poor book, so managed, would be nearly a miracle. We are all borrowers, by degree. Even a sentence of one's own might be an achievement.

Learning, therefore, is the initial bridge – like learning a language – in making the man an artist, or at least making him feel *like* one in contemplating the artist's work. Thereafter, feeling and memory, the artist recalling what others then feel they have always felt before, is the return movement which brings art and artist back to life. 'We should always *recollect*', said Reynolds on the subject of criticizing

Johnson, 'that it is he himself who taught us and enabled us to do it.'
Indeed, the fault that Johnson found both with the metaphysical
poets, Cowley and Donne, and also with Dryden was precisely the
failure thus to return art to life. The metaphysicals were artificially
learned, as though they had raised themselves by deliberately
forgetting what intelligence owed itself to; they did not move us:

> As they were wholly employed on something unexpected and
> surprising, they had no regard to that uniformity of sentiment
> which enables us to conceive and to excite the pains and
> pleasures of other minds: they never enquired what, on any
> occasion, they should have said or done, but wrote rather as
> beholders than partakers of human nature, as beings looking
> upon good and evil impassive and at leisure, as Epicurean
> deities making remarks on the actions of men and the
> vicissitudes of life without interest and without emotion...
> Their wish was only to say what they hoped had been never said
> before.[16]

To Johnson their 'particular character' is 'repugnant to the laws of
general humanity'. So too with Dryden:

> The power that predominated in his intellectual operations was
> rather strong reason than quick sensibility. Upon all occasions
> that were presented he studied rather than felt, and produced
> sentiments not such as nature enforces but meditation supplies.
> With the simple and elemental passions as they spring separate
> in the mind, he seems not much acquainted... He is therefore
> with all his variety of excellence not often pathetic, and had so
> little sensibility of the power of effusions purely natural that he
> did not esteem them in others.[17]

A poem that does not affect the emotions may still be art, but it is not
fully human. In both senses of the phrase, it has no feeling for us.
Congreve or Gray are opposed to Cowley or Dryden.

This present work is concerned with how to translate or embody
ideas and beliefs into real human recognition. It would be easy,
however, to parody this extraordinary insistence on the role of
emotion and identification in art as if it were no more than that
sentimental philistinism which is indeed one of its dangers. If it does
not move you, then finally it is no good, it does not feel real. Such an
attitude could prevent any learning for being artificial. For it is not
difficult, either, to see in that attitude an underlying anxiety about

art, even a fear of genius and of the freedom to create meaning. Indeed, it is to Reynolds's credit in his *Discourses* that he comes to recognize that anxiety in himself when putting his beloved, securing Raphael alongside the disturbingly individualistic Michelangelo – Michelangelo who, to Reynolds, is a sort of super-metaphysical poet with a language of his own: 'Michael Angelo's works have a strong, peculiar, and marked character: they seem to proceed from his own mind entirely, and that mind so rich and abundant, that he never needed, or seemed to disdain, to look abroad for foreign help.'[18] Johnson too, starting where he does, does not shrink from getting himself into great hesitations and difficulties with his principles in evaluating the sublime poet, Milton. *Paradise Lost*, for Johnson, is not emotionally a human book, for trying to be beyond and behind us who are latterly fallen.

In this way the idea of art in which Reynolds and Johnson were interested seemed to Blake, for example, closer to fearful compromise than to aweful transcendence.[19] And indeed, art in their view can seem like a compromise: between us feeling like the artist and him feeling like us; both parties perhaps having to adjust, even bend themselves to make the identification; but this against a background which recognizes the uncertain boundary between self and others as itself a human good. Uncertainty may be a licence not to be too fussy about drawing lines, and an intellectual failure to make utterly clear distinctions can also be the ground of a human solidarity even through and in such failures. For example, to translate: Johnson, while one day praising a certain prelate for building churches, found himself noting to Boswell the man's lack of commitment to learning –

> yet, it is well, where a man possesses any strong positive excellence. – Few have all kinds of merit belonging to their character. We must not examine matters too deeply – No, Sir a *fallible being will fail some-where*.[20]

In making the qualification upon his own criticism, Johnson remembered something. Relative fallibility – from the prelate not being learned to Johnson not attending church regularly – is a ground for mutual sympathy, the sympathy of *being* basically alike to start with, then by memory *feeling* it.

Let us at least imitate Johnson and Reynolds in this: in pursuing emotional principles which they knew would also get them into great difficulty; in refusing to give up needs without which their position might have been easier and less open to criticism. We are now entering a difficult area in thinking about emotion as a criterion in art. For the moment, we can simply tell it *is* difficult by recalling that, extraordinarily, Boswell quoted Johnson's remarks on Dryden as equally applicable to Johnson's own character and writing. 'There is not a single passage', Boswell concluded of Johnson's work, 'that ever drew a tear.'[21] Clearly, as we shall see in Chapter Two, Boswell and Johnson must have had an inherent disagreement as to what truly constituted feeling.

In the course of this book I shall often be looking very closely at the language of our texts. But this time – in order as it were novelistically to show the *story* of Johnson's relation to feeling in reading and writing, and the importance of that relation to art's own relation to living – I simply offer a reading demonstration of three passages, one after another, to be put together.

First, imagine Johnson reading the stanzas in Gray's *Elegy* that he praised for their re-creative resonance:

> Yet ev'n these bones from insult to protect
> Some frail memorial still erected nigh,
> With uncouth rhimes and shapeless sculpture deck'd,
> Implores the passing tribute of a sigh.
>
> Their name, their years, spelt by th' unletter'd muse,
> The place of fame and elegy supply:
> And many a holy text around she strews,
> That teach the rustic moralist to die.
>
> For who to dumb Forgetfulness a prey,
> This pleasing anxious being e'er resign'd,
> Left the warm precincts of the chearful day,
> Nor cast one longing ling'ring look behind?
>
> On some fond breast the parting soul relies,
> Some pious drops the closing eye requires;
> Ev'n from the tomb the voice of Nature cries,
> Ev'n in our Ashes live their wonted Fires.

'In the character of his *Elegy* I rejoice to concur with the common reader.'[22] The unletter'd muse and the letter'd one had something in common, and the reader of Gray's *Elegy* became the writer of *On the Death of Dr Robert Levet* in 1782. Levet, 'an obscure practiser of physick amongst the lower people', lived in Johnson's house and was dependent upon him. Boswell asked Goldsmith why Johnson had taken such a fellow on, uncouth as Levet was: '"He is poor and honest, which is recommendation enough to Johnson"; and when I wondered that he was very kind to a man of whom I had heard a very bad character, "He is now become miserable, and that insures the protection of Johnson."'[23] The final protection Johnson offered Levet's memory left Johnson himself vulnerable – imagine stanza four above calling for the poem ('On some fond breast the parting soul relies'), while stanza three above threatens Johnson with the thought of his own death even in writing it ('For who ... This pleasing anxious being e'er resign'd?'):

> Yet still he fills affection's eye,
>   Obscurely wise, and coarsely kind;
> Nor, letter'd arrogance, deny
>   Thy praise to merit unrefin'd.
>
> When fainting nature call'd for aid,
>   And hov'ring death prepar'd the blow,
> His vig'rous remedy display'd
>   The power of art without the show.
>
> In misery's darkest caverns known,
>   His useful care was ever nigh,
> Where hopeless anguish pour'd his groan,
>   And lonely want retir'd to die.
>
> No summons mock'd by chill delay,
>   No petty gain disdain'd by pride,
> The modest wants of ev'ry day
>   The toil of ev'ry day supplied.
>
> His virtues walk'd their narrow round,
>   Nor made a pause, nor left a void;
> And sure th' Eternal Master found
>   The single talent well employed.
>
> The busy day, the peaceful night,
>   Unfelt, uncounted, glided by;
> His frame was firm, his powers were bright,
>   Tho' now his eightieth year was nigh.

> Then with no throbbing fiery pain,
>   No cold gradations of decay,
> Death broke at once the vital chain,
>   And free'd his soul the nearest way.

'Some pious drops the closing eye requires'; 'Yet still he fills affection's eye.' Who 'this pleasing anxious being e'er resign'd'?; fighting for life with 'throbbing fiery pain', 'cold gradations of decay'. The voice of Nature cries, in both senses, through both poems, and no human can answer it as Levet did the summons of sick misery. The art is both more and less than Levet's own.

Likewise the poem has 'two characters', is both imitative and original, both common and, separately and tacitly, Johnson thinking of himself. Letter'd arrogance, Johnson could accuse himself, was what had also kept him from church attendance; at least Levet's art was useful amongst the common people and pleasing thereby to the Eternal Master. On the other hand, Johnson's own days did not pass uncounted, he was both less busy and more intelligent; also less limited but more anxious and imaginative: his own death might miss the blessing of Levet's appropriately *simple* release. The writer could not deceive himself either way: he was both uncommon in degree, in talents and levels of being, and common in kind, in basic fate.

Our third passage is pieced together by Walter Jackson Bate, on the life of V.J. Peyton. Who indeed? Peyton was one of Johnson's six assistants as he worked on his *Dictionary*; before that work Peyton had tried to keep alive by teaching French. Johnson chose his men nearly as much because of their wants as out of their abilities:

> After the *Dictionary* was finished, Peyton wrote a few works on language, and Johnson himself was occasionally able to hire him when he made revisions in the *Dictionary*. But after Peyton's wife had a stroke, he was reduced to complete penury, said Johnson, and 'sat starving by the bed of a Wife not only useless, but almost motionless, condemned by poverty to personal attendance...' Johnson's rough friend Giuseppe Baretti described Peyton as 'a fool and a drunkard'. But Johnson thought Peyton's life as moving as those of others that 'fill histories and tragedies' only because they are better known. When Peyton's wife at last died (1776), he was immediately 'seized by a fever' and died himself, and Johnson paid the burial expenses of both.[24]

Some may complain about treating literature as though it were real life. But Johnson's complaint here, when he finds Peyton's life as moving as tragedy, is against treating real life as though it were not up to literature, as if it were not as worthy of powerful language, as full of meaning, as are figments of imagination. In his *Confessions*, that other troubled, honest Christian, Augustine, worries himself that he was far more moved over the story of Dido's tragedy, dying for love of Aeneas, than by the reality of his own unsatisfactory relation with the God Whose Son died for love of mankind. In writing of Levet, at any rate, Johnson forces literature to admit real life – 'Nor, letter'd arrogance, deny/Thy praise' – while both equally and almost contradictorily admitting and integrating all that an intelligent, literate witness must in truth have to know in qualification of that real life ('coarsely kind', 'unrefined', 'narrow round', 'single talent', 'unfelt'). And all this, while the literary man is trying not to lurch from disdain to sentimentality, from sentimentality to envy, and so on. There is always an integrity behind Johnson's apparent contradictions and tensions: for his ambivalences and divisions are on behalf of, held together by, the same belief.

What holds our three passages together – the story of a man reading, a man writing, a man living? What holds them together, across their different compartments, is Johnson's deep sense of the experience and meaning of the word 'sympathy'. To illustrate his *Dictionary* definition of sympathy Johnson chose a passage from South's sermons:

> it is this noble quality that makes all men to be of one kind; for every man would be a distinct species to himself, were there no sympathy among individuals.

For Johnson – a man who trusted the wisdom of the species as it was preserved in its language – 'kind' was a noun long before it became an adjective: it is a basic condition rather than a mere favour or stray feeling. This has its consequence in what emotions meant to him. It is not merely that Johnson sympathized with ignored, forgotten souls with whose plight Gray also felt sympathetic; or sympathized with, was affected by, Gray's own affection and sympathy (though, unlike Dryden and more like Johnson, Gray's sympathy also included a more painful identification: the fear that he too might end a failure). It is not merely that Johnson happened to feel sympathetic towards the unattractive Levet or chose to feel sorry for the unlucky Peyton. It is less accidental, less individualistic than that, and more to do with the grounding of belief within the terms of human nature and biology. Our three passages hold together as it were generically, because of a deep, formal, not necessarily conscious sympathy with each other. They are of the same species; for they are the same not only because they come from the same basic nature, Johnson's, but because they arise from that same nature recognizing its own likeness to its own species.

> On some fond breast the parting soul relies,
> Some pious drops the closing eye requires;
> Ev'n from the tomb the voice of Nature cries,
> Ev'n in our Ashes live their wonted Fires.

It is language itself in Johnson that reminds us of our basic sympathy as a species, whether we wish to feel it or not. To take just a simple example from *The Adventurer*, 120: even a good man, says Johnson, may see 'his cares made useless by profusion, his instructions defeated by perverseness, and his kindness rejected by ingratitude'. On the other side of Johnson's publicly blurted thoughts and mutterings, said Reynolds, there were unconscious jerks and twitches as from the very mind of the man 'to reprobate some part of his past conduct': Johnson's reader often feels something *wincingly* analogous in private and particular response to his public and general language. 'Kindness rejected by ingratitude': such a phrase seems so formal and general, as though found in a dictionary; yet so much the greater is the shock of the reader who finds on the other side of such words their meanings in the feelings, memories and secret particulars of his own heart. How did the one, the words, ever lead to the other, the feelings, when they still seem so utterly different too?

Sympathy in Johnson is not just a particular emotion, it is the particular surfacing of the deep impersonal memory that we all belong to the same species. The language of 'kindness rejected by ingratitude' can strike almost with violence in its embodiment of the *two* characters of men at once: the differences of individual human beings held even within the terms of sameness. For the reader can feel at once the closeness *and* the separation between the general language and its particular felt meanings in a way that seems to register an almost biological memory of our evolution. Through such language, art and sympathy are thus near kin for Johnson. Life is full of particular lost stories, stories that art does not often recover but on the memory of which art draws and depends for its effect upon individual readers. In such a context, feeling comes from a memory, nearer to the origin of ourselves, which undermines compartmentalization and brings differences together in the very recognition of differences as evolved, through learning, upon a basic sameness beneath.

*

III   Discoursing like an angel, living like a man

Yet for all this basic sameness, Johnson did think himself in many respects superior to Levet. Reynolds reports that Johnson was too passionately proud ever to allow himself to be beaten in even the most minor verbal disputes: 'He thought it necessary never to be worsted in argument.'[25] Why so necessary, so competitive? His was already acknowledged to be one of the most powerful minds of the age. Yet when one day Johnson complained to a friend that Lord Chesterfield, the patron who failed him, was the proudest man living, the friend replied that he knew one prouder. 'But mine (replied Johnson instantly) was *defensive* pride.'[26] What is at stake in that distinction?

'Think with the wise, but speak with the vulgar' was Aristotle's dictum – in Reynolds's terms, Raphael as it were retaining Michelangelo within him in more common ways. But commenting on Aristotle's saying, Johnson says in *The Idler*, 70, that it is 'not always practicable': 'He that thinks with more extent than another will want words of larger meaning.' But the larger meaning, for example in the poem on the death of Levet, also consists in the greater thinker's increased self-blame for his increased pride. Tributes to Johnson's goodness ignore the struggle he always had to think and act as he wanted to, always seeming as he did to come at it the wrong way round through defensive fear and repentance of vice as much as love of virtue in the first place.

The mixture of particular aggression (towards both others and self) and general sympathy, the sense of a man working at different levels at once, an uncommon man defending commonness with extraordinary power of attack, must have been a startling and confusing spectacle to witness. An encounter with Johnson was an event, like trying to cross a minefield. Mrs Thrale recalled one notably explosive false step:

> What signifies, says some one, giving halfpence to common beggars? they only lay it out in gin or tobacco. 'And why should they be denied such sweeteners of their existence (says Johnson)? it is surely very savage to refuse them every possible avenue to pleasure, reckoned too coarse for our own

acceptance. Life is a pill which none of us can bear to swallow without gilding; yet for the poor we delight in stripping it still barer, and are not ashamed to shew even visible displeasure, if ever the bitter taste is taken from their mouths.'[27]

Emphatically this is said by one who, deeply read in the Gospels, has understood the way of Christ with Pharisees and disciples alike, as when he said to the Pharisees who would stone the woman taken in adultery: 'He that is without sin among you, let him first cast a stone at her' (John 8: 7). Or–more complicated but just as apposite in relation to matters both of the poor and of the sweeteners of existence – Christ's rebuke to his disciples' complaint against the woman who poured precious ointment upon him instead of selling it and giving the proceeds to the poor: 'Why trouble ye the woman? for she hath wrought a good work upon me' (Matthew 26: 10). Not that Johnson thought himself Christ. When he says bluntly: 'It is surely very savage to refuse them every possible avenue to pleasure, reckoned too coarse for our own acceptance', it is clear that he himself would sooner use bad temper and be coarse, with the poor, than be savage, with the refined. His un-Christ-like bad temper, albeit in defence of Christianity, is Johnson's acknowledgement of himself as still speaking only as a passionate man among passionate men. For the judge may condemn the poor with apparently dispassionate justice – you give them help, and look what they do with it – but the judge in such cases is also the witness who warmly affected the evidence before he coolly judged it: you give them enough rope and they hang themselves. The smoother savagery plays the levels game, but does not choose to see that it does. Johnson does see: as he puts it in *The Rambler*, 66, 'Before we permit our severity to break loose upon any fault or error, we ought surely to consider how much we have countenanced or promoted it.'

'Life is a pill which none of us can bear to swallow without gilding.' None of us: they have their gin, you the merely better equivalent. Sympathy is not as simple or easy for Johnson as it might have looked in our last section: it is for him the painful meeting-point of self-criticism with imagination of others. For there are two things I am thinking about in this section. One is the way there is something different about Johnson, something at a higher level of development which, however, also involves him in not quite fitting in, in being awkward with others and in being unsatisfactory and contradictory to himself. The other concerns the way Johnson, for all that, still uses his difference to look the same as the rest of us, and this, which must have to do with his being a writer, is perhaps the biggest contradiction of all about him.

'And why beholdest thou the mote that is in thy brother's eye, but considerest not the beam that is in thine own eye?' (Matthew 7: 3). In Johnson's fallen world, that sort of relativism is experienced as pain rather than easy tolerance or grace. Goodness for him seems to be created out of defence against the evils that attack it on both sides: a defence, in anger, against those who will not give halfpence to 'common beggars', through blindness to the word 'common'; a defence, in compassion, against the miseries of unhappiness and poverty which beset the beggar. 'Mine was *defensive* pride.' In her space fiction *The Sirian Experiments* Doris Lessing has a wonderful description of how it feels reluctantly to recognize such relatives through the power of a Wise Man. Ambien II, representative of planet Sirius, cannot understand why Klorathy, representative of planet Canopus, should want them both to bother to try to help the ruined planet Rohanda – our Earth:

> 'You have never told me *why*! Do you really have no inkling at all of why such care should go into these...these...'
>
> 'These murderous half-apes?'
>
> 'Or worse.' And I could feel how my mouth was twisted with distaste and dislike...
>
> And he, looking embarrassed, was *not* looking at me, but away.
>
> 'Oh, very well, very well, then! But you cannot possibly be saying, Canopus, that to an outside view, *yours*, Canopus, the inhabitants of Sirius, or at least some of us, the lower kinds of our Empire, strike you as repulsively as Rohandans strike me?' And, as he did not reply, I cried out: 'That cannot be!... We are not as bad... We are *not*.'[28]

For all the higher levels of class and intelligence, is the difference between them and you any different from that between a higher existence and your own? The mind swirls round in itself; things get blurted out.

But Johnson was not a creature from a higher planet, nor did he have – nor perhaps would he have allowed – anyone to educate him. He half-despised, half-blamed himself for despising his own often foolish parents. He had to be his own Klorathy, his own Ambien II. What Malamud's Dubin said in novelistic shorthand, 'He learned from life', looks deeper now, since life never proposes itself as a teacher in the first place.

To learn from life Johnson had first to incorporate it within himself, within a mind that could then contain the thoughts of it inside itself. He had to learn from himself, Canopus to his own Sirius. In that strong and weak self-dependence he was still the same half-blind child who, when the schoolmistress rushed to help him as he tried, gropingly, to cross the street on all fours, beat his Samaritan away; the same impoverished young student who violently threw away the new boots which a fellow-student had quietly left for him to replace his shameful old ones. Johnson had to learn from himself, even on the basis of his own inadequacies in so doing. Publicly to teach from the book of his own private errors, to raise himself above himself while still remaining defiantly within himself: this was the giant, tottering task he set himself on the very verge of self-destructive contradiction:

> For why did Wolsey near the steeps of fate,
> On weak foundations raise th' enormous weight?

There must come a time when the will-power of 'raise' is not as strong as the unbalancing interaction of 'enormous' with 'weak'. Johnson defensively tried to hold on to the very end. But here is Sir John Hawkins's description of him in 1784, the last year of his life:

> he, with a look that cut me to the heart, told me, that he had the prospect of death before him, and that he dreaded to meet his Saviour. I could not but be astonished at such a declaration, and advised him, as I had done once before, to reflect on the course of his life, and the services he had rendered to the cause of religion and virtue, as well by his example, as his writings; to which he answered that he had written as a philosopher, but had not lived like one... 'Shall I, who have been a teacher of others, myself be a castaway?'[29]

In contrast to Levet, Johnson felt that he had been given several talents and had employed none of them well. The reason why Johnson's sympathy is not simple is that he believed in the existence of levels: at one level he knew he was far more than Levet; at another much less: 'For unto whomsoever much is given, of him shall be much required' (Luke 12: 48). And even if Johnson was more than Levet, what was Johnson compared to, say, St Paul:

> St Paul, who wrought miracles, may have had a miracle wrought on himself, and may have obtained supernatural assurance of pardon, and mercy, and beatitude; yet St Paul,

though he expresses strong hope, also expresses fear, lest having preached to others, he himself should be a castaway.[30]

In quoting St Paul's words to Hawkins, Johnson is not so different from a man like Dubin quoting Johnson and finding what was learnt from literature come back to life again. For Johnson was both making an equation with St Paul and also feeling himself damned by it. It was not that he believed in absolute equality, right across the board from Levet to St Paul; he believed in different levels, up and down, but he also believed in analogy across those levels, setting the hierarchies spinning in the mind of a man in the midst of them. In quotation, said Johnson, there is a community of mind.

But Johnson's own strength had been that he had learnt from his own errors: *because* he had not lived like a philosopher, he was able at another level to write like one. By an act that was like his later sympathy for others but was an internal reverse of it, Johnson put himself into the place of seeing his own weaknesses – and he found that a strength, albeit a self-borrowed one that had constantly to be reconsolidated. Tolstoy said of his own brother that the brother had more sheer talent than he, but was never the novelist that Tolstoy was – because he had not made so many mistakes.

Yet perhaps the worst thing, for such an almost literally self-made man as Johnson, was to find this very strength to be still simultaneously a weakness: despite the literary contrition and compensation – that he had succeeded in writing like a philosopher – he still had managed it, he believed, while failing to live like one. The carefully raised levels were always perilously close to collapse, and that, ironically enough, by a sort of watchful integrity. In contrast, a man such as Dryden 'had so little sensibility of the power of effusions purely natural that he did not esteem them in others': Dryden lost twice over, in his nature and in his judgement's rationalization of it; what he did not have in himself, at another level he could not value in others. Such strength – of not even knowing that his deficiency was a deficiency – was a weakness. If, on the other hand, Johnson's weakness was a strength, if his sense of his failure at the highest levels made him sympathetic to failure at lower but analogous levels, still to him it remained a weakness, a pain and a rebuke. You could not get away from it, from your nature; you could repeat the words of St Paul, thinking that even a greater man has doubts, but the words and the doubts could still be true, for all that. You could apply the example to yourself and instead of the identification proving a relief, it might just stick, be translated and come home at that level. It was reading and writing, I believe, that made Johnson so aware of different levels of being. But they also made him wary of vicious circles: he who writes like a philosopher, although he does not live like one, still does not live like a philosopher, although he writes like one.

What was worse, perhaps, was the fact that Johnson had already anticipated the contradiction long before he made that final confession of it to Hawkins – and, like the quotation from Paul, the anticipation had described but not helped. To anticipate error and still to make it, to anticipate fault and still to have it was, confusingly, both a confirmation and a contradiction of the power of anticipation. Imagine Johnson writing the following, both out of and against himself:

> It is not difficult to conceive, however, that for many reasons a man writes much better than he lives... A man proposes his schemes of life in a state of abstraction and disengagement, exempt from the enticements of hope, the solicitations of affection, the importunities of appetite, or the depressions of fear...
>
> Nothing is more unjust, however common, than to charge with hypocrisy him that expresses zeal for those virtues, which he neglects to practise; since he may be sincerely convinced of the advantages of conquering his passions, without having yet obtained the victory. (*The Rambler,* 14)

Johnson wrote against idleness, yet feared he practised it, filling his loneliness with company and late hours, lying in bed until noon. It must seem incredible, none the less, for anyone to think of the author of *Rasselas, The Vanity of Human Wishes*, the great *Dictionary*, the *Lives of the Poets*, the edition of Shakespeare and a vast number of distinguished essays and sermons as an idle failure; but Johnson did so think of himself, in contrast to Levet – the more so as he considered those works of his as merely the inadequate products of his very fear of idleness, of wasted time and talents. The idleness itself seemed further prompted by a recognition of the vanity of preaching against idleness while still practising it; so the idleness could stop the preaching too, like a register of the vanity of that knowledge which cannot affect practice. Moreover, Johnson himself must have recognized that only a man of extraordinary ambition, in the first place, could have felt so disappointed and so guilty in the second. And if that pride was itself blameworthy, even with the pain it caused him, still its internal pressure might be no less than that of the external demand which the Eternal Master could rightly make. It all went round in circles like that. Johnson's very philosophy was based on Imlac's recognition in *Rasselas*: that philosophers discoursed like angels but lived like men. The philosophy thus at once contained and was itself contained by its own thought about philosophy's inadequacy – and again, the tension of such a double-bind might well set Johnson blurting. For so much of the contradictory power of his own writing derives from a tension analogous to that between discoursing like an angel and living like a man *and* discoursing about *that* discrepancy, in a spiralling, self-checking circle. No wonder the only thing that Johnson, the writer of sanity, feared more than hypocrisy was madness. He had to write himself into expecting contradictions, accepting them, even, as normal. Indeed, no writer is less anxious about his anxieties, more undisturbed by his own disturbances, more unsurprised by his own contradictions, than Johnson – even while still feeling them all so powerfully.

If Johnson discoursed like an angel, then, it was more like a chastened fallen angel than like Doris Lessing's Korathy. Johnson used his disappointment; he made his memory into a form of anticipation. In his writing he treats his own experience as if it were that of anyone else and the experience of anyone else as if it were his own. And when he finds that he cannot *quite* treat his own experience as if it *were* merely that of anyone else, and the power of personal feeling comes through, he still recognizes that that too is like everyone else; everyone else would be like that too. In a strange way, all the contradictions fit together. Similarly, the idea in *The Rambler*, 14, of the 'striking contrariety between the life of the author and his writings' characteristically becomes the paradoxical *link* between the writings and the life of Samuel Johnson. For although primarily he feared he had wasted his life, at a secondary verbal level he wasted nothing, not even those primary fears. Consequently, to complete the circle, he both relished *and* distrusted that secondary level.

It is therefore like Johnson to use literature to have doubts about a literary life, to use writing to have doubts about merely writing, and yet still to keep the pen going, on the very verge between tenacity and hypocrisy. Let us see this strange mixture of integrity and contradiction, of link and separation, difference and sameness, in action, by looking at a page and also trying to read what lies behind it half-admitted and half-repressed. Sermon 8, for example, is on the intellectual pride of men of learning:

There are some conditions of humanity, which are made particularly dangerous by an uncommon degree of seeming security; conditions, in which we appear so compleatly fortified, that we have little to dread, and therefore give ourselves up too readily to negligence and supineness; and are destroyed without precaution, because we flattered ourselves, that destruction could not approach us. This fatal slumber of treacherous tranquillity may be produced and prolonged by many causes, by causes as various as the situations of life. Our condition may be such, as may place us out of the reach of those general admonitions, by which the rest of mankind are reminded of their errours, and awakened to their duty; it may remove us to a great distance from the common incitements to common wickedness, and therefore may superinduce a forgetfulness of our natural frailties, and suppress all suspicions of the encroachments of sin. – And the sin to which we are particularly tempted may be of that insidious and seductive kind, as, that without alarming us by the horrours of its appearance, and shocking us with the enormity of any single acts, may, by slow advances, possess the soul, and in destroying us differ only from the atrociousness of more apparent wickedness, as a lingering poison differs from the sword; more difficultly avoided, and more certainly fatal.

To temptations of this subtle insinuating kind, the life of men of learning seems above all others to be exposed...

To these causes, or to some of these, it must surely be imputed, that learning is found so frequently to fail in the direction of life; and to operate so faintly and uncertainly in the regulation of *their* conduct, who are most celebrated for their application and proficiency.[31]

In a way, this is the language of the outsider – the man who had learnt more from life than from Oxford and who touchingly told Boswell he thought that, in the long run, he had managed to do better than those of his contemporaries who had been able to stay on at the great university. Taking his independent stand outside, Johnson is *basically* strong on the disposition of professions to insulate themselves, by their own rules and habits, from remembering the wider threats and efforts of a moral life on earth.

Yet on the other hand Johnson's position as outsider is essentially metaphorical, a translation through the act of writing. And it is meant to be decoded as such, for the tacit recognition of it is shared through the very word 'we' in the passage, an insider's word left behind as a clue and an admission. Johnson knew the dangers of his own pride. To insidious moral danger, he saw, literary people may not be more immune than others but in fact, just for thinking themselves more exempt, more liable. And he also includes, in that warning, himself in the very act of making it! 'Shall I, who have been a teacher, myself be a castaway?' Thus, although this passage from Johnson's sermon is indeed frightening, it also includes its own fear that even putting fears into words may be dangerously comforting – as though that were enough to allay them. How difficult, how almost impossible, Johnson made it for himself to write with honesty, for he was sceptical about everything: 'Mr Johnson's incredulity', reports Mrs Thrale, 'amounted almost to disease.'[32] Thus, when Johnson wrote: 'learning is found...to operate so faintly and uncertainly in the regulation of *their* conduct, who are most celebrated for their application and proficiency', although before his eyes he wrote 'their', behind them he also thought 'my'. For Johnson did not write like the metaphysical poets, 'rather as beholders than partakers of human nature'. The authorial strength of the moralist proceeded even while the man was twitchingly thinking of his personal weakness; the strength partly deriving from the memory of the weakness, even while simultaneously the weakness remained in shameful memory beneath the strength made out of it. Johnson was clearly terrified he had worked himself into subtly fatal habits – the lingering poison less detectable but more certainly fatal than the sword. And this was all the more ironic when the capacity to form habits could have been the means by which the man could have reformed his first nature through the acquiring from experience of a second. The writing became the attempt to found a better second nature – when the writing itself was not hampered by the very habits of depressive idleness.

But what were the weaknesses, memories, bad habits that set Johnson wincing even as he wrote against them? Let us try, like novelists, to imagine them. 'Learning is found so frequently to fail in the direction of life.' Suppose we let that take us back to the summer of 1729. Forced to be back home in Lichfield during the Oxford long vacation, Johnson found himself laid low with depression: lying in bed unable and unwilling to read or to write, staring at the movement of the hands of the clock outside his window, not telling the time but watching his life pass. For by the end of the year, as he must have already suspected, this proudly ambitious young scholar, seeking to get above and away from his parents, would have to leave Oxford without a degree, simply for lack of funds. Johnson's father, Michael, was an improvident bookseller: the books had given encouragement to the son, but the improvidence was that other hand which took away. If the son could get himself up, he would walk to Birmingham and back to try to shake off the depression...It must have been about a year later when Michael Johnson, now ailing and himself physically incapable of getting out of bed, asked his son, no longer at Oxford, to go to Uttoxeter market for him and work the bookstall there. 'To temptations of this subtle insinuating kind, the life of men of learning seems above all others to be exposed.' He, who had walked to Birmingham on his own account, refused to go and trade in Uttoxeter: perhaps, after all, for much the same reason. But in a few months his father was dead. In the last year of his own life Johnson confessed to a young friend:

> A few years ago, I desired to atone for this fault; I went to Uttoxeter in very bad weather, and stood for a considerable time bareheaded in the rain, on the spot where my father's stall used to stand. In contrition I stood, and I hope the penance was expiatory.[33]

This time he did not care what onlookers thought of the old man standing there bareheaded in the rain. It had been fifty years since he made the refusal. In trying to make himself a better man Johnson was always caught by the recognition that the uneasiness of guilt he felt was as much the consequence of the effort at reformation as of the original vices themselves. That was his purgatory. For memories like this one seem always to haunt, to lie just behind his prose, like a third dimension simultaneously summoned and held off.

And who could say, with confidence, that Johnson in his later years was really any less desperate; when his very lack of desperation at times made him feel *more* desperate about himself in 'the fatal slumber of treacherous tranquillity'. Only the levels changed, through experience and through writing about experience. On 26 April 1772, for example, Johnson, aged sixty-two, could write in his private journal:

> I have this week scarcely tried to read, nor have I read any thing this day...
> ...On this day little has been done and this is now the last hour. In life little has been done, and life is very far advanced. Lord have mercy on us.[34]

Through the act of writing, 'this day' could thus stand for Johnson as an analogy for the whole of his life. But there were also many more days 'in life' to waste and to lament wasting like this one in April 1772. The reality of time mocked his language even as it was named by it. Johnson lived, still uncertain, until he was seventy-five years old. There was always this tension between what appears to be his *finalized* knowledge of the human condition in his writing and his state of *still* continuing to suffer from that condition in time.

Discoursing like an angel, living like a man. It is both the discrepancy *and* the link between the stability of his words on the page and the shakingness of the experience which they describe, anticipate and remember off it, that gives Johnson's work its deeper meaning. Consider a sentence such as the following:

> A man proposes his schemes of life in a state of abstraction and disengagement, exempt from the enticements of hope, the solicitations of affection, the importunities of appetite, or the depressions of fear...

Johnson takes great pains to see that he himself in his writing is *not* free of the reality from which one sort of abstract writer is temporarily exempt. His 'abstraction' is only that of the power of his nouns to abstract experience into a common word; to grasp in the power of his writing hand, as it were, the multiple echoes of the words' own meaning. By the insertion of second, plural nouns (enticements, solicitations, importunities, depressions) within the catalogue of single, diverse emotions (hope, affection, appetite, fear), Johnson seeks to add to the authority of nouns, steadily seen, the summative power of verbs, still powerfully felt. The language does not seem exempt from the recognition of its own meaning: it has the power of renewed pain as well as, at different levels, both resistance and acknowledgement. 'The enticements of hope, the solicitations of affection, the importunities of appetite, or the depressions of fear.' This language registers within itself, in this way, a consciousness that 'a man writes much better than he lives'. For language here seems to be a form of signalling as well as naming, and as such it is a dual key system. For what this man is signalling through words is not only his meaning but also a simultaneous recognition that that very meaning is still being given only in *words*, with all their treacherous tranquillity and temptation to disengagement: not in life. Yet such a recognition is not simply a defeat: on second thought it is, as an acknowledgement of the convention of language, itself part of language's meaning. For the very limitation of language, within which one such as Johnson none the less tried as hard as he knew how, is itself a provocation of imagination, a signal of its necessity. When we read a Johnson essay or sermon, the power of his deliberately disproportionate language calls upon us to imagine or remember what it really means off the page to think and feel this on it. 'It is not sufficiently considered, that men more frequently require to be reminded than informed' (*The Rambler*, 2). I am suggesting that it would take a novel such as *Dubin's Lives* to begin to register the effect of such literature within a life. I am also now suggesting that what 'learning is found so frequently to fail in the direction of life' really means or stands for is, for example, Johnson crying out to Hawkins: 'Shall I, who have been a teacher of others, myself be a castaway?'. The 'frequency' of the thought can dull its meaning even for its own thinker, but that does not mean that in the end it will not come true again and have its natural effect, for all the proud anticipation of it, for all the literary familiarity of it. Johnson is above all a writer of memory and of reminding, who finds in language, as elsewhere, strength and weakness utterly entangled.

   Yet I am not arguing that the 'real' meaning of Johnson's words is to be found only in *Johnson's* life. For if we did not have the diaries and biographies we would not know so much, explicitly, about that life behind the work, and the meaning of the work cannot be dependent on the existence and survival of such contingencies. Without them we would simply have to imagine harder what the words really meant to Johnson and what the words really mean to us in order to get to that third dimension of meaning. But we have in Johnson's life, as it happens, an example of how serious the issues expressed on the page really are; he lived out his own meaning. For with Johnson the meaning is not just left passively on the page; it is not simply off the page either; at its most serious, the meaning on the page *means* the reality off it.

   For Johnson's language simultaneously recalls and represses that third dimension of meaning which lies in silence behind the foreheads of writers and readers alike. Thoughts of Uttoxeter; diary-bound shames; the unwritten, perhaps unwriteable novel that would connect the man's life with his work by being inside the movement and history of his very thoughts. When Johnson himself is writing, the woes which are so unbalancing in life are almost ironically balanced in his style; the very gap between the two entices thoughts to fill it. Thus, we 'are destroyed without precaution, because we flattered ourselves, that destruction could not approach us'; or, 'our condition admits many evils which cannot be remedied, but contains no good which cannot be taken from us'; or again, in a list of the pillar-to-post disadvantages on our every side, 'that in the dead calm of solitude we are insufficient to our own contentment, and that when weariness of our selves impels us to society, we are often ill received.'[35] Johnson piles up the contradictions of our near-helpless state with a paradoxically firm authorial balance, itself provokingly yet deliberately at odds with the very contradictions it describes *and* partakes of. He is on both sides of such sentences, sentencing and sentenced at once, delivering the rational form and receiving the emotional brunt of its content, educating himself too in the strength of his own weakness. Johnson positioned himself in sympathy as a sort of middleman between strong author and human sufferer. For he makes balanced sense out of what his own feelings cry out against from within their sentence; as though he were forced to read off and then verbally transmit the inferred lessons of life in lieu of that Eternal Master, the Great Author, who, we are tempted to think, *ought* to be offering us juster life-sentences, less ironic balances of frying pan or fire. But that is not how it is.

How it is *is* important to Johnson, above every other consideration. It is best to know, to acknowledge, that it is as it is. This conviction is at the very basis of Johnson's relationship to language, for it is no coincidence that Johnson Moralist is also Dictionary Johnson, the great definer. Words define our meanings regardless, in the first instance, of our feelings about those meanings. Thus Johnson can write as though from the outside, the dictionary other side, of human meaning:

> As cruelty looks upon misery without partaking pain, so envy beholds encrease of happiness without partaking joy.[36]

Yet our behaviour, even at its most apparently private, seems to be not only externally explained by these words but constituted by them, internally made up of them. When we read that sentence we think that that is both what it *means* and also what it *feels* like – to be cruel, to be envious, and so on. It is almost as though we could look ourselves up in a dictionary, when impersonal words stand thus as deep memories for personal feelings. We too feel ourselves to be on both sides of the language in such cases, inside it and out. For the nouns in Johnson's sentence seem linked in combinations whose inner logic of verbal connection is almost *independent* of our control, in life, even while also being paradoxically *internal* to both our natural constitution and our linguistic comprehension. Johnson wrote, mastering words even while simultaneously recognizing himself to be, at another level, composed by them. With him, we not only have to recognize, through the gift of language, that things are as they are; we also have to recognize that our relation to language is what it is. That is to say, we cannot expect to control ourselves even when, verbally, we can define ourselves – though language gives us that hope, that challenge. Nor can we expect language, because it seems to explain things, to justify things of which it appears to make sense. Sceptical Johnson always returns to say: 'The shame is to impose words for ideas upon ourselves or others', the error is to think that because language fits on the page its conclusions will therefore fit with experience off it.[37] There are different levels. Johnson is constantly worrying us whether even he can make the distinctions in life that his own words make on the page. Do we know the real difference between learning to reason and learning to live, or between living in peace and living in the fatal slumber of treacherous tranquillity? Yet even when we are right on the page, in our language, and wrong off it, in our lives, that is not simple hypocrisy – it is how it is with us and language: risks on both sides, threats of separation, challenges of reunion, attempts to move on one front, if not another, in the struggles of life, followed then by the necessity to try to fight again on the forgotten front.

Always in this tension and this acceptance of tension we sense Johnson's *need* for laws, for rules, for definition that offers a verbal *hold* on the world: for emphatically no one is a more mentally physical writer than Johnson, as his words try to grasp external reality. But those rules often have to be tautological or circular: things are as they are; the first rule often is that there are no rules as such.

Let us consider in this light the law that Johnson most of all admired, Christ's 'Whatsoever ye would that men should do unto you, even so do unto them'. In *The Rambler*, 81, Johnson says that this is 'a law, of which every man may find the exposition in his own breast' – where he is bidden to look. It must have seemed to Johnson the highest example of all he believed in. For like language itself, the dictum worked on both sides, from general to particular: that is to say, Christ says to everyone: 'What would ye have men do unto you? Go and do thou likewise unto them', and it is noticeable that he addresses everyone, but everyone singularly as 'you' rather than as 'men' (we all think everyone else is 'men'). The words are *so* general as to have to be taken individually. Even so, the saying then finds its way back from the particular to the general, from the individual to the social, by faith in that simple word with a complicated meaning: sympathy – the thing that Johnson himself also believed to be vital to literature. Do unto others as you would be done by: it is like a serious trick played upon self-centredness: now you think of yourself; now, even in so doing, you don't. This is the divine example of a self-dissolving rule, a rule that is also not a rule; for it both does and does not tell you what to do: leaving it *with* you, but not just leaving *you*.

With Johnson, human beings of course work on a much more primitive level than does Christ even when He addresses himself to us on it. One of the measures of that lower level is precisely and ironically our intelligence, because what He says simply, we find complicated. For it *is* complicated to us – so complicated, and so liable to be made even more complicated by abstract thinking, that Johnson always recognizes the need to combat overscrupulous intelligence by a still defiantly *intelligent* reclamation of the right to simplicity. So many of his long sentences are fighting within themselves to rescue something briefer or earlier. In the following he is, typically, fighting with the casuists' distinction between justice and charity, in the light of Jesus's saying. For justice requires that we treat everyone as we ourselves would expect to be treated; charity seems to require that we go beyond justice, treating some people better than we believe we might deserve in equivalent circumstances or better even than they would treat us were the circumstances reversed. Here is Johnson, definer and equivocator, separator and joiner at once:

> Justice is indispensably and universally necessary, and what is necessary must always be limited, uniform and distinct. But beneficence, though in general equally enjoined by our religion, and equally needful to the conciliation of the divine favour, is yet, for the most part, with regard to its single acts, elective and voluntary. We may certainly, without injury to our fellow-beings, allow in the distribution of kindness something to our affections, and change the measure of our liberality according to our opinions and prospects, our hopes and fears. This rule therefore is not equally determinate and absolute with respect to offices of kindness, and acts of liberality, because liberality and kindness, absolutely determined, would lose their nature; for how could we be called tender, or charitable, for giving that which we are positively forbidden to withhold? (*The Rambler*, 81)

The Rambler, 81, is Johnson at his greatest. Here is the man who at the first level would insist upon the existence of simple, basic principles, general and yet specific, essential to the grounding of ordinary lives in the practical ways that prevent chaos: 'what is necessary must always be limited, uniform, and distinct'. Do not pretend that you do not know these things, nor in 'letter'd arrogance' deny their merit, just because they have become common sense in the deepest sense of 'common'. A man as desperate for the terms of basic survival as was Johnson, and as convinced of their precariousness if not thoroughly relearnt down the generations, would not scorn to start with simplicity. For this is the man who, for all my use and defence of it, would quarrel with the novel, as we now know it, for too often despising the general and basic for the sake of particular, impressive complexity. There are rules and principles, is the down-to-earth insistence.

Yet at a second level, as he moves from justice to charity, Johnson finds himself having to provide a rule for there being no rules about kindness. No rules are, if you like, the rule here, for – and this is where the tautology of verbal definition works for an honourable purpose – kindness is a favour, charity is voluntary; that is what those words *mean*, otherwise they would not be kindness or charity as such but obligation, say, or justice. That paradoxically *voluntary requirement* in such things as kindness is the rule of freedom, as it were, for us as moral beings. That is what it seems to mean to be human. 'We may certainly...allow in the distribution of kindness something to our affections.' How like Johnson, at this second level, to put 'may' and 'certainly' together. And how like him too, when he found himself arguing from his first level that, strictly speaking, friendship was not a Christian virtue for preferring the interest of a friend before universal benevolence, to be moved and delighted for once by an opponent's reply:

> MRS KNOWLES 'We are commanded to do good to all men...But, Doctor, our Saviour had twelve Apostles, yet there was *one* whom he *loved*. John was called "the disciple whom Jesus loved" '.
> JOHNSON (with eyes sparkling benignantly) 'Very well, indeed, Madam. You have said very well.'
> BOSWELL 'A fine application. Pray Sir, had you ever thought of it?'
> JOHNSON 'I had not, Sir.'[38]

It was spoken like a Christian. And Christ had been incarnate, had had the generosity of emotion beyond rule.

At this second level Johnson makes a rule of no rules, a strength of human weakness, and it is to biography that we must go to see examples of how, for such a man, things get worked out, as he was dragged into deeper and deeper levels of particularity. It is here, at those limits within which Johnson is the protagonist of a life which he cannot entirely articulate but must live, that novel-like writing can help, in order to show what it might be like to take *The Rambler*, 81, seriously, lest reading might fail in the direction of life.

Here, then, is a sort of parable. There was once a dancing-master who, notwithstanding the genteel nature of his talent, delighted in low company and, when drunk, could easily be induced to sign notes of promise which subsequently he was unable to discharge. Eventually he was imprisoned for debt. His wife, reports Sir John Hawkins, 'through Mrs Williams, got at Johnson', and Johnson apparently turned to lawyer Hawkins for advice. Hawkins, a severe moralistic man, then questioned the woman. From her account Hawkins could find no principle in the man: rescue him now, he would only go down the drain again later – 'I therefore dismissed her with a message to Johnson to this effect: that her husband made it impossible for his friends to help him, and must submit to his destiny.' But Hawkins concludes the anecdote ruefully thus:

> When I next saw Johnson, I told him that there seemed to be as exact a fitness between the character of the man and his associates, as is between the web of a spider and the wings of a fly, and I could not but think he was born to be cheated. Johnson seemed to acquiesce in my opinion; but I believe, before that, had set him at liberty by paying the debt.[39]

'But': ah, if he had only waited to hear wisdom...yet it was clear from Johnson's own writings that he knew there was a difference between what was 'charity' and what was 'pusillanimity'. In Sermon 27 he distinguishes between right charity and that indulgence which may in fact 'contribute to the corruption of mankind' because the giver is not scrupulous in what he does: for 'tho' he has not hid his talent in the ground, he has scattered it in the wind, and emploied it indifferently, to good and bad purposes.'[40] To Hawkins, in retrospect, all this became evidence that Johnson was right to confess that he 'had written as a philosopher, but he had not lived like one'.

'Johnson *seemed* to acquiesce.' But while Hawkins laid down the

law to him, what was Johnson silently thinking, knowing he had
jumped the verdict? He could not be sure he had or had not wasted his
money or been a weak fool in contrast to lawyer Hawkins, man of
certainties. But in *The Rambler*, 79, it is said that 'it is better to suffer
wrong than to do it, and happier to be sometimes cheated than not to
trust'. Even thus Johnson's character is the benefit of his doubt: that
little bit of human excess that smudges the fine print of the rules. Even
Jesus loved one disciple better than the rest, and Johnson relished
that. For such moments are the *life*; the residue, after all, which goes
not into Johnson's work so much as Johnson's biography, is thought
and weighed and *still* uncertain. The life goes into his biography
partly because people who knew him could not let such moments as
Hawkins describes go forgotten or seem wasted; but also because
Johnson himself could suggest but not entirely convey such moments
of silent, inadequate knowledge in his own work, when that very
work was the struggle for adequate knowledge. Accordingly he
thought himself a failure, a writer of mere occasional pieces. But what
cannot be said cannot be said, and the victories of sheer character are
for Johnson inseparable from what also felt to him like the defeats of
his capacity to ground his actions in reason.

Charity and uncertainty seem so close here that Johnson's act of
benevolence towards the dancing-master looks like an even bet, even
to himself, between strength and weakness. Hence his equivocal
silence before Hawkins. What if he, Johnson, were that dancing-
master: would he not expect to be bailed out again and again and
again? Yet so what? – Johnson could not expect *that* of himself, to bail
the man out every time. No man is more aware than Johnson of the
limits of sanity, though even so Mrs Thrale feared that he put too
much of himself under his own microscope. He could not say the half
of it, dared not even for fear of losing such general bearings as he
had – the bearings, for example, which he gained even from the
thought that intolerable complexity was itself a licence for a person to
reclaim, for sanity's sake, practical simplicities.

When Johnson did break silence, the half of it he *could* say
appeared under correspondingly double pressure, pushing him to
grasp at reality with even greater, tighter precision of words: in the
rule that there are no rules eventually, in the generalized particularity,
in the impersonalized, disguised autobiography. We can feel that
pressure of precision, with the unspeakable behind it, in the very
verbs near the end of *The Rambler*, 81 – on doing to others, such as the
dancing-master, as you would be done by:

not therefore what we might wish, but what we could demand from others, we are obliged to grant, since though we can easily know how much we might claim, it is impossible to determine what we should hope.

How far do we have to go? Where may we properly draw the line? Above all, how much is *enough*? Johnson longed for the peace of definitiveness, to be given if not by God then by our own language. When Boswell says that he did not find Johnson's work really moving, he could not have recognized it as the *passionate* act of reason it was. For the verbs are passionately leant on here for their definitiveness and calm certainty, as though the distinctions between them, minute yet real, could offer a guide to life off the page as well as on it. 'Wish' as opposed to 'demand', though psychologically they often coincide; 'hope' in contrast to 'claim': we feel the struggle of emotion and justice and, more, the confusing overlap of requirements between pity for one's self and conscience towards others, all summoned from those verbs by the other verbs, 'obliged' and 'to grant', making their claim. Life feels here like a double-handed fight: between strength and weakness, between giving and taking, between self and others – without being quite sure of which is which.

And then suddenly, magnificently, Johnson opens the closing paragraph of his essay, directly after this one, by changing levels. He shifts his appeal from language to experience, in what is at once victory and defeat, as though the very use and defeat of words of desperate precision provoked the acknowledgement that life, even after all that, remains more than words:

> But in all enquiries concerning the practice of voluntary and occasional virtues, it is safest for minds not oppressed with superstitious fears to determine against their own inclinations, and secure themselves from deficiency by doing more than they believe strictly necessary. For of this every man may be certain that, if he were to exchange conditions with his dependent, he should expect more than, with the utmost exertion of his ardour, he now will prevail upon himself to perform; and when reason has no settled rule, and our passions are striving to mislead us, it is surely the part of a wise man to err on the side of safety.

Johnson is so wonderful at keeping going, even in his sentences. For there is a reservation here that could have stopped his thought:

namely, that overscrupulous people could drive themselves mad by adopting the rule-of-thumb always to do more than they wanted to. But the reservation is both granted and integrated within the sentence's big push for safety: 'it is safest for minds *not* oppressed with superstitious fears'. I have been saying that in order to see the full meaning of Johnson's shorthand on the page we need to look at his meaning with a novelist's eye, for this is a man who had more in him than he could quite say. But it is also my argument that Johnson's genius is for the most part implicitly opposed to what we might now call the procedure of the realist novel; for, while recognizing the force of complex particularities, Johnson sees it as his task not to let them destroy the possibility of general sense and sentence. His sentences are perhaps our race's last-ditch fight, against a different idea of what is literature, for general rules as though for sanity itself. For when Johnson found himself forced out of reliance on the definitive precision of a single word, or two in contrast, he restored precision at the level not of specific words so much as of syntax – in modified general sentences. The more general, the more sympathetic. The price he paid for this generality was to leave the particularities, of which his words so often remind us and are meant to, for the most part in silence – for others, his biographers and followers, to pick up and save from redundancy. The paradox is that we need the particulars to see all that is at stake in Johnson's brief but bulgingly compressed essays; yet Johnson himself needed to repress those particulars and compress them in order to write the essays in the first place. That measures both the price he paid and the loss we have suffered in being less able to understand general writing; but above all it measures the artful success of Johnson's means of procedure. For Johnson used the contradictions between writing and living, as between the general and the particular, precisely to occupy, rather than evacuate, the space between the two. He reminds us of what he also represses or compresses.

'Pause awhile from learning to be wise', Johnson tells the young student in *The Vanity of Human Wishes*, and that pause is what happens between the penultimate and the final paragraphs of *The Rambler*, 81. Johnson does not mean that we should pause awhile from learning-to-be-wise: he could never bring himself to mean that. He means we should pause awhile from Learning (comma understood), if we are also to learn to look up from the page and be Wise. As the words themselves suggest, there is a Difference between Learning and Wisdom, a change of level, though they are often along the same line – even of poetry. In the last paragraph of *The Rambler*, 81, it is 'the part of a wise man' that the man of strict precision should suddenly see the need to release himself and us by finally not being, on second thought, too fussy at all. Reason cannot help us, passion will mislead us, we naturally do not want to put ourselves out for others: what should we do? Make a mistake? Make a mistake, says Johnson, but err on the safer side. That's the rule when there are no rules. It is oddly reassuring in its flawedness.

Johnson's rough-and-ready moral mathematics is a form of precision at a level which allows no other: men should 'secure themselves from *deficiency* by doing *more* than they believe *strictly necessary*'. More, that is, than stricter men such as Hawkins would do. That 'more' is what human beings in trouble hope for but may not expect, desire but may not gain; a need that is in excess of what is 'strictly necessary'. That incalculable extra bit makes the difference which being human can simply constitute, and human beings may sometimes add that bit just because they do not know what else or how much they can do. Baffled by the sum, they put themselves into the equation, mucking up the strict rational solution, with reason of their own.

What we have been witnessing is this: that for Johnson the differences that can be made in the movement from species to individual or, within the individual, from first to second nature or from man to writer and back again – all these differences, I say, are never radical changes of our nature, which remains as a seemingly unalterable base, but no more and no less than important modifications of it when raised to levels at which it can be reworked. Paradoxically, the basic perception that *there is not after all that much difference* between individual and species or between the individual's strengths and weaknesses, for all the continuing necessity of the moral effort to improve, *itself makes a difference* when the perception becomes the feeling of sympathy and charity as a result.

What this looks like in practice may be seen, finally, in Johnson's reaction to the plight of Christopher Smart, the poet who was confined to a madhouse:

> I did not think he ought to be shut up. His infirmities were not noxious to society. He insisted on people praying with him; and I'd as lief pray with Kit Smart as any one else. Another charge was, that he did not love clean linen; and I have no passion for it.[41]

It must seem another of Johnson's vicious circles that he himself would know the relation between his sympathy for Kit Smart and his own fearful feelings of being in similar danger, but it is precisely the health and sanity of that sympathy and relativism that also saves Johnson from partaking the same fate. For there are virtuous circles too: 'I'd as lief pray with Kit Smart as any one else.' Rueful, comic, defiant, affectionate, supportive, and finally devout, together. Though at different levels, basically we are all praying in the madhouse. The author in Johnson could take for granted the very fact that the man in him could *not* take things for granted: Johnson had it, and caught it, both ways. Contradiction also seemed to make him whole, not least because of all his fears to the contrary.

*

IV   Concluding: 'The System of Life'

'Dr Johnson being asked by a lady why he so constantly gave money to beggars, replied with great feeling, "Madam to enable them to beg on".' Hawkins, asking himself why Levet and Johnson were friends, said this, 'that Levett admired Johnson because others admired him, and that Johnson in pity loved Levett, because few others could find any thing in him to love.'[42] What signifies giving halfpence to common beggars? In short, why bother with people whom no one would think it reasonable to trouble over? Because, says Johnson, no one would think it reasonable to bother with them. In Johnson that answer is a matter either of silence or of tautology.

It is when we see Johnson sticking to tautologies that his common sense comes closest to inscrutability too. It is as it is; the rule is there are no rules for kindness; it is part of his philosophy for the philosopher to know why he must live like a man in contravention of some of his own wisdom. It was this stance of Johnson's that baffled and fascinated Boswell, the man who wanted to imitate Johnson in a way far more suspect than that of Sir Joshua Reynolds:

> Upon being asked by a friend what he should think of a man who was apt to say *non est tanti*; – 'That he's a stupid fellow, Sir; (answered Johnson): What would these *tanti* men be doing the while?' When I, in a low-spirited fit, was talking to him with indifference of the pursuits which generally engage us in a course of action, and enquiring a *reason* for taking so much trouble; 'Sir, (said he, in an animated tone) it is driving on the system of life.'[43]

Non est tanti: it is not worth while. A *tanti* man such as Boswell would be just the one to ask the wise man the reason for bothering, the point of carrying on. But the wisdom of this wise man was not, as we have seen, strictly rational, as though life were solely a matter for reason. You can imagine Boswell thinking: how did this Johnson keep going, simply by believing in keeping going? It is a tautology which seems barely able to support itself. Why, for example, did Johnson carry on writing? By his own admission (in *The Rambler, 207*), 'Difficulties embarrass, uncertainty perplexes, opposition retards, censure exasperates, or neglect depresses'; 'Seldom any man obtains more from his endeavours than a painful conviction of his defects.' Why carry on? 'For money,' the wise man had been known to say to the *tanti* man, provokingly unidealistic. But in *The Rambler*, 207, he says with straightness, 'We proceed, because we have begun; we complete our design, that the labour may not be in vain.' For when the enthusiasm and the sense of heroism wane, 'we are compelled to implore severer powers', the grimmer power of just keeping going. That too is driving on the system of life.

When Hawkins complains that Johnson wrote like a philosopher but did not live like one – witness his action towards the dancing-master – it seems a sort of victory for Johnson. But when Johnson makes the charge against himself, and we think of his vices and errors as he did, it seems a defeat – and none the less so for the philosopher in him already, tautologically, knowing that. Victory? Defeat? It is as though the two terms are held together in solution in Johnson: one of the reasons he has lasted as a writer must be his leaving things still resonantly unsettled yet related. It all shakes down into a life-system: Johnson's. And it still leaves us, like Boswell, asking: Who, what was Johnson, at once so different from and so like others, so resistant and yet so accepting, so precise at one level and so defiantly unfussy at another, so complex and so committed to simplicity? Who and what was he that he could still hold all this together when it might have been expected to fall apart? The tolerance of Johnson seems very close to his mystery, for the mystery of 'the system of life' as he experienced it between his writing and his living has been the concern of this chapter. As Saul Bellow's protagonist puts it in *The Dean's December*: 'He was like everybody else, but not as everybody else conceived it'.

CHAPTER TWO

'You Tossed and Gored Several Persons'

I Johnson the Old Bear

Johnson's contemporaries were as likely to find him intimidating as sympathetic. As Carlyle was to put it, 'Johnson passed not for a fine nature, but for a dull, almost brutal one' – the irritable bear, the angry bull tossing and goring people even through the power of his words.[1] How did this apparently animal behaviour comport with the humanity and sympathy we witnessed in the last chapter? This chapter must take on a more unattractive Johnson and see the power of his compassion as only one part of the nature of his personal power.

For personal power was what Johnson had. Intimidatingly, he seemed to embody rules in his very act of being – rules that people around him often found themselves in danger of unthinkingly violating, rules that he himself often seemed to be contradicting in later or different circumstances. At once so formal and yet so violently unpredictable, Johnson was a source of frightened irritation and bafflement to one such as Mrs Thrale. She writes of him, with inadvertent comedy: 'Though thus uncommonly ready both to give and take offence, Mr Johnson had many rigid maxims concerning the necessity of continued softness and compliance of disposition'; 'Mr Johnson liked a frolic or jest well enough; though he had strange rules about it too: and very angry was he if anybody offered to be merry when he was disposed to be grave'.[2] Mrs Thrale is not slow to give instances. No sooner did she sympathize with him over the quarrelling of the people he had charitably admitted to his home, than he turned on her:

> He used to lament pathetically to me ... that they made his life miserable from the impossibility he found of making theirs

happy, when every favour he bestowed on one was wormwood to the rest. If, however, I ventured to blame their ingratitude, and condemn their conduct, he would instantly set about softening the one and justifying the other; and finished commonly by telling me, that I knew not how to make allowances for situations I never experienced.[3]

If, like a good moralist, Mrs Thrale rebuked the daughter of her own housekeeper for sitting down unpermitted in her mother's presence, Johnson broke out: 'Why, she gets her living, does she not, without her mother's help? Let the wench alone.'[4] Though this was certainly the bear against the bourgeoise, on the basis of a wider and more painful experience of the nature of economic life, still his sympathy seems to need and involve nervous anger too in both of the above instances.

'Strange rules': was Johnson's an arbitrary temperamental despotism, nervously fighting itself through others? Would he not have done more good, Boswell asked him, 'if he had been more gentle'?[5] For if his rules were not just temperamentally arbitrary and autobiographical, why did he not explain them without getting angry? In other words, does Johnson's power stand for anything more than the aggressive assertion of itself, filling in the gaps of his uncertainty?

Suppose for a moment it is not simply a personal issue. Suppose instead we consider the possibility that such resistance as we may well feel towards Johnson nowadays is in fact a resistance to what he has helped to make the eighteenth century stand for – even by berating the people of his own time. What may seem to us to be disagreeable in him could have some relation to a more general prejudice against what have come to be seen as eighteenth-century ways. Here, for example, is one confession of just such a prejudice:

The more I contemplate the eighteenth century the more interesting I find it. In my youth it seemed to me unworthy of a glance. The books and the men, Shelley above all, who stirred my young blood belonged to the early nineteenth century. I was led to regard the last century as a dull period of stagnation and decay, a tomb into which the spirit of man sank after the slow death which followed the Renaissance. The dawn of the nineteenth century was an Easter Day of the human soul, rising from the sepulchre and flinging aside the old eighteenth-century winding-sheet.

The author is Havelock Ellis, writing at the very close of the nineteenth century, and what he gives us here is a simple but honest and representative point of departure.[6] His young man's prejudice in favour of a vague, belated Romanticism is historical as much as personal and, as such, is I believe still the prejudice of many of *us* as well. We scarcely realize how (vaguely) 'Romantic' we are: if we did we might have to be more – or less – so. To a young Romantic Samuel Johnson must seem an essentially old as well as old-fashioned man, and it may be of no help that Johnson himself could almost foresee the reaction of such a youth to reading *The Rambler:*

> To a young man entering the world, with fulness of hope, and ardor of persuit, nothing is so unpleasing as the cold caution, the faint expectations, the scrupulous diffidence which experience and disappointments certainly infuse. (*The Rambler*, 69)

'Bliss was it in that dawn to be alive/But to be young was very heaven': Johnson died in 1784; the generation that was already leaving him behind, in virtually another world it sometimes seems, was one that was more than ever before a generation of youth and its visions, resistant to quasi-parental forewarnings. Reviewing the *Rambler* in 1802 in his *Critical Enquiry*, Mudford wrote: 'Life, in its very sunshine, is perhaps sufficiently beset with evil and we need not Monitors to tell us, at every step, that destruction may be the consequence. This is perpetually awakening the mind to a bitter consciousness of its situation ... A young mind rising from a perusal of the *Rambler* would conceive the most melancholy ideas of human nature and human events.'[7]

And yet, in the case of Havelock Ellis, the older man's partial recantation of his own youthful position constitutes a challenge to Romantic prejudice. For what if it is true that as we get older we also need something older, something that Havelock Ellis at least found by turning back to the eighteenth century? This present book is an attempt imaginatively to incorporate Samuel Johnson within life now. It results from being tempted, by such as Havelock Ellis, to ask what it would feel like, and whether it would help, to be an eighteenth-century man in terms that we might grasp in our own time. That is of course too demandingly crude a question for the taste of a professional scholar or historian, quite properly wishing to respect the past as something to be preserved from mere appropriation, and yet perhaps not too crude a question to act as a starting point for the

imagination of a novelist – certainly a novelist such as Ford Madox
Ford in his tetralogy *Parade's End.* For *Parade's End* is the story of
Christopher Tietjens, essentially an eighteenth-century man obliged
to live through the period of the Great War, during which he finds the
values of his old eighteenth century, already eroded by the nineteenth
century, finally collapsing at the beginning of the twentieth. To his
wife Tietjens 'was an eighteenth-century figure of the Dr. Johnson
type', and in his brother's last illness the book that Tietjens reads to
him is none other than Boswell's *Life of Johnson:*

> Over Boswell the two brothers had got as thick as thieves with
> an astonishing intimacy – and with an astonishing similarity. If
> one of them made a comment on Bennet Langton it would be
> precisely the comment that the other had on his lips. It was what
> asses call telepathy, nowadays... a warm, comfortable feeling,
> late at night with the light shaded from your eyes, the voice
> going on through the deep silence of London that awaited the
> crash of falling bombs.[8]

Free to imagine an eighteenth-century man alive in the twentieth
century, Ford has then, however, to confront himself with the
thought that such cultural memories are, like 'a warm, comfortable
feeling, late at night', no more than evasive nostalgia. Reading Dr
Johnson at times like these... Is not personal time, and the cultural
appropriations made within it presumably to protect and enlarge it,
always to be exposed by history as an ironically self-diminishing
refuge? Who needs another book about Samuel Johnson? If anyone
does, how much more than merely fictive, nostalgic, imaginary is that
need?

I leave these challenges to stand as worries, worries about fictive
cultural interests that Johnson himself had in mind when he criticized
Milton's use of the artifices of pastoral in relation to the realities of
death when writing *Lycidas.* We shall return to *Parade's End* again
soon. But for the moment, with these risks and doubts in mind, I
should still like to follow Ford in seeking to activate a novelist's
imagination and translate historical problems into personal terms, to
put ourselves in mind of Johnson. So let us first think again about the
young Havelock Ellis's adverse view of men such as old Johnson.
What I am about to do is probably neither entirely fair nor scholarly,
but I do it for the sake of finding an image of what it might be like, at
some authentic level, to consign the eighteenth century to the tomb. It
is this: that I find myself associating with young Havelock Ellis's

historical prejudice the following personal one from the pen of Mrs
Thrale. They are not the same thing, I readily grant: dismissing the
writer for cultural, historical reasons and freeing yourself from
somebody on your doorstep for personal ones. But as I see it, readers
of works from the past should always risk asking themselves: 'What if
this book were present and real, what if it wasn't a book but a person
embodying what it tries to say?' We owe such an effort to the
experimental possibility that we have even within our personal time
deep imaginative memories of other times and histories, reawaiting
activation. At any rate, here is a widow who, not yet aged,
is – understandably enough, I think – giving up on the great old
literary man of the eighteenth century for the sake, eventually, of a
new life and a new husband:

> I had been crossed in my intentions of going abroad, and found
> it convenient, for every reason of health, peace, and pecuniary
> circumstances, to retire to Bath, where I knew Mr Johnson
> would not follow me, and where I could for that reason
> command some little portion of time for my own use; a thing
> impossible while I remained at Streatham or at London, as my
> hours, carriage, and servants had long been at his command,
> who would not rise in the morning till twelve o'clock perhaps,
> and oblige me to make breakfast for him till the bell rung for
> dinner, though much displeased if the toilet was neglected, and
> though much of the time we passed together was spent in
> blaming and deriding, very justly, my neglect of economy, and
> waste of that money which might make many families happy.
> The original reason of our connection, his *particularly
> disordered health and spirits*, had been long at an end, and he
> had no other ailments than old age and general infirmity, which
> every professor of medicine was ardently zealous and generally
> attentive to palliate, and to contribute all in their power for the
> prolongation of a life so valuable. Veneration for his virtue,
> reverence for his talents, delight in his conversation, and
> habitual endurance of a yoke my first husband first put upon
> me, and of which he contentedly bore his share for sixteen or
> seventeen years, made me go on so long with Mr Johnson; but
> the perpetual confinement I will own to have been terrifying in
> the first years of our friendship, and irksome in the last; nor
> could I pretend to support it without help, when my coadjutor
> was no more.[9]

In this way Mrs Thrale parted from Samuel Johnson on 5 April 1783. He died in December 1784. In 1786 Mrs Thrale – who in July 1784, to Johnson's pain, had become Mrs Piozzi – published her *Anecdotes of Samuel Johnson*. As we can see, she goes to some trouble in her account to make it clear that she did not consider herself as delivering over to death an old man who truly must have seemed to her difficult, moralizing and jealous. He would keep her up, to listen and make tea, until four o'clock in the morning because, she says, he was terrified of retiring to bed and loneliness. But he did not mention the fear; he said instead that 'no one forbore their own gratifications for the sake of pleasing another' and, defiantly, that people stayed up with him simply because they really wanted to. Or when Mrs Thrale lamented the loss of a first cousin killed in America, he told her to stop canting: how would the world be worse if all her relations were spitted like larks and roasted for her dog's dinner?[10] Was it unreasonable to need to get away from what she took to be 'that natural roughness of his manner', demanding exactness in all things domestic save his own habits of rising, dress, eating, arguing and retiring at night?[11] Yet Johnson himself, on taking final leave of the Streatham house on 6 October 1782, a full eighteen months after the death of the master, must have felt himself given over, to face God and his own mortality again (for the two always appeared to him together). He had to make this prayer:

> Almighty God, Father of all mercy, help me by thy Grace that I may with humble and sincere thankfulness remember the comforts and conveniences which I have enjoyed at this place and that I may resign them with holy submission, equally trusting in thy protection when Thou givest and when Thou takest away. Have mercy upon me, O Lord, have mercy upon me.
>
> To thy fatherly protection, O Lord, I commend this family. Bless, guide, and defend them. That they may so pass through this world as finally to enjoy in thy presence everlasting happiness for Jesus Christ's sake. Amen.[12]

He was seventy-three; his own wife had been dead for thirty years. It shocked Boswell to read these two passages of farewell, Mrs Thrale's and Dr Johnson's, side by side.

It is not difficult to understand and even share Boswell's feeling. But perhaps there is room, even here, for some of that Johnsonian 'roughness' which first terrified and finally irked Mrs Thrale – only this time directing the roughness, as Johnson might almost have wanted, upon the case of Johnson himself. Take the second paragraph of Johnson's prayer. For the sake of 'this family', not himself, it is indeed truly Christian, in the spirit of loving thy neighbour as thyself and turning the smitten cheek. For Johnson himself had written in *The Rambler,* 74, against old age's 'fancying that we suffer by neglect, unkindness, or any evil which admits a remedy rather than by the decays of nature, which cannot be prevented, or repaired'. But, even more toughly, that second paragraph is also truly Christian in being thus formally, and not merely penitentially, the second thought; for the Christian's primary duty is first to save his own soul: 'that we may, as Chillingworth expresses it, consider things as if there were no other beings in the world but God and ourselves' (*The Rambler*, 29). 'Have mercy upon me, O Lord, have mercy upon me.' The underlying, fallen-psychological temptation – of putting yourself first and others second – is tacitly held, acknowledged and chastened within the still-abiding theologically formal requirement. The world may mis-interpret from the outside, but the prayer is to God. In contrast, Mrs Thrale's apologies, justifications and second thoughts have to reside, more uneasily, within the irregularities of a secular syntax: what does she feel about his 'deriding, *very justly,* my neglect of economy' or about 'a *yoke* my husband first put upon me, and of which *he contentedly* bore his share'? She cannot stop, even in the muddle; still has to carry on within the pull of her new life, despite old scruples. The old man's being a great man cannot make enough difference at this level – indeed, no great man ever so much concerned himself with such ordinary ironies as did Johnson himself; but the knowledge that people often would feel they had to do what Mrs Thrale did does make a difference. That is also how it is.

Yet in one sense Johnson was in a better, as well as a far worse, condition than Mrs Thrale: there are levels. He had said to Boswell that intelligence consisted mainly in the ability to abstract, and his own gift for abstraction raised his language from subservience under particular events to as general a view of human affairs under the eye of eternity as could be purchased by one still beneath it. It is a finally religious intelligence, formal and abstracting, where Mrs Thrale's is anecdotal or narrative. And in order to go on Mrs Thrale had to leave Johnson behind, or above. Such things the old man might have expected – were it not that he *also* expected his human nature not to be able to bear to expect them. On the death of his friend Levet at the beginning of 1782 Johnson had written:

> Condemn'd to hope's delusive mine,
> As on we toil from day to day,
> By sudden blast or slow decline
> Our social comforts drop away.

Hope was at once necessary and delusive. Like Levet, Mrs Thrale and the Streatham home had been one of those 'social comforts' on borrowed time.

So perhaps after all, considering their intimate relation, it is no wonder that it has been with the writings rather as it was with the life: the nod made to 'his virtue', 'his talents' and 'his conversation' – but finally, in historical terms too, Johnson got left behind, a Boswellian 'character' for years to come. For a writer so close as Johnson to virtual tautology is in grave danger of self-cancellation: he *expected* that he could not quite accept in his own case what he could so easily and generally predict of others; he knew the delusions under which he also knew we would all have to continue to suffer. Johnson's knowledge can look like a self-enclosed, circular system, resigned and rueful and wry and stoical, but also on the verge of declaring itself ironically redundant. At any time Johnson seems to write as an older, wiser man: it can seem, when you read the bear, as though life were always over, decided, fixed in memory; his sentences are always so ambitious of finality even through their own self-qualifications. In this way – too old, too final or simply too ordinary as a thinker – Johnson can appear to the young Romantic both limited and limiting, even in his practical wisdom. As Mudford suggests, his blanket common sense can hang over you like a pre-emptive limitation of what human beings through particular possibilities could become in a new, young future. 'To generalize is to be an idiot,' said Blake, burying the age of Johnson. 'He does not set us thinking for the first time,' complained Hazlitt. 'His reflections present themselves like reminiscences; do not disturb the ordinary march of our thoughts ... After closing the volumes of the *Rambler*, there is nothing we remember as a new truth gained to the mind.'[13] The old man's old, old story.

None the less, such criticisms bring me back to Havelock Ellis and the challenge that the older Ellis offers to youths such as he had been. And what is striking here is that what the older Havelock Ellis found himself approving in the eighteenth century was something not unrelated to 'that natural roughness of his manner' which Mrs Thrale found so difficult to live with in Johnson himself. 'Without the eighteenth century,' wrote Havelock Ellis, 'we should never have known many of the greatest qualities which are latent, and too often only latent, in our race.' The eighteenth century, he thought, recovered 'the old English spirit' lost or adulterated since the age of Chaucer: the great Englishmen of the eighteenth century possessed sobriety and sagacity, 'a mellow human solidity, such as the Romans possessed always'; these were men 'marked by sanity and catholicity, a superb solidity of spirit; they became genuinely cosmpolitan without losing any of their indigenous virtues.'[14]

It must seem an old-fashioned, fanciful, even chauvinistic vision, this nostalgia. And indeed Ford's Tietjens is himself driven to admit that 'it is not a good thing to belong to the seventeenth or eighteenth centuries in the twentieth'. For what Tietjens stands for, even in a conversation with a friend to whom he was previously admitted his wife's betrayals, is rules:

> Macmaster said:
>   'That woman's the cruellest beast...'
>   'You might,' Tietjens interrupted, 'remember that you're talking about my wife.'
>   'I don't see,' Macmaster said, 'how one can talk about Sylvia without...'
>   'The line is a perfectly simple one to draw,' Tietjens said. 'You can relate a lady's actions if you know them and are asked to. You mustn't comment. In this case you don't know the lady's actions even, so you may as well hold your tongue.' He sat looking straight in front of him.[15]

Rules established as such precisely because people will tend to break them; rules all the more necessary when others are breaking them and breaking you too: shall they also be allowed to break your belief in the rules? This particular conversation takes place early in the novel, but it is not hard to see what the dawn of the age of modernism will do to this sense of absolute rules of propriety and conduct – the more so when the rise of modernism is to be partly defined by the very way its consciousness of social context and historical relativism displaces the old effort towards fixedness. It becomes barely possible, for example, for Tietjens to use the phrase 'well bred', as Johnson does in the following, without consciousness of anachronism and even snobbery rendering its use now ironic:

> I expressed some surprise at Cadogan's recommending good

humour, as if it were quite in our power to attain it. JOHNSON: 'Why, sir, a man grows better humoured as he grows older. He improves by experience. When young, he thinks himself of great consequence, and every thing of importance. As he advances in life, he learns to think himself of no consequence, and little things of little importance; and so he becomes more patient, and better pleased. All good humour and complaisance are acquired. Naturally a child seizes directly what it sees, and thinks of pleasing itself only. By degrees, it is taught to please others; and that this will ultimately produce the greatest happiness. If a man is not convinced of that, he never will practise it. Common language speaks the truth as to this: we say, a person is well *bred*.[16]

Indeed, what is so astonishing about that old fixed idea of breeding is that within it the very idea of being fixed and unable to learn is rejected: Boswell 'expressed some surprise at Cadogan's recommending good humour, *as if it were quite in our power to attain it*'. Johnson can be caught in *ill* humour with the young, such as Boswell, when, putting their feelings first, they will not think they can learn feelings, like good humour, as if they were principles.

But where Dictionary Johnson could explain and redeem the deeper meaning of common social usage by uncovering the memory beneath the words 'well bred', as part of the effort to learn values that do not simply come as a gift of nature; further on down Tietjens is implicated in a class consciousness that his words are also those of the nineteenth-century public schoolboy he has been. Ironically, it is that sort of degeneration that Johnson was trying to use hard-thought language to prevent. 'You *would* think that sort of thing, wouldn't you?' the others can almost say to Tietjens, incapacitating him, as the Great War more literally does, through the insinuations of historical relativism. What can Tietjens say back?

'I stand for monogamy and chastity. And for no talking about it. Of course if a man who's a man wants to have a woman he has her. And again, no talking about it. He'd no doubt be in the end better, and better off, if he didn't. Just as it would probably be better for him if he didn't have the second glass of whisky and soda . . .'

'You call that monogamy and chastity!' Macmaster interjected.

'I do,' Tietjens answered. 'And it probably is, at any rate it's clean. What is loathsome is all your fumbling in placket-holes and polysyllabic Justification by Love. You stand for lachrymose polygamy. That's all right if you can get your club to change its rules.'[17]

Macmaster is writing a book on Dante Gabriel Rossetti: it is that wistful mixing up of physical desire within spiritual yearning that Tietjens accurately calls 'promiscuity'. Art now thrown into prominence as justification by words alone is precisely what stops Tietjens talking or makes him retire behind prosaically colloquial simplicities, his whole project of the accurate drawing of lines thus pre-empted. But again this is an early passage in the tetralogy. In the age of modern fluidity, when even the principles which oppose it can come to seem degenerated into obstinacy and priggishness, a man such as Tietjens must be tested by his author as much as rejected by his fellows if he is to stand for anything more than a fictive nostalgia. Accordingly, in the course of the work the man who stands for the rules of monogamy and chastity, who will not divorce his unfaithful wife and would rather sacrifice his reputation than his beliefs, is increasingly drawn into living with another woman. How far this is his defeat by the times, or how far his character and beliefs are deep enough both to withstand and to enable the mutation – this is Ford's serious concern.

It must be ours too if we are to think how to 'use' Johnson without a nostalgia itself as misleadingly artificial as was Rossetti's spirituality in Tietjens's eyes. For no one is more severely conscious of the dangers of literature in promoting a fictive sense of self-importance and imaginative self-deception than Johnson himself:

There is nothing more fatal to a man whose business is to think, than to have learned the art of regaling his mind with those airy gratifications. Other vices or follies are restrained by fear... But this invisible riot of the mind, this secret prodigality of being, is secure from detection, and fearless of reproach. The dreamer retires to his apartments, shuts out the cares and interruptions of mankind, and abandons himself to his own fancy; new worlds rise up before him, one image is followed by another, and a long succession of delights dance round him. He is at last called back to life by nature, or by custom, and enters peevish into society, because he cannot model it to his own will. (*The Rambler*, 89)

Fearful of what we can do to ourselves in 'secret', it becomes vital to *distinguish* (so often Johnson's word) between what can be properly acquired and learnt from books and what is merely fictive imitation, arty, wordy pretence. Johnson, following Jeremy Taylor, is not interested in the luxuries of hero-worship:

> Taylor justly blames some pious persons, who indulge their fancies too much, set themselves by the force of imagination, in the place of the ancient martyrs and confessors, and question the validity of their own faith because they shrink at the thoughts of flames and tortures. It is, says he, sufficient that you are able to encounter the temptations which now assault you; when God sends trials, he may send strength. (*The Rambler*, 29)

Like youth, literature can be a temptation towards a misplaced sense of specialness. What Johnson directs us to is where we are now, quite ordinarily, and such a direction is itself a mark of that mellow solidity and sobriety of spirit which Havelock Ellis spoke of as characterizing the age. 'Sufficient unto the day is the evil thereof.'

With Johnson, it is often quite sufficient – and too often more than enough – for us to consider the ordinary passage of our lives in time. Think, for example, of the change that took place in Havelock Ellis's views between youth and middle age. That difference prompts the strange thought which is one of the foundations of this book: that although at first *historical time* may seem to have taken us away from Johnson, *personal time* may still lead us back to him to meet a need. By personal time I am thinking of the reassessments that take place during that slow, gradual shift from youth to age. It is this, as it were, second stage of life after the preliminaries of infancy and youth which Johnson highlights in *The Rambler*, 151, on the climacterics of the human mind. For it is at this stage that he looks for the reign of judgement or reason, of prudence and foresight in the course of the transition from novelty to adult experience. And it is at this stage too that a potentially profitable uncertainty develops to replace a person's initial single-mindedness:

> Baxter, in the narrative of his own life, has enumerated several opinions, which, though he thought them evident and incontestable at his first entrance into the world, time and experience disposed him to change . . . we perceive that we have changed our minds, though perhaps we cannot discover when the alteration happened, or by what causes it was produced. (*The Rambler*, 196)

As Joseph Heller puts it in his novel of that name, 'something happened' – something we cannot quite put our finger on or specifically recall as a single event – to change or determine or confuse us *en route*, even by accidents; making us within our memories into more than one person even to ourselves; unfixing predispositions in the vital interchange between character and life over time. 'Every man . . . will by a slight retrospection be able to discover, that his mind has suffered many revolutions, that the same things have in the several parts of his life been condemned and approved, persued and shunned' (*The Adventurer*, 107). In this enriching and yet sobering second stage of life, we may need (as Imlac puts it in Chapter xxx of *Rasselas*) 'to recover some art lost to mankind' – a way of being, I shall argue, of which Johnson is in memory, for the sake of becoming fully grown up.

It is true that that appeal to grow up is sometimes given through a bear-like growl – as Mrs Thrale describes:

> On another occasion, when he was musing over the fire in our drawing-room at Streatham, a young gentleman called to him suddenly, and I suppose he thought disrespectfully, in these words: Mr Johnson, Would you advise me to marry? 'I would advise no man to marry, Sir (returns for answer in a very angry tone Dr Johnson), who is not likely to propagate under-standing;' and so left the room.[18]

But false tenderness misleads us if we merely suppose, with Mrs Thrale, that such behaviour is in simple contradiction with the advocacy of good humour. For consider a counter-example. At three one morning, after a night in the tavern, young Beauclerk and Langton came to knock up the formidable Johnson to get him to join them in a ramble; he appeared at the window, bewigged, growling and poker in hand, then recognizing them cried, 'What, is it you, you dogs! I'll have a frisk with you'.[19] Without mere self-pity for his own lonely widowerhood, Johnson *is* frisky. And we misread him in his work likewise if we do not feel, as Johnson himself did, the indignities of experience beneath his apparent authority over it. One final anecdote from the life may serve to show how, through his very conversation, Johnson prepared himself for this equivocal authority in writing from the book of his own remembered errors. Here is Boswell unwarily presuming to congratulate Johnson on not repenting his failure to attend his tutor at Oxford – stand back for the bite:

Mr Jorden asked me why I had not attended. I answered I had been sliding on Christ-Church meadow. And this I said with as much *nonchalance* as I am now talking to you. I had no notion that I was wrong or irreverent to my tutor. BOSWELL: 'That, Sir, was great fortitude of mind.' JOHNSON: 'No, Sir, stark insensibility.'[20]

– 'No, Sir': but this is not simply the victory of the old wise man. The negative here is indeed strong, because it defeats Boswell in the midst of his experiments with flattery. But without Boswell all this would be to Johnson on his own a matter not so much of the wit and wisdom of Dr Johnson (No, Sir, that is secondary!) but, more weakly, of the follies of the young Johnson in the first place. This very recognition is of course included tacitly in the robust, knowledgeable comedy of Johnson's tart reply. 'You showed great wisdom, Dr Johnson, in thus confuting Boswell.' 'No, Sir, I showed him my youthful inadequacy. But fortunately, Sir, he missed it, and I didn't.' Johnson was no great lover of apology, shame or confession, and could relish his own playfully devious honesty. For his retort to Boswell, at once masterful and modest, was his way of hiding his superiority within the very show of superiority, as well as ensuring that, with beautiful balance, he won and lost at the same time – the good humour of the bear, the frisky moralizer playing off against his younger self even as against Boswell. In Johnson we can still see the confident young fool behind the older man's achieving of wisdom on second thought. We recognized his translations of himself in Chapter One.

For in reading Johnson we can always see something of the personal history of what he has learnt, checked and acquired, in almost archaeological layers within the syntax, and we can recognize what younger primary forces beneath the achievements both challenge them and make them necessary, though difficult, to retain. Johnson knew that men like him, who were not going to be mediocre and were not going to be simply a pleasure to have around, tended to terrify people into discomforted alienation if not positive enmity. Yet this bear-like quarreller who would never own himself beaten in argument can turn round at the end of *The Rambler*, 188, and write: 'it is always necessary to be loved, but not always necessary to be reverenced'. Mrs Thrale had reverenced him, if anything.

The loneliness of his own intelligent awkwardness hurt Johnson, made him as he aged appreciate the social qualities of good humour he had earlier scorned. But his earlier scorn was only defensive, out of hopelessness as much as pride: for he told Boswell that he had despaired of ever pleasing – this twitching, pockmarked young man – and gave up thoughts of doing so until he was past thirty. In many ways Johnson barely had a real youth, befriended the young only when older – even at three in the morning. We can sense all this, I am suggesting, behind the back-to-front recommendation of good humour he makes in *The Rambler*, 72:

> Good humour is indeed generally degraded by the characters in which it is found; for being considered as a cheap and vulgar quality, we find it often neglected by those that having excellencies of higher reputation and brighter splendor, perhaps imagine that they have some right to gratify themselves at the expense of others, and are to demand compliance, rather than practice it.

The bear turns round on himself no less than he turned on others: we always feel the original power as true to itself even through its further self-modifications. And that seems not only more possible but also more frank than an attempt at wholesale reformation from scratch. Johnson sticks to his own basic nature, even in using it to amend itself. He does not merely tame the bear, in order to be apparently civilized.

Many critics have noted how Jane Austen inherited from her 'dear Dr Johnson' a belief in the necessity for strong moral principles; but the Jane Austen of *Persuasion* also repeated, in her own way, the Johnsonian capacity for turnarounds in the second stage of life. Anne Elliot gave up her young man on the advice of a relative: she was supposed to be too young and he – more to the point without fortune – too risky. Years later she believed that she would have been happier in maintaining the engagement than she ever became through the sacrifice of it; not only would she have been happier in adversity with him, but in fact he had gained a prosperity more quickly than even he in his confidence had supposed. What if now a young woman, in similar circumstances, sought her advice as she had sought Lady Russell's?

> How eloquent could Anne Elliot have been – how eloquent, at least, were her wishes on the side of early warm attachment, and a cheerful confidence in futurity, against that over-anxious caution which seems to insult exertion and distrust Providence! – She had been forced into prudence in her youth, she learned romance as she grew older – the natural sequel of an unnatural beginning.[21]

As with Anne Elliot and romance, so with Samuel Johnson and some of the ordinary values such as good humour: the achievements of second thought. In this chapter I shall therefore be arguing that for all Johnson's initially unpromising appearance in life, as witnessed by Mrs Thrale, and in writing, as described by Mudford, he is in fact deeply on the side of warmth, confidence and exertion rather than overanxious caution and distrust.

The bear snapped at the young man who asked him whether he should marry, 'I would advise no man to marry, Sir, who is not likely to propagate understanding', and left the room. But the story goes on:

> Our companion looked confounded, and I believe had scarce recovered the consciousness of his own existence, when Johnson came back, and drawing his chair among us, with altered looks and a softened voice, joined in the general chat, insensibly led the conversation to the subject of marriage, which he laid himself out in a dissertation so useful, so elegant, so founded on the true knowledge of human life, and so adorned with beauty of sentiment, that no one ever recollected the offence, except to rejoice in its consequences.

And there is a third twist too, more in memory than correction of the first:

> He repented just as certainly however, if he had been led to praise any person or thing by accident more than he thought it deserved; and was on such occasions comically earnest to destroy the praise or pleasure he had unintentionally given.[22]

That third movement, sometimes so comic, sometimes so bearish, is none the less as important as the more ostensibly attractive second; as though there was something deeper than guilt or good humour, something of which guilt and good humour are only sometimes the proper expression. We can think of Johnson going through these two or three different phases of thought in life, in response to incidents like the above, weighing the rival claims of anger, sympathy, manners, integrity and trying to make sure of the proper application of each. But the triumph of the archetypal Johnsonian sentence is to hold these several phases and differing centres of gravity together – in imitation of the co-ordination required in the very act of growing up into a complicated yet whole human being. When Johnson says in his poem that Levet is 'coarsely kind', he is not merely being ambivalent in his own mind, as though to say Levet was kind but he was also coarse. For Johnson is not interested in the two parts of his own mind here so much as the one thing in Levet whose reality compels the two to hold together. Johnson's robustness takes us beyond mere division even by working through it, and it is that eighteenth-century solidity which we must now test even as Ford did Tietjens. For if we are to use Johnson legitimately rather than fictively, in the service of the second stage of human formation, then we must not duck the challenge of his robustness in demanding real understanding rather than cant – especially as it is always easier to appreciate what at its very first appearance looks welcomingly tender, good-humouredly ambivalent or touchingly vulnerable.

*

II 'Suffering is no duty...' (The Rambler, 44)

Johnson was a good hater of fictively affected sensibility. A young man such as Boswell seemed encouraged in emotional pretences by the spectacle of Rousseau's Romanticism. Let Boswell try his almost endless complaining of inner misery on Johnson – misery, said Boswell, which was the worse for being quite without definitely pinpointable external causes! Here is Johnson's response:

> You are always complaining of melancholy, and I conclude from those complaints that you are fond of it. No man talks of that which he is desirous to conceal, and every man desires to conceal that of which he is ashamed... Make it an invariable and obligatory law to yourself, never to mention your own mental diseases; if you are never to speak of them, you will think on them but little, and if you think little of them, they will molest you rarely. When you talk of them, it is plain that you want either praise or pity; for praise there is no room, and pity will do you no good; therefore, from this hour speak no more, think no more, about them.[23]

Can this be the same man whom, a chapter ago, I praised for his tolerance and his sympathy? When he says 'every man desires to conceal that of which he is ashamed', is this not a clue that what is behind this rage is Johnson's own fear of *his* secret melancholy, the identification at one level actually preventing the sympathy at another? Had Boswell seen Johnson's diaries, he could have shown the man the mote in his own eye. But even on one occasion when

Boswell did dare to quote Johnson against himself in mere social argument, Johnson had exploded in anger against 'what he could least of all bear' and smashed Boswell with an accusation of drunkenness: 'There is no arguing with Johnson; for if his pistol misses fire, he knocks you down with the butt end of it.'[24] And all this violence is in defence against what Johnson took to be Boswell's breach of good manners! Well might Mrs Thrale wonder at Johnson's 'strange rules'. For is not this precisely that want of 'good humour' which Johnson himself laments in those who 'demand compliance, rather than practise it'? 'All should be warned', concluded Mrs Thrale, 'against such coarseness of manners, as drove even from *him* those who loved, honoured and esteemed him.'[25] Johnson, said many, kept beneath the old preacher in him a wild bear. Perhaps indeed he loved Boswell for not minding, even relishing that – as on their tour of the Hebrides, when Boswell notes Johnson's good humour ... for once:

> I told him, that I was diverted to hear all the people whom we had visited in our tour, say, 'Honest man! he's pleased with every thing; he's always content!' 'Little do they know,' said I. He laughed, and said, 'You rogue!'[26]

The laugh is fine here, but on other occasions is not the anger at being quoted against himself or at seeing his own neuroses in others a nervous fear lest 'we are known to others as well as to ourselves'?[27] Johnson often seems to be caught between seeing the whole and still being only a part within it.

Yet in this section I am concerned to deny that Johnson's mortifying attack on Boswell's complaint of melancholy is in fundamental contradiction of his belief in good social manners and Christian sympathy. Johnson's very roughness to Boswell is actually also the voice of eighteenth-century propriety made incarnate. For once abstracted, that propriety may be explained as it is in Adam Smith's *The Theory of Moral Sentiments*. One of Smith's central propositions in that work is this, toughly: 'Compassion can never be exactly the same with original sorrow'. After all what, for instance, was the death of a distant cousin really to Mrs Thrale? Johnson was first attracted towards Reynolds when he heard Reynolds say, tough-mindedly, to some ladies who were regretting the death of a friend to whom they owed great obligations, 'You have, however, the comfort of being relieved from a burthen of gratitude'.[28] The sympathizer always has the necessary thought of not really being the sufferer. In turn, the sufferer must acknowledge this truth with stoicism, even so far as lowering or compromising the violence of passion which he expresses – at, after all, another level – before the would-be sympathizer: 'His firmness, at the same time, perfectly coincides with our insensibility. He makes no demand upon us for that exquisite degree of sensibility which we find, and are mortified to find, that we do not possess.' This correspondence between the limited capacity of vicarious feeling and the accordingly reduced demands and thus increased resilience of the lonely sufferer both acknowledges and makes a bit more bearable the true state of the system of life, with its necessity for balances and for mind as well as feeling. Johnson was certainly less idealistic, more sceptical about this system of sheerly social balance than was Adam Smith in his rationalism. When the balance became impossible, Johnson ceased to be too fussy: his Christianity always required a tough *and* a soft recognition of fallen facts of human nature. But right up to the point of the balance breaking down, he clung to the help it offered as well as refused; what Johnson felt that Boswell was jettisoning upon others was the inner responsibility of being a separate person and of imagining himself as the spectator of as well as sufferer from his own trouble. For in return for such an imagination *ab extra*, the very duty of repression – informed by the natural threat of receiving less rather than more sympathy for making, out of pain, painful demands – strengthens a person innerly. In place of the wrong sort of identification, it gives discipline; in place of the artifice of wordiness, it offers silence or tact:

> In order to produce this concord, as nature teaches the spectators to assume the circumstances of the person principally concerned, so she teaches the last in some measure to assume those of the spectators ... conceiving some of that coolness about his own fortune, with which he is sensible that they will view it.

The socially reflected passion thus becomes weaker than the original, even in oneself, and the sufferer takes on 'a certain mediocrity' between a sense of original pain and a picture of its necessary reception and place among the concerns of other people.[27]

'Mediocrity is best,' said Johnson in *The Rambler*, 38. He was willing secondarily to assume that 'mediocrity' and allow the social man in him to make him appear and feel almost ordinary, as common as he could: he is the most apparently down-to-earth and common-sensical of great men. He was prepared to take that incarnation.

Boswell was not: in so far as Boswell was his own observer he was so only secretly and autobiographically, making the self-observer collude with the sufferer: 'You are always complaining of melancholy, and I conclude from those complaints that you are fond of it'.

Johnson was a man willing to borrow from outside a sense of reality in order to relieve himself from melancholy within. To fly from himself he must, in the words of *The Rambler*, 89, 'in opposition to the Stoick precept, teach his desires to fix upon external things; he must adopt the joys and pains of others'. Boswell, turning himself inside out and enjoying the sight, was making a chaos of the boundaries and levels between inner and outer: 'This great law it is the business of every rational being to understand,' Johnson wrote in *The Rambler*, 178, 'that life may not pass away in an attempt to make contradictions consistent, to combine opposite qualities, and to unite things which the nature of their being must always keep asunder.' Boswell refused to see that his troubles altered even in his talking about them; what felt like sincerity within became a demand without; even in confessing his sense of the truth, he was fictionalizing himself. Mental troubles that had no *external* cause were thus, by definition, to Johnson unreal even to the point of madness; not to see their unreality would be thus internally to *realize* them: 'Make it an invariable and obligatory law to yourself, never to mention your own mental diseases...from this hour speak no more, think no more, about them.' Speak no more, think no more is offered not just as an intensification but also as an equation: naming things calls them into being, gives them a substantiality they might not otherwise come to possess. Boswell at times must have seemed to Johnson his very opposite not only in youth but in modern ways; for Johnson turned to the externality of words to restrain rather than release himself. That is why we often feel the pressure of Johnson's own story behind or within his outward-looking words. An anti-Romantic, turned round on his very self.

Johnson exorcizes the mental devils not from inside out but from outside in. Speaking distressing thoughts, he told Boswell that they should be diverted, they could not be combated. Not combated? thought the would-be heroic, Romantic Boswell: might they not be thought down? Johnson: 'No, Sir. To attempt to *think them down* is madness.'[30] It is madness to try to make one's own mind think down its own thoughts, preside over itself to the point of even preying upon itself, seek to resolve the contradiction of using consciousness to make itself unconscious. All the mind can do is to make thoughts for itself into things external to itself; these thoughts Johnson called rules or laws: 'make it an invariable and obligatory law'; 'this great law it is the business of every rational being to understand'. But such laws are as much made as revealed, are things to be raised to the security of laws by habit in the guise of commandment. If to Boswell all this might seem to be carrying out an artifice upon oneself, the irony was that no one became more artificial than Boswell himself in trying to be so emotionally real all the time.

Indeed, confession to Samuel Johnson became for Boswell the means of finding in someone outside what he could not or would not find within. The biography of Johnson only came out of the essentially autobiographical journals of Boswell. It is like some terrible pastiche of what Johnson meant, as perhaps both Johnson and Boswell at times realized:

> Johnson said, 'A madman loves to be with people whom he fears; not as a dog fears the lash; but of whom he stands in awe.' I was struck with the justice of this observation. To be with those of whom a person, whose mind is wavering and dejected, stands in awe, represses and composes an uneasy tumult of spirits, and consoles him with the contemplation of something steady, and at least comparatively great.[31]

Boswell must have been thinking of himself, drinking and whoring then going to hear Johnson moralizing. But where it is heartening to find Johnson's 'the mind can only repose on the stability of truth' echoed in Reynolds's 'something steady, substantial, and durable on which the mind can lean as it were, and rest with safety', as we saw in Chapter One, now it is utterly disturbing to find it echoed in this context by Boswell's 'the contemplation of something steady, and at least comparatively great'. Boswell understands it only from outside, secondarily – and by a vicious circle makes his own inadequacy an instrument for investigating the adequacy of his hero. As Johnson says in *The Rambler*, 154, 'No man ever yet became great by imitation'.

The idea of 'the Social Man' endorsing mediocrity or ordinariness was the way for Johnson's extraordinariness to survive and live – with friends outside, without insanity inside. It is an idea perhaps half-forgotten to us now, just as it is difficult to peel off the layers that separate us from the serious meaning of being 'well bred'. But it is clear that Johnson's belief in the social was more to him than a mask or wig. 'Make it an invariable and obligatory law to yourself, never to mention your own mental diseases . . . from this hour speak no more, think no more, about them.' We may recover an intimation of how the refusal or inability to wear social clothes has a more than superficial significance if we listen to those words again with the ear of a poet, born 1731 died 1800, of the generation which followed Johnson's and lived into Wordsworth's. In his final depression, when he seemed in his unresponsive silence beyond any human help and convinced of his own damnation, the poet William Cowper was tended by his cousin John Johnson who, like Christopher Tietjens nursing his brother, tried reading aloud to him Boswell's *Life of Johnson*, presumably for the sake of its picture of a deeply troubled but still strong life. John Johnson read out with particular emphasis our passage, Johnson criticizing Boswell's inward-turning disposition to nurse melancholic thoughts: 'from this hour speak no more, think no more, about them':

> John Johnson: 'What do you think of that advice, my Cousin?
> William Cowper: 'It may be good – but no man can follow it.'[32]

It is a terrifying rejoinder, when practical good sense turns out to be impractical. Johnson is no use?

Cowper had to say no. But according to Boswell, one of Johnson's own most frequent expressions in conversation was, quite bluntly, 'No, Sir':

> *No, Sir,* was not always to intimate contradiction; for he would say no, when he was about to enforce an affirmative proposition which had not been denied . . . I used to consider it as a kind of flag of defiance; as if he had said, 'Any argument you may offer against this, is not just. No, Sir, it is not.'[33]

This is precisely the robust, no-nonsense force of Johnson's 'No' to Boswell. 'Speak no more, think no more, about them': any argument you may offer against this will get you nowhere. Johnson's is always a strong, active negative, a resistant response to his own fear or pessimism; but Cowper was in the nowhere that Johnson feared. When Cowper says of Johnson's advice, 'It may be good – but no man can follow it', the response is more passive and more hopeless than Johnson's. What was offered as rationality was granted as plausibly such but still received as impossibility, and that is much more frightening than if its rationality had simply been denied. It leaves Cowper a stranger to the rational system and the social order, a man caught between being an outcast from it all and a rejecter of it all, without recourse to feeling the forces within him as his own power rather than his own weakness. Cowper cannot *stand* for something as Johnson can, save as a kind of victim. It is as though for Cowper life does not really take place in the ordinary, common-sense world but in an inner realm where although rationality is not as rational as it likes to suppose, the denial of such reason is still felt as no safeguard against insanity. To Cowper at his most desperate it was as if the whole world might be right in its own terms, but those terms were unprovably yet wholly inapplicable. This is the deepest sense in which Cowper was a *Nonconformist*, essentially a Calvinist convinced of his own damnation. When he was offered a virtual sinecure and had only to pass a simple test to secure the position, he felt driven to the very verge of suicide. In a letter written in May 1781 he says: 'What nature expressly designed me for, I have never been able to conjecture, I seem to myself so universally disqualified for the common and customary occupations and amusements of mankind.' It is Johnson's rule to offer a double perspective on such a view: we are at one level so *alike*, he says, in thinking ourselves at another level, within us, so different and exceptional and alone. But Cowper cannot use the words 'common' and 'customary'; the word 'universal' replaces the word 'common' only to signal 'disqualification' from it; 'I *seem* to *myself*', he is left strandedly saying. To the subjectivism of the Puritan tradition at its most piercing, the sanity of a Johnsonian double view is itself a wordly madness, or a mad secondary attempt to distract ourselves from real, primary madness. Cowper seems unconfidently caught between two views: neither 'mad' enough, in one sense, not to feel humilated by being incapacitated for the ordinary world; nor 'mad' enough, in another sense, to feel that the deepest sense of life is to conform to the world's ways. He is damned by the religion that also makes the world impossible for him and he barely has recourse to a language of sanity and reality together.

We shall consider Johnson's own religion in Chapter Five. For the moment we may see what is at stake between Johnson's way and Cowper's, between the strong *no* and the weak one, in terms which, though at bottom 'religious', are recognizable at many other levels of life and being. Consider the two following passages together: the first a letter by Cowper to his religious mentor, John Newton, on 24 September 1785, the second Number 207 of *The Rambler*, published on 10 March 1752.

Speaking of a 'certain perverseness' in himself, Cowper explains:

I mean that temper, or humour, or whatever it is to be called, that indisposes us to a situation though not unpleasant in itself, merely because we cannot get out of it. I could not endure the room in which I now write, were I conscious that the door were locked. In less than five minutes I should feel myself a prisoner, though I can spend hours in it, under an assurance that I may leave it when I please, without experiencing any tedium at all.

Speaking of pressing on and finishing, Johnson writes, more publicly:

every day brings its task, and often without bringing abilities to perform it: Difficulties embarrass, uncertainty perplexes, opposition retards, censure exasperates, or neglect depresses. We proceed, because we have begun; we complete our design, that the labour already spent may not be in vain... Whatever motive first incited action, has still greater force to stimulate perseverance... To faint or loiter, when only the last efforts are required, is to steer the ship through tempests, and abandon it to the winds in sight of land; it is to break the ground and scatter the seed, and at last to neglect the harvest.

Cowper here unable to write because the door was locked is an image: an image of a refusal to accept that literature can solve in the second place what is not solved in life, in the first. It is as though he was more concerned with the freedom than with the writing, and freedom existed by the door and not on the page. Cowper himself could barely (afford to) understand it: if the door was unlocked, he would simply stay in the room; if the door was locked and he did not know it, he would carry on. But to Johnson himself to stop because the door was locked, or was even thought to be locked, was simply to double-lock it. It is that area of consciousness, concerning our surrounding context, that Johnson was so adamant about repressing – 'speak no more, think no more about it' – and that the apostles of modernism, even Ford himself, have been at such pains to stress. Press on with the work, Johnson insists, whatever you suspect of the circumstances surrounding it. It is as though the task of a man was to be and to remain the *content* of life, its raw, struggling material-impetus, its passion, whatever the changes wrought upon him by the form or force of circumstances he found around him. The consciousness of circumstance and history is like your own mental disease: you don't talk of it, so as not to think of it; you assume that those forces are *not* there – lest by thinking that they are, you make them present anyway, whether they really are or not – until or unless they prove themselves by forcing themselves upon you. A strong *no*. Of course, such a way is less dramatic, less terrible than Cowper's: it exists precisely by *not* making the problems which it tries to solve articulate, conscious, interesting. Accordingly its implicit intelligence is easy to underrate: so much of its force goes into ordinary continuance and resolute character such as leave an impression deeper than they can quite say on Johnson's biographers.

The great admirer of both Johnson *and* Cowper is, most immediately, Jane Austen – a fact that should remind us how unfair it would be to take the two as simple opposites. After all, Cowper himself continues with his *Task* from within his own prison of damnation – yet with what must have seemed to him an almost maddening sanity. Jane Austen is a less equivocal Johnsonian than Cowper. When Mary Crawford in *Mansfield Park* argues the counterproductiveness of compulsory public worship, for causing in people feelings of unwillingness, Edmund demurs in the very spirit of Johnson and a revealing debate ensues:

> 'What would be expected from the *private* devotions of such persons? Do you think the minds which are suffered, which are indulged in wanderings in a chapel, would be more collected in a closet?'
>
> 'Yes, very likely. They would have two chances at least in their favour. There would be less to distract the attention from without, and it would not be tried too long.'
>
> 'The mind which does not struggle against itself under *one* circumstance, would find objects to distract it in the *other*, I believe ...'[34]

The line taken is very like that which Johnson himself takes against Cowley in *The Rambler*, 6. Cowley is no Mary Crawford; he is arguing the other way in favour of complete, voluntary retirement from the world into the country – the very thing Cowper himself did, though by a typical paradox desperately seeking that freedom as if he had no choice. Cowley's desire for a hermitage, says Johnson, is only a literary man's wishful thinking:

> He forgot, in the vehemence of desire, that solitude and quiet owe their pleasures to those miseries, which he was so studious to obviate ... he, who has so little knowledge of human nature, as to seek happiness by changing any thing, but his own dispositions, will waste his life in fruitless efforts, and multiply the griefs which he purposes to remove.

The mind that will not struggle with its difficulties in one place will find them again in but a different form in another.

Johnson's is the way of resolute flexibility, not that all-or-nothing way into which Cowper is so often in danger of being forced. Boswell was once told by a friend that men like him who got drunk had no right on the next day to take the moral line against atheists and refuse to mix with them. But when Boswell reported this view of cancellation to Johnson, Johnson made a characteristic retort:

> Nay, Sir, this is sad reasoning. Because a man cannot be right in all things, is he to be right in nothing? Because a man sometimes gets drunk, is he therefore to steal? This doctrine would very soon bring a man to the gallows.[35]

The strong *no* of principle maintains itself through all the unsatisfactory, mixed and partial circumstances of its applications and failures. The tolerance of being able to stay right after doing wrong makes 'tolerance' a tougher word than we usually remember it being.

Johnson would rather be right, downright right, than literary-existential as Boswell prefers; for to Johnson to be right is more important, even in literary terms, than being wrong, even when wrong looks to be more impressively at the heart of the problem. It would be an interesting thought-experiment to imagine how far Byron, that later Romantic Calvinist, might have agreed, committed as he was both to a Johnsonian aversion to the merely fictive and to his own deep and guilty love affair with damnation.

*

Still, confronted with Boswell's moaning introspection, Johnson is all for turning inside out again – out into a world the consciousness of which is itself to a large extent kept out of mind while the task is to be done. But for all the turning outwards, there is still an internal factor to Johnson's rage. Johnson knew when to trust his angers, could distinguish between anger as mere fear and anger as the reflex of belief – that passionate impatience with anything that imperils the clarity of principled survival and practical necessity. While the anger flashes outwards aggressively, there is always something within the man which that anger is sympathetically and implicitly defending. For in its own way the anger against Boswell is no less a part of Christian charity than the indignation which Johnson had displayed as a younger man, not in attack but in defence of a dissolute friend.

Here is Johnson, then, on his ruined friend Savage – whose friends, having agreed to maintain him providing he retired from London to Swansea, finally, in weariness of his antics, withdrew their support:

> It may be alleged, and, perhaps, justly, that he was petulant and contemptuous, that he more frequently reproached his Subscribers for not giving him more, than thanked them for what he had received; but it is to be remembered, that this Conduct, and this is the worst Charge that can be drawn up against him, did them no real Injury; and that it, therefore, ought rather to have been pitied than resented, at least, the Resentment that it might provoke ought to have been generous and manly; Epithets which his Conduct will hardly deserve, that starves the Man whom he has persuaded to put himself into his Power.[36]

'No *real* injury' – it is a sense of what constitutes reality, in an already confusing world, that Johnson's anger defends from unnecessary complications. It often comes as a shock to find a man of such intelligence eschewing complexity, even as Boswell must have been shaken to find him refusing sympathy; but this is a position Johnson takes up with all the force of character and conviction together: 'The student must learnt by commerce with mankind to reduce his speculations to practice, and accommodate his knowledge to the purposes of life' (*The Rambler*, 137). *Reducing* here is an act of sanity, is 'real' life rescued from impossible consciousness of, say, the Henry James variety:

> It sometimes happens that too close an attention to minute exactness, or a too rigorous habit of examining every thing by the standard of perfection, vitiates the temper, rather than improves the understanding, and teaches the mind to discern faults with unhappy penetration. (*The Rambler*, 74).

Look what happens if we do not 'reduce': the tender nicety of principle in Savage's friends, feeling his lack of gratitude, did not stop them being finally punitive; a brutality betraying itself only in the sophisticatedly indirect means of cutting off the petty cash behind the man's back. Johnson was a big man as well as a highly intelligent and critical one: he had to hold himself back from being embroiled at the level of minutiae in his moral discriminations. For it is better to be sheerly, physically angry like Johnson, and charitable only later, than mentally refined like Savage's other, richer friends and yet repressedly brutal beneath the well-mannered veneer. As always Johnson gets the order of things naturally right. The word 'real', moreover, is associated in this passage from *The Life of Savage* with the word 'manly' rather than the word 'power'. 'Manly' is both a proud and a modest word here, one that these days, for some good and some bad reasons, we have had to put by, but indeed the sort of thing towards which Havelock Ellis was gesturing in his sense of something basic and firm. Tietjens himself has recourse to the word in resisting that more 'modern' idea of art which I have called literary-existential:

> The exact eye: exact observation; it was a man's work. The only work for a man. Why then, were artists soft, effeminate, not men at all; whilst the army officer, who had the inexact mind of the schoolteacher, was a manly man? Quite a manly man, until he became an old woman![37]

Johnson's is the manliness of not stooping to bother so much about mere small sums of money; the manliness of not wanting to go too much into mere refinements of feeling in urgent, practical matters of sheer economic survival, on the other hand; the manliness of knowing the world – which made Johnson see Reynolds as a fellow-spirit for saying to the mourners, 'You have the comfort of being relieved from a burden of gratitude'. Character of this kind means the balancing of scepticism and generosity in a way that goes deeper than any merely mental calculation of their relation could provide. Two things have grown together into one, as in the way Johnson noted that Levet was 'coarsely kind'. Mrs Chapone, in talking with Johnson, 'wondered to hear a man, who by his actions shows so much benevolence, maintain that the human heart is naturally malevolent, and that all the benevolence we see in the few who are good is acquired by reason and religion.'[38]

Why should she wonder? The benevolence was defensively borrowed – 'acquired' – from the threats of one's own recognized malevolence, by another sort of reflection outside in or back to front. As we saw in Chapter One, Johnson thought of us all in our infirmities having to borrow both from others and from ourselves. Yet, confronted by his mixture of toughness and tenderness, we can often find ourselves confused, like Mrs Chapone, by the combination of the weak and the strong until we hardly know which is which. Consider, for instance, Johnson's relation to a man from whom he himself did borrow, if only by bad example – Richard Savage again, that older rake figure with whom Johnson, as a poor young married

man who had lately quarrelled with his wife, roamed the streets of
London. Savage had fallen by then. Lord Tryconnel had been his
patron; Savage repaid him by impudently commanding his wine
cellar and pawning his books; Lord Tryconnel had sent Savage
packing but, more, had made his complaints public, while Savage, as
proud as ever, counterattacked publicly even as his reputation sank
lower and lower. Here is Johnson in defence of human kindness in his
usual aggressive manner:

> These mutual Accusations were retorted on both Sides for
> many Years, with the utmost Degree of Virulence and Rage,
> and Time seemed rather to augment than diminish their
> Resentment; that the Anger of Mr *Savage* should be kept alive is
> not strange, because he felt every Day the Consequences of the
> Quarrel; but it might reasonably have been hoped, that Lord
> *Tryconnel* might have relented, and at length have forgot those
> Provocations, which, however they might have once inflamed
> him, had not in Reality much hurt him.[39]

'In *Reality*': 'we may think the blow violent only because we have
made ourselves delicate and tender'; 'Mr Johnson had indeed a real
abhorrence of a person that had ever before him treated a little thing
like a great one'; 'Poh! poh! Madam; who is the worse for being
talked of uncharitably?'.[40] Comedy, contempt, a sense of reality
strong enough to make distinctions while seizing essentials: these are
the means by which Johnson dealt unsympathetically with both a
lack of sympathy and a demand for it, when only internal feelings
were at stake. 'You are always complaining of melancholy,' Johnson
told Boswell, and here is Lord Tryconnel complaining that his
feelings are affronted while Savage is starving. Johnson hated
complaint and complainers (while Savage practised the virtue of his
own vice in 'the art of escaping from his own Reflections', in the
vanity of 'a steady Confidence in his own Capacity' and an 'obstinate
Adherence to his own Resolutions').[41] Complaint was the privilege of
those who thought themselves special, rather than ordinary; such
pride pre-empted the very grounds of sympathy which it presumed to
claim:

> for as every man has in his own opinion, a full share of the
> miseries of life, he is inclined to consider all clamorous
> uneasiness, as a proof of impatience rather than affliction, and
> to ask, What merit has this man to show, by which he has
> acquired a right to repine at the distributions of nature? Or, why

does he imagine that exemptions should be granted him from the general condition of man? (*The Rambler*, 50).

For it was the very principle that lay behind sympathy that such complainers flouted: the principle of commonness. In that sense, Johnson's anger is not against sympathy but for it: the hard and the soft are united in him. 'No man', he told Mrs Thrale, 'should be expected to sympathize with the sorrows of vanity'; 'All censure of a man's self', he told Boswell, 'is oblique praise. It is in order to show how much he can spare.'[42] Johnson's attack on false sociability – he growled at poor Boswell, 'You may *talk* in this manner; it is a mode of talking in Society: but don't *think* foolishly'[43] – made room for the authentic language of real fellow feeling, such as he could then feel for Savage. And this more real feeling was such as could still bear the presence of tough-minded judgement alongside it: 'he scarcely ever found a Stranger, whom he did not leave a Friend; but it must likewise be added, that he had not often a Friend long, without obliging him to bcome a Stranger'; 'it was not always by the Negligence or Coldness of his Friends that Savage was distressed, but because it was in reality very difficult to preserve him long in a State of Ease. To supply him with Money was a hopeless Attempt...'[44] 'In reality' – again; Johnson had to find a language and a syntax large enough to hold together simple emotion within complex thought or the claims of judgement and of feeling which in theory might look incompatible. You can feel the two coinciding as one near the conclusion, with both justice without and pain within: '*His* Friendship was therefore of little Value'.[45] But *Johnson's*, though hurt, was not. His friendship abided, in the midst of its own judgements, though it pained Johnson and could not save Savage.

This sort of toughness, at once hard and soft in its tolerance, may be conveniently forgotten and easily misinterpreted. At first sight, for example, it must seem to us like further evidence of bullying dogmatism that Johnson thought the best friends were those united in the same principles as well as by reciprocal affections. But as usual when we turn to his own words – in *The Rambler*, 64 – his commitment to uncover the memory of a meaning beneath its later surface-degenerations reopens for us the possibility of conviction about things that have seemed to become commonplace, taken for granted or redundant. The language, predating us, seems to disclose predispositions within which we work, perhaps the more easily for forgetting them:

That friendship may be at once fond and lasting, there must not only be equal virtue on each part, but virtue of the same kind; not only the same end must be proposed, but the same means must be approved by both. We are often, by superficial accomplishments and accidental endearments, induced to love those whom we cannot esteem; we are sometimes, by great abilities and incontestable evidences of virtue, compelled to esteem those we cannot love. But friendship, compounded of esteem and love, derives from one its tenderness, and its permanence from the other; and therefore requires not only that its candidates should gain the judgement, but that they should attract the affections.

The integration sought here between *esteem* and *love*, the *judgement* and the *affections*, is just that which, at another level, Johnson sought in literature: 'Poetry', he wrote in his 'Life of Milton', 'is the art of uniting *pleasure* with *truth* by calling *imagination* to the help of *reason*.' More often the unity is missing – in friendship with Savage, on reading Cowley's poetry ('the power of Cowley is not so much to move the affections as to exercise the understanding'). The two sides of one's nature should appear as one: so often Johnson's long sentences are struggling after that almost prelapsarian harmony (for it is no coincidence that he speaks of it most powerfully in relation to the problems of reading *Paradise Lost*). But those sentences are hampered by difficulties that almost eclipse the unifying idea – principles without feelings, affections without sense, reason without imagination, imagination without reason. The achievement of friendship in such a world of splits and tangles means more than liking or choosing, and makes for a bit of that rare peace, found in just a part of the personal sphere, which reminds us of how it ought to be. Friendship *stands for* something in Johnson: that we need principles as well as affections even for our affections to survive; that we need feelings as well as reasons in order to act in accordance with our nature. The pressure on Cowper made it impossible for him equivalently both to use *and* to enjoy the world. But Johnson's definitions remind us of our needs when the failure to satisfy those needs often leads us to bury their memory.

It makes me think: perhaps we should bear to remember to ask more of friendship as distinguished from acquaintance, and as beyond the lazy relativism of thinking we just happen to like some people more than others. If things 'just' happen to happen, we shall have stories but we shall not have thoughts or meanings; things will be just what they are, they will stand for nothing more than themselves even within themselves, it will merely be chance likes without a function for liking in a wider order of things; it will just be a personal liking for the works of Dr Johnson, say. Easy-going liberal humanism, almost begging for a reactive scepticism to follow it, has its origin in the secular reasonableness of that eighteenth-century enlightenment which, in many ways, Johnson actually conservatively resists. I will risk sounding like a second-hand Tietjens to say: I think we are often squeamish now about anger, we are weak about strong things; for we are strong about weak things, relativizing, tolerating. 'The best lack all conviction' in Yeats's phrase – on the whole we do not like to make generalizations, even that one. But Johnson had convictions, toughness, made generalizations. If we were to imagine what it would be like to try to regain such tough-mindedness, on purpose, we would have to take seriously the project of Friedrich Nietzsche in revaluing post-Romantic values:

> In man, *creature* and *creator* are united: in man there is matter, fragment, excess, clay, mud, madness, chaos; but in man there is also creator, sculptor, the hardness of the hammer, the divine spectator and the seventh day – do you understand this antithesis? And that *your* pity is for the 'creature in man', for that which has to be formed, broken, forged, torn, burned, annealed, refined – that which has to *suffer* and should suffer? And *our* pity – do you not grasp whom our *opposite* pity is for when it defends itself against your pity as the worst of all pampering and weakening? – Pity *against* pity, then![46]

'Pity against pity' as if to rediscover something older in the word; in our terms, something closer to Samuel Johnson than perhaps to George Eliot, closer to *The Rambler* and *The Life of Mr. Richard Savage* than to the realist, humanist novel. Yet to call man a 'creator' in the way that Nietzsche does, even as he reacts with exaggeration against 'pampering', is still to use a sort of Romanticism to replace the loss of God in the nineteenth century. In Chapters Five and Six we shall see what a belief in a divine Creator meant to Johnson and how foolish it is to take him without it. What I am offering in this chapter is the picture of Johnson untamed, a living reminder, a one-man cultural bastion, incorporating principles implicitly within passions and the passions in memory of both principles and their exceptions.

*

III 'Lest we should think ourselves too soon entitled to the mournful privileges of irresistible misery' (The Rambler, 32)

We barely know how to 'read' strength, seeing it from outside as an off-putting manner rather than as the upshot of inner beliefs. Here is old Johnson, still toughly proud *and* toughly humble near the very end of his life:

> When I was ill, said Johnson, I desired Mr Langton to tell me sincerely in what he thought my life was faulty. Sir, he brought me a sheet of paper on which he had written down several texts of Scripture, recommending christian charity. And when I questioned him what occasion I had given for such an animadversion, all he could say amounted to this, – that I sometimes contradicted people in conversation. Now what harm does it do to any man to be contradicted? BOSWELL. 'I suppose he meant the *manner* of doing it; roughly, –and harshly.' JOHNSON. 'And who is the worse for that?' BOSWELL. 'It hurts people of weak nerves.' JOHNSON. 'I know no such weak-nerved people.'[47]

Exit Boswell, trembling... The comedy, the resilience of spirit, the commitment to simplicity, the essential health, indomitable and incorrigible – all these belong together as only the other side of Johnson's also saying, through his very fear of death, 'I will be conquered, I will not capitulate'.[48] This is the same Johnson as he who kept in his bureau a letter from someone who knew him well, listing Johnson's faults and failings as a man, and so positioned it that whenever he opened the bureau 'it might look him in the face'.[49] He ignores the weak nerves. Johnson – who, after all, filled his own house following his wife's death with a bundle of outcasts and misfits who repaid him by quarrelling amongst themselves and finding fault with him – was not going to be spiritually blackmailed or bullied, even when frightened and ill; was not going to believe the Enlightenment view that mere tolerance was the greatest thing and call that Christian charity. 'No, Sir.' This is not a man whose first word towards life is Yes; he is often a *not* knower but a knower of what is *not*; a back-to-front man who is to be found via his refusals, antagonisms, limits of thus far and no farther. See him in that light, try to turn the back-to-front man round through his own mind, and this great resister, giving us more of himself through his very reluctance than ever could be given more directly, is closer than one would at first imagine to that spirit of basic, large disclosure of being which D.H. Lawrence, in his essay on John Galsworthy, warns us against losing:

> While a man remains a man, a true human individual, there is at the core of him a certain innocence of naiveté which defies all analysis, and which you cannot bargain with, you can only deal with it in good faith from your own corresponding innocence or naiveté. This does not mean that the human being is nothing but naive or innocent. He is Mr Worldly Wiseman also to his own degree. But in his essential core he is naive.[50]

Naive – namely: what harm does it do any man to be contradicted? Who is the worse for that? In reality?

Are we the worse for hearing Johnson's truth? Johnson, said Reynolds, was rude only because he put truth before anything else. But how shall we feel if we now put on the receiving end of Johnson's dismissiveness not Boswell but, say, our younger selves? To the young mind perusing *The Rambler*, said Mudford,

> life would appear...as one incessant warfare with envy, malevolence, and falshood; as the precarious tenure of a minute, never free from open assault or secret undermining; as beset on every side with misery, with want, with disease; as a road for ever obstructed by the pitfalls of infamy and remorse, and into which every step may plunge us.[51]

Imagine a young person having to read this from *The Rambler*, 196:

> It is impossible, without pity and contempt, to hear a youth of generous sentiments and warm imagination, declaring in the moment of openness and confidence his designs and expectations; because long life is possible, he considers it as certain, and therefore promises himself all the changes of happiness, and provides gratifications for every desire. He is, for a time, to give himself wholly to frolick and diversion, to range the world in search of pleasure, to delight every eye, to gain every heart, and to be celebrated equally for his pleasing levities and solid attainments, his deep reflections, and his sparkling repartees. He then elevates his views to nobler enjoyments, and finds all the scattered excellencies of the female world united in a woman, who prefers his addresses to wealth and titles; he is afterwards to engage in business, to dissipate difficulty, and overpower opposition; to climb by the mere force of merit to

fame and greatness; and reward all those who countenanced his rise, or paid due regard to his early excellence. At last he will retire in peace and honour; contract his views to domestick pleasures; form the manners of children like himself; observe how every year expands the beauty of his daughters, and how his sons catch ardour from their father's history; he will give laws to the neighbourhood; dictate axioms to posterity; and leave the world an example of wisdom and of happiness.

Johnson is so terrifyingly good at driving into language what most of us can keep on thinking only by keeping it out of words: the unadmitted secrets for which language acts as a reality-test. That great belated Romantic George Eliot, with her Maggie Tullivers and Dorothea Brookes, would say: it is folly to be disgusted at the illusions of youth when you remember you had them and were not then disgusted by them; projective sympathy should take you back inside the remembered reality of what is felt at the time. But to Johnson it is folly *not* to be disgusted at the illusions of youth simply because you remember having them. Trust your anger, not just your sympathy, or you will be deceiving yourself a second time round. Thus he immediately puts up against the paragraph of prospects a second paragraph of retrospect:

> With hopes like these, he sallies jocund into life; to little purpose is he told, that the condition of humanity admits no pure and unmingled happiness; that the exuberant gaiety of youth ends in poverty or disease; that uncommon qualifications and contrarieties of excellence, produce envy equally with applause; that whatever admiration and fondness may promise him, he must marry a wife like the wives of others, with some virtues and some faults, and be as often disgusted by her vices, as delighted by her elegance; that if he adventures into the circle of action, he must expect to encounter men as artful, as daring, as resolute as himself; that of his children, some may be deformed, and others vicious; some may disgrace him by their follies, some offend him by their insolence, and some exhaust him by their profusion. He hears all this with obstinate incredulity, and wonders by what malignity old age is influenced, that it cannot forbear to fill his ears with predictions of misery.

Perhaps it is unfair to think of the Johnson of *The Rambler* as old rather than young; his natural ambivalence either way makes him

essentially middle-aged here. Life for such a man goes before he knows
and while he waits for it, until the young innocent has become the old
failure, without there ever being a strict boundary point (like the
boundary point between *paragraphs* which acts like a rule or law) at
which you ceased to be one and became the other. All the time you are
being young in paragraph one of our passage, you are becoming old
in paragraph two: that is how indefinite it really feels beneath the
formal division. Yet for all that, is not this pessimism precisely the
dead hand of the eighteenth century which Havelock Ellis felt in his
youth: crushing the rising hope, using memory and experience to
finish with things rather than re-enter them, ironically setting itself up
for the revenge of the emerging Romantics?

Johnson himself, as ever, gives warning against his own dangerous
possibilities when in *The Rambler*, 59, he speaks of the human
screech-owl, the habitually malign lamenter and aged prophet of evil.
But in the way that first paragraph also seems set up in order to be
knocked down by the second, is not Johnson another screech-owl,
serving to 'weaken for a time that love of life, which is necessary to the
vigorous prosecution of any undertaking'? In *The Rambler*, 11, he
warns against those who use anger as an expedient 'for procuring
some kind of supplemental dignity'. The thought survives even the
self-interest of a hurt youth in thinking it: is not Johnson's anger
somewhere the revenge of a frustrated, redundant bigger self,
provoking that natural roughness of manner whenever he confronted
anyone passing for the heroism he himself had had to forgo? Nearly
sixty years later, in his magnificent 'Answer to Mathetes',
Wordsworth himself cautions us against teachers who, not knowing
when to be silent, intervene to correct and depress youthful spirits just
when they must find their own way. Does not Wordsworth in that
essay embody the corrective necessity of the Romantic movement's
coming into being, in offering more faith, and less contempt, in
considering the young mind? To put it another way, is not Johnson an
old screech-owl – even as he circles round and covers himself in saying
that he gives his dire warning 'to little purpose' and predicting that his
very prediction will be seen nullifyingly as mere 'malignity'?

Yet Johnson is not Mudford's screech-owl. Just as Mrs Chapone
did not understand the mix of hard and soft in Johnson, just as
Boswell in his confessions could not tell the artificial from the real
and needed Johnson to see the difference between what was really
strong and what really weak, so here we too can fail to make the right
distinctions. For it is the man of rigidity such as Johnson – far better

than a more pliable, optimistic and determinedly conscious believer
in 'the possibilities of life' – who creates the idea of possibility as a felt
reality: precisely for wanting initially to tie things down but finding
himself on second thought unable to do so. Near the end of his
Rambler on the human screech-owl, for example, he says with
apparent conclusiveness, like Adam Smith, '*he suffers most like a hero
that hides his grief in silence*'; but though a hater of complainers,
Johnson was also, we may recall, not very much interested in the
heroic: 'Heroic virtues', he told Mrs Thrale, 'are the *bon mots* of life;
they do not appear often, and when they do appear are too much
prized I think.'[52] So, on second thought, he adds, beautifully: '*yet, it
cannot be denied that he who complains acts like a man, like a social
being who looks for help from his fellow-creatures*'. It is itself a lovely
reassuring reminder of what it is to act – not like a hero, but (less)
more, 'like a man'. 'It cannot be denied': a genuine charity *in* thought
rather than merely added to it. Johnson is always ready to spoil the
heroism or the neatness of his essays by an appeal left unashamedly
open to nature, even in mid-sentence.

Consequently when, in *The Rambler*, 196, Johnson turns from the
list of youthful hopes to make his own (still to them incredible) list of
what will become of those hopes, what seems to be on first thought a
rebuke from experience can be seen on second thought, released from
vulnerability by anger, to be an experience of pain:

> that uncommon qualifications and contrarieties of excellence,
> produce envy equally with applause; that whatever admiration
> and fondness may promise him, he must marry a wife like the
> wives of others, with some virtues and some faults...

The older man does not want it to be like that either; he still has the
young man that he was within him, in memory of hope. But the older
man has to have two views, two necessities, in mind at once: 'he *must*
marry a wife like the wives of others' but, inside, must retain 'that love
of life, which is *necessary*'. It is like the double-think, inside and
outside of self, that takes place in *The Rambler*, 160: 'the truth is, that
no man is much regarded by the rest of the world. He that considers
how little he dwells upon the condition of others, will learn how little
the attention of others is attracted by himself.' Think of how common
it is in youth to think oneself special. To see that hope which is also
presumption, to see it pass into a maturity which is also a
disappointment, is to recognize that experience is both loss and gain,
gain and loss. 'Such is the condition of life,' for both young and old,

says Johnson in *The Rambler*, 196, 'that something is always wanting to happiness':

> In youth we have warm hopes, which are soon blasted by rashness and negligence, and great designs which are defeated by inexperience. In age we have knowledge and prudence without spirit to exert, or motives to prompt them; we are able to plan schemes and regulate measures, but have not time remaining to bring them to completion.

While the pain of experience in an older man may look like a specific rebuke to a younger one, it is founded more generally in the same experience of youthful hopes wounded or destroyed. The deeper *sympathy*, deeper than individual emotion, is in this sense formal, generic.

Experience is simultaneously a loss *and* a gain. That is why Johnson writes:

> It is impossible, without pity *and* contempt, to hear a youth... declaring in the moment of openness and confidence his designs and expectations.

Pity *and* contempt: we are pitiable because we are also pitiful, pitiful. The two are one complex feeling: tough and tender, tough because tender, tender because tough. Johnson is always near his best when he has already incorporated his second thought and his first thought into one holding sentence – a sentence in which two divided feelings, such as pity versus contempt, have become whole again; in which experience, going beyond melancholy and the disappointment of hope, becomes again character and instinct:

> There is in the commerce of life, as in Art, a sagacity which is far from being contradictory to right reason, and is superior to any occasional exercise of that faculty, which supersedes it; and does not wait for the slow progress of deduction, but goes at once, by what appears a kind of intuition, to the conclusion. A man endowed with this faculty, feels and acknowledges the truth, though it is not always in his power, perhaps, to give a reason for it; because he cannot recollect and bring before him all the materials that gave birth to his opinion; for very many very intricate considerations may unite or form the principle, even of small and minute parts, involved in, or dependent on, a great system of things: though these in process of time are forgotten, the right impression still remains fixed in his mind.

This impression is the result of the accumulated experience of our whole life, and has been collected, we do not always know how, or when. But this mass of collective observation, however acquired, ought to prevail over that reason, which however powerfully exerted on any particular occasion, will probably comprehend but a partial view of the subject; and our conduct in life as well as in the Arts, is, or ought to be, generally governed by this habitual reason: it is our happiness that we are enabled to draw on such funds. If we were obliged to enter into a theoretical deliberation on every occasion, before we act, life would be at a stand, and Art would be impracticable.

It appears to me therefore, that our first thoughts, that is, the effect which any thing produces on our minds on its first appearance, is never to be forgotten.

'I caution you against... an unfounded distrust of the imagination and feeling, in favour of narrow, partial, confined, argumentative theories.'[53] Thus Sir Joshua Reynolds privileges over cold surface reason and theory a faith in the general power of intuition, rising almost mysteriously from the depths of memory and experience. If that seems more Romantic than Augustan, it can only be because of our misunderstanding – like the young Havelock Ellis's, like Mrs Chapone's, like Boswell's – of the old eighteenth century. No words more than Reynolds's here give a deeper recognition of the relation of experience and practical thinking to 'our whole life', our being, our character, and make habit and practice seem wonderful, not dull. 'Men more often require to be reminded than informed.' Reynolds's words help us to remember, just as do Johnson's in *The Rambler*. For in this sense of 'the accumulated experience of our whole life' *The Rambler* is Johnson's autobiography and embodied 'system of things' – in which, none the less, he uses reason to try to remember those 'very many and very intricate considerations' which, for the most part forgotten, thus shake down into general, representative feelings in most of us as by second nature. But Johnson's reason never breaks up his big sentences as they purposefully push on, beyond the partial or momentary consideration, to a generality, weight and largeness commensurate with their foundation in a lifetime's experience and a whole human life behind this writing. This is the Johnson who could be big enough to say, 'Who is the worse for being talked of uncharitably?'

*

To take Reynolds's words as the best account we have of the weight of
Johnson's prose is also to admit that Johnson is in fact no sceptic as
to the quality of the growth of experience in the human mind. Yet Mrs
Thrale thought him a sceptic and Mudford considered him a
misanthrope and cynic. I propose we take a little extra time to
consider what is at stake here by comparing Johnson's life-thought
with the procedures of thinking of a true eighteenth-century sceptic,
David Hume.

Hume was the philosopher whom Johnson particularly hated. Yet
what Leslie Stephen suggests in his *History of English Thought in the
Eighteenth Century* is that such hatred was really fear – fear of a figure
who embodied the secular way that history was taking men even in
their minds, fear of a scepticism from which Johnson himself suffered
at the very back of his mind, with all his equivocal cries of 'No':

> A kind of implicit consciousness of the difficulties signalized
> by Hume is shown in the aversion with which many forcible
> thinkers of the time regarded all philosophical speculation.
> Johnson, for example, represents the most thoroughly national
> frame of mind... If you once ask the ultimate question, he
> seems to have thought, you will get no conclusive answer, and
> be left without a compass in the actual conduct of life.[54]

It is Johnson's instinct or prejudice to reject Hume with apparently
blind quickness. Yet a later reader, in mind of Johnson but working
more slowly, can still find good implicit reasons for this hasty action.
Take as a starting point, perhaps, the most famous passage in *A
Treatise of Human Nature*, in which Hume turns round upon his own
sceptical activity within the book:

> I am first affrighted and confounded with that forlorn solitude,
> in which I am plac'd in my philosophy, and fancy myself some
> strange uncouth monster... When I look abroad, I foresee on
> every side, dispute, contradiction, anger, calumny and
> distraction. When I turn my eye inward, I find nothing but
> doubt and ignorance... Where am I, or what? From what
> causes do I derive my existence, and to what condition shall I
> return? Whose favour shall I court, and whose anger must I
> dread? What beings surround me? and on whom have I any
> influence, or who have any influence on me? I am confounded
> with all these questions, and begin to fancy myself in the most
> deplorable condition imaginable, inviron'd with the deepest
> darkness, and utterly depriv'd of the use of every member and

faculty.

Most fortunately it happens, that since reason is incapable of dispelling these clouds, nature herself suffices to that purpose, and cures me of this philosophical melancholy and delirium ... I dine, I play a game of backgammon, I converse, and am merry with my friends; and when after three or four hour's amusement, I wou'd return to these speculations, they appear so cold, and strain'd, and ridiculous, that I cannot find in my heart to enter into them any farther.[55]

It was perhaps this passage more than any other that created, as though from the Johnsonian side of things, the Scottish school of Common Sense philosophy in reaction against Hume. To Thomas Reid and his followers, the theorist's own unavoidable practice was itself an inadvertent admission of the untenability of the theory; Hume had created an impossible disbelief which quite dissociated philosophic thinking from the ordinary experience of life. But Hume would have agreed that nobody *could* really believe in his philosophy – because that philosophy threatened the very possibility of our real beliefs. The failure of practice to bear out the theory was as much (or as little) a proof of the *truth* of the theory – namely, of the necessary delusions of practice – as the opposite. Hume wrote to Reid ironically thanking him for the so-called refutation – because it demonstrated how much original, common-sense principles had simply to be taken on (unphilosophic) trust. The circle can turn either way. To Hume the fact that in him writing and living, or reason and nature, were separate was not a contradiction of his whole way but an expression of it; for his whole way was rooted in contradiction: scepticism sceptical both of itself and of what was sceptical of itself. Visitors such as Boswell were disconcerted by Hume's blank stare. Something in him blankly presided over the mutual destruction of arguments between philosophic thinking and ordinary social living, and remained secularly undisturbed, where Johnson would have been horrified. For Johnson's world is real and whole, albeit a world of different levels. There is still room for negotiation and translation between levels.

Did the blank stare belong to a human being? To Boswell it seemed that Hume spoke like an alien when he said that 'he was no more uneasy to think he should *not be* after this life, than that he *had not been* before he began to exist'. Memory, being, living from the inside seemed to be dissolved: when it came to isolating something called 'myself', 'I never can catch *myself* at any time without a perception,

and never can observe any thing but the perception.'[56] Hume, it
seems, lived externally in a mere series of present moments. Not only
does the *Treatise* simply argue for such an existence, it is itself just
such an existence: it is 'Hume' without anything behind it 'unknown
and mysterious, connecting the parts, beside their relation'. For the
Treatise leaves nothing external or anterior to the interior moment-
by-moment present of the all-encompassing masterwork it was meant
to be; a mind turning itself around within itself. Thus from faith to
doubt: 'I begun this subject with premising, that we ought to have an
implicit faith in our senses...But to be ingenuous, I feel myself *at
present* of a quite contrary sentiment, and am more inclin'd to repose
no faith at all in my senses, or rather imagination.'[57] And so it is again,
on the way back from doubt to that doubt of doubting that Hume still
cannot call faith but only, more blankly, 'the course of nature' or 'this
indolent belief': 'I dine, I play a game of backgammon ... and when
after three or four hour's amusement, I wou'd return to these
speculations, they appear so cold, and strain'd, and ridiculous.'
'Where am I?' asks Hume; and the only answer comes from his own
words 'I feel myself at present' or the argument in which 'I find
myself' here:

> I am ready to throw all my books and papers into the fire, and
> resolve never more to renounce the pleasures of life for the sake
> of reasoning and philosophy. For these are my sentiments in
> that splenetic humour which governs me *at present*.[58]

Nevertheless he writes this *in* his books, *in* his papers. Hume loves the
circles that Johnson would have to call vicious. Even to get out of the
head, Hume still argues within it; and even outside the head, in the
world of connections between cause and effect, we are still, according
to Hume, inside our own minds, interpreting it like that. Reading
Hume, we find not only our fictions, which are almost everything we
call knowledge, but also our continuing need of them, for all that.
But if the philosopher too must finally go with, not against, the
current of nature in this respect, returning to ordinary assumptions,
still nature must enter his philosophic book to make him do so, make
him write as much; even as thinking turns against the idea of thinking
precisely through thought. The conservative return from thinking to
living is, for Hume, merely the Pyrrhic victory of thought's defeat and
remains, none the less, an internal movment of thought.

To Johnson this would have seemed to make thought into madness
and writing into solipsism: the book turned round on itself. Hume's

thinking itself turned external things, such as cause and effect, inside
our own minds; turned internal things of mind and feeling into
externally explainable mechanisms. Had he read Hume carefully
(and thus no wonder he did not) Johnson would have felt that he was
seeing himself and his whole world through the looking glass, turned
back to front, inside out. The same return to the ordinary out of the
very turns of scepticism, the same inclusions of doubt about the work
within the very work itself: how Hume delighted in abolishing the
difference that belief made, thus leaving what believers and non-
believers seem to think the same! So much of the covert strategy of the
Dialogues Concerning Natural Religion depends upon using the
scepticism of the religious to knock out the rationality of the deists
and then play into the hands of the scepticism of the irreligious
themselves: 'how do you mystics, who maintain the absolute
incomprehensibility of the Deity, differ from sceptics or atheists, who
assert that the first cause of all is unknown and unintelligible?'[59] On
Hume's paper, not at all. 'The total infirmity of human reason, the
absolute incomprehensibility of the Divine Nature, the great and
universal misery, and still greater wickedness of men – these are
strange topics, surely, to be so fondly cherished by orthodox divines
and doctors.'[60] To the agent of reason, blandly embodying himself in
different persuasions for secret purposes of his own, one thing
becomes another. Even the scepticism of reason became a reason for
continuing to follow custom.

Hume abolishes differences, or only sets them up again on a less
secure basis. To Johnson this was precisely what someone would do
in a book, not in a life; in a diagram rather than a realistic picture.
What Johnson insists upon *is* the very difference between a writing
such as his own, which sacrifices itself to the memory of the reality of
which it treats – 'there is always an appeal open to criticism from
nature' – and a writing such as Hume's that sets itself up outside
reality in order to criticize that reality, and then criticize itself too, in a
dismantling that is also ironically the creation of itself.[61] To Johnson,
Hume's writing would have seemed guilty of the shame of imposing
'words for ideas upon ourselves or others'.

The *Treatise* does seem, magnificently, to be created straight off in
one long sitting, with pauses only for that rest which made for doubt
in Hume; it seems passionately followed through, made new moment
by moment in living thought as it occurs to an ingenious young man.
But the *Treatise,* as Hume famously declared, fell dead-born from the
press; its writer had to spend virtually the rest of his life rewriting and

translating it into essays which seemed to offer the more ordinary illusions of opinion and argument in the hands of an author of recognizable personal identity. Without ever looking at the *Treatise* as such, Johnson would always have been the inveterate enemy to that form of original writing, committed to its own pure existence as thought on the page, and would have judged it damagingly significant that Hume's thoughts could only have been thought that way, blindly, straight off – where Hume himself offered them precisely as those thoughts which we could not bear customarily to think. 'If I could have allowed myself to gratify my vanity at the expence of truth,' Johnson told Boswell, 'what fame might I have acquired. Every thing which Hume has advanced against Christianity had passed through my mind long before he wrote.[62] But the ancients, in contrast to the moderns, notes Johnson, hesitated long before publication, weighed and tested novelty – perhaps because they had the old idea of truth that Hume himself in his work was virtually declaring a fiction. Should the young Hume have paid attention to the advice of *The Rambler,* 169, had it appeared in time to warn him; or are the following the words of an old and conservative man?

To him, whose eagerness of praise hurries his productions soon into the light, many imperfections are unavoidable, even where the mind furnishes the materials, as well as regulates their disposition, and nothing depends upon search or information. Delay opens new veins of thought, the subject dismissed for a time appears with a new train of dependant images, the accidents of reading or conversation supply new ornaments or allusions, or mere intermission of the fatigue of thinking enables the mind to collect new force, and make new excursions. But all those benefits come too late for him, who when he was weary with labour, snatched at the recompence, and gave his work to his friends and enemies, as soon as impatience and pride persuaded him to conclude it.

One of the most pernicious effects of haste is obscurity. He that teems with a quick succession of ideas, and perceives how one sentiment produces another, easily believes that he can clearly express what he so strongly comprehends; he seldom suspects his thoughts of embarrassment while he preserves in his own memory the series of connection...

Authors and lovers always suffer some infatuation, from which only absence can set them free; and every man ought to

restore himself to the full exercise of his judgement, before he
does that which he cannot do improperly, without injuring his
honour and his quiet.

Of course such an account does not – and was not intended
to – describe Hume's own practice with anything like fairness. But it
does describe something like it from Johnson's point of view. If the
Treatise is a succession of 'present moments'of thought, that sense of
the present was one such as to terrify or disgust Johnson by its claims
to be both predominant and, as it will turn out, relative. A continuous
succession of moments each of which gives a mental conviction which
always becomes relative again: this very notion of time is a denial of
the ballast of knowledge in experience. For Johnson commits himself
to a double sense of time in his work: the writing-time and the life-time
behind it. Hence he is not as single-minded a writer as Hume but tries
to site himself between writing and that which in reality he is writing
about. He works on both sides of his texts. Intermission followed by
recollection and then return; commitment to paper, withdrawal from
it, absence, restoration: all these, in sequence, attest to a felt necessity
in Johnson for the writer to be more than a paper tiger, to find, even
in himself, a bridge between writing and the world. Delay lets time,
lets life in, where haste makes self-enclosed systems. Johnson does
not want to preserve merely 'in his *own* memory' the implicit
connections between his thoughts; he wants also to be able to see
them, and to have them seen, on the other side of writing where it is
human, public, ordinary again.

But was not Johnson, notoriously, a last-minute, short-essay
composer rather than a deliberating rewriter of a large work? How
does *The Rambler*, 169, with its emphasis on delay, square with other
Ramblers such as 135, warning against procrastination:

> he whose penetration extends to remote consequences, and
> who, whenever he applies his attention to any design, discovers
> new prospects of advantage, and possibilities of improvement,
> will not easily be persuaded that his project is ripe for execution;
> but will superadd one contrivance to another...till he is
> entangled in his own scheme.

Was not the essay-form the compromise of writing quickly, for fear of
procrastination, but writing briefly, for fear of extended literary
solipsism?

It was more than that. When Johnson urges in one essay to delay
and in another not to delay, it is as it is in *The Rambler,* 63:

Thus men may be made inconstant by virtue and by vice, by too much or too little thought.

This is how time becomes a factor in *The Rambler*, for all its apparently permanent language. At different times, different thoughts and aspects of truth are appropriate, different essays are written or remembered. The present of mere procrastination, belonging as it does to those 'who sacrifice future advantage to present inclination' (*The Rambler*, 134), is the very opposite of that delay by which 'the future is purchased by the present'. For the latter is a present in which an awareness of the levels of existence is reopened and temporary room is found for the man to recall the relation of what he does on the page to the wider world of his being. Thus the hostility to procrastination and the support of delay are governed – very flexibly and very much according to time's occasions – by the same principle. For not only with regard to the future, not only with regard to the past, but with regard to time itself as a whole, Johnson sought to include human experience within the external measures of the clock. A future to be gained more thoughtfully than through the mere lapse of the present; a past to be recalled in the present as much as left behind by it; a sense of time incorporated as a thing of the passions too – hope and fear and change – and as the way the multi-facetedness of truth is disclosed to human experience.

*

In this way *The Rambler* is, in Reynolds's words on habitual reason, 'the result of the accumulated experience of our whole life, and has been collected, we do not always know how, or when'. It lets in – to books, to the scheme of things as described – a sense of human experience, of what it means, *pace* Hume, to be a person who can live and die.

No wonder, then, that Hume can write in support of suicide. His essentially secular greatness always consists in his giving us *less* purposeful human meaning than we had before, and yet – as though by sheer grandeur of liberated intelligence – continuing to rest on that 'less' as also 'more', 'more complicated'. His is the quiet new voice on suicide:

> *But you are placed by Providence, like a sentinel, in a particular station; and when you desert it without being recalled, you are equally guilty of rebellion against your Almighty Sovereign, and*

have incurred his displeasure – I ask, Why do you conclude that
Providence has placed me in this station? For my part, I find
that I owe my birth to a long chain of causes, of which many
depended upon the voluntary actions of men. *But Providence
guided all these causes, and nothing happens in the world without
its consent and co-operation.* If so, then neither does my death,
however voluntary, happen without its consent...[63]

His is the easy tone of one blankly starting again in a post-religious
world:

Heaven and hell suppose two distinct species of men, the good
and the bad; but the greatest part of mankind float betwixt vice
and virtue.[64]

But when *Johnson* offers us less, he refuses to be stoical even in a
modern fashion; he forces us to have our feelings even when he
challenges them:

Among other pleasing errors of young minds, is the opinion of
their own importance. He that has not yet remarked, how little
attention his contemporaries can spare from their own affairs,
conceives all eyes turned upon himself, and imagines every one
that approaches him to be an enemy or a follower, an admirer
or a spy. He therefore considers his fame as involved in the
event of every action. Many of the virtues and vices of youth
proceed from this quick sense of reputation. This it is that gives
firmness and constancy, fidelity and disinterestedness, and it is
this that kindles resentment for slight injuries, and dictates all
the principles of sanguinary honour.
    But as time brings him forward into the world, he soon
discovers that he only shares fame or reproach with
innumerable partners; that he is left unmarked in the obscurity
of the croud... (*The Rambler*, 196)

'Who is the worse for being talked of uncharitably?' All the more
when, as above, it is not simply uncharitable – can't the Young bear to
hear this? They, we can. The bully who makes us admit that we can
bear the sight of our own weakness and survive it is a friend of the most
real kind to that complicated and equivocal strength of ours which we
gradually learn. Johnson always brings his sense of experience back
to its own starting point – the problems of youth – and so we end this
chapter by returning to *The Rambler*, 196.
    The bad news is always what Johnson offers first: in this case the
bad news of our individual *un*importance. This is a thing to be known

of oneself first of all before ever we apply it to others, but in this world it may be that we have to learn it of our own selves back-to-front by first seeing how *we* think of *others*: 'He that considers how little he dwells upon the condition of others, will learn how little the attention of others is attracted by himself.'[65] Do unto yourself as you see you do unto others. For individual unimportance is a hard thing for human beings to begin to take, and we often have to learn bits of it in reversed ways, through our angers and frustrations and boredoms and disappointments rather than through our 'better' feelings. In the words of William Tyndale, one of the fathers of English Protestantism, 'God worketh backwards' – and it is back-to-front, outside-in that Johnson also finds himself working, bad news first. 'Whom he loveth, him he chasteneth.'[66] Johnson found himself chastened from the moment he found that he could not be a God-like speculatist but a reporter from experience; he was himself one of those who 'instead of gratifying their vanity by inferring effects from causes . . . are always reduced at last to conjecture causes from effects' (*The Rambler*, 13). Theory was reduced to memory, and Johnson himself then acts as a chastener, urging a sense of individual unimportance which he also knows is impossible wholly to take – and which he would not be urging were it not impossible wholly to take. For 'no man can live only for others, unless he could persuade others to live only for him' – and he could hardly do that, as tough-minded Johnson knows well enough. But to force ourselves to take the idea of unimportance just a bit more seriously than our egoism naturally allows – we can afford that, we need it in the name of morality, and that is Johnson's strategy, balancing as we go, pushing on even by going against the grain. One step back to force two forward.

The hard news is hard to take and, characteristically of life, it is sometimes even good that we cannot take it. This may sound like Hume resting ironic and nearly content in the system by which we have practically to reject our own scepticism about it. But this time the flesh and blood is put on the mind, which is precisely the difference here under consideration. For if we could take the idea of individual unimportance fully to heart, it might be heart that we lose; the fact that we cannot – that we, like children of Israel, have enough fallen stubbornness in us – is itself heartening. Johnson's Imlac in Chapter xxxii of *Rasselas* finds himself thinking that the Egyptian pyramids are both magnificent and useless, ridiculous and incorrigible, in the sheer vain perseverance of that human 'hunger of imagination'. Likewise the vanity of youth is both 'error' and 'pleasing', responsible for 'many of the virtues *and* vices' involved in youth's caring so much about what affects it. It may be good that we cannot quite take the bad news, but we hardly know and barely choose when it is good. There are times when folly is wiser than wisdom, or even when life is more important than knowledge, and there are not many intellectuals who know how or why to celebrate that. Johnson is one, ruefully, zestfully, in his two minds; again, Nietzsche is another:

> First of all, there is an observation that everyone must have made: a man's historical sense and knowledge can be very limited, his horizon as narrow as that of a dweller in the Alps, all his judgements may involve injustice and he may falsely suppose that all his experiences are original to him – yet in spite of this injustice and error he will none the less stand there in superlative health and vigour, a joy to all who see him; while close behind him a man far more just and instructed than he sickens and collapses because the lines of his horizon are always restlessly changing, because he can no longer extricate himself from the delicate net of his judiciousness and truth for a simple act of will and desire.[67]

It may be that Levet, in his way, did better than Johnson. There is always a sort of common peasant, a simpler man, in Johnson robustly warning the wise man and the literary man in him against themselves. For no literary man has ever waged a keener war than does Johnson against pure intellect such as Hume's or intelligent cowardice and artificial self-dramatization such as Boswell's. Common sense is a name for something also more spirited when Johnson uses it to attack intellectuals and their specializations: 'they have annexed to every species of knowledge some chimerical character of terror and inhibition, which they transmit...' (*The Rambler*, 25). Hope here becomes a bold but rational (what Tietjens might call a manly rather than wistful) pursuit.

In the light of Nietzsche's observation, the defeat of one's own judiciousness, the reduction of oneself from wise writer to same old Adam, may be a wry, backhanded gift. Yet the fact that there are always at least two sides to things, like gain *and* loss in both youth *and* age, does not mean that for Johnson there is always therefore a nice, comforting, liberal mixture of good and bad, pessimism and optimism, swings and roundabouts in human life. On the contrary, it means that we hardly know just *where* we are between the two poles, the snags and compensations on each second thought only increasing almost to the point of unreality the mental confusion when everything is so plausible and well rehearsed. We are left on our own, surrounded by general plausibilities, to try to work out the precise, particular degree of loss and gain at each stage; all life being a matter of balance, the uncertainty and loneliness calling for the very necessity of thought. It is at that point that the peasant and the pessimist in Johnson begin with the reality, at least, of the bottom-line, bad news first. For if the bad news has some good in it, that at least is the kind of good news one might begin safely to trust.

Johnson therefore tells the young his good bad news: namely, not to be so bothered about themselves, *because* other people aren't so bothered about them as they half-like, half-fear to believe. This may be particularly difficult to take for those who have been brought up with vague ideas of Romantic individualism. To Thomas Hardy, for instance, this might be a reason for being *more* bothered: precisely because 'they' don't care. Indeed, I know a man who could be said to have spent his whole adult life trying to hold off the pessimism of Hardy precisely through the pessimism of Johnson: it would be a great thing to think *which* of the two was the human screech-owl. For Johnson is travelling in the opposite direction from Hardy, working backwards, outside-in, complaining against our complaints as if that were the best thing he could do for us:

> By such acts of voluntary delusion does every man endeavour to conceal his own unimportance from himself. It is long before we are convinced of the small proportion which every individual bears to the collective body of mankind; or learn how few can be interested in the fortune of any single man... Mankind are kept perpetually busy by their fears or desires, and have not more leisure from their own affairs... (*The Rambler*, 146)

Again, first the bad or sad news as our pity goes out to ourselves: single, unimportant, small, neglected from without and having to hide it all within. Pitiful, pitiful. And then a shift as the 'mankind' which has been neglecting us becomes the mankind which feels neglected too, with its own fears and desires. Thus the way we learn to feel sorry for ourselves at the end of the passage is different from the way we felt sorry for ourselves at the beginning. It is a more social sentiment; the self-pity is not further punished but, chastened, is educatively transformed until it is glad to recognize itself as a misplaced form of the later, more collective compassion to which it gives way. We are not now dealing with society as It or They, neglecting me, but we, us, neglecting and neglected. Johnson has this powerful higher sympathy which hardly looks like sympathy at all but suddenly becomes it. So it is with so many names of things in Johnson: we begin to remember how one, its base assured, can then become another; how the apparent unattractiveness at first sight becomes a later authentication of the process of transformation. 'Common sense', 'tolerance', 'pessimism', 'angry resistance': these qualities begin to mean more and go further in Johnson. These re-educating transformations are quite different from Hume's secular shedding of weight; in Hume it just is as it is, or how it has to seem to be.

But, without shedding the truth for which his pessimism serves as a disciplining reminder, Johnson never wants to leave without helping those to whom he has first given his diagnosis. He says, for instance, that it is sadder than you think when you feel sad alone – sadder, but more real. For many people are feeling the same thing even at this moment in their – apparently – subjectively unique loneliness. Yet somehow, and for reasons beyond malice, that more general sadness is almost heartening, more solid, more a generic and formal fact than a matter of the perilously arbitrary content of personal feeling; less lonely. Thus we know *why* 'how few *can* be interested in the fortune of any single man', for the many are all those single men too. It is as though Johnson thought this: that if through language something can be understood, it can be borne – the more so since it naturally is our *shared* language, offering not only the support of human reason but also the emotional memory of our basic solidarity. For using language with that depth of understanding, Johnson, even in his down-to-earth prosaic toughness, is a poet by that very grace which makes a way suddenly from the hard to the soft or, rather, finds the one arising even within the very terms of the other. A miracle of language by the great educator.

There are other ways and Wordsworth, in his 'Answer to Mathetes', offers one which seems much closer to what one might call the faith and spirit embodied in poetry, less than twenty years after Johnson's own death. For like a true poet, Wordsworth, even here in his prose, gives us an image to think about: the image of the dying light of a candle. Look at the flame:

It fades and revives – gathers to a point – seems as if it would go out in a moment – again recovers its strength, nay becomes

brighter than before: it continues to shine with an endurance
which in its apparent weakness is a mystery.[68]

To a child, watching it, alone, just before sleep, the thought must be
of death. Nature, says Wordsworth, here teaches the child
immediately through the emotions: the child naturally thinks of
someone he or she has already lost or a guardian he or she will in time
lose. The thought goes with the feeling, is naturally inside it:
mortality, loneliness the dying flame. So much for the first natural
stage of life.

But there is another stage, beyond youth, and it is a necessary one.
An older person skilled in language knows that there are different
ways of taking the same thing, different meanings within the same
words. 'Mathetes', the pseudonym of the young man who, like a
latter-day Boswell, wrote to Wordsworth seeking his teaching, ended
his letter like a child, with an emotion: we might lose our way on our
own – that was virtually his cry. But what to Mathetes was a natural
emotion, a natural fear at the end of the first stage of youth, is to
Wordsworth a condition of being at the very entrance to manhood:
we *might* lose our way, that is what is implicit and essential in the task
of finding it. The emotion becomes a recognition of a condition; the
fear becomes a thought. Similarly there are two ways of looking at the
dying flame.

For the child grows older and, in Wordsworth's beautiful parable,
sees the dying flame again: 'It continues to shine with an endurance
which in its apparent weakness is a mystery.' He no longer feels so
directly the sense of sadness, or the specific reminder of losing people
he depends upon. The loneliness gives way to the thought that he is on
his own, always dying, always dependent upon no one but himself.
The light, struggling with a sense of inward decay, is now to the
maturing youth the light of his own fragile spirit, his own life until it
ends in death. Early on, thoughts come easily within feelings. Now
the thought goes *against* the natural grain of emotion: the feeling of
loneliness has to give way to the responsibility of thinking I am on my
own – whatever my feelings about it. And if my self-pitying feelings
about it paradoxically *prevent* my being in myself and making what I
can of what *is* my own, then my light will not endure through its
apparent weakness. When thought, as in adulthood, has to go *against*
the natural grain, going through feelings to go beyond feeling
towards what they stand for; when thought reaches what lies 'too
deep for tears' – then we have what Wordworth calls not Nature but
Reason. For Reason is the faculty which makes of loneliness the

responsibility of independence: let me not pity my own flame, if *not* pitying it *adds* a strength to make the flame brighter: 'With trust-worthy hopes; founded less upon his sentient than upon his intellectual Being – to Nature, not as leading on insensibly to the society of Reason; but to Reason and Will, as leading back to the wisdom of Nature.'[69]

Such Reason is, I believe, Wordsworth's own translation of what one such as Johnson stands for in the history of human feeling. For this book's consideration of the strengths and disadvantages of Johnson's position is also implicitly the story of why Wordsworth, more than any of the Romantics save perhaps Byron, had both to include and to modify what Johnson stood for, within his own project of being. But where Wordsworth wants to show the necessity of going against the grain – if ever to return to it – as a second stage in the human chronology, Johnson begins with it, the bad news first: a cross-grained, back-to-front man whose first word is *No*. In the next chapter we shall see why Johnson needed his passionate *No* to the forefront – in order both to prevent the dissolution of his faith and to discourage its more fictitiously consoling semblances. For the moment we may conclude that there is something in Johnson's cussed roughness, for all its strange mixture of scepticism and conservatism, agedness and anger, which is far more attractive and valuable than we might have suspected.

CHAPTER THREE

On the Strength of Limitation (1): Johnson's Realism

I Boswell's Dilemma

The Rambler, 196, maintains that it is impossible, without pity and contempt, to hear a young person openly declaring his or her fond expectations of life. Yet, as so often in Johnson, the trouble does not stop when the person in question begins to realize it. As Johnson says of the island peasantry during their historical transition from a feudal to a money economy, 'Their ignorance grows every day less, but their knowledge is yet of little other use than to shew them their wants. They are now in the period of education, and feel the uneasiness of discipline, without yet perceiving the benefit of instruction.'[1] A state of personal transition similarly may leave us questioning the benefit of new, uncomfortable self-knowledge. Accordingly, a young person, beginning to suspect how his expectations may sound in the ear of experience, may decide no longer to be open but closed: making the inner expectations of deeper, secret and less conscious hold, because he 'knows' he may not openly hold them himself. Probably such a youth will have to learn from experience, can only learn from time. That feels like youth's right: the right to find it anew, even though the old may wonder what was the point of their learning so much at such a cost, and often too late, if the next generation cannot take anything from them as given, and each generation seems doomed to repeat the old mistakes in a new way. If there are problems about ignorance, there are problems about learning. Youth's cover-up begins precisely when the young person has learnt too much too soon for his own good, and when hopeful innocence has learnt, usually through words alone, to cover its important naiveté in premature consciousness.

Suppose, like novelists, we try to imagine just such a young person. We shall say he is aged twenty-two, a Scotsman just arrived in London, grateful to meet another young Scot who impresses him with his cool elegance, indifference, and utter scepticism about the importance of life. The date is 11 December 1762 and our young man is James Boswell, who in a few months' time will first meet Samuel Johnson, but who is now so impressed by cynical young Captain Erskine. Here is Boswell's journal:

> I was mentioning Erskine's character to Sir James Macdonald, a young man who has made a great figure at Eton school and the University of Oxford and is studying hard to fit himself for Parliament, being full of notions of the consequence of real life, and making a figure in the world, and all that. When he heard Erskine's sentiments (which, by the by, are much my own, and which I mentioned just to see what he would say), he was perfectly stunned. 'Why,' said he, 'he must not be a man. He is unfit to live in human society. He is not of the species.' I was really entertained. 'Ah!' thought I, 'little do you know of how small duration the pleasure is of making one of these great figures that now swell before your ambitious imagination.'
>
> Yet I do think it is a happiness to have an object in view which one keenly follows. It gives a lively agitation to the mind which is very pleasurable. I am determined to have a degree of Erskine's indifference to make me easy when things go cross; and a degree of Macdonald's eagerness for real life, to make me relish things when they go well. It is in vain to sit down and say, 'What good does it do to have a regiment? Is a general more happy than an ensign?' No. But a man who has had his desire gratified of rising by degrees to that rank in the Army, has enjoyed more happiness than one who has never risen at all. The great art I have to study is to balance these two very different ways of thinking, properly. It is very difficult to be keen about a thing which in reality you do not regard, and consider as imaginary. But I fancy it may do, as a man is afraid of ghosts in the dark, although he is sure there are none; or pleased with beautiful exhibitions on the stage, although he knows they are not real. Although the Judgement may know that all is vanity, yet Passion may ardently pursue. Judgement and Passion are very different.[2]

In content this may seem, for its sheer intelligence, impressive; but in context, just because of that, there is cause for shame in the very attempt at an older, articulate dignity. Only a young person, all too defensively conscious of himself as yet unformed, could write such philosophy in his own diary. We might well think: Why didn't he wait, keep quiet, till he was older? but then if we all wait until we are 'mature', who will ever be ready to say anything? A few weeks before, the young man had written to himself: 'I have discovered that we may be in some degree whatever character we choose', and this basic uncertainty is also, to his mind, freedom.[3] Everything is (only?) possible. Perhaps one forgives the youthfulness for the sake of the interest of the more general problems which its troubles uncover.

But then confusion sets in to this young mind precisely because the youth does not want to entertain this possibility of a distinction between the problems of his time of life and the problems of life itself. That would be too humiliating; it would take too much steam out of his intelligence's conversion of psychology into philosophy. We may notice how he tries, in that first paragraph, to imply that it is *he* who listens to Macdonald with 'pity and contempt'. But who is he fooling? The pity and contempt, so slyly unexpressed and condescendingly bracketed off to match the very withdrawal of an Erskine himself, nevertheless give way in the second paragraph to envy of Macdonald. Unlike Johnson, Boswell will not work his first and second thoughts together in a paragraph, in a sentence, but prefers to split his thinking up as if into two opposed people: Erskine versus Macdonald. On the private stage of his own journal, in which he is anyway both actor and spectator, Boswell dramatizes his own self-divisions in the opposition which he creates between two other young Scots of his acquaintance; he borrows his sense of himself from both of them, even as he looks down on them both.

For Erskine versus Macdonald becomes Judgement versus Passion, 'two very different ways of thinking': the detachment of consciousness from the commitments of emotional involvement; the capacity to take up a position outside yourself 'when things go cross' but inside yourself only 'when they go well' – as though the two were distinct and choosable. It is clear that the words 'Judgement' and 'Passion', though said to be 'very different', are at any rate alike in being similarly psychologically split off from each other. Thus the word 'real' sometimes goes with Macdonald and Passion – 'eagerness for real life', 'the consequence of real life' – but sometimes is associated with Erskine and Judgement – 'I was really entertained', 'a thing which in reality you do not regard', 'although he knows they are not real'. But we may suspect that passion is 'really' conventional ambition here, just as judgement is 'really' cynicism's disguise for fear. Where is the reality of life, the young man is worrying, is this *it*?

Yet all the time in this passage Boswell is playing unreal games. He is the manipulator ('which I mentioned just to see what he would say') and he is the aesthete ('an object in view . . . gives a lively agitation to the mind which is very pleasurable'; 'the great art I have to study . . . '). Everything is choice, nothing can be chosen; objective values become subjective sensations rather than beliefs in anything real outside; abstract language has become innerly psychologized and distorted. Boswell is living in a play of life and, 'with beautiful exhibitions on the stage', he is its author, characters and audience, in various turns.

The real Hero was about to enter: Samuel Johnson. It was Johnson who made Macdonald's passion – 'Why, he must not be a man. He is unfit to live in human society. He is not of the species' – into a form of judgement in Boswell's eyes; though Boswell himself never quite recognized, in all his confusions, the emotion in Johnson's reason. Macdonald's outraged disgust at Erskine's position as outsider, as though looking down on what human beings do on this planet, is taken up into Johnson's undaunted judgement of the metaphysical poets:

> they never enquired what, on any occasion, they should have said or done, but wrote rather as beholders than partakers of human nature, as beings looking upon good and evil impassive and at leisure, as Epicurean deities making remarks on the actions of men and the vicissitudes of life without interest and without emotion.[4]

They were not of the species, not even in the way they thought they were. For Johnson is resolutely unashamed before any man of what he, like other human beings, finds himself committed to or impassioned about, however small or absurd that might look from above. He is tough-minded enough, as well as linguistically precise enough, to use that word 'interest' at the end of the above passage in the sense both of sympathetic involvement and of gainful prejudice, knowing that it *is* our condition to combine the two in that way, however dispassionately fairer some higher, inhuman being might be. Unashamed before man, Johnson is ashamed only before God – the sole Being who may judge us, even as we cannot really see ourselves, from above. Johnson refuses to think a Cowley or Donne superior: they are inferior, Sir, even in their unreal pretensions.

Yet if Johnson replaced Macdonald in Boswell's mind, there was a maturer replacement for Erskine there too. Seven years later, in 1769,

Boswell is still trying out his experiments of the mind amidst his outside acquaintance:

> I told him that David Hume said to me, he was no more uneasy to think that he should *not be* after this life, than that he *had not been* before he began to exist. JOHNSON: 'Sir, if he really thinks so, his perceptions are disturbed; he is mad: if he does not think so, he lies. . . . When he dies, he at least gives up all he has.'[5]

Take a pistol to Hume's breast, said Johnson, and then see how he behaves, what he believes. The logic of Johnson's argument asserts itself with comic relish through the appropriate violence of its own chosen illustration, as if to say: I could kill Hume for thinking that. Yet when Boswell had gone, incredibly enough, to see how Hume was taking the thought of his own imminent death, he could hardly believe the almost playful equanimity before him: 'I asked him if it was not possible that there might be a future state. He answered It was possible that a piece of coal put upon the fire would not burn . . .'[6] With characteristic irony, Hume himself was taking as an illustration of the unreasonable the very thing his own *Treatise* had shown to be un-discreditable. For we cannot entirely trust the belief that we none the less have to have in practice: that coal will always burn, that the relation of cause and effect will always hold true. This was no final concession to Boswell, however, for what Hume was doing was revolving everything still within the implacable grandeur and self-subsistence of a rationality which his own death would not affect. 'He is not of the species' is still the basic protest that religious, social and biological Man, in the person of Johnson, had to make against the scepticism of the relativizing, secular Philosopher in Boswell's mind.

This is the Johnson whom Boswell himself so often deliberately provoked to *kick* the Erskine side of him out of mind, just as Johnson had kicked a stone to confute what he took to be Berkeley's case against the existence of physical reality. Remember that when Boswell asked Johnson for a *reason* for bothering with all those routine acts which generally engage us in life, Johnson replied 'in an animated tone': 'Sir, it is driving on the system of life'. There was only one sense in which Johnson agreed with the young Boswell that we could be anything: it is stupid, Johnson scolded Mrs Thrale, to 'ask a baby of seven years old which way his *genius* leads him, when we all know that a boy of seven years old has no genius for any thing except a peg-top and an apple-pye'.[7] There are no special 'reasons' or 'calling', it is all more chance than choice, he feels. And it is as though

Johnson could almost persuade himself to want to abolish the burdens of individualism and unexercisable choice by a sort of radical Toryism or enlightened personal despotism on the model of more ancient societies: 'I have often thought those happy that have been fixed, from the first dawn of thought, in a determination to some state of life, by the choice of one, whose authority may preclude caprice, and whose influence may prejudice them in favour of his opinion' (*The Rambler*, 19). The Bear! But Edmund Burke (besides Sir Joshua Reynolds, the other great graduate of the school of Johnson) put it thus, in arguing similarly that a foolish modern arbitrariness had been substituted for an old-established wise one:

> It has been the misfortune (not as these gentlemen think it, the glory) of this age, that every thing is to be discussed, as if the constitution of our country were to be always a subject rather of altercation than enjoyment.[8]

The *tanti* men will want everything talked out – as if it could be. They do not understand the importance of 'the system of life' predating us, invented by no one. They want not the system but the choice of life.

For indeed the young Boswell was not looking for the system of life so much as for a person with a theory of how to live and what to live for. Thus in 1762 he was in much the same position as Johnson's own Rasselas; *The History of Rasselas, Prince of Abissinia* having appeared in 1759. Both were trying to make 'the choice of life', from outside life, by looking at people in it. Life approached in that way so often describes a vicious circle. For as Imlac says to Rasselas, just as Johnson might say to Boswell, 'It seems to me . . . that while you are making the choice of life, you neglect to live'. For Rasselas was the sort of young man who 'past four months in resolving to lose no more time in idle resolves', who, regretting the time he has wasted, then spends more time regretting the time he has wasted even now in regrets![9] Poor Boswell, likewise, spends so much time putting himself into Erskine and into Macdonald that he has no time to be wholly himself except in so doing. Where Johnson speaks of 'driving on the system of life', Imlac says that 'some desire is necessary to keep life in motion'.[10] But with Boswell, as with Rasselas, 'every thing' – as Burke put it – 'is to be discussed'.

So what do Johnson and Imlac mean? Their language is vigorous, driving life on, keeping it in motion, but to what purpose? Is the very vigour a half-bullying, half-fearful substitute for a felt want of direction? That is to say, is 'the system of life' the language of a basic conservative – that certain things have to keep going in order to keep us going, even though it is all repetitive and tautological and circular? We do it because we need to do something and so need something to do. 'Some desire is necessary to keep life in motion': some desire, but what desire? Any desire – it doesn't matter which? One couldn't tell which was best? In the *Happy Valley* Rasselas says, poignantly, 'I have already enjoyed too much; give me something to desire'.[11] Even if it makes him *unhappy*? Sickeningly, question after question. But all this is just what was troubling Boswell in 1762: that hope, desire, passion were necessary for life as it is lived from within, though also (as Hume-like judgement tells us from without) fallacious, arbitrary and irrational:

> It is very difficult to be keen about a thing which in reality you do not regard. But I fancy it may do, as a man is afraid of ghosts in the dark, although he is sure there are none; or pleased with beautiful exhibitions on the stage, although he knows they are not real. Although the Judgement may know that all is vanity, yet Passion may ardently pursue.

Boswell's problem is: How can we *believe* in what we also know to be a useful fiction? We need to believe in something – in anything, perhaps just to keep going; but if we know we can believe in anything, we can believe in nothing really. If we have to make things which are essentially unimportant important to us in order to find meaning in life, then life is implicitly meaningless; our emotions are acts and fictions; our values are inventions, toys, distractions from mortality. Yet somehow we do continue to play this trick upon ourselves and suspend disbelief as in a theatre. The absurdity is not only that we look down on our commitments from outside and see their vanity but also that we know, even in thus looking down, that we will still continue with them. The levels of wisdom and life, judgement and passion, external and internal points of view, seem irreconcilable.[12] Is it any comfort to know that man lives by self-deception and still to be able to deceive oneself even about that?

The Rambler itself is full of this sort of problem. Take as just one example two paragraphs from Number 67. One begins:

> Hope is necessary in every condition. The miseries of poverty, of sickness, of captivity, would, without this comfort, be insupportable...

Then the next follows with:

Hope is, indeed, very fallacious, and promises what it seldom gives; but its promises are more valuable than the gifts of fortune...

Hope, as the wise man knows, is delusive; the sort of thing a child clings to in order to hide the reality of present time in the hope of future. But though delusive, hope, as the wise man also knows, is necessary for us even so; we cannot live without hope. 'Hope is necessary', 'Hope is fallacious': are those two statements to be joined by a 'but' or a 'because'? It is a trick and a comfort. The wise man feels stranded: he can neither believe nor disbelieve in hope; his wisdom is to be sceptical of it, but his wisdom is also, if he is Johnson, to be sceptical of his own scepticism: you may not believe in hope but you hope in lieu of belief; that is what 'hope' means; you cannot stop hoping, even hoping for legitimate hope, to keep you going. The wise man cannot simply grow up and leave the child's hope behind him, without becoming a cynical inhuman figure like Erskine. For Johnson, growing up cannot be merely about disenchantment, about the loss of hope; it has to be about ways of reclaiming hope, honourable ways of saying, as it were, 'people need their illusions' – without thereby making us all impossibly conscious self-deceivers.

Johnson really saw many of the same things that Boswell presumed to, as to 'the vanity of human wishes'. But Johnson was not the same as Boswell – fictive Boswell who would run before he could walk or limp to show he knew suffering, who never began at the beginning but prematurely joined in, imitating his heroes. Let us ask the question Boswell must have asked: What did Johnson have that Boswell did not?

*

II Johnson's fallen 'angelick counsel'

Here is Johnson against Boswell translated to a higher, poetic level:

> Solicit not thy thoughts with matters hid;
> Leave them to God alone; him serve and fear.
> Of other creatures as him pleases best,
> Wherever placed, let him dispose; joy thou
> In what he gives to thee, this Paradise
> And thy fair Eve; Heaven is for thee too high
> To know what passes there. Be lowly wise;

> Think only what concerns thee and thy being;
> Dream not of other worlds, what creatures there
> Live, in what state, condition, or degree –
> Contented that thus far hath been revealed
> Not of Earth only, but of highest Heaven.

These lines are actually from Milton's *Paradise Lost* (viii, 167–78), but here is Johnson's commentary on them:

> Raphael, in return to Adam's enquiries into the courses of the stars and the revolutions of heaven, counsels him to withdraw his mind from idle speculations, and employ his faculties upon nearer and more interesting objects, the survey of his own life, the subjection of his passions, the knowledge of duties which must daily be performed, and the detection of dangers which must daily be incurred.
>
> This angelick counsel every man of letters should always have before him. (*The Rambler*, 180)

The greatness of Socrates, says Johnson in *The Rambler*, 24, consisted in his turning the attention of the Greeks from vain speculation about the *stars* to the nearer task of moral enquiry about the conduct of human life on *earth*. This is down-to-earth Johnson: a Johnsonian realism, sanctioned both by Socrates and by Raphael, by philosophy and religion, and founded in the experience of human limitation:

> 'Books,' says Bacon, 'can never teach the use of books.' The student must learn by commerce with mankind to reduce his speculations to practice, and accommodate his knowledge to the purposes of life. (*The Rambler*, 137)

What Johnson says to the world of literature is what Raphael says to Adam: 'Dream not of other worlds'. It is in this respect that one thinks of Johnson in relation to that history of literature which later involved the development of the realist novel:

> In the romances formerly written, every transaction and sentiment was so remote from all that passes among men, that the reader was in very little danger of making any applications to himself; the virtues and crimes were equally beyond his sphere of activity; and he amused himself with heroes and with traitors, deliverers and persecutors, as with beings of another species, whose actions were regulated upon motives of their own, and who had neither faults nor excellencies in common

with himself. (*The Rambler*, 4)

What old romance does not bear, in Johnson's eyes, is the mark of the real: for Johnson, that is to say, the force of personal application within the common resonance offered to the species. I am concerned in this work to tease out the complex of implicit ideas and beliefs that Johnson held together and lived out in his very character: what we see here is precisely how he embodied a virtual theory that always retained together in his mind three things – the real, the sympathetic and the limited – in all their reciprocal combinations. Of romance, he goes on to write: 'the reader was in very little danger of making any application to himself'. And here Johnson is not just being ironical, he means that word 'danger'. For it is vital to his practical theory that the literature of the limitations of reality would be quite the opposite of comfortable or small – quite the opposite of the sort of book which was produced 'without fear of criticism, without the toil of study, without knowledge of nature, or acquaintance with life' (*The Rambler*, 4). Unrealistic romances, made up from their own special terms, are to Johnson 'safe': grant their imaginative premises and you need not quarrel with them, you need not find that they embody real beliefs to challenge your own. But the sort of writings Johnson supports are, on the contrary, 'in danger from every common reader'. We all share their subject matter; the books are open to an appeal to or criticism from nature, from a reader's own experience of life; we have to take on issues of truth and belief.

Thus 'the student must learn by commerce with mankind to reduce his speculations to practice, and accommodate his knowledge to the purposes of life'. But what, we may ask, *are* the purposes of life by which 'to reduce' is not merely reductive? Or, like Boswell, are we not allowed to ask that either? A hostile reader might well wonder if it is not significant and odd that Johnson, a literary man, should most exercise this apparent repression upon literature and men of letters. We have constantly come up against his deep distrust of fiction's temptations for the delusive imagination, and Boswell himself must often have seemed to Johnson a prime example of the man who confused life with literature. But is Johnson's Realism both antagonistic to art and reductive of life, a symptom of the fear and failure of imagination in both (perhaps falsely separated) realms?

In other words, how 'angelick' is the counsel of reduction? Here, as an initial test case, is the final paragraph of *The Rambler*, 19 – on the danger of ranging from one study to another and the importance of an early choice of profession:

It was said of the learned Bishop Sanderson, that, when he was preparing his lectures, he hesitated so much, and rejected so often, that, at the time of reading, he was often forced to produce, not what was best, but what happened to be at hand. This will be the state of every man, who, in the choice of his employment, balances all the arguments on every side; the complication is so intricate, the motives and obligations so numerous, there is so much play for the imagination, and so much remains in the power of others, that reason is forced at last to rest in neutrality, the decision devolves into the hands of chance, and after a great part of life spent in enquiries which can never be resolved, the rest must often pass in repenting the unnecessary delay, and can be useful to few other purposes than to warn others against the same folly, and to show, that of two states of life equally consistent with religion and virtue, he who chuses earliest chuses best.

Imagine Matthew Arnold, *the* great man of letters a century after Johnson, reading that. To Arnold, I suggest, this would have seemed practical yet limited, in a most damaging sense; not so much angelic as Hebraic. For Hebraism as Arnold defines it *Culture and Anarchy*, in opposition to Hellenism, puts conscience before consciousness, the rigour of moral rules and laws before the flexibility of disinterested thinking for its own sake, literalness before literariness. To Arnold it must have seemed that Johnson embodied Hebraic strengths of duty, practicality and concentrated, common-sense endeavour that, by Arnold's own time, had degenerated into philistine forms of the Protestant work ethic. Johnson in Arnold's eyes was significantly not a real poet: that was his limitation in the very name of practicality.

Indeed, from a position like Arnold's, Sanderson's hesitation might be seen as plausibly seeking to hold off the practical finality of choice. Hesitation tries to prevent life merely coming down to the narrowness of a mutually exclusive this-*or*-that. 'You have to choose between the two', a Hebraic view of life might insist. 'Now choose.' But after the choice it also adds: 'Now see that almost always you feel you have made the wrong choice.' As the princess puts it in Chapter xxix of *Rasselas*, 'nature sets her gifts on the right hand and on the left . . . as we approach one, we recede from another.' Those who would have both, lose each. Yet a learned man such as Bishop Sanderson might well want room and time for more thoughts, when thought itself suggests that any conclusion will be reductive and premature. Indeed, a learned man might even suggest that a notion of life as always 'either/or', as always a matter of mutually exclusive choices you are only ironically *free* to *have to* make, is bound to be linked with pessimism. One produces the other, whichever way round it is. So what price Johnson's Hebraism, if its very attempt to forge and discipline a life only darkens and narrows it?

That is not how Johnson would see it. For him, hesitation, so far from being about not yet deciding upon a course, is in reality itself a course of indecision even before you know it. In *The Rambler*, 135, he clearly has in mind the example of his own procrastinations, made for all too plausibly learned reasons:

> He whose penetration extends to remote consequences, and who, whenever he applies his attention to any design, discovers new prospects of advantage, and possibilities of improvement, will not easily be persuaded that his project is ripe for execution; but will superadd one contrivance to another, endeavour to unite various purposes in one operation, multiply complications, and refine niceties, till he is entangled in his own scheme, and bewildered in the perplexity of various intentions.

For Johnson, where epistemology reaches its limits, human psychology takes over. When we cannot know for sure but can only think, the mind, without the security of external knowledge, falls prey to those internal mental forces of its own which have little to do with pure intellect but everything to do with the passions that invade its doubt. Anyone who has tried to write a book knows what it is like to be lost in it: lost in one's *own* work or head – it is a terrible fear for Johnson; the fear of becoming unreal even by adding one thought about reality to another and another, until the reality itself has gone into the thinking. If all this does not lead to self-entanglement, it leads at least to self-destruction – self-destruction with particular relation to time, in the matter of procrastination. My project is not ripe for execution, a Coleridge might say. But Johnson says:

> The disposition to defer every important design to a time of leisure, and a state of settled uniformity, proceeds generally from a false estimate of the human powers. If we except those gigantick and stupendous intelligences who are said to grasp a system by intuition, and bound forward from one series of conclusions to another, without regular steps through intermediate propositions, the most successful students make their advances in knowledge by short flights between each of which the mind may lie at rest. (*The Rambler*, 108)

What is crucial here is Johnson's re-estimate of the human powers: what naturally must be their business is to be deduced from their scale and range. It is with Johnson as it is with that other great eighteenth-century Anglican, Bishop Butler, in his sermon 'Upon the Ignorance of Man':

> If to acquire knowledge were our proper end, we should indeed be poorly provided: but if somewhat else be our business and duty, we may, notwithstanding our ignorance, be well enough furnished for it; and the observation of our ignorance may be of assistance to us in the discharge of it.[13]

We know what an eye is for, we know that it fulfils its ordinary function in the act of seeing, for its function is naturally appropriate to and determined by its characteristics. But what is a human being for? Clearly not for knowledge: the struggle that Johnson's Bishop Sanderson has to complete a thought or sentence may be summed up in Butler's remark, 'Nor can we give the whole account of any one thing whatever; of all its causes, ends, and necessary adjuncts, those adjuncts, I mean, without which it could not have been.'[14] Johnson, as we have seen, hated those *tanti* men who thought they needed a reason to live. For him the problem of how to live (as it were) *ordinarily* without extra *reasons* was a formal question to be asked first of the species as a whole rather than the individual especially. As in Aristotle's *Nicomachean Ethics*, which Johnson once had vague plans to translate, a type of natural wisdom should be able to infer what is the business of mankind from the clues offered by the limitations of its constitution. As Butler again puts it, harnessing Aristotle to Anglicanism, 'If the real nature of any creature leads him and is adapted to such and such purposes only, or more than to any other; this is a reason to believe the Author of that nature intended it for those purposes.'[15] We know how sceptical Johnson can be – about the possibility of knowing our 'real nature' anyway, about the danger of inferring that how we are is how God meant us to be. Indeed, such thoughts keep Johnson quieter than Butler. Yet *The Rambler* does carry tacitly within it the Aristotelian thought that function and nature are interrelated, that our limitations are clues to our proper business, and that the sphere of what is practical is not therefore, as Arnold might want to say, a falling away from our 'higher' possibilities but the place in which we may see their reality in action. Since the nineteenth century, with its Industrial Revolution, we have somewhat lost sight of the meaning of 'practical' by seeing it as conflictingly opposed to theoretical; but in the Aristotelian world human practices are the arena in which the theoretical takes place, as the nature of man viewed holistically simply undergoes translation from one realm to another. Holism rather than conflict is the distinction at stake here.

It is that different order of understanding for human practice and human limitation that Johnson is seeking, even for such conflicts as he undoubtedly does have. Hating as he did those literary existentialists who wanted a reason to live, Johnson was none the less a man deeply troubled by the question: What are we *for*? What he did was take his fear of having nothing to do into the very writing of *The Rambler*, to seek and define there normative conditions for the species. Johnson clearly did think of himself as a representatively limited man, trying to use a sense of limitation as a clue to the understanding of normal human purpose within our bounds. He did not think of himself, therefore, as one of those 'gigantick and stupendous intelligences' he mentions in *The Rambler*, 108: men such as Newton or the scholars of the Renaissance period who could seem to take in something of the whole of things rather than having to take short flights, dividing and conquering, like the rest of us. Yet on the other hand Johnson did not consider himself merely the sort of mediocrity who, gloomy over mediocrity, does not sufficiently consider 'how much less is the calamity of not possessing great powers, than of not using them aright' (*The Rambler*, 38). For he did blame himself for having great talents yet not using them aright – though even those talents were not 'gigantick', any more than they were mediocre. He felt himself to be an in-between man: he knew too much, for he knew that he knew too little. This is to know limitation very well, but very equivocally.

Equivocally, for this reason. It was not as if Johnson felt securely limited, sanctioned by limitation simply to know what was therefore his business within its bounds. On the contrary, this sense of limitation could make him feel indefinite rather than defined. The state of in-betweenness, in the sense of something being neither this nor that, was to Johnson's mind both a common and yet an essentially impossible position in which to find oneself. He felt himself in between knowledge and ignorance, for example. The question he had then to face was this: Could limitation be a blind guide within for the inference of our station and purpose in the scheme of things without – as Butler implies when he talks of our very ignorance being of assistance to us? Or is limitation, conversely, the very sign of indefiniteness, the being too limited to know even whether we have a purpose at all? He needed to know the legitimate uses of a sense of limitation, be it as a strengthening or weakening recognition, for faith or despair.

*

For the moment let us simply continue to try to understand what Johnson meant by human limitation. I have said that 'limitation' often implies something definite and bounded – and that indeed is what a thinker such as Montaigne tries to make of it:

> to affections that distract me from myself, and divert me elesewhere, surely to such I oppose myself with all my force. Mine opinion is, that one should lend himself to others, and not give himself but to himself... Thou hast business enough within thyself, therefore stray not abroad: men give themselves to hire. Their faculties are not their own, but theirs to whom they subject themselves...The more we amplify our need and possession, the more we engage ourselves to the crosses of fortune and adversities. The career of our desires must be circumscribed, and tied to strict bounds of nearest and contiguous commodities.[16]

This is the *deliberate* self-limitation, self-control, of stoic quietism. However much one can imagine the circumstances in an age of civil war that can make people feel the need thus to limit themselves, only the force of such circumstances could restrain the twinge of disgust one otherwise feels at the artifice of making life smaller, as well as safer, than emotion suggests it can be. Yet the sanity of this position was, perhaps, something Johnson could respect for its attempt to limit mentally from within, the damage that can come to a person from without. 'The cure for the greater part of human miseries', wrote Johnson in *The Rambler*, 32, 'is not radical, but palliative': if one cannot entirely abolish one's dependence on the outside world, there is in that a licence at least to reconsider and modify one's conscious inner commitment to that dependence. But Johnson then adds this to the widom of Montaigne:

> In calamities which operate chiefly on our passions... many expedients have been contrived, by which the blow may be broken. Of these the most general precept is, not to take

pleasure in any thing, of which it is not in our power to secure the
advantage to ourselves. This counsel, when we consider the
enjoyment of any terrestrial advantage, as opposed to a
constant and habitual solicitute for future felicity, is undoubtedly just ... but in any other sense, is it not like advice,
not to walk lest we should stumble, or not to see lest our eyes
should light upon deformity? (*The Rambler*, 32)

That is the human limitation with which Johnson is most concerned:
the limitation which exactly prevents our consciously, artificially
limiting our passions. This is, as opposed to Stoicism, Johnson's
natural Christianity deeply and implicitly in memory of St Augustine:
'The Stoics, to be sure, are in the habit of extending their
condemnation to compassion; but how much more honourable
would it have been in the Stoic ... to have been "disturbed" by
compassion so as to rescue someone.'[17] There is a humbling, a
stumbling, which is greater than the apparently higher dignity of
merely sitting still. Johnson was always prepared to let admitted
snags and stumbles ruin the elegant self-containedness of his essays,
the appeal always left untidily open to nature and human feelings.
Augustine, like a model for Johnson, recalls those almost inadvertent
principles which become so implicit as to be in danger of neglect:

Thus we sometimes weep, even when we do not want to, though
we may be moved not by any blameworhthy desire but by
praiseworthy charity. That implies that we have these emotions
as a result of the weakness of our human condition; but this was
not true of the Lord Jesus, whose weakness resulted from his
power. Yet if we felt none of those emotions at all, while we are
subject to the weakness of this life, there would really be
something wrong with our life.[18]

At some level it is right that we cannot help feeling, that we cannot
abolish the weakness.

The limits in which Johnson was finally interested were not
deliberately made in the head, nor were they the work of Arnold's
philistine. 'I am far from any intention', he says in *The Rambler*, 180,
'to limit curiosity, or confine the labours of learning to arts of
immediate and necessary use.' What he is concerned with are the
limits we *find* even in trying our very utmost or in feeling most
anxious to transcend limitation. Such limits are, as I have said,
equivocal: they have as much to do with our finding ourselves
indefinite, and therefore inadequate, as with finding ourselves

definitely, physically constrained. Examples of such equivocation are not hard to find in Johnson: 'It is beyond the powers of humanity to spend a whole day in profound study and intense meditation'; 'Few minds will be long confined to severe and laborious meditation'; 'Irresolution and mutability are often the faults of men, whose views are wide, and whose imagination is vigorous and excursive, because they cannot confine their thoughts within their own boundaries of action.'[19] That is to say, are we to call this limitation of our ability to limit ourselves our freedom or our inadequacy? Through our strengths and our weaknesses alike, we keep breaking out – breaking out of our confines, our definitions, but only to find just beyond them that we have still brought our limitations with us, even in the very restlessness of breaking bounds. Thus, the in-between man has to see, we *are* and also *will not be* limited. If we rejoice in freedom, we suffer from a loss of necessity for what we are or do. This under-determination, this equivocal, impossible in-betweenness, can feel like the worst of both worlds: neither limited nor unlimited enough to rest content. We have sufficient free choice to know that there is not one compulsory or destined role for us in life, we have insufficient freedom either to know what to choose or to feel certain that freedom is more our purpose than our lack of purpose. 'Thus men may be made inconstant by virtue and by vice, by too much or too little thought' (*The Rambler*, 63).

If to Boswell judgement and passion seemed to point in opposite directions, so may the needs of intellectual freedom and certainty of purpose. Near the beginning of *Rasselas* the young protagonist asks: 'what makes the difference between men and all the rest of animal creation?' Like a beast, says Rasselas, I am 'pained with want, but am not, like him, satisfied with fulness' – again, it seems the worst of both worlds. But is that need for *more* – which ever prevents the definition of what is securely *enough* – is that dissatisfaction our nature or our resistance to our nature? The worst, and likely, answer is, confusingly, both. In Chapter XXII a philosopher advises Rasselas to live according to nature, the actions corresponding to the nature of the agent; to which Johnson slyly offers the young man's modesty in reply: 'Let me only know what it is to live according to nature'.

I do not think that Matthew Arnold ever saw that Johnson, as much as any Romantic, believed that our definition was that we did not have a definition. And even this state, ungrounded in nature, could not be described as either one thing or another, a pain or a freedom. We always see more than we can do: in one sense that is our limitation, our inadequacy; in another, simultaneously, that is our lack of limitation, the lack of fixed sanction for what are thus uncertain human creatures.

These mutually entangled yet irreconcilable positions were precisely what precipitated in Johnson a sense of *levels*: a sense of levels between seeing and doing, between mind and body: 'For such is the inequality of our corporeal to our intellectual faculties, that we contrive in minutes what we execute in years, and the soul often stands an idle spectator of the labour of the hands, and expedition of the feet' (*The Rambler*, 8). Johnson could hardly bear such delay; in reading and in writing his impatience is a fundamental resentment of physical limitations to mind. He gutted books rather than read slowly through them. In writing he set himself a regular deadline or fixed number of verses in order to force himself through the detailed execution of what his mind had already anticipated: he worked as fast as he could, slipping his constraints from one level to another and back again. But the soul as idle spectator – that was what Johnson feared lay behind his own idleness: an admission of the frequent redundancy of the soul within our bodily life on earth. The recognition could make the body go on strike, depressively, at the thought of a homeless spirit of transcedence constantly having to recoil from its own unsatisfiable search for the absolute and un-conditional on earth – the state without 'if' or 'and' or 'but' – and settle instead for limitation. Johnson needed a steadying sense of levels, but he also needed not to get stuck on any one of them, to be able to work and translate quickly between them.

Thus Mrs Thrale praised Johnson for what actually he most feared in himself when she said, 'whatever work he did, seemed so much be-low his powers of performance that he appeared the idlest of all human beings'.[20] Nor does she seem ever to have linked this perception to something that in fact irritated her about Johnson – his obsession with redundancy: 'The vacuity of life had at some early period of life struck so forcibly on the mind of Mr. Johnson, that it became by repeated impression his favourite hypothesis, and the general tenor of his reasonings commonly ended there, wherever they might begin.'[21] It was an obsession with a sense of essential undefinedness, arbitrariness, in life, implying the mere filling in of time's emptiness in often ungrounded ways:

> So few of the hours of life are filled up with objects adequate to
> the mind of man, and so frequently are we in want of present
> pleasure or employment, that we are forced to have recourse

every moment to the past and future for supplemental
satisfactions, and relieve the vacuities of our being, by
recollection of former passages, or anticipation of events to
come. (*The Rambler*, 41)

The present was like the body: the mind could hardly stay in it, the
soul was only sporadically at home in it, with the force of suddenly
remembering. There was nothing specifically to do, nothing that *had*
to be done at this time, no heroic vocations or missions; time went on
almost deceitfully as if it was not a matter of life and death. For time
keeps going, in both senses; only on the inside, as it were, for human
beings does time begin to run out, even as they play about with it and
lose the present. It seems so frighteningly unsanctioned that time
which outside is so indifferent, neutral, marking time, should matter
so much to us inside, be our lives. And it is not as though intelligence
can allow the emotions to project all suspicion of meaninglessness
simply externally on to 'time'. There is inside us a consciousness
equivalent to time's apparent indifference, a sceptical intelligence
itself created to inhabit the gaps and indeterminacies increasingly
revealed in any system of life. What is so disturbing about Johnson's
complex account of human limitation is the relation in it between an
intellectual sense of sheer arbitrariness in the making of commitments and an emotional sense of restlessness in the need still to find
commitments to make. In one way those two things – cool
intelligence and warm passion – are travelling the same journey: alike
unfixed and homeless. At another level, however, they remain
opposed and in conflict: the intellect threatening to preside,
redundantly and yet mockingly, over the futile, desperate yet defiant
needs and imaginations of the passions. This is typical of Johnson's
view of life: that the simplicities of heroic conflict, as with a merely
external foe, are pre-empted by the recognition that the conflicting
parts inside you are even so parties in a perilous but balancing unity;
or that a quality such as suspicious intelligence, which is so plausibly
useful in one context, must also be remembered to be generally
harmful in the light of another. That is why Johnson needs so many
differing and responsive shades of meaning in words and such
carefully intricate, knotted and unknotting, sentences. If only we
were *more* limited, he could think, if only we were more defined, more
single-mindedly concentrated in the purposes of the present. Or, if only
we were *less* limited; more capable of lasting transcendence or of
adequte knowledge. Johnson could think both of these things but not
just one of them, and so still ended up in between the two.

It was Johnson's sense of levels, then, that rescued some sense of integrity out of the conflict or confusion of things. He turned Boswell's sense of completely opposed persons – Erskine versus Macdonald, Hume versus Johnson – into a subtler perception of different states of mind, contexts of circumstance, levels of being within the *same* person. Moreover, instead of then keeping those levels defensively separate within his own mind, he next began to test all the fluidities and snags, conflicts and connections by working these levels within linear *sentences*. For now we may see how big a project it was for Johnson to 'reduce' all this to sentences made by one mind travelling through different states or times or centres of mind. For as he said when writing of Bishop Sanderson, 'the complication is so intricate, the motives and objections so numerous' that it is barely possible to form it all into single sentences: to know where to stop them, what to exclude from them, how to link them. Take just a clause or two from a Johnsonian sentence – one we have already encountered, concerning the intelligent procrastinator who 'will not easily be persuaded that his project is ripe for execution':

> but will superadd one contrivance to another, endeavour to unite various purposes in one operation, multiply complications, and refine niceties, till he is entangled in his own scheme, and bewildered in the perplexity of various intentions.

That sort of writing both includes and pushes against its own sympathy with complications and perplexity, and is part of a constant struggle to hold the large *within* the small. This last is a two-way movement, for to hold large issues within the terms of our limited capacities for them means at once stretching those capacities *and* disciplining the threats and appetites of the impulse to excess within them. Incarnating that tension within the very syntax of his sentences is Johnson's powerful alternative to Boswell's way of splitting himself between two opposed people. 'Accommodation' in Johnson is not a sell-out: it is a way of inhabiting that tension, living with and in it, rather than letting it make life impossible.

Relative accommodation thus begins to look more like a maturer commitment, as when Johnson warns the overdramatizing Boswell not to make too much of any one moment, since no one thing on earth will stand what we will want to put into it:

> think of happiness, of learning, of friendship. We cannot tell the precise moment when friendship is formed. As in filling a vessel drop by drop, there is at last a drop which makes it run over; so

in a series of kindnesses there is at last one which makes the heart run over. We must not divide objects of our attention into minute parts, and think separately of each part.[22]

We must not say of each little thing, 'What's the point, the good, of it?', but let life run on until we see that even this is 'the system of life' and of being alive in time. I doubt that Boswell was sure whether Johnson here was attacking or defending a large sense of life: that is the masterful beauty of Johnson's *general* style, poised between the particular and the universal. It is likewise the beauty of the literature of experience that what at a primary level seems like a loss – the loss of one big occasion in life – becomes at a secondary level something else: a sense of life bigger than any of its own particular occasions or memories.

We can try to paraphrase what Johnson means, but only an analysis of his prose shows what it really felt like for him to think it. Clearly 'reducing' did mean making things initially smaller and more manageable: the limited task – of completing an essay, a chapter, a sentence, a rhyme – at least temporarily created a space which had to be filled, a room to be accommodated by the self-imposition of a consciously artificial necessity. You had then at least to think *inside* that space rather than merely of it, as of all the other empty spaces in life. And on the inside of that externally self-imposed limitation, things found room to make resistance and get bigger again. 'Reduce' to Johnson is a means of preventing our 'always breaking away from the present moment';[23] it means treating as for the time being final a condition which dissatisfaction, with some truth, declares to be conditional, relative and incomplete. For the consequence of *not* settling for what can be said and done inside life and human practices lies in the terrors of vacuity, unreality and silence, such as procrastination affords. But look how Johnson makes us feel all this in concrete abstraction as something common:

> Thus life is languished away in the gloom of anxiety, and consumed in collecting resolution which next morning dissipates; in forming purposes which we scarcely hope to keep, and reconciling ourselves to our own cowardice by excuses, which, while we admit them, we know to be absurd. (*The Rambler*, 134)

That last complex clause (from 'and reconciling ourselves') is vital to an understanding of Johnson's reducing-by-sentences: we know what we are doing, while we act to ourselves as if we did not, and that is the misery which results from the failure to apply such practical knowledge as we can have. 'Own' stands there within 'reconciling ourselves to our own cowardice by excuses, which . . . 'like a strong appeal for acknowledgement as something in the sentence tries to go past it. But it is the link word 'which' that does even more damage to our delusions, even as 'while' tries to temporize: 'excuses, *which, while* we admit them, we know to be absurd'. So it is too in the part of the sentence about Bishop Sanderson that went: 'a great part of life spent in enquiries *which* can never be resolved'. In his *Life of Mr. Richard Savage* Johnson uses parenthesis to similarly devastating effect when he says of Savage that Reason would have 'shown him, what he never wished to see, his real State'. A Johnsonian sentence thus finally 'reduces' to almost judicial sentencing that human tendency to be close to reality yet twisted by hiding from it even as it inexorably takes a person along and away; the parenthesis is being at once tough and tender, the crime and its mitigation. For what used to be at least two *levels* – inside and outside the condition; the experience of self-delusion and the memory of knowing that it *is* self-delusion – are now held together in one *line*, incarnating Boswell's two selves and making them struggle to live together: 'reconciling *ourselves* to *our own* cowardice' not by excuses but by acknowledgement. These are insider or incarnate sentences, they hold the big within the small or intricate turns of the sentence just as *The Rambler* incorporates what seem to be almost absolute statements within an acknowledged relative context of topic and essay.

For Johnson insists that we are all always insiders; that an Erskine when he is cynical or a Sanderson when he is delaying are both really damaging themselves inside life while they are pretending or aspiring to be outside it; that we cannot really be outsiders looking down on our own limited condition as though we were not in it or as though it were not still us. Yet on the other hand Johnson will never deny himself, for the sake of emotional security, the intelligence of a self-objectifying stance, according to which you are no longer, as you first supposed, the centre of the world but merely one of many similarly disposed selves, without special claims but with a new ability to generalize. But such intelligence is not simply a view from outside oneself; it has to struggle to incorporate itself back within the self, as within its sentences, as another inner level of being.

Intelligence has to hold the fort because the edifice is crumbling, because intelligence sees how things do not quite hold together and the seeing has to stand as a sort of strength. It is intelligence in *The*

Adventurer, 120, that sees 'we do not always suffer by our crimes; we are not always protected by our innocence' and has to struggle to incorporate those insights within a scheme that still makes sense, for all the apparent senselessness. Johnson's sort of intelligence is precisely that which can see how intelligence itself will not survive by merely hovering over the spectacle of the damaged fortress. It is his practical intelligence which dares to become smaller, reduce itself, in order to enter the building. Inside it all Johnson can say, in a marvellously typical mixture of rebuke and encouragement, to the impractical procrastinator of *The Rambler*, 134:

> To act is far easier than to suffer.

Is that a big or small saying? Is it heroic or precisely anti-heroic for its use of 'easier'? Our way of judging the size and perspective of things is itself here undergoing re-education, since we suffer, says Johnson, from 'a false estimate of the human powers' when egoism seems big and limitation appears like defeatism. He does not say, you notice, that to suffer is *harder* than the difficulties of action; this back-to-front man turns it round, finds even in the negative a hold from which to start. 'To act is far easier': the real and relative difficulties of acting are then committed to go on *within* the determination to act notwithstanding. As Johnson said to Boswell, 'Every man is to take existence on the terms on which it is given to him' – not 'accept' or 'resign himself to' or even simply 'fight against' but unspeakably in between active and passive, '*take*'.[24] And what Johnson takes is a little certainty, such as 'To act is far easier than to suffer', so that to suffer is seen by intelligence as not invariably necessary. Then that small relative certainty is forced to go on to produce, and secure internally, a larger consciousness of what even in itself is missing, of the acts which outside its terms are still uncertain and challenging – in other words, of all that, beyond limitation, may none the less be felt and lived with within it. That is how Johnson makes one sense of limitation – strict boundedness – carry *within* it another: a dissolving indefiniteness that feels like inadequacy. *The Rambler* in that sense saved Johnson's life; for in writing it this most physical of writers reincarnated his soul and his mind within the body of his words, saving himself from the redundancy of an unlimited aspiration to transcendence.

*

'To act is far easier than to suffer' – let us finally take this back to the case of the learned Bishop Sanderson, 'the state of every man who, in the choice of his employment, balances all the arguments on every side'. Let us take two paragraphs more to examine the predicament.

First, Johnson clearly knew in himself the scruples of a Sanderson, but that only made him value all the more the survival instinct of common sense, of getting on with it without unnecessary complications. Doubts about this practical sanction for a return to simplicity were always in danger of merely taking one back into vain scruples again. So Johnson settled for living in time, with 'the knowledge of duties which must daily be performed, and the detection of dangers which must daily be incurred'. For it was the idea of a day, an ordinary day rather than an extraordinary inspiration, that offered him the possibility of a life of 'short flights' instead of the frustrating impossibility of giant leaps. It was a day, and the routine of the daily, day by day, that could keep a man sane, busy and ordinary.

None the less, if there is in Johnson a problem on one side (say, procrastination) and a solution on the other (resolving to get on with it) – such that the practical separation of the two can seem disconcertingly over-simple and unreally decisive to the would-be procrastinator – still, the solution then has its own problems too, even descended from the original apparently resolved dilemma. For Johnson is at once a very solid and definitive separatist in entanglements and yet also a great re-engager with the slippery and the overlapping when once he has set up his firm terms of operation. In this case of Bishop Sanderson, for example, the very ordinariness to which the solution of routine could 'reduce' Johnson was also felt as a disavantage: 'He that condemns himself to compose on a stated day', he notes in his final *Rambler*, 208, 'will often bring to the task an attention dissipated, a memory embarrassed, an imagination overwhelmed, a mind distracted with anxieties, a body languishing with disease.' This is the niggling other side of Johnson's transformation of bad into good news which we witnessed at the end of Chapter Two: good news can be transformed too in time, by a consciousness of its relative snags. There is, I must conclude, no position you can possibly take up in between these two paragraphs or in between the problem and its flawed solution – you must go one way or the other; yet you cannot possibly rest absolutely content in either of them alone and simply ignore the other!

Yet sometimes there is a third turn to affairs. When one reads of 'an attention dissipated, a memory embarrassed, an imagination overwhelmed' it is just this that seems so marvellous in Johnson: the inclusion in this extraordinary man of his ordinariness unabolished by 'art'. For who else could preface a *magnum opus* with such an *unashamed* apology as does Johnson in the Preface to his great *Dictionary*? Consider, he says, that this work cannot possibly be perfect:

> that a whole life cannot be spent upon syntax and etymology, and that even a whole life would not be sufficient; that he whose design includes whatever language can express must often speak of what he does not understand; that a writer will sometimes be hurried by eagerness to the end, and sometimes faint with weariness under a task which Scaliger compares to the labours of the anvil and the mine; that what is obvious is not always known, and what is known is not always present; that sudden fits of inadvertency will surprise vigilance, slight avocations will seduce attention, and casual eclipses of the mind will darken learning; and that the writer shall often in vain trace his memory at the moment of need for that which yesterday he knew with intuitive readiness, and which will come uncalled into his thoughts tomorrow.[25]

Yesterday, today, tomorrow: those basic units, at once so regular and so inconsistent, are the reality of that 'whole life' which cannot let itself be simply dedicated with one-hundred-per-cent purposiveness to one mental thing. The impossibility of total concentration and consistent high achievement is, confusingly, both a limitation and an incapacity for limitation: the inability of the mind to limit itself and the life of its thinker to one task is itself part of human inadequacy. Yet here it is also almost a celebration that 'a whole life' should include the contingencies of the ordinary and that a professionally finished work should still bear the mark of being one person's daily work: at times flawed, personal, accidental, struggling, routine, with only that amateurism which is compatible with a High Tory disdain of narrowingly dehumanizing specialism. The work feels more real for that, with *more* of a whole life behind it.

For all his appetite for relatively distinguishing, Johnson never believed, as a Boswell wanted to believe, in the absolute separation of problem and solution, of strength and weakness. It was not that there was some hovering position in between the two, but whichever way you moved you found one implicated within another. Ironically, Boswell's very attempt at creating black-and-white splits – between

Erskine and Macdonald, for instance – only left him further adrift in the sea of relativism: the spectacle of two different people viewing the same thing in the mutually exclusive lights of their own perfectly self-consistent systems of perception left Boswell with an impossible choice between them. Johnson knew the complication whereby for every strength there was a weakness, for every weakness a strength, but for him that was just mental knowledge. You had then still to choose the most rational way – getting on with it rather than procrastinating – even if that way was so often that of disappointment at the want of something better. And it was only when you had had to resign the *idea* of compensation that the reality of compensation might come through: the pain so evident in the Preface to the *Dictionary* is part of an achievement which would *not* be an achievement had he congratulated himself on the pain, on the weakness as strength, or asked for a reason for carrying on so apparently unrewardingly. At such points, precisely when a person goes *beyond* his ability mentally to preside over the fluctuating transformations of his condition, he knows *limitation* as the human situation.

Perhaps nowhere in literature is this clearer than in the case of Tolstoy's Levin in *Anna Karenina*. For here, at the end of Chapter 16 of Part Seven in Aylmer Maude's translation, is Levin immediately after his wife has given birth:

> Smiling, and hardly able to keep back tears of tenderness, Levin kissed his wife and quitted the darkened room.
>
> What he felt toward this little creature was not at all what he had anticipated. There was nothing merry or joyful in it; on the contrary, there was a new and distressing sense of fear. It was the consciousness of another vulnerable region. And this consciousness was at first so painful, the fear lest that helpless being should suffer was so strong, that it quite hid the strange feeling of unreasoning joy and even pride which he experienced when the baby sneezed.

Levin here has reached his sheer limits as a human creature in the very face of creation. Precisely through the very virtue of his dogged honesty, he cannot know what his fear really stands for. But we know that the real name for that fear which seems to have replaced the naively anticipated joy is still in fact *love* for his child – though the continued joy in it all seems both unreasoning and hidden. Levin's own frightened joy is hidden from him because for the moment he can only honestly experience that love as fear – the baby is yet another hostage to fortune.

> To have voluntarily become to any being the occasion of its existence, produces an obligation to make that existence happy. To see helpless infancy stretching out her hands and pouring out her cries in testimony of dependence, without any powers to alarm jealousy, or any guilt to alienate affection, must surely awaken tenderness in every human mind. (*The Rambler*, 148)

Tenderness: meaning in Johnson's *Dictionary* both 'state of being easily hurt; susceptibility of the softer passions' and 'state of being tender; kind attention; anxiety for the good of another' – care as both love and fear. At that moment Levin is Tolstoy's version of 'every human mind': however complex, he is also just a good simple creature who cannot get above his own experience, cannot even authentically have it and at the same time say what it is. To Tolstoy, and later to Levin himself, such an experience of limitation is an indirect sign of the existence of God – alone understanding us above us.

Even when we try to be intelligently honest, there are thoughts which, however much we cannot quite ignore them, we cannot *really* think: thoughts which, I fear, Boswell loved best to think artificially – thoughts of compensation, of wanting to believe in something for the utility of it even if the belief itself is fictitious. Boswell is like an unreconstructed Levin trying to stick with the fictional emotions he anticipated. But with Johnson, as with that fearlessly frightened man Levin, you cannot get above yourself, you cannot be in between one position and another without making that in-betweenness into another position. You just have to go on – the cliché almost hides the truth; but it never quite does so in Johnson or Tolstoy, those two great religious realists, alike. By the strength of such limitation, baffled agnosticism itself becomes the beginning of a religious mode of apprehension, as we shall see again later in this book.

*

III   Conclusion: On settling down – the life of limitation

'Johnson was a strong force of conservation and concentration in an epoch which by its natural tendencies seemed to be moving towards expansion and freedom.'[26] Thus Matthew Arnold on the limitations of Samuel Johnson, the last strong anachronism before the modern age, the man of resistance and reaction in the face of history. To Arnold, Johnson must have seemed essentially a prejudiced man, lacking in pliability of thought because opinionated, a man both strong and narrow in his limitations. 'Johnson's mind, acute and robust as it was, was at many points bounded, at many points warped. He was neither sufficiently disinterested, nor sufficiently flexible, nor sufficiently responsive, to be a satisfactory critic of Milton.'[27] Indeed, Johnson was not going to be Milton; he was going to take his own stand on human earth. Certainly therefore Johnson was not – to use one of Arnold's key words – 'disinterested'. Nor was he (to use the language of Eliot and Leavis in Arnoldian mood) 'impersonal' either. Johnson was unashamedly limited in so far as that meant being passionately interested, personal and prejudiced. But it takes someone born in the eighteenth century to help us remember how prejudice might be greater than our cant talk of disinterestedness: for surely Burke had Johnson very much in mind when he wrote that 'many of our men of speculation'

> instead of exploding general prejudices, employ their sagacity to discover the latent wisdom which prevails in them. If they find what they seek, and they seldom fail, they think it more wise to continue the prejudice, with the reason involved, than to cast away the coat of prejudice, and to leave nothing but the naked reason; because prejudice, with its reason, has a motive to give action to that reason, and an affection which will give it permanence. Prejudice is of ready application in the emergency; it previously engages the mind in a steady course of wisdom and virtue, and does not leave the man hesitating in the moment of decision, sceptical, puzzled and unresolved. Prejudice renders a man's virtue his habit; and not a series of unconnected acts. Through just prejudice, his duty becomes a part of his nature.[28]

Let me issue an immediate caveat here in partial concession, as it were, to Arnold. It must be admitted that on turning from Johnson to Burke, we find a greater emotive emphasis on polemical key words such as 'prejudice', under the 'practical' pressure of a sense of history about to happen or happening immediately. Burke, after all, is here writing in reaction against the French Revolution, amidst fears of its repetition in England. Thus whereas in Johnson a sentence would have to contain the struggle of a single thought to maintain itself justly in relation to all the other thoughts it provoked in opposition or modification, in Burke one thought is now making a number of sentences, one after another, in order to characterize itself dramatically. Johnson would never have used the word 'prejudice' so unequivocally and provocatively, save perhaps in conversation. Dictionary Johnson never favours linguistic singularity, and respects the unfavourable connotations of the word 'prejudice',[29] for the history and wisdom of human experience held within the memory of language goes deeper with Johnson than does history itself.

That said then, Burke's belief in prejudice nevertheless does identify, with a simplifying boldness, something contained and complicated in Johnson's sense of limitation. For Johnson did keep himself incarnate within the clothing of his prejudices, not willing 'to cast away the coat of prejudice, and to leave nothing but the naked reason' when reason itself too often postured as a naked emperor. Johnson could work and translate himself within the clothing of human emotions and traditions; he told Mrs Thrale: 'let us all conform in outward customs, which are of no consequence, to the manners of those we live among'.[30].

Moreover, he also managed to do subtle work within the body of his own prejudices. Item of prejudice: the dangers of imaginative fantasy. Yet in *The Rambler*, 125, Imagination itself, 'unsusceptible of limitations and impatient of restraint', is sickened by the theoretical definitions which mere critics impose and suddenly, in the very name of human practice, bursts through those 'inclosures of regularity' which Johnson himself, in his general stance, would (only) generally observe. Imagination is suddenly not the enemy of the practical but the very spirit of it. For imagination *is* part of the life-force of Johnson's practicality, but it is imagination worked within the human system of the moral essays rather than allowed the separate autonomy of 'art'. Constantly in *The Rambler* Johnson bursts through the pros and cons of any question, impatiently so relishing the very limitation of our ability to weigh it all up and choose properly as to abolish all other restraints. At points of stalemate, there is something liberatingly large about the way he lifts himself from the level of the page to the life behind it and, finding a licence to strike through the knots and trammels, carves out a crucial, limited simplicity for the time being.

Or again: item of prejudice – Johnson's scorn towards complainers, human screech-owls as he calls them in *The Rambler*, 59. Yet he can still turn round in that essay and say it is none the less like a man and a social being to complain. Johnson shifts so brilliantly from one centre of gravity to another in himself, from one level to another, when suddenly he sees how one prejudice (against imagination, against complaint) has crossed over into the realm of another (in favour of the practical, in defence of sympathy). These are changes and consistencies at once, as subtle as the movements of the brain's network. For this is the believer looking in the world for his beliefs, seeking to match general beliefs with particular instances, more open in his interests than disinterestedness could ever be.

Disinterestedness for Johnson does not come despite prejudices but through them. Even in trying to be disinterested we are always interested, always someone rather than everyone, an insider rather than a impartially detached reasoner. Disinterestedness does not come from *not* being someone in the first place, but from being someone first with prejudices, then with doubts and changes within them. We shall see this again when we return to Arnold and the ideal of the Poet in Chapter Five.

Through just prejudice, says Burke, a man's virtue may become his habit, his duty may become a part of his nature. Similarly, on the strength of limitation, Johnson used his own character to stand for his beliefs so that the changes that the realization of those beliefs sometimes forced upon his mind or behaviour were still expressed within those emotions of anger or charity that remained characteristically his own. How many changes were contained within Johnson's capacity to remain the same!

For Johnson made the commitment, as Boswell never did, to incarnation in a particular person, with prejudices, beliefs and doubts, to growing up and settling down and dying in one life rather than in the imagination of many lives. Boswell never recovered from being the young man who thought, 'I have discovered that we may be in some degree whatever character we choose'. But with Johnson we have to commit ourselves to being responsibly someone in order to be really anyone at all. For our limitation is not that we are only one thing, one predestined type, but that though we are general and could potentially do many things, we are baffled by choice and confounded by such freedom as we do seem to possess. 'Nor can we give the whole account of any *one* thing whatever,' said Bishop Butler; yet we lose ourselves when we try to take on many things. The most practical, ordinary incarnation of what is at stake in all this is to be found, in Johnson, in the decision to marry, the belief in marriage:

It has long been observed that friendship is to be confined to one; or that to use the words of the axiom, 'he that hath friends, has no friend'. That ardour of kindness, that unbounded confidence, that unsuspecting security which friendship requires, cannot be extended beyond a single object. A divided affection may be termed benevolence, but can hardly rise to friendship; for the narrow limits of the human mind allow it not intensely to contemplate more than one idea. As we love one more we must love another less; and however impartially we may, for a very short time, distribute our regards, the balance of affection will quickly incline, perhaps against our consent, to one side or the other. Besides, though we should love our friends *equally*, which is perhaps *not* possible; and *each* according to their *merit*, which is *very difficult*; what shall secure them from jealousy of each other? Will not each think highly of his own value, and imagine himself rated below his worth? Or what shall preserve their common friend, from the same jealousy, with regard to them? As he divides his affection and esteem between them, he can in return claim no more than a dividend of theirs; and as he regards them equally, they may justly rank some other in equality with him ... [31]

Marriage, deliberately partaking of neither the egotism of the individual nor the dispersedness of social relations, is a passionate act of prudence: a decision to settle, to make an enclave for being, rather than to transcend. Commitment here is grounded in natural limitation: we can cherish intensely only one person, one idea; more is more casual, less rooted, more overweening. Inadequacy may also serve unapologetically as a sanction, at another level, for a more narrow concentration on a practical station in life. Unapologetically: for the absolutism that Johnson had to give up at one level is here brought back in the very name of pragmatism at another: the reducing thought that 'friendship is to be *confined*' itself makes for the expansive ideal of '*unbounded* confidence' as a real possibility. 'However impartially we *may*' is a less powerful consideration than 'as we love one more we *must* love another less'. In the same way the distinction between loving our friends '*equally*' (which is 'perhaps *not* possible') and loving *each* of them 'according to their *merit*' (which is '*very difficult*') – another of those sentences fighting for its point with and against the distinctions offered by the dictionary – is emphatically less conclusive than the distinction between '*friendship*' and what 'may be termed *benevolence*'. Johnson is an absolutist in a world fallen to the level of relativism, in which he has to find and make his terms.

Thus Johnson clearly cannot speak with the authority of St Paul on marriage: 'I would that all men were even as I myself'; 'It is good for a man not to touch a woman'; 'It is good for them if they abide even as I' – '*Nevertheless*, to avoid fornication, let every man have his own wife, and let every woman have her own husband'; '*But* every man hath his proper gift of God, one after this manner, and another after that'; '*But* if they cannot contain, let them marry.'[32] For 'but' in Paul is a secondary level, since he says of his own argument for chastity and singleness, 'But I speak this by permission, and not of commandment' and, with that proviso, may lay down the law from above and outside. Johnson has to work it out from experience within – it is 'we', even in our incapacity to get along with each other, rather than the single 'I' of St Paul. Johnson was no saint and he had to fight for his definitions not in some preordained way – 'one after this manner, and another after that' – but in a movement constantly swaying 'to one side or another': 'however impartially we may, for a very short time, distribute our regards, the balance of affection will quickly incline, perhaps against our consent, to one side or the other'. He works, moreover, at two levels of insecurity: within the relationships, with regard to jealousy and emotional partiality, and then within the meta-level of enquiry itself, in all the hesitations of 'perhaps', 'hardly', 'may'. He is with us at St Paul's fallen, secondary level.

We have to make such security as we can. If there is something tough-minded about Johnson's sense of emotional economy and how much we can afford to feel, or trust ourselves to continue feeling, for how long, it is none the less a tough-mindedness on behalf of an equally strong ambition for the heart: 'that ardour of kindness, that unbounded confidence, that unsuspecting security which friendship *requires*'. (Indeed, I remember a student saying: Who could expect even one such friend? Was that why we often have to have many 'friends'?) What Johnson is writing about even in his general language is in fact the need to cease to be merely general and mental and become riskily particular in the commitment to one person and one life. Someone outside life, someone looking down on the planet or on the verge of existence, might find it incredible that human beings take this particular risk again and again, as if it were (what it also therefore is) general and ordinary.

Johnson himself settled for a woman twenty years his senior, a widow who in this her second marriage became increasingly susceptible, it seems, to alcohol. There were difficulties in the marriage, yet the loss of his wife devastated Johnson: the commitment so partial in one sense, so total in another. The loss of the one person to whom one committed one's life means finding oneself more limited than was one's choice in the first place. 'Inconsistencies', said Imlac, 'cannot both be right, but, imputed to man, they may both be true.'[33] Johnson had to live on for over thirty more years, conscious of himself as a straggling social being, making his house a place for unfortunates, knowing still that 'he that hath friends, has no friend'. That too is what limitation meant.

In Section I we saw how Boswell's youthful question came to this: How can a man, knowing he can to some extent be anything, ever commit himself to being just something? How can we know we are just like others, even in always wanting to believe ourselves special, and still be ourselves? Johnson knows about those two levels. In *The Rambler*, 196, he tells us that a man – even he himself –

> *must* marry a wife like the wives of others, with some virtues and some faults.

Yet the princess Nekayah tells us during the marriage debate that though 'there are a thousand familiar disputes which reason never can decide', they are still 'cases where something *must* be done, and where little can be said'.[34] We *must* marry a wife, like the wives of others; for with all of us, as we love one more we *must* love another less. Always Johnson sought to hold two thoughts in one, so that at least he 'has fought the battle, though he missed the victory' (*The Rambler*, 134). Though he missed the victory, he fought the battle; though he fought the battle, he missed the victory. With Johnson, we have to lead a double existence as though it were a single one, 'for the narrow limits of the human mind allow it not intensely to contemplate more than one idea'. The one idea he had was, perhaps, to hold two or more inconsistencies together in one incarnation. Thus he puts one 'must' up against another in the struggle for something like freedom; we *must* stumble but we *must* walk anyway, and only the latter – the walking – is at all up to us. We must make mistakes, even as we must also do something. In Johnson our doubts and fears do not preside over our limited capacities but are contained within them with fortitude and intelligence. We do not preside over ourselves but let God be God: for perhaps sometimes, even by grace, our disadvantages may be turning themselves to our final advantage, behind our backs. We do not know about that (any more than did Levin in his divine comedy); we are too limited to have the right to judge our own lives, only be them. But *be* them.

CHAPTER FOUR

On the Strength of Limitation (2): Johnson's Practical Art

I Practical Reasoning

In order to see how far we have got in understanding Johnson from the inside, let us start by trying to make out, in another imaginatively practical test, what Johnson would have thought of the following. For the following is written by a painter recording his feelings when years ago, as a young Romantic, he first started painting seriously:

> People say to me: 'You can't be expected in your second picture to paint like Titian and draw like Michel Angelo'; but I will try ... I have heard that Nelson used to say: 'Never mind the justice or the impudence, only let me succeed'. This is what no man, of the common timid feelings of mankind, would have dared to say or feel, and what is the world's opinion of Nelson?
>
> The danger is, if you put these feelings off until you are older or more capable, that you will put them off until death interrupts the possibility of accomplishment. It is very easy to say, 'Stop till I am thirty'; but thirty so gradually approaches, that your excuses will become habitual, and every year, every hour, you will be the more incapable of a beginning. Therefore, whatever you feel, do.

The writer is Benjamin Robert Haydon (1786–1846), friend of Wordsworth and of Keats.[1] He was a painter who constantly sought to inspire himself into heroic imitation through his reading, Vasari's *Lives of the Artists* being a principal text. For Haydon did not just read the books of his heroes, he pictured them, he tried to make his heroes come back to real life in him and his imagination. Here he is, for example, reading Boswell's *Life of Johnson*:

> Was excessively affected at the account of Johnson's death. When Boswell says: 'In the morning he asked the hour? and

they told him six; he answered that all went on regularly, and he felt that he had but a few hours to live', everything rushed into my mind – all the accompaniments, the expiring rushlight, day just beginning to break, the attendants gently stepping towards the window, whispering to each other, and holding back the curtain to see how day was breaking, the stars twinkling in the clear blue sky before the blaze of sunlight drowned their splendour, and now and then Johnson's awful voice asking pardon of his Creator. It brought many, many things crowding in on my mind.[2]

Real engagement or self-indulgent fantasy? What should a person's relation to books and their authors be like?

In our first passage, on trying to paint like Titian and draw like Michelangelo, it is clear that Haydon is aspiring to give virtually Johnsonian advice. 'It is very easy to say, "Stop till I am thirty"': Haydon at such moments seems to be offering just that sort of sceptical, back-to-front courage from experience which Johnson himself borrowed from his fear of death.

I want to ask this: a generation after Johnson – indeed, *the* generation after Johnson, when he seems to have been forgotten and shelved in the Romantic movement – had Haydon, addressing himself in Johnsonian terms on a Johnsonian subject, in fact got Johnson right or, even, gone further?

Compare Haydon's voice with that of the closing words of *The Rambler*, 134:

> The certainty that life cannot be long, and the probability that it will be much shorter than nature allows, ought to awaken every man to the active prosecution of whatever he is desirous to perform. It is true that no diligence can ascertain success; death may intercept the swiftest career; but he who is cut off in the execution of an honest undertaking, has at least the honour of falling in his rank, and has fought the battle, though he missed the victory.

Johnson was not too proud to be what he was often ashamed of not being, a good trier. But he also says you should persevere though you might still fail – where 'though' itself is poised on a knife's edge which makes acceptance and resistance unexpectedly close to each other. In contrast, Haydon uses his sceptical knowledge not for but against common 'probability' and on behalf of risk, saying words to this effect: we are told that it is unrealistic to aim at being great, when the only 'certainty' is that if Titian, Michelangelo or Nelson had not aimed to be great, they would not have been. Haydon would chance the big failure of many to produce the great success of one or two. For all his tone of common sense – 'The danger is, if you put these feelings off...' – Haydon is committed to exceptional heroism and particular success in defiance of 'the common timid feelings'; whereas Johnson is concerned with general survival as long and as honourably as possible. Haydon ended in bankruptcy and suicide. Which, the generalizer or the particularizer, was (in Blake's phrase about generalizers) the idiot?

But, says Blake, again in *The Marriage of Heaven and Hell*, 'if the fool would persist in his folly he would become wise'. The persistence of Haydon in risking his life rests on the chance that what is not reasonable may yet be true, what is not probable may yet be possible. 'Never mind the justice, or the impudence, only let me succeed.' In such a chance, that we may create *facts* where anticipation saw only improbabilities, real life alone seems to exist for Haydon: uniquely real life as opposed to those notional and external estimates which are made from common sense and everybody else's past experience, not your own. To a Haydon, as we may imagine him, Johnson's wisdom might even seem to be that of the very Outsider towards whom, I have argued, Johnson was actively hostile and sceptical. Haydon's individualistic experiment is to ignore probable limits until they are really proved upon his very flesh, as it were, by the brand of failure.

Yet in this almost Faustian privileging of risk over probability, of life over thoughts of life, Haydon in fact resembles Johnson's astronomer in *Rasselas*. Here is the astronomer telling Imlac that for ten years now he has been secretly controlling the world's seasons and climes:

> 'I sometimes suspected myself of madness, and should not have dared to impart this secret but to a man like you, capable of distinguishing the wonderful from the impossible, and the incredible from the false.'
>
> 'Why, sir,' said I, 'do you call that incredible, which you know, or think you know, to be true?'
>
> 'Because,' said he, 'I cannot prove it by any external evidence; and I know too well the laws of demonstration to think that my conviction ought to influence another, who cannot, like me, be conscious of its force.' (Chapter XLII)

The astronomer is driven back upon Haydon's defence: he concludes,

'It is sufficient that I feel this power', just as Haydon says finally, 'whatever you feel, do'. Now Johnson, we know, is no simple truster in feelings, as was Boswell. Of the sentiments of youth we may recall Johnson writing in *The Rambler*, 196, 'because long life is possible, he considers it as certain'. Dictionary Johnson is very alive to the difference in meaning between what is *possible* and what is *certain*, or between what is probable and what is unlikely. Emotion tries to blur those distinctions in hope or fear. Indeed, what the astronomer himself ironically tries to work upon in Imlac is precisely the capacity which Imlac shares with Johnson himself – the capacity of 'distinguishing'. It is a capacity which depends upon an outside force just as surely as Johnson, like Adam Smith, was willing to borrow moderation from the thought of external, social views of the self. For the capacity to distinguish depends heavily upon that *limitation* from outside which linguistic definition provides: 'distinction will perhaps assist us', says Johnson in *The Rambler*, 129, 'in fixing the just limits of caution and adventurousness.'

Even so, the astronomer is not making a mistake in appealing to this capacity in Imlac, albeit for the sake of adventurousness rather than caution. For it is Johnson's genius – and one reason why he is not simply the enemy of a later Romanticism – that he sees that irrationality is also, in one sense, itself disturbingly rational. Rational not only because the astronomer can diagnose the doubt and the risk as though from outside himself – that position of plausibility, not physical reality; but also because, in so far as life is not always or certainly a matter of reason, it is sometimes internally reasonable to act outside reason itself. Hope, for example, has a reason for its own irrational persistence:

> We are unhappy, at least less happy than our nature seems to admit; we necessarily desire the melioration of our lot; what we desire, we very reasonably seek, and what we seek we are naturally eager to believe that we have found. Our confidence is often disappointed, but our reason is not convinced, and there is no man who does not hope for something which he has not, though perhaps his wishes lie unactive, because he foresees the difficulty of attainment. (*The Rambler*, 63)

Almost terrifyingly, the self-deception of hope may itself be reasonable: no one is clearer than Johnson about the logic of psychological knots. Yet equally it is unreasonable to suppose that just because it is hope, it is always therefore self-deception. It would be easier if in all contexts hope was always good or always bad: the fact that it is not so forces knowledge back into the practice of life in each particular eventuality. There are so many levels, with reason moving so disturbingly and adaptively across the bounds that should separate psychology and logic, or the truth of belief and the utility of hoping, that we may easily become entangled in varying mental plausibilities. Practical thinking is like that: always defeasible, endlessly modifiable as fresh circumstances and considerations are added. The astronomer's particular chink of possibility – that what is *incredible* may still plausibly be *not false* – is an enormous temptation even for sceptical Johnson's ambitious hopes, for his own weapons of verbal distinction are being turned against him. The *incredible* is not necessarily the *impossible*: tautologically, that is precisely what the words mean. Johnson's defence against his own psychology is opened up.

This is to trade upon his very flexibility. For reason in Johnson is always adaptive rather than prescriptive: in a specific set of circumstances he could imaginatively throw over his general position for the sake of the exception which his general position itself had previously acknowledged as latent. Thus on imagination as truth in *Paradise Lost* he writes: 'It contains the history of a miracle, of Creation and Redemption: it displays the power and the mercy of the Supreme Being; the probable therefore is marvellous, and the marvellous is probable.'[3] This is the very opposite of Hume's encircling irony in his essay 'Of Miracles' when he says that for a man actually to believe in miracles is itself a – miracle: unbelievable to any man of understanding! Single-minded Hume loved to express one world-view in terms of another and reduce their differences to word play; Johnson was always closer to genuine conflict: where Hume put all his doubts into his work and lived a life of calm, Johnson's division between belief and doubt carried over into both life and work – a half-and-half integrity, so to speak. And potentially, at least, Johnson was always close to the possibility of conversion: potentially he would always throw over his own earthly guides of probability for a believable sign of God. I doubt he ever found one, where trust was contaminated even by his own hope for it. But Milton had almost done in art what Johnson would have hardly dared dream of in life: Milton had brought probability to heel, restored it to a lesser place in the original system. Genre in art was, after all, very like the work of moral rules themselves, functioning relatively in respect of differing circumstances. Milton's triumph, to put it another way, had been to take one genre, the epic, and make it in *Paradise Lost* the story of how, as it were, all rules and all genres subsequently came to be. 'The moral of other poems is incidental and consequent,' wrote Johnson; 'in Milton's only it is essential and intrinsic.'[4] Johnson never found in either his work or life exactly what source human probabilities were grounded in, governed under, although he knew well enough that they were indeed secondary. To stay the course in what was also known to be unsatisfactory was the honour of limitation in this consciously second-order man. His first thought is always that there is life before ever there is thought concerning it.

But what if his powers of thought could be in charge? For a long time Johnson remains fascinated by the incredible possibility of the astronomer – or some man – being Superman. For if no one could ever prove it, someone might still be it; while everyone remained quite reasonable in continuing to doubt it. Hence Johnson's ambivalence about Milton too: a superman but inhuman in the same breath, one possibly at the height of religious vision but also probably without human interest at the passionate ordinary level of fallen lives. Again and again in his *Life of Milton* Johnson sees how, improbably, Milton keeps countering his objections, yet at levels still influenced by what Johnson calls the 'original deficience'. There are for Johnson simple, original starting points behind people's lives which become necessarily complicated, modified, half-buried in the course of existence. Milton's original deficiency can be masked but not lost: it is implicit in the very act of seeking and needing to transcend the human condition, even with all the strengths and virtues of such an ambition. Johnson's original feeling in relation to *Paradise Lost* is that he simply is not moved by it, although he is impressed: both, because the achievement seems to him not quite human. To argue this, without succumbing to the opposite extreme of a merely vengeful reduction of Milton's genius, is to enter into increasing sophistication, hesitation and refinement of that initial but necessary naiveté of instinctive conviction. Even so the increased complexity is not allowed to forget the starting point from which it descends and to which it can, when necessary, still be related if not reduced. Such is Johnson's tightrope.

The sense Johnson had of the original flaws in his *own* design meant that his commitment to practical thinking, on the basis of human limitation, could not be in mere opposition to visionary views. In so far as limitation was related to indeterminacy, the practical thinking which resulted from it was committed both to being provisional and yet to doing something, now, even so. Moreover its pragmatism was that it always thus included *within* its very nature the properly shaking possibility of the visionary and the exceptional as above or outside itself. That is to say, it still bore the marks of its own genesis, begotten out of uncertainty as a response to uncertainty, as its conscious limitation.

There is always an admirable 'to and fro' movement like this in Johnson's way of thinking. The public, social world had indeed to be based on the majority of cases, the reasonably probable order of things; but that leaves, if not even creates, the eighteenth-century private world as the place where it might just be reasonable to be unreasonable, where it might just possibly be heroically sane to be 'mad'. The poet Smart was mad, for wanting people to pray with him? Well of course, Johnson's bottom-line instinct for sanity still meant fearing any automatic assumption that an individual is defined by some private as opposed to some outer, social self. But even so, it is almost tautological in his 'system of life' that the man who has an unreasonable – because socially unconfirmed – conviction of his own possible greatness, and knows that the world may think him mad for thinking so, has to retreat further into private silence because he has no acceptable language by which to prove his own sanity or contest the world's. For the madman who thought he was superman was, I believe, a repressed part of Johnson himself. When we thus weigh the to and fro of thoughts involved in this silence, we are following Johnson within the inner convolutions of his own mind; for it is always as though his writings were – as indeed they must have been – thoughts in his head fractionally before, and even while, they also became separate pieces of published literature, of apparently closed history. Inside that mind, behind the distilled sentences that could barely end if they admitted all he thought and doubted, or tried to trace all the contexts in which good became bad and vice versa, we can sense a life less limited and more complicated than the lives of those who more openly speak on behalf of human possibility. So much seems to go into such only apparently limited sentences: 'Many complain of neglect who never tried to attract regard' (*The Rambler*, 168); 'A man once persuaded, that any impediment is insuperable, has given it, with respect to himself, that strength and weight which it had not before' (*The Rambler*, 25). It would take a novelist to spell out from these sentences all that was thus at stake in securing a proper confidence in our own lives.

'He may therefore be justly numbered among the benefactors of mankind, who contracts the great rules of life into short sentences, that may be easily impressed on the memory, and taught by frequent recollection to recur habitually to the mind' (*The Rambler*, 175). Just such a benefactor is Johnson, at once reducing and expanding within the contraction; a man with imagination more powerful than many who would praise imagination more highly. Imlac has to rebuke the princess and her lady when they laugh at the account of the astronomer: there is no one – he says, looking at the others while also thinking of himself – who may not be driven to 'hope or fear beyond the limits of sober probability'.[5] Johnson had to fight off his own mad ambition while also not allowing himself to subside into a depressive idleness as a result. As usual finding himself almost impossibly sited between two opposing forces, he had to use reason to prevent himself being at the mercy of his own emotional mechanisms. Here he is in *The Rambler*, 25, fighting against that repression of hope which at other times he needs to employ in order not to trangress the sober limits of probability. Experts in any field, he notes, will tell you that their field is too difficult for you, unless you have some so-called natural talents of an almost miraculous kind – but that is not the true spirit of education:

> To this discouragement it may be possibly answered, that since a genius, whatever it be, is like fire in the flint, only to be produced by collision with a proper subject, it is the business of every man to try whether his faculties may not happily co-operate with his desires; and since they whose proficiency he admires, knew their own force only by the event, he needs but engage in the same undertaking, with equal spirit, and may reasonably hope for equal success.

'To try' here includes the sterner meaning, 'to test'. Whenever he wrote, Johnson was always testing himself and the validity of remembered wisdom in application to each new practical context. He was testing himself, even more than usual, between Imlac and the astronomer. For a person can make a sanely plausible case for the sanity of his presumed madness and may well, for all that, be truly mad anyway – as the astronomer is finally seen to be. In the course of experience things can become simpler as well as more complicated, and this itself is as often confusing or strange as it is either securing or disappointing. We only know 'in the event' that the Superman is an ordinary man with an extraordinary delusion. 'He that will eat bread, must plow and sow; though it is not certain, that he who plows and sows shall eat bread'; 'We are not to imagine, that God approves us because he does not afflict us, nor, on the other hand, to persuade ourselves too hastily that he afflicts us because he does not love us.'[6] Because that which is opposed to us may not be right, that does not mean that we still may not be wrong. Johnson makes himself a sort of secondary rule out of the lack of rule as to reversibility in such statements; for in the realm of practical thinking, the sentences of logic are always open to an appeal to nature and contingent event.

Indeed, it is the nature of practical thinking that the particular case can be dealt with only as the sum and modification of a whole set of prior generalities testingly applied to it by the mind of the person involved. What is left over is then the particular case's own further characteristics. As Hazlitt was to put it, in arguing against the view of Locke and Hume that our sense of the general is merely built up out of our experience of the particular: 'All particulars are nothing but generals, more or less defined according to circumstances, but never perfectly so. The knowledge of any finite being rests in generals.' General terms are the necessarily limited basis for language: 'Language without this would be reduced to a heap of proper names: and we should be just as much at a loss to name any object generally, from its agreement with others, as to know whether we should call the first man we met in the street by the name of John or Thomas.'[7] In reading Johnson we can feel the power of general terms increasingly modifying each other to get down to a provisional imagination of the sort of thing he has in mind: only the inexperienced mind would wish to shun such modification-by-conflict in the hope of a simpler, heroic life:

> He never imagines that there may be greatness without safety, affluence without content, jollity without friendship, and solitude without peace. He fancies himself permitted to cull the blessings of every condition, and to leave its inconveniences to the idle and the ignorant. (*The Rambler*, 196)

For Johnson, characteristically, 'without' is an ironically linking word, for consciousness precisely does add to us a sense of what is always missing and incomplete. There is solitude-without-peace: the two generals begin to form the imagination of a particular, precisely through their limitations and life's own difficulties.

Yet there is also a richness of possibility released out of such difficulty, conflict and indeterminacy. Here is Johnson relishing his thinking about life when he considers why, in contrast to youth's eagerness, we paradoxically 'grow negligent of time in proportion as we have less remaining':

> and suffer the last part of life to steal from us in languid preparations for future undertakings, or slow approaches to

remote advantages, in weak hopes of some fortuitous occurrence, or drowsy equilibrations of undetermined counsel. Whether it be that the aged, having tasted the pleasures of man's condition, and found them delusive, become less anxious for their attainment; or that frequent miscarriages have depressed them to despair, and frozen them to inactivity; or that death shocks them more as it advances upon them, and they are afraid to remind themselves of their decay, or to discover to their own hearts, that the time of trifling is past. (*The Rambler*, 111)

The shift from 'we' and 'us' in the first sentence to 'they' and 'them' in the second shows no lack of sympathy but the effort to imagine a future condition which will increasingly resist thinking or being thought about. It is a shift equivalent to the change of gear from the cumulative 'or' in apposition in sentence one to the more many-minded 'or' in alternation in sentence two. The richness of sentence two bespeaks a mind able to reconcile itself to the varied plausibilities of a relativism without being harassed into not treating each of the parts or possibilities as absolutely true to imagination for the time it is entertained. That combination – of clauses within a sentence, of differences within the same effect, of different minds held within still one mind which is able to entertain them all and move between them – is an achievement that leaves the reader thinking: How did he know all this? Where could he have got it all from? How could he entertain so much and keep it all stable when it is also so much a series of inferences and guesses? A mind alone could not have produced such a sentence as by rules of logic, one statement produced from another. The very uncertainty, on the one hand, that prevents an exclusively logical use of mind seems, on the other, to let life in, and feeling and freedom too – in the nearest thing to inexhaustibleness of which a finite mind, knowing itself to be so, is capable in considering its own species' also finite nature. All these general considerations – that age gives up because of knowledge, or despair, or fear – would have to be brought to a consideration of the case of any particular old man 'in the event', like lens upon lens to sharpen the insight. Johnson is not ashamed to think that all this goes into being what we merely call common-sensical, for that is better than offering discouragement by insisting upon natural genius.

The paradox of this sort of limitation is that the state of being *finite* is also productive of a certain *loosening* of certainties. The double-bind by which freedom is tied to uncertainty means that this of itself is a cause for neither complete joy nor unequivocal sorrow. For always being more than nature, we are also always incomplete: as Johnson puts it in *The Rambler*, 111, again: 'A perpetual conflict with natural desires seems to be the lot of our present state. In youth we require something of the tardiness and frigidity of age; and in age, we must labour to recal the fire and impetuosity of youth; in youth we must learn to expect, and in age to enjoy.' The way the sentences balance our precisely unbalanced tendency to go from one extreme to another, from pillar to post, implies an acceptance of a sort of equivocal order even in that. But it is an order inferred by intelligence working on experience: it is not directly revealed as part of the divine plan, nor could it be said to be naturally sanctioned except in some secondary sense, by saying it is our nature precisely to be in conflict with our nature. Something is always missing: in youth the virtues of age, in age the merits of youth; all the unfittingness also fits, regularly, generally. The way of being that can accept this ironic order of things can make only relative use of words, for there are no words that may be allowed absolutely to fix an attitude to what is going on. In *The Rambler*, 29, Johnson argues against anxiety about the future precisely *because of* the uncertainty involved:

> It has been usual in all ages for moralists to repress the swellings of vain hope by representations of the innumerable casualties to which life is subject, and by instances of the unexpected defeat of the wisest schemes of policy, and sudden subversions of the highest eminences of greatness. It has, perhaps, not been equally observed, that all these examples afford the proper antidote to fear as well as to hope, and may be applied with no less efficacy as consolations to the timorous, than as restraints to the proud.
>
> Evil is uncertain in the same degree as good, and for the reason that we ought not to hope too securely, we ought not to fear with too much dejection.

This is quite different from Hume and the wit of secular liberation. Look at the changes of attitude, says Hume in his *Dialogues Concerning Natural Religion*. In ignorant times, the religious stressed that 'human life was vanity and misery': melancholy and terror were used to turn the masses towards another life. But in late years, when it is educated sceptics who cite just that vanity and misery of life as evidence against a benevolent deity, 'divines, we find, begin to retract this position and maintain, though still with some hesitation, that there are more goods than evils, more pleasures than pains, even in this life.'[8] Does this not show that religion is only history, not truth? For Johnson, however, what the divines said in *both* ages was relatively true: there is hope as well as fear in different degrees and contexts, and our equivocal misery, or equivocal comfort, is that we cannot say we are completely miserable – 'lest we should think ourselves too soon entitled to the mournful privileges of irresistible misery' (*The Rambler*, 32). Life is terrible, Johnson might well say in one context; and in another, that there is probably nothing that we cannot bear with; the two thoughts can work together in almost endless, plausible combinations of encouragement, rebuke, admission, dismay. Again Johnson, as ever inhabiting both the state of ignorance *and* the state of education, has to hold on in between hope and fear, good and evil, even while knowing himself also still liable to feel both. What is extraordinary about him is his capacity to see and still to feel, to recognize the relativism and, without an absolute position for himself as a finite creature to rest in, none the less preserve a toughly intellectual neutrality even in the midst of strong feeling. Thus: 'It is not sufficiently considered in the hour of exultation, that all human excellence is comparative; that no man performs much but in proportion to what others perform' (*The Rambler*, 127). Or again: 'Nor has any man found the evils of life so formidable in reality, as they were described to him by his own imagination' (*The Rambler*, 29). Whether it is good or bad news or something in between the two, Johnson will not let us stay fixed, since time ticks on alike past the hours of exultation and of fear.

Practical thinking is thus a response to a constantly changing world. A practical thought is not like a logical argument whose purpose is to establish rules for the preservation of truth, from step to step, on the page and outside time. Practical thinking is defeasible in time – a problem is posed, a plan is put forward, the two are then put together to see if the plan meets the problem or has forgotten something. Say the problem is sorrow at the loss of a friend; the plan offered by the Stoics is not to indulge in such commitments, to make such emotional hostages to fortune, 'but to keep our minds always suspended in such indifference, that we may change the objects about us without emotion' and thus replace our losses continually. In *The Rambler*, 47, Johnson then puts problem and strategy together to test what ends such means will serve:

An exact compliance with this rule might, perhaps, contribute

to tranquillity, but surely it would never produce happiness...
If by excluding joy we could shut out grief, the scheme would
deserve very serious attention; but...

Practical thinking is always seeking to find a plan by which to operate
itself. It is always seeking successful translations into new contexts
and levels. In the middle of life, it is concerned with means towards
ends, but with Johnson it is the trial of those means which so often
reveals – in their failure, and so back-to-front – the ends which we
may have forgotten. Thus here the Stoic strategy serves only the end
of tranquillity, not *happiness*. Can we forget the ideal of *happiness*? It is
possible we could choose to try to forget it, if with it *sorrow* was alike
abolished. But if anyway excluding *joy* does *not* shut out *grief*, then all
the more do we need such joy as we can reasonably gain. 'We may
surely endeavour to raise life above the middle point of apathy at one
time, since it will necessarily sink below it at another.' Trying it out in
this way means that the key words begin to give way to each
other – 'tranquillity' to 'happiness' precisely because of the necessity
of 'grief' – so that they cease to be the names of static ideas in history
and come to life as real thoughts, things really remembered in the
weighing of options by soberly intelligent courage level by level,
down to the bottom of grief and back up to the reclamation of
ordinary efforts at happiness because of it. Strikingly, this movement
in the midst of blocked avenues is what Johnson implicitly
understands as our freedom, even in its very limitations.

Here again, moreover, there is a fundamental difference from
Hume. For Hume seeks to abolish the distinction between words
such as – for example – liberty and necessity: 'According to my
definitions, necessity makes an essential part of causation; and
consequently liberty, by removing necessity, removes also causes,
and is the very same thing with chance.'[9] For Hume, my reason for
doing something is the same as the cause that makes it be done – in
this he is thinking of human beings as though they were no different
from external objects. The fire heats the water; the desire causes the
action. If I act out of generosity, that is not an act of free will, as
subjectivity suggests, but an act to which my generosity itself
compels me. For the philosophers of the Scottish school of Common
Sense – the formal equivalent to Johnson in the field of academic
thought – Hume was ignoring and betraying the sense of mankind
retained in the structure of its very language: the sense according to
which my voluntary actions are not *caused* by anything, even by their
own voluntariness, for that is just what the word 'voluntary' means. It

is Hume, radically translating one word into its apparent opposite, who by his own definitions becomes a 'reducer'. Johnson is always productive of language, to meet the branching changes of direction that take place in practical thinking's response to time; his sense of indeterminacy in existence always seeks to hold open a space for meaning in between the distinctions that different words exist to make possible again. The proliferating language, the rich uncertainty of changing contexts, the freedom we paradoxically *have* to have through the very limitations of knowledge: all three of these are aspects of one another.

'For it is necessary to act,' says Johnson in *The Rambler*, 184, 'but impossible to know the consequences of action.' There is in him a sort of inscrutable poise, knowing that of any two ways both will have their disadvantages and one only must be chosen. This intelligent poise takes on a more recognizable incarnation when he moves in his thinking from the level of knowledge to the level of ethics. We can feel that level-movement being registered as the realistic equivalent of simile in *The Rambler*, 29, when Johnson writes of the folly of anticipating future misfortunes: 'Anxiety of this kind is nearly of the same nature with jealousy in love'. Similarly, he can find within himself that tolerance of the provisional and the uncertain is 'nearly of the same nature' at the level of knowledge as is the practice of charity at the level of ethics:

> We know not to what degree of malignity any injury is to be imputed; or how much its guilt, if we were to inspect the mind of him that committed it, would be extenuated by mistake, precipitance, or negligence; we cannot be certain how much we encrease the mischief to ourselves by voluntary aggravations. We may charge to design the effects of accident; we may think the blow violent only because we have made ourselves delicate and tender; we are on every side in danger of error and of guilt, which we are certain to avoid only by speedy forgiveness. (*The Rambler*, 185)

It seems to be one of Johnson's most freeing lessons that there should be this equivalent loosening of the bonds of bitter anger: bonds always based on mere inference, always damaging to our own quiet. 'We cannot be certain.' Anger, like envy, restricts meanings and even thus narrows the soul: 'to him who studiously looks for an affront, every mode of behaviour will supply it; freedom will be rudeness and reserve sullenness; mirth will be negligence, and seriousness formality' (*The Rambler*, 172). Practical thinking will constantly have to consider turning back to check what its conclusions would be had it started from the perception of 'reserve' rather than 'sullenness'; will constantly have to consider 'what degree' of difference might be sufficient if not wholly to convert 'negligence' back to mere harmless 'mirth', at least to find extenuation of 'negligence' through a complex modification of one general word in terms of another and yet another in the intricate working out of a sentence. There are no rules as to what to include, what to exclude, in such thinking; it is always open to nature and to error and never safe in self-sufficiency. But with Johnson it is for all that never an apologetically weak, but riskily reasonable, way of thinking. It is important that our eyes are opened to charitable interpretations only through weighing them alongside less charitable interpretations, and that we measure externally the relative truth of both interpretations as well as the relative internal damage they might do to him who holds them. We must not be with our morality as the unconfident man is with his modesty – owing it to his weakness. For Johnson is not like those inexperienced people who are absolutely impressed by the appearance of sheer liveliness in others, when in fact those others 'proceed not from confidence of right, but fearlessness of wrong'; he is not taken in by the free-and-easy friend 'who thinks his forgetfulness of others excused by his inattention to himself.'[10] We are constantly in a world where one thing looks like, or is changing into, or needs to be distinguished from, another. 'None can tell whether the good that he peruses is not evil in disguise.'[11] With that fear, practical thinking is no soft option.

For practical thinking is the art of inference, of inadequate means trying to satisfy ends which it cannot even wholly articulate, of action without full knowledge of what else in the situation might render it unnecessary or misdirected. It is, *in medias res*, Johnson's fallen form of human thinking, reducing the aspirations of super-theorists: 'instead of gratifying their vanity by inferring effects from causes, they are always reduced at last to conjecture causes from effects' (*The Rambler*, 13). We work through the veil of inference. And what is most terrible in Johnson is that though the boundaries between one thing and another are always shifting and unclear, they nevertheless do always exist. What we are uncertain about may certainly be doing us definite harm even in that. That is to say, within Johnson's sense of life's relativism there remains a strict requirement for moral absolutism at each point:

Some have advanced, without due attention to the consequences of this notion, that certain virtues have their
correspondent faults, and therefore that to exhibit either apart
is to deviate from probability. Thus men are observed by Swift
to be 'grateful in the same degree as they are resentful' . . . .
Though it should be allowed that gratitude and resentment
arise from the same constitution of passions, it follows not that
they will be equally indulged when reason is consulted . . .

It is of the utmost importance to mankind, that positions of
this tendency should be laid open and confuted; for while men
consider good and evil as springing from the same root, they
will spare the one for the sake of the other, and in judging, if not
of others at least of themselves, will be apt to estimate their
virtues by their vices. To this fatal error all those will
contribute, who confound the colours of right and wrong, and
instead of helping to settle their boundaries, mix them with so
much art, that no common mind is able to disunite them. (*The
Rambler*, 4)

He mentions Swift, but he may as well have said Hume or
Mandeville – all of whom show how good is inextricably related to
bad; how effort, for instance, is also a compound of emulation.
Against them all Johnson offers something at once looser and tighter.
The room we have for painful freedom means a looser relation than
we might prefer to suppose between our strengths and their
corresponding weaknesses: there is a higher level at which we can
interfere with their relation. It was not necessary for the so-called
free-and-easy friend to combine 'forgetfulness of others' with
'inattention to himself' and think of the two as guaranteeing the
irremediable wholeness of his personality. Language and thought, in
significant relation to each other, can allow room between what is
'mirth' and what 'negligence': the two do not have to go together as
two sides of the same thing, if morality is to mean anything. And this
looseness which allows distinctions both needs and creates the
tightness which makes them. It is a constant support to find how
deeply and subtly Johnson has it all worked out and together, for the
sake of the common mind.

Johnson can look utterly different from and opposed to a
Romantic such as Haydon, but I have argued that he has a far subtler
sense of possibility in life – 'in the event', as he puts it. He always
offers us rules to break rules in sentences that refuse to be chop-

logically reversed: 'instead of rating the man by his performance, we rate too frequently the performance by the man'; 'practice has introduced rules, rather than rules have directed practice'; 'it ought to be the first endeavour of a writer to distinguish nature from custom, or that which is established because it is right, from that which is right because it is established.'[12] This is the authentic image of what open-mindedness is like: often something you do not want, that opens up painfully real doubts, rather than standing comfortably and tolerantly in place of any beliefs. Johnson is a back-to-front man; he is not simply an anti-Romantic limiter and reducer. For, conscious of superior abilities, immensely proud and ambitious originally, he himself remains deeply attracted to the astronomer's idea, the silent secret of being the greatest of all men. But by a characteristic paradox, his greatness actually lies in his own determined and secondary resistance to such ideas. Whereas for Haydon procrastination was an act of unheroic timidity, Johnson on the contrary saw it as a result of the opposite, of hubris. It was through such reverses, not only directed against others but also suffered in himself, that Johnson emerges as more authentic in his 'nature' than any of the categories of 'custom' used to define or criticize him ever suggest – he is a more real human being.

More real because more tested. It is a process Johnson himself recognized:

> He whose courage has made way amidst the turbulence of opposition, and whose vigour has broken through the snares of distress, has many advantages over those that have slept in the shades of indolence, and whose retrospect of time can entertain them with nothing but day rising upon day, and year gliding after year. (*The Rambler*, 150)

Yet he had also to fight against the distress of thinking that there might be nothing to fight against, for his diaries reveal a man racked with being both underemployed and unsure whether life *could* be employed rather than merely filled up: 'A kind of strange oblivion has overspread me, so that I know not what has become of the last year'; 'I have now spent fifty-five years in resolving; having, from the earliest time almost that I can remember, been forming schemes of a better life. I have done nothing'; 'Make me remember, O God, that every day is thy gift, and ought to be used accordingly to thy command.'[13] Year after year, day after day, which was it – the shades of indolence or the snares of distress? Johnson made indolence into distress, but remained distressed lest such resolving was only another guise for indolence's continuance. If his equivocal fight thus offered equivocal 'advantages' (in the words of *The Rambler*, 150, above), still those advantages, he would *have* to say, neither justified adversity nor exonerated those who factitiously seek adversity in the name of 'experience'. He is more real, less controlled, more limited than that, in a tight ball of mutually qualifying thoughts and feelings which kept him within his own boundaries. In a world in which it is so easy merely to lapse gradually into going wrong because there is no one to tell you except yourself and he is unwilling or unreliable; in a world in which it is so hard to fight against the thought that there is nothing to fight against, unless fighting takes on a subtler, more adult meaning; a world which is hard to live in because it is also easy to live in; Johnson serves as both a subtle and a solid reminder in his looseness and tightness together. He reminds us of the old voice of seriousness that we try to keep down, but is still kept, in our minds:

> Nothing but daily experience could make it credible, that we should see the daily descent into the grave of those whom we love or fear, admire or detest; that we should see one generation past, and another passing, see possessions daily changing their owners, and the world, at very short intervals, altering its appearance, and yet should want to be reminded that life is short... [14]

That it *is* incredible makes Johnson's deep common sense begin to seem soberly wonderful in contrast.

*

Matthew Arnold does not seem to have thought that Johnson's practicality was art. To Arnold the poetic was – often self-damagingly – opposed to the merely practical; the eighteenth century was the age of prose; Johnson was a characteristically prosaic and Hebraic figure of that age.

But we must offer a quite different conclusion. For consider the force of Johnson's practical reasoning when he writes of the refusal of Martha Blount to attend Pope near the very end of his life. She had been a great favourite of the poet's, but she refused his messenger, Lord Marchmont, with the words: 'What, is he not dead yet?'. What did Pope think of her neglect of him, Johnson asks himself:

> Perhaps he considered her unwillingness to approach the chamber of sickness as female weakness or human frailty, perhaps he was conscious to himself of peevishness and impatience, or though he was offended by her inattention might yet consider her merit as overbalancing her fault; and if he had suffered his heart to be alienated from her, he could have found nothing that might fill her place; he could have only shrunk within himself; it was too late to transfer his confidence or fondness.[15]

Those alternatives come from the very habit of strong practical consideration of possibility and probability. An almost infinite imagination works here within what remains a sense of finite truth, possibilities limited but complex, barely knowable by another mortal yet guessable too. This, emphatically, shows that Johnson's practical reasoning *is* a form of art, and it is a shame that a narrow, transcendent account, offered by some post-Romantics, of what 'literature' is should have consigned the tradition of letters and discursive prose to a place outside the mainstream of writing and thinking. This is particularly hard to take when a prose work such as *The Rambler* existed precisely to *avoid* the splitting-up of human writing into exclusive specialist categories of art as opposed to philosophy, or philosophy as opposed to theology, or biography as opposed to criticism. For *The Rambler* offered profoundly common, non-specialist guidance instead. By way of insisting that Johnson's moral essays are art, I shall next stress their strong connection with the writing of *Rasselas*, Johnson's novel.

*

II *Rasselas: in memory of The Rambler*

Consider one of Johnson's reminder-sentences, from *The Rambler*, 28: 'One sophism by which men persuade themselves that they have those virtues which they really want, is formed by the substitution of single acts for habits.' That is to say, once upon a time a dishonest man made a single great effort to be honest and now he thinks (dishonestly) that that was 'really' himself. To be fully realized, such a sentence needs to reawaken in its reader a memory in illustration or a story which itself would subdue his more dramatic fictionalizings. These days, of course, a novel would take a much longer time to tell such a story, taking practical thinking perhaps even further into artistic particularities but also possibly even further away from common resonance. Throughout this book I have been ambivalent as to how far the novel is an advance and development or a retreat and artifice in comparison with the austere, discursive prose of Johnsonian realism in the moral essays. I put that crudely but basically. To bring this chapter to a close, I now want to look at Johnson's own novel, *Rasselas*, in relation to *The Rambler*, to see if *Rasselas* truly is a novel and to try to clarify what is at stake in my crude ambivalence. I also want to imagine the problem considered in Chapters Two and Three: Boswell in his existential anxieties confronted by Johnson's apparently straightforward and yet also inscrutable poise – as though Boswell were Rasselas and Johnson Imlac, more or less. For I shall argue that *Rasselas* offers us a concluding picture of what is implicit in the strong limitations of the *Rambler* essays.

*

Here, first of all then, is Rasselas – a young man trying to break out of limitation as much as any Boswell or Haydon, thus searching for a way out of the Happy Valley so that he might find outside this apparent Eden the best life a person could *choose*:

> In these fruitless searches he spent ten months. The time, however, passed cheerfully away: in the morning he rose with new hope, in the evening applauded his own diligence, and in the night slept sound after his fatigue. He met a thousand amusements which beguiled his labour, and diversified his thoughts. He discerned the various instincts of animals, and properties of plants, and found the place replete with wonders, of which he purposed to solace himself with the contemplation, if he should never be able to accomplish his flight; rejoicing that his endeavours, though yet unsuccessful, had supplied him with a source of inexhaustible enquiry. (Chapter V)

It looks like a powerful satire against human perverseness that the purpose of finding an escape from the valley should have provided Rasselas with the means of enjoying it. Indeed, Rasselas actually thinks that this will solace him even if he cannot leave after all. He thinks so – but the hunger of his nature is always in advance of his belated recognitions and resolves, and by a further irony that 'inexhaustible' pleasure will be pretty near exhausted by the very next paragraph. Yet though in *The Rambler* this would indeed be irony, here it seems more like good news in what could have been the tone of bad. For it is not only despite but through his resolves to get out that Rasselas gets into life here. The *system of life* itself – as that movement in time which can never be fully registered in a moral essay for want of narrative – takes Rasselas beyond his own consciously 'important' questions and into itself, however much he still feels that life is not living up to his ideals. It is as though his question of *what one should do with life* was like what Burke said about the science of government: 'a matter which requires experience, and even *more* experience than any person can gain in his *whole life*'.[16]

'What egregious fools are we!' a Stoic wise man once concluded, 'Hee hath past his life in idleness say we; alas! I have done nothing this day. What; have you not lived?'[17] Yet Rasselas's need for backing to life, through purpose behind him, *before* being able to live in it or even see what is in front of his eyes, is to Johnson a matter of impossibility indeed but not of simple irony. When in Chapter xv Rasselas's sister, Princess Nekayah, first leaves the valley, she experiences a truly Johnsonian horror of emptiness before her: 'The princess and her maid turned their eyes towards every part, and, seeing nothing to bound their prospect, considered themselves as in danger of being lost in a dreary vacuity.' What, are they not living? But for what? Living to be alive? Why was not that – or should it indeed be – enough? Reading Johnson, one senses in him not only subtle levels of different forms of being but also almost archaeological layers of classical and Christian ways of thinking remembered and re-combined by one man. Thus the human search for purposes beyond immediate self-preservation could seem to Johnson both 'a strong proof of the superior nature of the soul of man' – going beyond the Stoic desire of merely avoiding disturbance and affirming instead the reality of the passions – and yet also part of the human unreality of the *tanti man*, diseasedly asking for an external reason for everything before ever being willing to participate in it.[18] For different times and circumstances, Johnson will bring back to mind the thought of different ages.

A moral essay would challenge Johnson immediately to struggle with that ambivalence about the search for purpose in life and to try to resolve it through qualifications and distinctions, as the man fought to preserve, amidst the grinding small of thought upon thought, the general largeness and experiential reality of what was at stake. More perkily, the novel can relish the irony as also life's little bonus: 'he discerned the various instincts of animals, and properties of plants, and found the place replete with wonders'. The comedy of this so-called pessimistic novel lies in its resistance to the idea that life may be used as a means applied to the end of an individual's plan. What he presumed to be irrelevant or disappointing or distracting will begin to come back upon the individual with renewed life just when direct access to the end of the plan recedes. Story can show what otherwise can only be argued – that life cannot be taught *a priori*.

But this is how it looks when it is discursively argued – Burke again:

> Old establishments are tried by their effects ... They are not constructed after any theory; theories are rather drawn from them. In them we often see the end best obtained, where the means seem not perfectly reasonable to what we may fancy was the original scheme. The means taught by experience may be better suited to political ends than those contrived in the original project. They again re-act upon the primitive constitution, and sometimes improve the design itself from which they have departed.[19]

The story of Rasselas is the other side of what Burke calls 're-action': what were supposed to be the means in the mind of the planner or seeker re-act back upon that mind to question not only the end of the original theory but the whole idea of an artificial theory being grafted on in the first place. Moreover, the failure of a *theory* of life, as a backing for living it, seems to be the very working out of the *system* of life itself, using the theory as its own means. There is a subtle configuration working itself out in *Rasselas*.

In Burke's terms, Rasselas repeatedly finds life's 'primitive constitution' obstinately reformulating itself behind his back or beneath his plans, just when he thinks he is pushing on ahead. But if we want to know what this feels like, we should also turn to that realistic descendant of *Rasselas*, Tolstoy's *The Cossacks*. For in almost every sense Tolstoy's young Olenin is trying to establish a fixed philosophy:

> 'What then are the cravings that can always be satisfied, independently of external circumstances? What are they? Love for others, and self-sacrifice.' He was so pleased and excited at this discovery, which seemed to him a new truth, that he sprang to his feet and began impatiently thinking to whom he could sacrifice himself, whom he could do good to, and love, immediately.[20]

Immediately! Every time Olenin wants to stop and fix things once and for all, the novel says through its story, with silent cheek, 'Come on, come on a bit further! Life isn't having you stop there!' That is how story speaks to character in *Rasselas* too, making it a novel in so far as it goes for things that do not *feel* like mere static ideas – as two further examples may show.

Chapter x consists of Imlac's magnificent dissertation on poetry, containing his *idea* of the Poet: 'The business of a poet is to examine, not the individual, but the species...He must write as the interpreter of nature, and the legislator of mankind, and consider himself as presiding over the thoughts and manners of future generations; as a being superior to time and place.' Chapter xi begins immediately thus:

> Imlac now felt the enthusiastic fit, and was proceeding to aggrandize his own profession, when the prince cried out, 'Enough! Thou hast convinced me that no human being can ever be a poet. Proceed with thy narration.'

Now the way Chapter xi reacts back upon Chapter x is no merely sceptical cynicism about ideas, but offers a *joie de vivre*. The novel, said Lawrence, is the great book of life. Here time steps in to bring a magnificent mind back within the body of the tale; the shift in chapters, like a shift in levels, hinting at the incompleteness of even our most complete ideals. The shortness of the chapters, on the other hand, lets life in as time. 'Proceed with thy narration' is the keynote here: life goes on beyond the ideas of it which are not so much over and above life as still going on within it. Indeed, according to Johnson, as a person ages and the forward-looking ideals of youth are chastened while memories of experience take their place from the opposite direction, then that older person becomes more interested in stories of real life. 'Age delights in narratives,' he says in *The Rambler*, 203 – because sentences in narratives are based upon what *happened*, whereas thinking about life without the aid of narrative left a man such as Johnson struggling, amidst almost unendable considerations of probability and possibility, to finish a thought. It is Johnson's subtle joke – the tough side of sympathy – to express his own flawed wisdom through the sane and ordinary instincts of Rasselas's also comic naiveté: 'No human being can ever be a poet'. Even Johnson could not quite make it.

Here is a second example of how in *Rasselas* life *won't* be used as an illustration of a human idea or as a mere means to an individual's end.

This is not simply a negative statement, for as Imlac says, 'To a poet nothing can be useless'. Equally, what Rasselas at first finds to be 'useless' is not so simply so to his author, be he poet or no. In Chapter XVIII the young man finds a wise man whose philosophy, like the precepts of the Stoics, promises an end to the tyranny of feeling and, whatever happens externally, an internal life of invulnerable calm. But when Rasselas goes to visit this potential mentor, he finds the man, despite the philosopher in him, utterly broken by the death of his own daughter. Why does he weep when his reason tells him that that will not bring her back? He weeps *because* that will not bring her back. When he hears this tautology, Rasselas gives up repeating to this now useless hero his own philosophy of but a few days previously – the chapter ends accordingly:

> The prince, whose humanity would not suffer him to insult misery with reproof, went away convinced of the emptiness of rhetorical sound, and the inefficacy of polished periods and studied sentences.

To Rasselas, what Imlac could only tell him about beforehand – 'the teachers of morality: they discourse like angels, but they live like men' – has to be repeated in practice for him really to know it. And indeed it is by perception of its practice that the philosopher's theory becomes disqualified in Rasselas's eyes, in bitter irony. It looks as though Rasselas, in the name of empirical practice, could now go on to write a *Rambler* about this in the very spirit of Johnsonian limitation. But just as Johnson's ideas are more like memories than theories, more like Imlac's than the philosopher's, so through this novel we can see how much subtler is Johnson than a Rasselas might take him to be. For he is here as much interested in the way in which the young man holds the thought as he is in the truth of the thought *per se*. And this not because Johnson, like one sort of secular-aesthetic novelist, puts truth and belief second to psychology; but because he knows that the way a position is held in practice changes the truth of the position. And what Johnson likewise sees with respect to the mourning philosopher – which Rasselas does not – is that the life of a man is at least as important as the belief of a thinker. To Rasselas this fact was a matter of disappointment, an ideal philosophy ruined by a chance death; but this disappointment has as much to do with his personal expectation of heroes, teachers and answers as it has with the 'Vanity of Human Life' itself. What Rasselas thinks of it all may be the end of the chapter, but human ends are not

truly conclusive. The issue will return in the book's repetitive pattern-
ing, though Rasselas thinks he has moved on beyond it. The story of
his own life does not simply belong to the protagonist.

For Johnson himself is always one thought further on from the
vanity of initial disappointment, because he uses it as a clue to
reassess the scale of reality. To Johnson, in contrast to Rasselas, it is
no simple hyprocrisy that the teacher should discourse like an angel
but live like a man. The sort of novelist that Johnson was could see,
beyond hypocrisy, that what the father felt was more valuable than
what the philosopher had thought. Being a novelist was the final logic
of Johnson's effort to make his scepticism compatible with his
humanity. Thus for Johnson it is almost as it should be that a man,
whatever his rational principles or scholarly thoughts, should be
utterly damaged by the death of his own daughter. It is common,
ordinary, felt as unjust as one level and yet also felt as proper at
another, that the man should be suffering so. It would take the
complexity of a *Rambler* sentence to explain and hold together as one
thing the thought that in one form or another Johnson lived to
embody: that it is *good* as well as *bad* that man should feel the pain
and loss, and that limitation means that he must feel it regardless.
Bad, if we were in charge of the universe (for Johnson is no apologist
for the reality of unjust suffering); good, from below, since it is the
mark of being human to bear, feel and even insist upon the meaning
of what the universe seems to treat as meaningless: a lost daughter here
or there.

Rasselas may be disappointed with such behaviour on the part of a
philosopher, though at least he had the 'humanity', our passage says,
to keep that to himself and not 'insult misery with reproof'. But he
does not see how that 'humanity' corresponds to something in the
philosopher which makes the fact of his suffering like a man more
than a satiric irony. As editor of Shakespeare, Johnson must have
remembered what Macduff, on the murder of his wife and children,
replied to Malcolm's exhortation to 'dispute it like a man': 'But I
must also feel it as a man'.

Readers of *The Rambler* should have learnt to expect what
disappointed Rasselas: for human beings to be mistaken, 'if they
thought themselves liable to mistake', could not be considered 'as
either shameful or wonderful' (*The Rambler*, 31). But note '*if*': what is
wrong is that the bereaved man's philosophy had never included, as
does Johnson's, the circular and self-checking thought that
philosophy would barely help in such cases. Johnson's own essay on

bereavement (*The Rambler*, 47) is a masterpiece in balancing the irreconcilable feelings that it is good and bad to feel this loss. It may be as the princess says in Chapter XXXVI of *Rasselas*: 'that happiness itself is the cause of misery' – that the sorrow of loss is something we at one level seem to cause ourselves, proportionate to our former pleasure of possession. But we cannot remove misery simply by never allowing ourselves to be happy in the first place, any more than we should try forcibly to prevent our bereavement-pain from giving way gradually to the pull of life again later. To carry on without either justifying or ignoring what has happened *by* carrying on; to carry on without indifference or martyrdom alike, when the apparent normality is actually the result of the mutual cancellation of more extreme responses under the stress of complication – that is Johnson's way, extraordinarily ordinary. For so much of his achievement consists in arriving from higher levels and reverse directions, at positions nevertheless confirmingly translatable into the limits of ordinary and common sense.

This form of cancellation must be responsible for many of Johnson's readers having felt that they were not dealing here with a 'real' flesh-and-blood novel. William Mudford went so far as to say that there was nothing in *Rasselas* 'which bears any resemblance to the real events of life'. With a view of Johnson quite the opposite of that taken in this book, Mudford concluded that Johnson is not so much realistic as literary: 'The disquisitions which [*Rasselas*] contains are indeed valuable, but as they are literary, they can have but few admirers.'[21] We can see something of the reason for this sort of criticism if we compare the passage from *Rasselas* that we started by considering with an equivalent passage from a novel that was one of Johnson's favourite books – Defoe's *Robinson Crusoe*. For *Robinson Crusoe* must seem to us what we call a 'real' novel, a novel of psychological individualism in the tradition that links Puritan to Romantic self-consciousness. First, here is Johnson's passage again:

> In these fruitless searches he spent ten months. The time, however, passed cheerfully away: in the morning he rose with new hope, in the evening applauded his own diligence, and in the night slept sound after his fatigue. He met a thousand amusements which beguiled his labour, and diversified his thoughts. He discerned the various instincts of animals, and properties of plants, and found the place replete with wonders, of which he purposed to solace himself with the contemplation, if he should never be able to accomplish his flight; rejoicing that

his endeavours, though yet unsuccessful, had supplied him with a source of inexhaustible enquiry.

Life not as a means to the individual's ends; our need for purpose, yet our need also for the bonuses that come from the defeat of purpose. Here now is the *Rasselas* passage translated into the terms of the Puritan novel and seen from the opposite side as bad news, when Crusoe finds himself about to be carried out to sea and lost while trying to explore the coast of his desert island:

> And now I saw how easy it was for the providence of God to make the most miserable condition mankind could be in, *worse*. Now I looked back upon my desolate solitary island as the most pleasant place in the world, and all the happiness my heart could wish for was to be but there again.... Then I reproached my self with my unthankful temper, and how I had repined at my solitary condition; and now what would I give to be on shore there again! Thus we never see the true state of our condition till it is illustrated to us by its contraries, nor know how to value what we enjoy, but by the want of it.[22]

This is just the same as when, later in the novel, the lonely man finds himself in a mortal panic at discovering what for two years he thought he had been longing for: the sign, the footprint, of another human being in his world. To Crusoe this relativism which, taking present feelings in the wake of events, provokes thoughts which themselves turn back upon past feelings, is something so terrifyingly beyond the certainty and control of humans as to constitute intimation of a Higher Power, of Providence. It is characteristic of Puritan psychology that insecurity and fear should provoke the thought of punishment and the feeling of guilt: 'I reproached my self with my unthankful temper.'

For an Anglican Tory the account would have to be less dramatic and direct, the relativism indicating a sort of looseness in human affairs. In Edmund Gibson's fourth *Pastoral Letter* as Bishop of London, written in 1739 against both lukewarmness and enthusiasm in religion, it is the Anglican middle way to insist that

> the extraordinary Operations [of the Spirit of God] were those, by which the Apostles and others, who were entrusted with the first Propagation of the Gospel, were enabled to work Miracles, and speak with Tongues, in Testimony that their Mission and Doctrine were from God. But these have long since ceased; and

the ordinary Gifts and Influences of the Spirit which still
continue, are conveyed in a different Manner.[23]

The work of God is now more 'ordinary' and more indirect than some
Puritan enthusiasts, speaking as though they were the ancient
Apostles, suggest. As with Johnson in relation to the great
Renaissance scholars, so here, in a different sphere, an eighteenth-
century Anglican in comparison with the first great men of religious
inspiration.

It is not difficult, then, to set Tory Prudence and Puritan
Enthusiasm so far apart as to appear to be Ordinary versus
Extraordinary, Social Man in the national Church of England versus
Individual of Religious Dissent. In such an over-simplified sketch the
so-called Augustan age would be very much an age of Anglicanism,
while the voice of Puritan individualism was to find expression only
later as part of the tone of Romanticism, of rediscovered enthusiasm.

There is some truth in that contrast, and we shall be considering the
meaning of eighteenth-century Anglicanism in Chapter Five. But it
cannot be the whole truth, if Johnson so deeply admired *Robinson
Crusoe*. *Rasselas* and *Robinson Crusoe* are, after all, not mere
opposites. Rasselas saw more to enjoy in the Happy Valley while
trying to find a way out of it than he ever did when he thought he
would never leave it. Robinson Crusoe finds that the danger he
experiences on leaving land makes the extreme misery he had
previously felt on being confined to it seem like a happiness he would
gladly now have in exchange. To both we may apply what Johnson
himself says in his *Journey to the Western Islands*: 'When the islanders
were reproached with their ignorance, or insensibility of the wonders
of Staffa, they had not much to reply. They had indeed considered it
little, because they had always seen it; and none but philosophers, nor
they always, are struck with wonder, otherwise than by novelty.'[24]
What I am suggesting is that so far from being opposites, *Rasselas*
and *Robinson Crusoe* treat of the same general experience translated
into different experiential levels. To see it like this would change our
way of reading Johnson. For *Robinson Crusoe* is, as it were, what the
Western Islanders imaginatively need in order fully to re-realize what
has become overfamiliar to them; while *Rasselas* is a later
consolidating translation into ordinary, general terms of the issue of
survival on earth that is so dramatic, extraordinary and particular in
Robinson Crusoe.

Both books start with a young man's question about the life he
seems merely to have been thrown into. The context in which Defoe

places Crusoe gives him an extraordinary purchase upon the ordinary: should Crusoe bother to start all that up again or become a savage or an animal? What in civilization have become habits to be taken for granted, 'the system of life', become to this unaccommodated man reopened as the realities of human survival. The practical has restored to it the element of the necessary. Considerations which have become secondary in civilized England – matters of shelter, food, comfort, happiness and basic purpose – are restored to a primary status. What is he for? What is he to do? How will he live? What difference does it make that he is on his own? Always? How make a home? – these are primary questions predating the privilege of Rasselas's way of asking them and yet also serving as a latent memory within Rasselas's enquiry. One man on an island: Robinson Crusoe must have seemed to Johnson an imaginative microcosm wellsuited in scale to what human capacities can take in. For in Johnson's tradition it is the small-scale which recovers personal access to echoes of what is too generally original, too much the ground of experience, to be individually experienced at all most of the time in our social world – 'The object is too vast. . . . Therefore persons more practical have, instead of mankind, put our country', 'To be attached to the subdivision, to love the little platoon we belong to in society, is the first principle (the germ as it were) of public affections.'[25] And *Robinson Crusoe*, like a kinder *Gulliver's Travels*, was only the small made imaginatively large again.

Johnson must have loved the subtle expansion and contraction of the boundaries of the human home within the world of this book. After finding his first journey of exploration to the other side of the island, 'without settled place of abode', to have been a disturbing experience, Crusoe returns to what he now familiarizes as 'my own house'. 'It rendered every thing about me so comfortable' – though his home is still only more or less a cave on the worst side of the island, where he merely happened to be cast up – 'that I resolved I would never go a great way from it again, while it should be my lot to stay on the island.'[26] Yet an expanding range of need and desire, at first apparently basic but later more to do with psychology, draws him out again. When he fears invasion by savages, however, the fear alone makes a difference from that earlier time when 'I was as happy in not knowing my danger, as if I had never really been exposed to it'.[27] Reality is becoming more complex, less immediate; the man seems to be relearning what we would call the lessons of evolution. And now the anxieties of consciousness 'put an end to all invention, and to all the contrivances that I had laid for my future accommodations and conveniences'.[28] As security gives way before the threat of invasion, the thought of sheer preservation becomes primary again and invention becomes secondary: a luxury, adding to life, but one which looks like folly if life is going to be taken away. All this is like a dramatic mapping out of the flexibility and the defeasibility of Johnsonian practical thinking! For if *Robinson Crusoe* is an imaginative microcosm of problems of survival and purposive invention, Johnson himself keeps an equivalent little world in his own head, a microcosm realistically translated into a mere person still in the ordinary world. So often he is like literature come to real life, without literary self-consciousness such as Boswell's as part of the package.

For the author of *Rasselas* could feel himself at other times transported back, like Robinson Crusoe, into the mind, as it were, of one of the First Men. Thus Johnson standing in one of the barren places of the Western Isles, on tour, in no danger, and yet mortally afraid:

> We were in this place at ease and by choice, and had no evils to suffer or to fear; yet the imaginations excited by the view of an unknown and untravelled wilderness are not such as arise in the artificial solitude of parks and gardens, a flattering notion of self-sufficiency, a placid indulgence of voluntary delusions, a secure expansion of the fancy, or a cool concentration of the mental powers. The phantoms which haunt a desert are want, and misery, and danger; the evils of dereliction rush upon the thoughts; man is made unwillingly acquainted with his own weakness, and meditation shows him only how little he can sustain, and how little he can perform.[29]

Our social comforts drop away, the social world vanishes: what, then, are we here for, in this space on this world? Why carry on with it all, going back on tour, visiting and talking? Just to forget the reality? And why does Johnson not reveal this big terror in the writing of his novel, as Defoe essentially does, as well as in the living of his life? A moralist and a biographer always, but not the powerfully imaginative novelist: is that not, with its refusals, the weakness of Johnson's strength and his limitation?

If we are to answer those questions and refute those criticisms, it must be by turning to Imlac. For it is Imlac, more than any other character within the work, who knows and signifies how and why *Rasselas* is conceived as it is and not otherwise. It is through Imlac that Johnson embodies what is of value to him in his reading of *Robinson Crusoe* – we may put it like that. For what Johnson must have relished in *Robinson Crusoe*, in seeing it as his sort of book, for all its differences from the sort of novel he did write, was the book's own shift from individualism to representativeness. For on the desert island on which he is marooned the young man, who so ironically had wanted to determine life on his own despite his father, becomes the one isolated representative of the human species. Imlac watching Rasselas is, as it were, like Johnson reading *Robinson Crusoe*; for Rasselas's is an unconscious attempt to imitate a Robinson Crusoe first-man view of life, but not on an island this time, rather in the world of later men. Those later men, of whom Imlac himself is one, seem to the young man to have forgotten the big questions, to have repressed them as Johnson might be accused of doing, in order to let the world take its own continuance for granted without the individual having to reopen the issue. But Johnson has his own view, as ever. To him, 'why do we carry on with it all?' is only a dramatically simplified question when imaginatively transformed back, even by Defoe, into a personal question of beginning, with the responsibility sheerly one's own. No doubt Johnson is grateful for the imaginative highlighting; but the problem it throws light upon is, in common life, not so simply a personal question. And so, as the next stage, Johnson in his own novel returns the extraordinary question with characteristic cancellation to ordinary life – to a young man half-immersed in a world which often seems to him to have survived by making its own inhabitants oblivious or distracted. Imlac is not only the witness of Rasselas, then, he is a trace of Johnson and his project; he is that something left over in Johnson which is so extraordinarily ordinary, after making some accommodation with the extraordinary in him. To understand this better, we must look to Imlac. I do not see him as merely that passive and ironically redundant wise man whom some critics take as a sign of Johnson's own failure of life and creativity in the face of intelligence.

*

'Example is always more efficacious than precept,' says Imlac. It is Rasselas himself who exemplifies the way we need but cannot possibly have a backing for life before being able to live in it. And this he shows even while his *story* discloses how, by not getting answers and learning to change the questions in the act of practical thinking, such a background can begin to be attained back to front only. But it is Imlac who exemplifies the mysterious, almost self-supporting nature of Johnson's work. For Imlac, like Johnson at times, seems a man so close to what he takes to be the terms of life as to make it difficult for an outsider to see where the bits of him that were different or resisting had gone. 'Why should he keep going?' young Boswell might well have asked, naggingly, from the outside. 'We proceed because we have begun,' is the almost tautological, circular return, taking life on its terms.

It is Imlac who has already found a backing purpose for human life: one which provides a purchase on life but provides it with the least possible distortion or restriction of the world's variety:

> Being now resolved to be a poet, I saw everything with a new purpose; my sphere of attention was suddenly magnified: no kind of knowledge was to be overlooked. . . . To a poet nothing can be useless. (Chapter x)

The poet's vocation – of knower and witness – is here offered as an initially particular interest, the fulfilment of which, however, lies precisely in the dissolving or effacing of that special motive in the contemplation of ordinary life. Johnson seems to have loved the idea of a secret two-in-one: the viewer from outside put inside that which he still views, but now from a level of mind firmly implicated in a particular body of experience; a purpose upon life almost mysteriously reconciled with what is also an acquiescence in life; the large held within the small, the absolute within the relative. He relished figures such as Imlac who had pulled down the overweening astronomer within themselves – figures, that is, who have a *double* existence which still looks like a mundanely *single* one: a poet, yet an ordinary man; an ordinary man who at first seems to be merely drifting in time, going along with life, but who on second thought seems somehow also to *believe* in drifting in time, though he has to anyway. This is like *The Rambler*, 112, where Johnson, putting accommodation ahead of over-nicety, seems almost deviously to praise that very limitation which, at another level, we have to have anyway: 'In things which are not immediately subject to religious or moral consideration, it is dangerous to be too long or too rigidly in the right.' The two-in-one is there again: for this lovely acceptance is about learning from limitation to make limitations and allowances; it is about trying to make proportionate our physical condition and our mental estimates of it, so that we can live with ourselves as we really are. For 'the right' is not where we can long remain and stay right. 'Perhaps if we speak with rigorous exactness,' says Imlac in Chapter XLIV, 'no human mind is in its right state.' There is a lovely, practical expedience in Johnson's acquiescence in being always *human* rather than always purely 'right'.

What makes *Rasselas* more than a moral essay, adding the dimension of a novel to what was practical but not quite seen in practice in *The Rambler*, is its recognition that life is above and beyond, as well as also in, the simultaneous disappointment of the young man and the suffering of the bereaved philosopher. And it is Imlac above all who seems to incorporate that understanding: that none of our ways of taking life completely catches life. *The Rambler* is magnificently and courageously self-flawed, caught in the circle of its own knowledge, an example of its own problems in trying to be practical about the uncertainties of practice; but in the novel all the apparent scepticism is truly revealed as relativism: problems can become events and situations. It is as though Johnson always feels that human life, in the strength of its weakness, can be *more* than a matter of truth – in feeling, in resolve despite logical impasse, in comedy and in hidden resistance – when truth is anyway beyond us. *Rasselas* embodies – just as *The Rambler* prepares the way for – that licence to be human, not perfect. As Johnson's beloved Jeremy Taylor had put it: 'to admit mankind to repentance and pardon was a favour greater than ever God gave to the angels and devils; for they were never admitted to the condition of second thoughts.'[30]

With Johnson we are always in the condition of second thoughts, for good and for bad, in all the wrong-headedness or defeasibility of our dimly perceived first principles. The marriage debate, on the respective advantages and disadvantages of both early and late marriage, ends in that irresolution which actually reveals more, humanly, than Rasselas's own earlier conclusiveness ever deliberately did. Significantly it is Imlac who signals the necessity for ending the discussion incomplete. Rasselas had been arguing for the prudence of delayed choice, but his sister, the princess Nekayah, stressed the drawbacks; the debate goes on in the absence of Imlac, who could have given them both sides together before they ever started:

' It is dangerous for a man and woman to suspend their fate
upon each other, at a time when their opinions are fixed, and
habits are established; when friendships have been contracted
on both sides, when life has been planned into method, and the
mind has long enjoyed the contemplation of its own

prospects.... And even though mutual esteem produces mutual desire to please, time itself, as it modifies unchangeably the external mien, determines likewise the direction of the passions, and gives an inflexible rigidity to the manners. Long customs are not easily broken: he that attempts to change the course of his own life, very often labours in vain; and how shall we do that for others which we are seldom able to do for ourselves?'

'But surely,' interposed the prince, 'you suppose the chief motive of choice forgotten or neglected. Whenever I shall seek a wife, it shall be my first question, whether she be willing to be led by reason?'

'Thus it is,' said Nekayah, 'that philosophers are deceived. There are a thousand familiar disputes which reason never can decide; questions that elude investigation, and make logic ridiculous; cases where something must be done, and where little can be said.' (Chapter xxix)

'Something must be done', with its tone of 'even so', is another version of 'proceed with thy narration', the human story still having to continue even if reason has come to a stop. *Rasselas* is the work that had to be written to prove the impossibility of working from the outside – after *Rasselas* it is as though we can understand why novels exist, why we have to settle into telling stories, particular stories, from within it all. As such, perhaps the writing might seem to us to occupy the middle ground between *The Rambler* on the one hand and what we might crudely but perhaps forgiveably think of as 'a real novel' on the other, where something must really be done on the inside of a particular physical context. Yet when I think of what all that is at stake in the marriage debate would look like in just such a novel or nearer our time, I find that, though done is a quite different way, the following seems to me to reveal more of the spirit of Johnson's meaning than could anyone more intent on being on Johnson's side:

' – And why this desperate hurry? She's a child of eighteen, and you're a boy of twenty. You're neither of you of age to do as you like yet.'

Will Brangwen ducked his head and looked at his uncle with swift, bright mistrustful eyes, like a caged hawk.

'What does it matter how old she is and how old I am?' he said. 'What's the difference between me now and when I'm thirty?'

'A big difference, let us hope.'

'But you have no experience – you have no experience, and no money. Why do you want to marry, without experience or money?' asked the aunt.

'What experience do I want, Aunt?' asked the boy.

And if Brangwen's heart had not been hard and intact with anger, like a precious stone, he would have agreed.

(D.H. Lawrence, *The Rainbow*, Chapter IV)

For all their differences, both *Rasselas* and *The Rainbow* are dedicated to one big thing: the idea of the basic repetition of the same human story in all its variations down the generations or across borders. Like Will, Rasselas finds that there is no prelude to experience, it begins as soon as we do and it carries on and on; we cannot first get experience, like a qualification, in order then to have an experience more safely. Yet not only the uncle but Lawrence calls Will 'the boy' even in the very moment of his victory: ' "What experience do I want, Aunt?" asked the boy'. Where there are no answers, there we find human beings doing something, taking chances, naively having to live again and again, with only the increasing wisdom of there being no certain wisdom.

It is a back-to-front, cross-grained feeling, this, that Johnson's pessimism is actually something which comes over almost as optimism, for Johnson himself powerfully resisted Leibniz's cheering philosophy that this is the best of all possible worlds, that whatever is is right. Moreover, many readers from Sir John Hawkins onwards have found *Rasselas* an essentially negative achievement: 'Johnson, after speculatively surveying various modes of life, had judged happiness unattainable, and choice useless'.[31] Yet life seems such a huge thing in *Rasselas*, even as revealed through human difficulty and inadequacy, that there seems to be something more-than-humanly awesome, as well as negatively corrective, in the conclusions Imlac draws: 'It seems to me . . . that while you are making the choice of life, you neglect to live'; 'This is often the fate of long consideration: he does nothing who endeavours to do more than is allowed to humanity.'[32] *Rasselas* seems to push the moral essay into the pre-novel, understanding the epistemological conditions that later made for novels while refusing to relinquish the language of philosophy that provided the understanding even through the circle of its own defeat. But *Rasselas* also pushes on beyond the pre-novel into the novel precisely through the ambition of a language which for want of being purely philosophic becomes almost poetic in raising statement to the level of seeming to realize its own meaning – as when, for instance, the astronomer begins to understand his own delusion and to hope that to see it is even thus not to have it:

> 'I hope that time and variety will dissipate the gloom that has so long surrounded me, and the latter part of my days will be spent in peace.'
>
> 'Your learning and virtue,' said Imlac, 'may justly give you hopes.' (Chapter XLVII)

The words could not be more carefully chosen by a poet; the language is here the human memory's deepest hold on truth and sanity down the generations. 'Hopes' says Imlac, picking up that beginning which may so easily be forgotten in the hope of its own end: 'I hope that ...'. Just *hopes*, not certainties: '*may* give you *hopes*'; but *just* hopes, too, to be proved in the event: 'may *justly* give you hopes'. It is tightly balanced, yet not so tightly as not to be able to bear doubt and allow hope, equally with reason, challenging and maintaining each other. That is the Johnsonian sentence, and it goes so deep as to be close to that very origin of language-making which brings all genres of writing, from essay to pre-novel to novel to poetry, much closer together than we usually remember.

Like the movements within sentences in *The Rambler*, the shifts between speeches or between paragraphs in *Rasselas* are a sort of poetic syntax within the prose, changing the levels of being. There is just this movement in *Rasselas* between the figure of the Thinker – like Imlac's poet, 'a being superior to time and place' – and the man of Narrative ('Proceed with thy narration') concerned with the course of a life in time. Imlac moves between the two, and Johnson himself quickly turns from one to another, as between the aspiration to the Eternal and the gravity of the Temporal, never letting the two draw too far apart.

In Chapter XXI, to take an example, Rasselas finally reaches the hermit from whom he had expected to hear of the happiness of solitude. What does he find by the second half of the chapter but that the hermit, sick of solitude, is on the very point of returning to society! Rasselas then retells the story in Chapter XXII as if it were over and he had learnt (or unlearnt) from it. But one of the hearers, who remains anonymous but is surely kin to Imlac and Johnson, is more affected by the narrative than the others and opens it up again by a thought: he 'thought it likely, that the hermit would, in a few years, go back to his retreat, and, perhaps, if shame did not restrain, or death intercept him, return once more from his retreat into the world.' Not just: he will go back to solitude, but: after that he will return to society again. The sequence is marvellously wrought, the wise man being the one who goes one step further in thought, then another, while still remaining in the same place. When you think you have finished, you have not finished; the fresh start is the same old beginning; we rush around and get nowhere, until thinking can return us to the same place from a higher level. For thinking here has not become so abashed at the thought that everything in life is relative and conditional as then to suppose that the only possible discourse for life is a particularizing one unable to refer to anything beyond the present. There are thinkers who already know.

Just such a thinker is Imlac himself, a man not limited to the present. In Chapter XLV he can hear his young friends trying to explain away the black view of life given them by an old man whom they have met. Their explanations are indeed plausible, the sort of things we have heard Johnson himself say in other contexts: old age is peevish and depressed, everyone calls his own condition *the* condition of life; but Imlac, like a novelist, also knows that really, relatively, they are trying to comfort themselves even so; he 'remembered that at the same age, he was equally confident of unmingled prosperity, and equally fertile of consolatory expedients' – that is their liveliness. 'He forbore to force upon them unwelcome knowledge, which time itself would soon impress.'

Yet Imlac, who can thus anticipate time, still goes along with time, his memory keeping in the background, until what in him is more than the mere present can become present and save itself from redundancy. For the movements we have been looking at in Johnson's prose are such as follow the practical exigencies of thought: thoughts, above and behind any particular time, held by men of experience such as Imlac, Johnson and the anonymous hearer, waiting to find the necessary occasion or right time in which to make themselves manifest. 'We are so frequently condemned to inactivity, that as through all our time we are thinking, so for a great part of our time we can only think' (*The Rambler*, 8). *Rasselas* itself, so full of wisdom, is none the less an occasional work, written to defray the cost of the funeral expenses of Johnson's mother. Each short chapter is an occasion for admitting the adventitiousness of thought especially in one who has had so many thoughts at so many different times, all of which now has to shake down to this, just as on one day Johnson was clearer about the full meaning of a word in his *Dictionary* than he was on another; an occasion for art to stand to brevity and chance like a virtue made out of necessity. Seven years after writing the last *Rambler* Johnson wrote *Rasselas*, itself a sort of collected memory of the essays, in just seven days.

> Great powers cannot be exerted, but when great exigencies make them necessary. Great exigencies can happen but seldom, and therefore those qualities which have a claim to the veneration of mankind, lie hid, for the most part, like subterranean treasures, over which the foot passes as on common ground, till necessity breaks open the goldern cavern. (*The Idler*, 52)

Necessity, in the form of moral and humane need, often breaks open the golden cavern within those prose sentences that Johnson had to treat as occasional work, prompted by chance more than choice and by economics far more than by heroic exigencies. Just as Imlac's thoughts as a thinker will have to come out in events in time, so there are times in the midst of Johnson's sentences when he finds he has to recall the hope or the experience he has long had hanging around in him outside his writing. As when he interrupts his own tirade against the complaints of the human screech-owl to say that to complain is also to act like a human being in need of human beings; or when bad news suddenly also seems to be good news and a boundary or level is crossed by suddenly realizing that 'to act is far *easier* than to suffer' or that 'something must be done'. These sudden, present needs arise in the very teeth of the temporally unlimited thought that our lives are unnecessary.

At the beginning of Chapter Three, in contrast, we saw Boswell unable to live in the present and torn between Erskine's outsider and Macdonald's insider position. We can imagine him asking of Imlac: How can you see so much of the world and still be in it as just a part, but a living part, of it? That is a problem that Imlac poses, for the book needs the life and folly of Rasselas too, and Imlac himself recognizes that. Imlac sees the danger of being the wise man as ineffectual outsider, when he recognizes that the Egyptians' building of the pyramids was both stupid *and* magnificent: another unnecessary monument made of the human resistance to redundancy to which even wisdom itself can fall prey. Boswell might ask: How could Imlac see that mixture of brave folly in all of us, including himself, and thereafter be the same or, indeed, different either?

By the end of *Rasselas*, Imlac, with the chastened astronomer, seems oddly 'contented to be driven along the stream of life without directing [his] course to any particular spot'. For when Rasselas tried

to direct his own journey it turned into a circle, the narrative turning
back on the idea of getting somewhere merely physically. What Imlac
stands for is vital to the whole here, and it is not mere defeat. It is
Imlac who is purged to something that has gone through both search
and hopelessness, before ever Rasselas set out, to a third term as of a
sort of purposive neutrality. He may not be seeking a particular
direction, but there is still behind this a general purpose, at once built
up and subdued by time itself. It is something warmer than that 'frigid
tranquillity, having little to fear or hope from censure or from praise'
with which Johnson himself dismissed his own *Dictionary*. It is more
like what it would be to find oneself in the *middle* of a characteristic
Johnsonian formulation in *The Rambler*, 184: 'for it is necessary to
act, but impossible to know the consequences of action'. Above all
Johnson is a master of periods, of holding complex thoughts and
relations together in whole sentences, so that the mind can seek to
contain it own difficulties. In *Rasselas* those sentences are translated
on to an enlarged linear level of narrative, keeping 'life in motion'
chapter by chapter. Life rather than mind seems a large invisible
power beyond human manipulation yet inside our very reactions; and
what it feels like to live out a Johnsonian sentence is exemplified in
Imlac. For although there is undoubtedly a sense of loss as well as
gain when we compare Imlac to Rasselas, who is far more in the
foreground of life, the relation is just that of old and young described
inside the book itself, *but* with the book's own knowledge of that
relation included within Imlac himself, a character in it. That sort of
loop of consciousness is important to Johnson, even though it only
returns Imlac to himself again, for it is much the same as the complex
effort to live unfretfully in the present with all that inside us, for better
and for worse, does not simply belong to it. With Imlac, we have to be
a part of time, going along with its resistance to our madly emotive
attempts to dramatize or hijack it; but within that embodiment we
also have to be that part of time which human beings add to time's
meaning beyond the endless, finite tick-tock. That is to say, we have
to try to go with time's grain and against it *at the same time*. Imlac
leads a double existence as though it was a single one: author and
character at once.

For there are strange moments when levels are crossed, and what
we suffer from is also what we are. To the Stoic who is committed not
to be emotional, not to get involved, we may recall Johnson's great
reply: 'is it not like advice, not to walk lest we stumble, or not to see
lest our eyes should light upon deformity?' The stumbling is *part* of

our walking, not just an aberration from it. And knowing that, we still continue to walk by stumbling. In the same way, Imlac's knowledge often seems to make no difference, involving as it does a realistic acknowledgement which leaves everything as it is. But even by being able to leave everything as it is, that at another level changes everything utterly, in the very acceptance that it remains the same. That is the double-bind of Imlac's mystery at the centre of a novel which ought to be pessimistic and seems often to be the opposite, almost in spite of itself. That Imlac or Johnson can hardly lift up their heads from realistic acceptance to see that that very acceptance partly changes what it accepts, is itself according to the terms of human limitation. Even in the keeping us down and in, it can guarantee authenticity in us which if we knew about it, as the mad astronomer thinks he does, we would damage. If I had to point to something which expressed a little more of what was at stake in *Rasselas* than perhaps even Johnson quite expresses, it would be this:

He travels on, and in his face, his step,
His gait, is one expression: every limb,
His look and bending figure, all bespeak
A man who does not move with pain, but moves
With thought. – He is insensibly subdued
To settled quiet: he is one by whom
All effort seems forgotten; one to whom
Long patience hath such mild composure given,
That patience now doth seem a thing of which
He hath no need. He is by nature led
To peace so perfect that the young behold
With envy what the Old Man hardly feels.

It is Wordsworth's 'Animal Tranquillity and Decay', the poetry held down inside Johnson's prose. The poem holds open a middle ground of observation ('expression', 'look', 'bespeak', 'seems', 'doth seem') between the young and the old, with their reciprocally independent gains and losses on each side. The young want what the old man hardly feels the need of: the irony of desire (since we almost have to *want*, by definition, what we do not have) is played off against the equivocal achievement of an insensibility of which, by definition, the insensible one cannot be conscious ('He is insensibly subdued'). If the old man cannot be conscious of the achievement of his growing down into a sort of natural unconsciousness again, then is it an achievement? And if so, for whom? For those who are conscious and thus project out of their own difficulties? For is it not mere decay, animal decay, portrayed as spiritual tranquillity? Isn't it no achievement as such but the natural product of time ('He is by nature led')? Or if we were conscious of our achievements, if we could get outside and on top of ourselves in that way, would that destroy us, them? Johnson thought himself a failure; without that, I take it, he would not be the man we today admire. The poem holds open these questions and thoughts as it examines the stance of a man whom time has incarnated so deeply within the ways of life as seemingly to have purged all difference between what is life and what is he, what is nature and what is his nature within it: 'One to whom/Long patience hath such mild composure given,/That patience now doth seem a thing of which/He hath no need.' This is a dissolving into life which also transforms life in so doing, without even seeing that it does. The story of patience in that sentence is contained within a journey of just 'travelling on', which, with its gains and losses, stands over against Rasselas's more apparently purposive quest for life. Only Wordsworth, perhaps, is as concerned with the syntactical shape and journey of thought as was Johnson. At any rate, it is in this context that the young feel bound to ask the almost impossible question that the young Wordsworth posed the leech-gatherer: 'How is it that you live, and what is it you do?' – the question that Boswell was always really asking of Johnson. Why, how do you keep going in purposive neutrality? What is it – which for other people is something external to them, a word, an idea – what is it that has grown down into being in you? An extraordinary ordinariness.

*

It is true that we sometimes need exceptional art – poems, stories, novels, our own memories supported and enlarged – to help us see what Johnson's sentences stand for. It is, as Johnson surely knew, both the strength and weakness of *The Rambler* that it should need, and its resonances almost demand, such extension; for to Johnson himself, *The Rambler* as a whole is only part of its own larger view: namely, that incarnation both commits and limits the soul within the body of earth. I have tried to show how *Rasselas*, written in memory of *The Rambler*'s wisdom, is the fruit of this ambivalence and of a language itself hovering between the particular and the universal. For *Rasselas* is the culmination of *The Rambler* but also the limit of how far Johnson thought he could go, beyond the moral essay, without, as it were, losing the wood for the trees. Quoting Johnson as she sometimes does, did George Eliot ever put to herself the thought that *Middlemarch* was a successor to *Rasselas* in seeking transaction between the particular and the general, the fictional and the morally discursive? Such questions help, I think, to restore Johnson to the so-called mainstream of the history and purpose of literature. In him the qualities that make up art and artists are returned to ordinary being and thinking, making them less visible in one way, more approachable in another.

CHAPTER FIVE

An Anglican Saint?

*I 'The right path ... at an equal distance between
the extremes of error' (The Rambler, 25)*

Although we know from Boswell how emphatically High Church and
Tory his hero could be, Johnson none the less admired Dissenters,
such as Bunyan and Baxter, who had added to the country's spiritual
stature. He made a particular, stretched point of including the
Dissenter Isaac Watts in his *Lives of the Poets*, insisting: 'I shall do
what I can for Dr Watts'.[1] In his account Johnson praises Watts for a
flexibility which he acknowledges to be closer to the habit of religious
vocation than to sheer natural inclination:

> By his natural temper he was quick of resentment; but, by his
> established and habitual practice, he was gentle, modest, and
> inoffensive. His tenderness appeared in his attention to
> children, and to the poor. To the poor, while he lived in the
> family of his friend, he allowed the third part of his annual
> revenue, though the whole was not a hundred a year; and for
> children, he condescended to lay aside the scholar, the
> philosopher, and the wit, to write little poems of devotion, and
> systems of instruction, adapted to their wants and capacities,
> from the dawn of reason through its gradations of advance in
> the morning of life. Every man, acquainted with the common
> principles of human action, will look with veneration on the
> writer who is at one time combating Locke, and at another
> making a catechism for children in their fourth year. A
> voluntary descent from the dignity of science is perhaps the
> hardest lesson that humility can teach.[2]

The use of the word 'common' there ('Every man, acquainted with the
common principles of human action ...') is strikingly different from

Johnson's more customary, celebratory usage: 'I rejoice to concur with the common reader'. 'The common principles of human action' concern man's fallen nature here, habitually addicted to pride. Yet the 'humility' that Watts learned, against both that general disposition and his own particular temper, was a commitment to ordinary life involving the better, redeemed meaning of 'common'. During Watts's lifetime Bishop Gilbert Burnet expressed concern that his own Anglican clergy had relaxed the power of the English Reformation and were failing in the ordinary duties that the people could now see Nonconformists to be more conscientiously fulfilling. In his *Discourse of the Pastoral Care*, written in 1692 for those intending to undertake Anglican priesthood, Burnet points to the ideal humility of the man of uncommon commonness:

> A Man of this Disposition affects no Singularities, unless the faultiness of those about him, makes his doing his Duty to be a Singularity.[3]

It is society that makes such a man singular, not he himself, for even thus his life, like Watts's, is an incarnate, educative example and a tacit social reproach. In writing *The Rambler*, could Johnson see himself, I wonder, as an Anglican version of Watts?

Perhaps not, for two reasons. First, there was the particular way in which Johnson admired Watts: less as a model and more as a rebuke. For although the Blake of the *Songs of Innocence* was later to satirize Watts's religious songs for children, to Johnson Watts none the less had constituted just the sort of implicit reproach to his own pride in learning that Burnet would have wanted the Anglican priest to provide: 'A voluntary descent'. It was in the same self-troubled spirit that Johnson admired the Reverend Philip Skelton, as Thomas Campbell reports:

> I mentioned Skelton to him as a man of strong imagination, and told him the story of his selling his library for the support of the poor. He seemed much affected by it, and then fell a rowling and muttering to himself, and I could hear him plainly say after several minutes pause from conversation, 'Skelton is a great good man'.[4]

I think Johnson was affected and muttering because he suspected that he might not do the same – sell his books – as Skelton had. Johnson was no voluntary descender; he loved as a schoolboy to be carried to school by his contemporaries, shoulder-high; he had to push himself to descend.

But there is a second reservation muffled behind Johnson's mutter. His clear intelligence also forced from him, albeit mutteringly, a tough recognition with regard to Watts – a recognition as tough as Imlac's saying that 'nature sets her gifts on the right hand and on the left':

> His character, therefore, must be formed from the multiplicity and diversity of his attainments, rather than from any single performance; for it would not be safe to claim for him the highest rank in any single denomination of literary dignity; yet perhaps there was nothing in which he would not have excelled, if he had not divided his powers to different pursuits.[5]

The strength was also, at another level, a weakness. On the one hand, 'Dr Watts was one of the first who taught the Dissenters to write and speak like other men, by shewing them that elegance might consist with piety.'[6] But on the other hand, to do this, ceasing to be simply elect and becoming instead an insider to the common language of the country, Watts had also to descend into being much more like other men. Against that flexible charity of thus virtually giving oneself away for the sake of others, Johnson hints at an almost regretted regret in that last clause, 'if he had not divided his powers to different pursuits...' – as if he still could not prevent thoughts of excellence and single-mindedness of purpose. For the regret is all Johnson's. He may have been like Watts in one respect, in being naturally 'quick of resentment'; but he could also accuse himself of managing *neither* the 'single performance' of a great masterpiece *nor* a willing diversity of (to use his own phrase about Dr Levet) 'useful care'. The in-between man again. Did Watts sacrifice his ability to do one great thing, for the sake of a Christian flexibility in attacking Locke at one moment and educating children at the next? Yet, impatient of both his own intrusive obsessions and over-theoretical dialectics, Johnson sets up his life of Watts just *inside* the general issue of single purpose versus general flexibility, and treats it not as an abstract problem but as the shape and meaning of one man's life on earth.

But how much Johnson would have wanted to be Watts at an even higher level of achievement is clear from his evident desire to live the life of one of the great Renaissance scholars. His brief *Life of Dr. Herman Boerhaave* betrays his ambition to be greatly *un*ambitious. All of Boerhaave's life holds together in a way that Johnson, in his contradictions, must have felt his own did not. Boerhaave trained in philosophy and divinity and wrote a thesis on the relation of soul and body. Running out of funds, he had to resolve to study for a profession and chose medicine as a career which would support his theological studies. It was perhaps an arbitrary choice, yet it maintained the interest of his thesis on the relation of soul and body. It also harked back to Boerhaave's childhood illness, an ulcerated left thigh, which no doctor had been able to cure and which the child himself had had to find means to heal. Yet not only did Boerhaave seek complete medical knowledge alongside his search for the largest possible theological understanding, he next began to consider his own branch of science in relation to all the others. At the same time, however, he began to question why men of great learning did less for religion than did illiterate persons. Trained as a doctor, he still wished to use his academic success to find funds to enable him to become a minister, but his desire for knowledge raised prejudice and made him seem suspect. He had to continue his holistic mission in the garb of physician, and his theological concerns were so far from being now a mere background part of his life, and so far from rendering him incapable of mundane practice, that they precisely defined the limits and conduct of his medical skill. For he not only declared but proved by experiment, says Johnson, 'that we are entirely ignorant of the principles of things' – all his apparently superhuman intelligence went into carefully showing how we are not God. 'He examined systems by experiments', showing their emptiness or uncertainty for all their speculative impressiveness or antiquity; but he also 'formed experiments into systems' rather than leave behind merely sceptically negative conclusions. All this became concentrated within the very moments of his medical practice: 'so far was this great master from presumptuous confidence in his abilities, that in his examination of the sick he was remarkably circumstantial and particular.'[7]

This was the great balanced life of classical, Christian humanism – holding together knowledge and practice, faith and science, soul and body. In a lesser age Watts's failure to limit himself in one way, by concentration of his efforts, had meant limitation in another; it is a measure of Watts's achievement that Johnson could not bring himself to call Watts what to some extent he actually was: jack of all trades, master of none. But Boerhaave's life belonged to an earlier, higher model than Watts's and put it all the other way round: Boerhaave's Renaissance unlimitedness at one level, in seeking knowledge about everything in order to hold everything together, was still entirely and consciously limited beneath the eye of God. And knowledge for Boerhaave was no different from humility in making him content that it should be like this, even at the personal level where his way had to be that of physician, not priest as he had hoped.

What was terrifying to Johnson, I think, was that the opposite of such a coherent and balanced life was not simply an unbalanced one but a life in which the balance was taken over, from within, by the matching of forces against each other. He had seen in the life of his ruined friend Savage that chaos itself could be an ironic and terrifying form of order: 'if his Miseries were sometimes the Consequences of his Faults...his Faults were very often the Effects of his Misfortunes'; 'him, to whom Life afforded no other Comforts than barren Praises, *and* the Consciousness of deserving them'; 'he scarcely ever found a Stranger, whom he did not leave a Friend; but it must likewise be added, that he had not often a Friend long, without obliging him to become a Stranger.'[8] The fact that there is a pattern even to a life of self-destruction must have been to Johnson a massive inducement to the writing of *The Rambler*. For there was always control: the issue was to see whether you could control the forces rather than let them control you, turning you into strange shapes. Either you use your thoughts or they begin to use you.

One particular movement was vital to Johnson, and again *Robinson Crusoe* may serve to illustrate it. For he must have looked keenly at the almost biological ebb and flow between the secular and the religious life within the mind of Crusoe. There is a moment, for example, when the man first thinks of actually thanking God for bringing him to this island, because this alone has opened his eyes to the Lord. But there immediately follows a second, cross-grained thought in which it is hard to separate, yet equally hard to combine, secular snag and religious scruple:

> I know not what it was, but something shocked my mind at that thought, and I durst not speak the words. 'How canst thou be such a hypocrite,' said I, even audibly, 'to pretend to be thankful for a condition, which however thou may'st endeavour to be contented with, thou would'st rather pray heartily to be delivered from?' So I stopped there.[9]

If he is silent for the sake of his religious sincerity, part of that equivocal sincerity lies in a mortal stubbornness which is still far from truly thankful to God. Johnson himself was both honestly down-to-earth and determinedly religious, but he was also terrified at times that he could not hold the two together. He must have been deeply impressed not only by Puritan honesty but also by the agonizing pressures it was under. Johnson greatly admired Bunyan's *The Pilgrim's Progress*: it would have been like him to have been particularly impressed by the way in which the Man at the beginning of the book, fleeing from the City of Destruction, still has to say, with utter honesty to Evangelist's tempting 'Do you see yonder Wicket-gate?' – 'No'. 'No' is so often Johnson's own first word, strong and weak, reluctant and honest at once. And indeed all the Man can manage on second thought in reply to Evangelist's 'Do you see yonder shining light?' is not 'Yes, yes, I see the light' but simply 'I think I do'. Jeremy Taylor said that God gave man alone second chances: 'Lord I believe, help thou mine unbelief'.

There was in Johnson's Anglicanism, for reasons both of personal temperament and national history, a deep attraction to the seriousness of English Puritanism alongside a need also to transform it. Johnson not only admired the cultural achievements of Nonconformists such as Bunyan and then Watts in bringing religious culture to the common people, he also felt a tacit, controlled kinship with the religious fervour of Reformation Puritanism, justified not by reason but by faith beyond reason's capacity. Sir John Hawkins said that Johnson's religion 'had a tincture of enthusiasm' which was particularly revealed in 'an habitual reverence for the name of GOD, which he was never known to utter but on proper occasions and with due respect'.[10] This is the Johnson who when asked by Dr Adams, in an Oxford-donnish way, what he meant by being damned, said '(passionately and loudly) "Sent to Hell, Sir, and punished everlastingly"'. 'I am afraid I may be one of those who shall be damned.' It is clear that Johnson really meant 'afraid', passionately and loudly; for when Dr Adams told him that he had good evidence, evidence enough, for the existence of another world, Johnson answered as to Evangelist, 'I like to have more'.[11] The rueful cheek is just a cover.

'I like to have more' could almost be Johnson's motto. For it is still startling to realize that Johnson thought of himself, for all his pride, not as a great man like Boerhaave but as a failure. The poem 'Know Thyself', which he wrote in 1773 after finishing his final revision of the *Dictionary*, reveals a man who thought himself a pigmy in comparison with the great scholars of the past such as Scaliger, also a compiler of a lexicon. 'Know Thyself' actually bears its title in Greek and its verses are in Latin. It is as though the use of the great old languages is both a tribute from a fallen age and a buried confession of personal inadequacy. At one and the same time, Johnson is a man of culture and, behind that translation, a man of common disappointments still. How can I, he says, compare with a Boerhaave – or with you, Scaliger:

> A large example is dangerous. The dunciad of learned dolts presume
> to glare and grumble, presenting their case, princely Scaliger
> as if it were yours, master. Let each mind his measure!
> I, at least, have realized that to be your rival (in rage
> or in knowledge) was never part of my nature. Who can know why? . . .
> As for me, my task finished, I find myself still fettered to myself:
> the dull doom of doing nothing, harsher than any drudgery,
> stays with me, and the staleness of slow stagnation . . .
> Trembling, I trudge everywhere, peering, prying, into everything, trying
> passionate to know if somewhere, anyhow, a path leads up to a more perfect pasture,
> but glooming over grand schemes I never find my growing-point,
> and am always forced finally to face myself, to own frankly
> that my heart is illiterate, and my mind's strength an illusion
> I labour to keep alive.[12]

This, I think, is why Boswell was rightly attracted to Johnson, as though Johnson were a sort of bridge for us between the ordinary and the great: a Johnson who enables us to see what is at stake in that range which lies between our own frustrated needs, potentialities or aspirations and the achievements of our heroes who seem to speak and act for us, in place of us, but also still somewhat beyond us. *The Rambler* uses all the resources of literature and culture to make a translation, prosaically, of that wealth into the currency of ordinary lives.

Nowhere is the example of Johnson more important than in the matter of making a balanced and coherent life, for he had to make of himself this bridge between the ordinary and the great. 'To walk with circumspection and steadiness in the right path, at an equal distance between the extremes of error,' he wrote in *The Rambler*, 25, 'ought to be the constant endeavour of every reasonable being.' Balance is a dull-sounding word; but what it really means to get it right becomes clearer from thinking of the opposite in the case of such as Savage. Johnson himself recurrently and privately felt himself divided and unbalanced between forces – between the secular and the religious, between flexibility of accommodation and fixity of serious purpose, between pride and fear . . . and so on. His achievement was to hold on and to hold together, with more difficulty, it seems, than did Watts. It was this that, as we have seen, continually astonished Boswell; as though he thought: How can a person who feels partial and inadequate yet settle for that? and as though Johnson replied in his very person: How can he not? It is because of the unshowy mystery of Johnson's abiding, closer to tautology than to drama, that we turn now to think finally about his religion as the last sustaining expression of what he kept private behind his published translations of himself and his wisdom.

In this chapter I shall argue that Johnson's survival and coherence were based upon belief, so let me close this introductory section by considering a somewhat contrary view which itself has mileage in it. To that most acute of Victorian critics, R.H. Hutton, Johnson's ability to survive was less a mystery than a matter of sheer resistance. Hutton has this to say on Johnson's place within the possible modes of human being:

> Most men of letters, like most men of science, have gained their reputation by their power of entering into and understanding that which was outside of them and different from them. Johnson gained his reputation by his unrivalled power of concentrating his own forces, of defending himself against the aggression of outer influences, – and striking a light in the process . . . Admitting freely that it both takes a man of some character as well as insight, to understand distinctly what is beyond his own sphere, and a man of some insight as well as character, to teach others to understand distinctly what is within himself, it is clear that Johnson's genius lay in the latter, not in the former direction – in maintaining himself against the encroachments of the world, and in interpreting himself to that world, not in enlarging materially the world's sympathies and horizons, except so far as he taught them to include himself.[13]

If we want to know what it would feel like to be the opposite of Johnson, as Hutton sees it, then we need to think about the example of Keats – as we shall see in our next section. For Keats was indeed one who set himself the task of 'entering into' what was outside of and different from himself. This for Keats was the way of the Poet, with a power of flexible Imagination which did not need to be simply feared.

To Keats poetry existed to enlarge the world's horizons and limitations; a way of being, not otherwise available, which took us beyond the confinement of our selves. In this he seems to have been following Coleridge's account of Shakespeare, who turned himself into all things, where Milton drew all things into himself.[14]

But Keats's way clearly is not Johnson's. Hutton is right about that. Johnson was the sort of man who said not 'yes' but 'no' to life, for his first word at any rate. Perhaps 'but' was his second. He was the sort of man who used words in order to lay hold of life and pass the whole world through his own consciousness. 'I like to have more.' Such a position in contrast to Keats's must raise the issues about boundaries which, I suggested in Chapter Four, so interested Johnson in *Robinson Crusoe*. For Crusoe's movements are always asking, implicitly: How far do I go? Where are my boundaries and limits? Do I consolidate behind their defence? Take them as a base for further outward movement? Where is home? What is the place of invention and the human arts? A figure such as Boswell thus exists virtually to ask Johnson this: How do people 'decide' (if that is the word) the boundaries of their own sphere and their relation to what lies beyond it? As Johnson himself indicates in *The Rambler*, 63, the presence of imagination and the desire for wider views in human beings makes them disturbingly unable to 'confine their thoughts within their own boundaries of action'. It is as though his writing of that tendency also put it just where Johnson could maintain himself against its encroachments – outside.

Hutton seems right, therefore, when he describes Johnson's stance as one based on opposition to the outside world – the Protestant Hebraism of Luther's 'Here I stand'. But in my view, such opposition is secondary to the initial effort which Johnson made to incarnate his knowledge of the world and his species, almost greedily, within himself as Knower. That is partly his ambition but also partly his mystery, for nothing is more awesome in Johnson than his apparently common-sense ability to remain undisturbed at the thought that he, like all other human beings, will have disturbances. That is the familiar yet strange voice of tautology in *The Rambler*: How can you bear it? Well, how can you not bear it? Always Johnson accepted life's terms as knowledge, the Great Accepter as much as the Great Fighter. His knowledge felt to him like a higher form of ignorance; his effort to balance was created solely by his intelligent recognition of the tension of his imbalances. Even so, Johnson was a knower and balancer the second time around. For this, above all, is what distinguishes him: the ability to bring within himself constraints or negations which might have been thought of as outside himself or preventing him from being himself. The Poet in him, Imlac's 'being superior to time and place', did not preside over the world, floatingly split off from any body while ready for temporary incarnations of the spirit of imagination anywhere. The converse was true in this back-to-front man: he kept that high spirit deep down within himself, as knowledge, and let the world come in, make and enforce its changes within him, as though he were a latter-day microcosm. In that sense he had bounds, but only externally; the world also went on within him mentally while he meanwhile carried on like an ordinary person within the world. A two-in-one man, like Imlac – or like Newton, whom Johnson praised, in *The Adventurer*, 131, for a superiority which was all the more superior for not appearing singular. This was Johnson's equivalent to that achievement of Isaac Watts about which Johnson himself was so ambivalent: Johnson the microcosm, the would-be Renaissance knower, lived on inside an exterior of ordinariness, by a barely visible strategy. To make it all more visible is the purpose of this chapter.

*

II   A Thought-Experiment

Because Johnson offers himself as a useful writer and because we see more of what he stands for by filling in the context – recalling in ourselves the difficulties he speaks to, creating alternatives to measure him against – there is, I hope, some justification for constructing an imaginatively practical test upon his wisdom: especially with regard to this problem of creating a balanced and coherent life. Throughout this chapter I have at the back of my mind, therefore, something like the following case-history, in search of help. It is the sketch of a man who made the wrong choices and went badly wrong, like another version of the Savage story:

> It was very early – he was not more than twenty-five years old – that he succumbed. Furthermore, he knew that he was doing something wrong. The young often have moments of clear thinking, which as they grow older become fewer, and muddied. He had kept alive in some part of him a knowledge that he was 'destined' to do something or other. He felt this as pure and unsullied, but – more often and more deeply as he grew older – 'impractical'.

He was in his early fifties, that is, he was well past the halfway mark... He was handicapped because of his self-division. His suppressed inner qualities made him disappointed with what he was. He knew he had greater qualities than any he was using but did not know what they were. The restlessness had caused him to drink too much, indulge in bouts of self-denigration and cynicism. He was not respected in ways that matter, and he knew it.[15]

This is something like Savage, 'to whom life afforded no other Comforts than barren Praises, and the Consciousness of deserving them': barren, something having happened or not happened somewhere between twenty-five and fifty; limited in the wrong way as a result; self-divided through the working of internal forces against each other to sustain a sort of life, but only of lost purpose.

This sort of figure stands in the background as I try now again to come at Johnson backwards, for the sake of such help as he can offer, from the twentieth and nineteenth centuries that have gone on past him. What I propose is this, by way of time-experiment. Recognizing that Johnson himself was so deeply concerned about a split between the religious and the social, between the important and the normal, between the purposive and the acquiescent or flexible, I intend in this section to examine, as it were through the eyes of Dr Johnson, a nineteenth-century split which it seems to me we have also inherited: the split diagnosed by Arnold as being essentially between Hebrew and Hellene. I shall set up – I hope not improperly – a quarrel between a Hebrew and a Hellene, between a Puritan religious called John Foster and the poet and aesthetic thinker John Keats; and I shall try to imagine both Arnold and Johnson witnessing it. But within this time-experiment I shall be tacitly imagining, at the personal level, what happens in our culture to a person who starts, when young, as hard and ambitious in his determination to get a single hold upon life; but who begins to get tired, begins to find the initial, narrow drive too self-destructively single-minded to enable him to live properly; and then has to try to readjust and rebalance in the second stage of life without toppling over into a relaxed or dissolute loss of original purpose. Johnson himself, ambitious, anxious and frustrated, could have become one of the last, roaming the London streets with Savage.

*

In 1805 a Radical Baptist, John Foster, published a book entitled

Essays in a Series of Letters. Much read, it went through many editions throughout the century. One essay was concerned to try to heal the split between Evangelical Christians and men of culture and learning (as Watts had tried to do for Dissenters generally, teaching them 'to write and speak like other men'). Another puritanically attacked the impractical extravagances of Romantics (drawing on the example of Rasselas to show the natural dangers for the young in a prevalence of imagination over judgement). But the essay with which I am here concerned is the second, 'On Decision of Character'. Typically, it was this essay, rather than the Romantic corrective, that our extravagant friend Benjamin Robert Haydon used to fuel his enthusiasm: 'I read it and re-read it, prayed with all my heart, and resolved, come what would, to proceed with a greater work, to avoid the errors or extravagances of this and try to produce a faultless production.'[16]

Decision was for Foster the test of character. The person who could not make up his mind – and Foster himself was chronically indecisive – seemed to be one who did not know who he was or what he was for. In a world of clear functions and purposes, who one was would perhaps in part determine, in part be settled by, what one was for. There would be no waste, no redundancy, through the inner divisions of uncertainty. One instance of decisiveness, on the verge of constituting a sense of personal destiny, was, says Foster, the commitment of Martin Luther at the Diet of Worms. Another which he hardly dared mention was the calling of Christ to incarnation and crucifixion. But at a more mundane level, one of Foster's major examples of a person with a decisive sense of vocation was Lord Howard of Effingham, conqueror of the Spanish Armada, a man who could almost literally turn himself into action. In such instances there were no longer two things – the individual and the world – with a space of hesitation between them but one fused: the individual used up, pulled out in a way which was none the less the releasing fulfilment of himself.

Imagine what it was like to be heroic Howard, with a sense of one main object in life to which he dedicated his whole being:

> The importance of this object held his faculties in a state of determination which was too rigid to be affected by lighter interests, and on which therefore the beauties of nature and of art had no power. He had no leisure feeling which he could spare to be divested among the innumerable varieties of the extensive scene which he traversed; his subordinate feelings

nearly lost their separate existence and operation, by falling
into the grand one. There have not been wanting trivial minds,
to mark this as a fault in his character.[17]

This is the very absoluteness and exclusivity of the Hebraic character
at its most extreme. To everything else, besides his main purpose, the
man single-mindedly said no. This is the type that thrives on being
opposed or deserted; the very individuality is aggressively dependent
upon those obstacles which constitute a defining opposition; the
individual has to suspect ease, if not actively create difficulties;
temptations have to be seen as enemies, even where those temptations
are provided by family and friends – lest one lose one's way in a life
which must be viewed as a career or a mission. Howard had

> an inconceivable severity of conviction, that he had *one thing to
> do*, and that he who would do some great work in this short
> life, must apply himself to the work with such a concentration
> of his forces, as, to idle spectators, who live only to amuse them-
> selves, looks like insanity. (p. 124)

Such a life is 'rigid' and 'severe' in so far as everything in it is to be
referred to the one end; life is lived forward as a plan and within an
economy; it is 'unsparing', as far as possible avoiding relaxation,
construed as distraction. A man such as Howard 'loves to be actuated
by a passion so strong as to compel into exercise the utmost force of
his being', finding his power in using his strength against himself as
pressure. Compared with such violence of commitment, 'the gentle
affections, if he had felt them, would be accounted tameness'; for
such a man 'values not feelings which he cannot employ as weapons
or as engines' (p. 144).

Clearly Foster had his own subdued misgivings about such single-
mindedness, at once so Puritanical and so Romantic. And well he
might have doubts, for is it only to idle spectators or secular relativists
that this commitment to an absolute purpose and vocation, to which
all the rest of life is sacrificed, looks close to insanity?

Matthew Arnold, I imagine, could have provided instances from
his own time. James Mill's rigidly Utilitarian education of his son
ended in John Stuart Mill's nervous breakdown in 1826, when the
boy was twenty. It is an irony of this mixed-up time of dawning
secularism to see Utilitarianism, in its belief in a rationalism so
contemptuous of personal feeling, as having strong antecedents in the
enthusiasm of Hebraic evangelicalism. Yet that is precisely the
ironical history that Arnold was to trace in *Culture and Anarchy*,

wherein James Mill, like any Puritan, 'values not feelings which he cannot employ as weapons or as engines'. Men on whom, in Foster's words, 'the beauties of nature and art had no power' were possessed of a particularly narrow view of what 'power' had to be as well as a wide one of its place in the human world. Aesthetics, accordingly, did not compel a place in James Mill's ungentle curriculum – no more than did play in the programme he devised for his child; the equation between the two being left as implicit. And indeed, even when the adult son did turn to art after his nervous breakdown, he did so only under his father's revised criterion, still: the criterion of utility. Art must be useful, he found retrospectively, for all his father's prospective exclusions; art must have a sort of negative power; for *without* it and without what it stands for in human psychology, there were – by a sort of protesting revenge of human nature within itself – nervous breakdowns. The son's was still a ruined, if patched-up human life, for there was in him an unwilling witness to the strong relation between creating an exclusivist self, with only 'one thing to do', and actual self-destruction. That internal witness or scar haunted John Stuart Mill for the rest of his life. Ironically, it was his deepest self. Such was one of the Victorian sages who displaced the old-fashioned *Rambler*.

Here, in necessary counterweight therefore, is the voice of a poet, who, writing in 1819 about an old acquaintance, may be taken as speaking against the Hebraic force and anxiety of John Foster:

> I explained what I thought of Dilke's Character. Which resolved itself into this conclusion. That Dilke was a Man who cannot feel he has a personal identity unless he has made up his Mind about every thing. The only means of strengthening one's intellect is to make up one's mind about nothing – to let the mind be a thoroughfare for all thoughts. Not a select party. The genus is not scarce in population. All the stubborn arguers you meet with are of the same brood – They never begin upon a subject they have not preresolved on. They want to hammer their nail into you and if you turn the point, still they think you wrong. Dilke will never come at a truth as long as he lives; because he is always trying at it. He is a Godwin-methodist.[18]

I perhaps leave signs of having lived too long in Foster's camp by putting the two adjectives together, but I was going to say that there are *gentler* and *weaker* souls than Dr Johnson's – for example, William Cowper's; souls in need of the defence provided by those

words of John Keats against Hebraic decision of character. And the
virtues of something other than a direct confrontation with the truth
of the world need to be expressed for the sake of those who, like Mill,
begin life with the idea of a single all-subordinating purpose and find
the exclusivist tension of that position eventually impossible for
living. Sometimes all such people are left with is the opposite fear of
having sunk into jog-trot habits of self-protectively forgetful living, in
order to get away from their own self-destroying need for a purposive
hold on existence. As they turn from youth to the second stage of life,
when the initial energy is no longer sufficient, people increasingly
need advice. Suppose this time we do not look to *The Rambler* for it
but to Keats versus Foster. The mention of Dilke enables us to see
how Keats's letter of 1819 goes with another of his written late in
December 1817:

> I had not a dispute but a disquisition with Dilke, on various
> subjects; several things dovetailed in my mind, & at once it
> struck me, what quality went to form a Man of Achievement
> especially in Literature & which Shakespeare possessed so
> enormously – I mean *Negative Capability*, that is when man is
> capable of being in uncertainties, Mysteries, doubts, without
> any irritable reaching after fact & reason – Coleridge, for
> instance, would let go by a fine isolated verisimilitude caught
> from the Penetralium of mystery, from being incapable of
> remaining content with half knowledge. This pursued through
> Volumes would perhaps takes us no further than this, that with
> a great poet the sense of Beauty overcomes every other
> consideration, or rather obliterates all consideration.[19]

It is Keats's achievement to begin to show that the problem of
identity as thus conceived is actually, before that, a problem of
knowledge: 'Dilke was a Man who cannot feel he has a personal
identity unless he has made up his Mind about every thing'. For
Foster the inability to make up your mind likewise seemed a terrible
intimation that you did not exist as a whole person. Decision did
indicate 'the full agreement of the mind with itself, the consenting co-
operation of all its powers and all its dispositions' (p. 132). For the
self was then even as it had made its subject matter – namely, whole:
'he sees the different parts of the subject in an arranged order, not in
unconnected fragments; . . . in each deliberation the main object
keeps its clear pre-eminence, and he perceives the bearings which the
subordinate and conducive ones have on it' (p. 110). The pressure for

an integral self so expressed itself in an anxious need for a manageable, coherent subject matter that the existence of any problem or situation which was not tidily susceptible to resolution threatened the very existence of that self. After all, it might well be that it was the situation which was unresolvable, without any necessary implication as to the integrity of the character implicated in it. But, by a species of nemesis, such a situation cracked the sense of self with that very doubt which, it had been assumed, was necessary to be exorcized for there to be a whole self in the first place.

How did identity become so confused with, and threatened by, problems of knowledge outside itself? 'It is', says Foster, 'one of the nicest points of wisdom to decide how much less than complete knowledge, in any question of practical interest, will warrant a man to venture on an undertaking' (p. 160). But the issue became more paranoid, less susceptible to prudent and impersonal calculation, when the idea of self had been tacitly founded upon a particularly unfortunate model of what knowledge was: the knower – separated off from what, external to him, was to be known – stood in tense, vulnerable and aggressive relation to the confronting world of knowledge; a world conceived of as almost waiting to see whether the would-be knower was up to it: as if knowledge were a fight across a gap between inside and out, a test of the knower by the objects of knowledge already existing outside him. It is this model of knowledge which caused the problem of beleaguered identity, confusing epistemology at one level with psychology at another. Coleridge, it might be said, was one who sought to change the model. But to Keats, I suspect that Coleridge and Johnson, metaphysical and practical thinker, were still only two sides of much the same coin. Neither of them satisfied with half knowledge, one went too high for the sake of entirety, while the other was too limited to be complete; both achieved agonizingly less than their own potential suggested to them.

Through Keats, then, we may recognize that Foster's sense of one life for one purpose is an act of will in lieu of a more certain state of predestination. It is precisely this *ugliness* of a person sticking to his views *as if* his very life depended upon it that Matthew Arnold was to characterize as run-down Hebraism, as the English disease of philistinism, limited and reductive in its practicality. This helps us see, retrospectively, why Keats wanted to use the word 'Beauty' in a deep sense as an alternative to impossibly complete knowledge. Foster himself had sufficient scruple to concede that the key test of character was the ability to feel 'free' to change one's mind in the face of what now appeared as a fresh truth, without self-destruction as a necessary consequence. But too much of his model was already founded upon the idea of strength, as *opposed* to both the world outside and weakness inside, for it to be possible for the ego to tolerate uncertainty as Keats proposed.

For what of Keats's way? It is clear that 'Negative Capability' is different from that Puritanism which had Bunyan's Man admitting 'No' when asked if he saw his way to belief. 'Negative Capability' is proposed as a halfway house, innocent of a sense of defeat as the Hebraic positive incapability is *not* in its guilt and conflict and need for self-testing. Negative Capability, on the other hand, offers a chance, beyond ego, 'to let the mind *be* a thoroughfare for all thoughts. Not a select party' – in contrast to 'irritable reaching' for truth, entire, at all costs; in contrast to the hammering of the nail. By 1869 Arnold had made the contrast polemically definite:

> while Hebraism seizes upon certain plain, capital intimations of the universal order, and rivets itself, one may say, with unequalled grandeur of earnestness and intensity on the study and observance of them, the bent of Hellenism is to follow, with flexible activity, the whole play of the universal order, to be apprehensive of missing any part of it, of sacrificing one part to another, to slip away from resting in this or that intimation of it, however capital. An unclouded clearness of mind, an unimpeded play of thought, is what this bent drives at. The governing idea of Hellenism is *spontaneity of consciousness;* that of Hebraism, *strictness of conscience.*[20]

Arnold offers the distinction between Hellenistic and Hebraic, where Keats defines Men of Genius in contrast to Men of Power: 'they have not any individuality, any determined Character. I would call the top and head of those who have a proper self Men of Power.'[21] The Poet is one type of the Man of Genius: 'he has no Identity – he is continually in for – and filling some other Body'.[22] But Keats's Men of Genius were, it seems, either men who gave their lives to poetry in this way, such as Shakespeare, or those who led such incarnately poetic lives, like Socrates and Jesus, that others felt bound to devote writings to them. In this reckoning, therefore, Johnson is a Man of Power, not a Poet. And it is Poetry, implicit or explicit, that is beginning to stand for the highest human meaning of life.

'He must divest himself of the prejudices of his age and country...He must write as the interpreter of nature and the legislator of mankind, and consider himself as presiding over the thoughts and manners of future generations; as a being superior to time and place.' Yet who is this speaking? Not Keats or Shelley but Johnson's Imlac at the end of Chapter V of *Rasselas*.

In what way, then, was Johnson no Poet? We can guess at Keats's view. What Poetry stands for in Keats is Imagination. Imagination, moreover, not as a dangerously delusive reflex of frustrated desire – as though to say: if I can't be it, at least I can imagine it; but, less fallen, Imagination as a form of innocent potential. As if we could be anything, anything. 'It is an old maxim of mine and of course must be well known,' wrote Keats, 'that every point of thought is the centre of an intellectual world.'[23] This is what Hutton might have called turning inside out. For with the mind as a thoroughfare for all thoughts, each thought, being detached from sequence, may grow independently into the world which a person centred upon that thought thereby brings into being. It is as though, neo-Platonically, people are essentially who they are, and things what they are, because of the particular Thought they incarnate. How many such thoughts, I wonder, make up a person; how many may a person bear to hold and still remain one? Is there room for more than a single thought, with clarity? For if there are people such as Howard who, for practical purposes, decide they have 'one thing to do', there are others who, for better and worse perhaps, lose themselves in fragmentary and diverse purposes, too multiple to offer distinction. In that case, the thing that the Poet exists for, as Keats sees it, is to hold in mind, like a memory or reservoir, the lives of those many, manifest there as thoughts, populating the imagination – to which the Poet himself sacrifices personal identity, while his anxieties about so doing are steadied by his impersonal sense of vocation. That is what, I think, Negative Capability and Keats's own poem 'The Fall of Hyperion' are about. Where direct knowledge fails, we may ask: Shouldn't the quest for what human beings are *for* be conducted more in the realm of poetry than biography or morality, when in poetry the destruction of the ego can mean something much finer than it normally does in mere ordinary life?

For to the ordinary, practical urgency of a voice such as Foster's, insisting that we *must* be *something*, the voice of the Poet says chasteningly: we can be anything. Imagination will not surrender threshold-possibilities once and for all to the limitations of decisions of choice. Those who commit themselves to one way, not letting their minds *be* but making their minds *up*, thus scorn imagination in the first place and find in the second their imaginations returning upon them in twisted, inner forms, not now as the intimator of other possibilities but as the ghost of nagging doubt, harassing regret and frustrated desire, tormenting their own narrowness. This, plausibly, was the tragedy of the Poet in Thomas Hardy as in Samuel Johnson: the fear of imagination. 'The desires of mankind are much more numerous than their attainments, and the capacity of imagination much larger than actual enjoyment' (*The Rambler*, 104). Where Keats turned his thoughts into worlds and travelled through them, Johnson pulled past ages and speculations into his own mind, moving internally between different centres of gravity. That is to re-paraphrase Hutton's diagnosis.

What is more, Johnson himself may have recognized something disabling in him – even as he wrote such poetry as he did contrive. 'Great powers cannot be exerted,' he wrote in *The Idler*, 52, 'but when great exigencies make them necessary.' But since great exigencies are now few, great qualities 'lie hid, for the most part, like subterranean treasures, over which the foot passes as on common ground, till necessity breaks open the goldern cavern'. What then were the exigencies of Johnson's poetry? All too often, the mere exigencies of rhyme, the poet counting his lines to see where he could stop. For there is always a sense when reading Johnson, even at his most apparently final, that he tacitly thinks he could have written almost anything, something different under even slightly different circumstances. If this is testimony to the potential of his talent and to his endless capacity for improvisation, it is also a sign of his uncertainty about knowledge, his conviction that human work was always incomplete, and his sense of the almost endless permutations of human vanity. In *The Vanity of Human Wishes* (1749) there are no longer those moments when the 'treasure' of his thought is conclusively displayed as in the earlier *London* (1738):

> This mournful Truth is ev'ry where confest,
> SLOW RISES WORTH, BY POVERTY DEPREST.

That sort of worth, rising through what tries to depress it, is more incarnate within the very movement of *The Vanity of Human Wishes* as it unrolls; a giant intellect within pigmy couplets:

> For why did *Wolsey* by the Steps of Fate,
> On weak Foundations raise th'enormous Weight?

> Yet hope not Life from Grief and Danger free,

Nor think the Doom of Man revers'd for thee:
Deign on the passing World to turn thine Eyes
And pause awhile from Learning to be wise;
There mark what Ills the Scholar's Life assail,
Toil, Envy, Want, the Garret, and the Jail.
See Nations slowly wise, and meanly just,
To buried Merit raise the tardy Bust.

Yet ev'n on this her Load Misfortune flings
To press the weary Minutes flagging Wings:
New Sorrow rises as the Day returns,
A Sister sickens, or a Daughter mourns.

Through rhyme Johnson could push himself to fill in the gaps, limiting the task from without, formally, and filling the dreaded vacuity, inside the lines themselves, until the light transience of verse across the page gave way to a sense of 'weight' down it, strugglingly. The treasures are subterranean indeed: 'buried Merit', 'raise', 'revers'd', 'rises as ... returns'. It is the verse of one who, like Archimedes, would raise the world if he could but find a point for a lever. The lines slip by, like moments, the cumulative weight falling on him like memory of losses again and again. Johnson's work becomes always based on experience, on second thought, on his own difficulties with work. After *The Vanity of Human Wishes*, both so final and so endless, he is a poet only within his prose: 'over which the foot passes as on common ground' – until, that is, the sheer care of the words reopens a deeper sense of meaning. In *Rasselas*, likewise, 'the load of life was much lightened' at times ('Proceed with thy narrative'), for as Imlac says, 'great works are performed, not by *strength*, but *perserverance*'.[24] But *The Vanity of Human Wishes*, though indeed magnificent, is a work of sheer, final *strength*. The poem could build itself once only upon its own defeats, make that its very subject, with perilous, tottering courage, and then no more. Such is Johnson at the very limits of poetry.

But poetry can take us further than that, if we believe as Keats does. Yet does Negative Capability really take us further than the desire or demand for Belief? There is something not quite right here. Arnold's sense of opposition between Hebraic and Hellenistic seems harder and more dogmatic than Hellenism itself would seem to consider healthy for the balance of the human mind. Partly, no doubt, that has to do with the nature of mid-nineteenth-century social conditions: the pressure of Hebraism transforming itself into the blinkeredess of hard-working, competitive capitalism at the height of the Industrial Revolution. Partly too, as Keats might be the first to suggest, it results from the over-literal and over-irritable nature of public prose that it should thus give *opinions* of things rather than *be* them incarnate. But it also goes deeper. For when Keats himself complains of Dilke's literally *making up* his 'Mind' 'about *every* thing', his own position becomes too emphatic in reaction: 'The *only* means of strengthening one's intellect is to make up one's mind about *nothing*'; Beauty '*obliterates all* consideration'; the Poet has '*no* Identity' and Men of Genius '*not any* individuality'. 'Only'? 'Nothing'? 'All'? 'No'? It is as though the very century deserves the title that Kierkegaard gave his major work – *Either/Or*.[25] Even those arguing against splits seem torn by them. Where is 'the right path' 'at an equal distance between the extremes of error'?

*

We have been using the imaginary quarrel between Foster and Keats as another, historically later way of reimagining the Johnsonian problem of finding a balance in life – of finding something in between purpose and acquiescence, in between seeking and finding meaning in existence, in between living without tension and living without wakefulness. In the second period of life, I have suggested, people often *need* advice, in the effort to balance themselves as adults, all the more so for there being no external necessity to prevent drifting. It is that mixture of internal necessity and the external lack of it that gives 'advice' its status as such. And advice on going through the eye of this needle is precisely what *The Rambler* offers in the very face of its own recognition that 'Of the numbers that pass their lives among books, very few read to be made wiser or better'.[26] As the man puts his self, his character, his identity, memory and experience into his writing, so he asks that we should only do likewise in relation to books. Is this beyond or below the aspirations of Keats's Negative Capability?

For the whole point about Johnson from a Keatsian point of view is that he can *only* give advice, only make literature a matter of powerfully explicit but still secondary edification. Yet is not putting it like that to miss something truly fine in Johnson's endeavour to find, as in *The Rambler*, 129, the middle way of prudence? Emphasis may serve here to highlight the complex turns and joins:

> Every man should, *indeed, carefully* compare his force with his undertaking; *for though* we ought *not* to live *only* for our own

sakes, and *though therefore* danger or difficulty should *not* be avoided *merely because* we may expose ourselves to misery or disgrace; *yet* it may be *justly required* of us, *not* to throw away our lives, upon inadequate and hopeless designs, *since* we might by a *just* estimate of our abilities become *more* useful to mankind.

That is advice fighting for access to the mind through a whole series of clauses that prepare the way for the balance of justice. Advice in *The Rambler* has to have just such a strategy if it is to have any hope of reasoned acceptance:

> All the force of reason and all the charms of language are indeed necessary to support positions which every man hears with a wish to confute them. Truth finds an easy entrance into the mind when it is introduced by desire, and attended by pleasure; but when she intrudes uncalled, and brings only fear and sorrow in her train, the passes of the intellect are barred against her by prejudice and passion; if she sometimes forces her way by the batteries of argument, she seldom long keeps possession of her conquests, but is ejected by some favoured enemy, or at best obtains only a nominal sovereignty, without influence and without authority. (*The Rambler*, 165)

You can feel just such a Johnsonian sentence having to work its way through long, fallen clauses of uncertainty, temptation and reconsideration of alternatives (not, but, if, or, though, without) in order to try to convince the enemies of truth, inside and out. It is indeed a way that assumes, unlike Keats's, that the thoroughfares of thought are customarily blocked and that in the postlapsarian world pleasure and beauty will reopen the passage more like gildings than like principles. An Arnoldian might well call that Hebraism indeed, in its very struggle to give general laws particular application as well as internal balance; though it also has within it more than a little of Hellenism's 'flexible activity'.

As Johnson keeps telling Boswell, we must *distinguish*; acts of distinguishing and abstracting being the very hallmarks of intelligence. There is, accordingly, a world of difference between Foster's 'severity of conviction, that he had *one thing to do*' and Johnson's belief, in his sermon on marriage, that 'the narrow limits of the human mind allow it not intensely to contemplate more than *one* idea'. And we can try to explain that difference, since between the two we may place in explanation Johnson's opposition to Pope's notion of the one Ruling Passion that each naturally had within him, the clue to the course of his whole subsequent life. For this was, said Johnson in his *Life of Pope*, a pernicious as well as a false doctrine in proposing a sort of irresistible moral predestination overruling our other efforts. For we need to recall that for Johnson life was looser than that, with an intrinsic uncertainty that a Foster could barely tolerate, and that life thus called for a more subtle discipline and intelligence than Arnold's later description of Hebraism allows. But these explanations and descriptions are themselves not Johnson's way. They miss that translated poetry which his own prose affords and which is itself one of the marks of his difference from men such as Foster. Let Saul Bellow's old man, Mr Sammler, a man who feels he does not belong to his own age, indicate what is at stake here:

> Intellectual man had become an explaining creature. Fathers to children, wives to husbands, lecturers to listeners, experts to layment, colleagues to colleagues, doctors to patients, man to his own soul, explained. The root of this, the causes of the other, the source of events, the history, the structure, the reasons why.

Is this not on the side of Negative Capability? Yet read on, it becomes truly Johnsonian:

> Not really. One had to learn to distinguish and distinguish and distinguish. It was distinguishing, not explanation, that mattered. Explanation was for the mental masses.

Johnson would not despise Isaac Watts, the popular explainer – far from it – as he would, however, despise the *tanti* men for always seeking reasons. But what lies behind the preference for distinguishing over explaining is not simply a sense of poetry but a belief that is religious:

> But inability to explain is no ground for disbelief. Not as long as the sense of God persists.[27]

Distinguishing is religious as well as practical, where explaining is neither; because to distinguish is to work on what is given, whereas to explain is to try to get behind it. Accordingly, what Johnson has to offer against the degenerated form of himself that Foster represents – and thus also against the necessity of Keats's complete overhaul of the unbeautiful, positive-seeking stance of character – may be expressed in the typical Johnsonian form of anecdote on the verge of parable. I have abstracted it from Boswell's *Life*, to show Johnson's very use of distinguishing as essential to the problem of balance, and I call it Johnson's parable of the Magistrate and the Martyr.

One day the argument had turned to matters of toleration. Johnson argued the Tory case as follows. It was reasonable of the magistrates, he said, to persecute the first Christians in order to uphold the integrity of the country for which they were responsible: 'Every man has a right to utter what he thinks truth, and every other man has a right to knock him down for it.'[28] The Christians could not expect tolerance if they wanted to spread the Word actively throughout the land; for tolerance was not primarily what they were seeking. They were seeking radical conversion. In such circumstances, at the level of the ways of the world where each side claims and disputes truth alike, disinterestedness becomes simply one prejudice knowing from its own side that it cannot expect the opposing prejudice to tolerate it. God knows, and each party only claims to know, which if any holds the truth. The magistrate from his point of view has a right to enforce what he thinks: he may be ultimately wrong within that but, relative to the form of things here, while he thinks himself right as to the welfare of his charge it is his duty to enforce his will. There is no disagreement about that from the other side, simply opposition according to those agreed terms. Within this form of things the Christian has a relevant content in the world but not of it. He has to ask: Is the magistrate right absolutely? But not only does he have to try to know the truth beyond the world's ways, he has to return with that truth into a world where he must still expect to suffer for it in the effort to establish it from within. 'The magistrate has a right to enforce what he thinks,' says the Tory in Johnson, and without disagreeing the Christian in him adds, 'and he who is conscious of the truth has a right to suffer.'[29] Martyrdom is the risk and the test. Johnson's conservatism goes hand-in-hand with a belief in the risk of individual radicalism within it: the two are not opposed but cover for each other, in rough justice. Johnson could see at one and the same time the necessity of both Magistrate and Martyr, though he knew that at any one time he could only be one or the other. Yet though he could only be *one at one time*, his way of thinking could enable him to be *one at a time*, either one depending on the circumstances and the belief; although his way of thinking also meant that he could not be certain in being *this one at this time*.

This form of practical thinking is quite alien to Arnold's liberal, cultural disinterestedness, quite different from Keats's imaginative disembodiment. At the very least it offers something valuable in between Foster's insistence that we must be somebody and Keats's recognition that we could be anybody. For it lets in purpose and flexibility, embodiment and temporality. Moreover, it is the expression of an eighteenth-century Anglicanism which has had to accommodate within its history both the break from Rome and its own resistance to dissenting breaks in England; both the necessity of the Civil War and the changes made and accepted in 1688. From its own days of disestablishment, Anglicanism had developed a tradition of what Johnson's beloved Jeremy Taylor called 'Christian Prudence': 'Be ye therefore wise as serpents, and harmless as doves'.[30] Better, says Taylor, an 'honest evasion' within the clothing of conformity to outward rules, than 'an open prostitution of our lives' in the glory of useless martyrdom. The Christians, in opposition, have a duty to buy their time before they can redeem it. This is what lies behind writings such as *The Rambler*, 129, on prudence as a middle way, distinguishing between that overcaution which is a parody of prudence and that overboldness which is a mere reaction to it. There Christianity inherits the tradition of Aristotle on virtue as the mean between false and extreme versions of itself. Prudence is the incarnation of the Christian in the world, when headstrong enthusiasm is ironically both too much of the world, in being an all too human version of religion, and yet too little really in it. When a woman poured precious ointment on the head of Jesus the disciples rebuked her for not having sold the ointment and given the money to the poor instead: it seemed to be one of their Master's Rules about wealth. But the Master's Rules are not Rules in the old, outwardly fixed sense; Jesus rebuked his disciples: 'Let her alone; why trouble ye her? she hath wrought a good work on me'.[31] We must distinguish. Although this is not Taylor's own example, the spirit of it lies behind his commendation of a fallen, human prudence which looks not for simple rules but for subtle patterns and openings. 'It is the duty of Christian prudence to choose the end of a Christian': for prudence is about recognizing the Christian end even in different or unusual appearances, and then finding the means to translate such an end into being.[32]

Thus in both Taylor and Johnson prudence has to do with *language* as an act of weighing the form and distinguishing the circumstance in which the spirit has to make its earthly way. Without prudence, says Taylor,

> simplicity would turn to silliness, zeal into passion, passion into

fury, religion into scandal, conversation into a snare, ambition into temptation, courtesies into danger.[33]

What is that which I am now doing properly to be called? This is what language offered as an act of moral *practice* for the Rambler himself, with all the problems of fitting words to things rather than things to words. For as Johnson typically puts it on the difficulty of application:

> There may be zeal without sincerity, and security without innocence.[34]

Even thus Johnson, sceptical of ever finding pure 'x' in human life without 'y', can make his scepticism productive of nearer, not farther, application. Anglicanism stressed the resources of the English language, such resources as we, as Christians, have in this place at this time; even though our language is not the tongue in which original Truth was told but a translation which has become our second nature and accommodation. For these are the terms in which we happen to live our lives: absolutely from our point of view, though relatively in the whole scheme of meaning. Here is Johnson steering his way:

> security and despair are equal follies, and as it is presumption and arrogance to anticipate triumphs, it is weakness and cowardice to prognosticate miscarriages.

> A student may easily exhaust his life in comparing divines and moralists, without any practical regard to morality or religion; he may be learning not to live, but to reason.[35]

Abstraction, division, distinction: these are the means by which we can at least see one thing at a time and modify confusion. In his struggle for balance which was also precision rather than fudging, Johnson was glad of the clarity of Dissenters such as Isaac Watts who, in returning Dissent to the common language, must have seemed to him to be remembering belatedly Anglicanism's own founding of principles. 'Since our Minds are narrow in their Capacity,' wrote Watts in a favourite book of Johnson's, 'and cannot survey the several Parts of any complex Being with one single view, as God sees all Things at once; therefore we must as it were take it to Pieces, and consider of the Parts separately that we may have a more complete Conception of the Whole.'[36] Words are those pieces to our mind, but even as we break it all down we have to build it all back up together again, precisely since no one word alone can distinctly manifest all the parts of a single complex idea and so must call for others. Even breaking it down opened it all up to come together again.

There is more to Johnson, therefore, than just failure – of knowledge, of poetry, of full imaginative actualization of all that he thought. Something apparently less than the richness of Negative Capability might actually turn out to be more. Often in this book, through anecdotes and novels, I have been trying to translate Johnson's prose wisdom, almost as austere in sheer language on the page as poetry itself, into terms that make what is at stake more recognizable. We have now to recognize that this is precisely what Johnson himself was doing: translating himself, his memory of culture and learning, his religion, into ordinary applications, as he testifies in the final *Rambler*:

> The essays professedly serious, if I have been able to execute my own intentions, will be found exactly conformable to the precepts of Christianity, without any accommodation to the licentiousness and levity of the present age. I therefore look back on this part of my work with pleasure, which no blame or praise of man shall diminish or augment. (*The Rambler*, 208)

Like 'prudence' or 'application', 'conformable' is not an exciting-looking word. Yet I do not think that this is just a tacked-on, apologetic nod to conventional religion. Such words give a clue as to what it might mean to have religion in a life or a life in religion without a great gulf between those two ways of seeing it. With Johnson as Anglican lay preacher we see a possible translation between the two, which itself may stand our own secular age in good stead if it ever wants to remember what having a religion in ordinary life was really like.

*

III   Johnson's Anglicanism (i): of prayers and silence

Those who doubt how deep Johnson's Protestant centre goes should listen to the following voice, earthily rooted in a common language and a native ground:

> 'When I am assailed by tribulation, I rush out among my pigs rather than remain alone,' he said on one occasion at table. 'The human heart is like a millstone in a mill; put wheat under it, and

it grinds the wheat to flour; put no wheat, and it still grinds on;
but then 'tis itself it wears away.'[37]

With some modification of style, this could almost be the voice of
Samuel Johnson: down-to-earth, roughly but humanely common-
sensical. It is in fact the voice of Martin Luther, another tough
Hebraic man, offering from the Reformation a voice of faith rooted
in the ordinary life and rich vernacular of a limited and familiar
homeland. Consciously living in a later, less dramatic and arguably
more civilized age than Luther's, Johnson provides a Protestant voice
which, in the next three sections of this chapter, I shall be arguing is
the deliberately unheroic lay tone of the Church of England. It is a
faith that has much to do with balance and with practice.

Luther's words may remind us how astonishing it is to realize that
so much of *The Rambler*'s practical advice about how to spend one's
time is actually what *morality* is: how we are to spend our time. 'A
wise man will make haste to forgive, because he knows the true value
of time, and will not suffer it to pass away in unnecessary pain'; 'It is a
maxim commonly received, that a wise man is never surprised . . .
[But] if a wise man is not amazed at sudden occurrences, it is not that
he has thought more, but less upon futurity'; 'He that can only be
useful in great occasions may die without exerting his abilities, and
stand a helpless spectator of a thousand vexations which fret away
happiness, and which nothing is required to remove but a little
dexterity of conduct and readiness of expedients.'[38] I think I have
learnt a lot, and have still a lot to learn, from Johnson on the many
forms of staying the right size: controlling anxiety and suspicion,
working in short stages and amidst ordinary circumstances, not
finding too much fault. These are at once both little things – being
manageable – and big things – being important; only Johnson makes
them both.

Yet for all the religious use of a common language, there is finally
in Johnson and in his Anglicanism a point of silence, where the
ordinary runs out and the extraordinary is not allowed to take over.
This is where we find Johnson saying 'no': he found his sense of
bounds, of what he was *for* at least negatively, when he found he had
to say 'no'. This was the man whom Boswell could hardly prevail
upon to speak of death. This is the Johnson whose scepticism
demolished Soame Jenyns's *A Free Enquiry into the Nature and Origin
of Evil* for claiming that everything on earth could be shown
rationally to be worked out for the best. The embargo Johnson

placed upon Jenyns – the shame is 'to think that there is any difference between him that gives no reason, and him that gives a reason, which by his confession cannot be conceived' – was an embargo he placed upon his own lips too.[39] But most of all this is the Johnson who, literary man as he was, declared in his *Life of Waller* that he did not believe poetry could be directly religious: poetry could not, that is to say, speak to God, in its artifice, as a much simpler prayer could. Thus, this is the Hebraic Man who did not think, as Keats or Shelley seem to have believed, that to be a Poet took a man to the height of being:

> Contemplative piety, or the intercourse between God and the human soul, cannot be poetical. Man admitted to implore the mercy of his Creator, and plead the merits of his Redeemer, is already in a higher state than poetry can confer.[40]

Poetry must fail and seem puny when 'applied to the decoration of something more excellent than itself'. Its tools of invention, selection, fancy and persuasion seem foolish before the thought of GOD: 'Omnipotence cannot be exalted; Infinity cannot be amplified; Perfection cannot be improved'.

This is the voice of Johnson, the great literary man, speaking of what is beyond literature. To some it must seem even in that to be betraying its limitations, and yet to me the stopping short seems to give more real intimation of seriousness and reverence than almost any articulate continuance might:

> The employments of pious meditation are Faith, Thanksgiving, Repentance, and Supplication. Faith, invariably uniform, cannot be invested by fancy with decorations. Thanksgiving, the most joyful of all holy effusions, yet addressed to a Being without passions, is confined to a few modes, and is to be felt rather than expressed. Repentence trembling in the presence of the judge, is not at leisure for cadences and epithets. Supplication of man to man may diffuse itself through many topicks of persuasion; but supplication to God can only cry for mercy.[41]

That voice, in 1781, is described by Boswell as having 'though I do not entirely agree with him . . . the merit of originality, with uncommon force and reasoning'.[42] But it goes deeper than that; it is the austere voice of high Anglicanism itself, to which Johnson had once specifically directed Boswell: on prayer being for neither information nor persuasion:

> He is beforehand with all our prayers, (Matt. vi. 8), 'Your
> Father knoweth what things ye have need of before ye ask him';
> and (Psal. cxxxix. 2), 'Thou understandest my thoughts afar
> off'. God knows our thoughts before the very heart that
> conceives them. And how, then, can he who is but of yesterday,
> suggest any thing new to that eternal mind! how can ignorance
> inform omniscience!
>
> 2dly, Neither does prayer prevail with God by way of
> persuasion, or working upon the affections, so as thereby to
> move him to pity or compassion. This, indeed, is the most usual
> and effectual way to prevail with men; who, for the generality,
> are, one part reason, and nine parts affection. . . . But God, who
> is as void of passion or affection, as he is of quantity or
> corporeity, is not to be dealt with this way. . . . In all passion, the
> mind suffers (as the very signification of the word imports), but
> absolute, entire perfection cannot suffer; it is and must be
> immovable, and by consequence impassible.[43]

The preacher is Robert South (1633–1716), much read by Johnson,
much quoted in his *Dictionary* and recommended by him to Boswell,
particularly for the Sermons on Prayer, in 1769.[44] The sermon is
virtually a defence of the *Book of Common Prayer*, being an attack
against the long extempore prayers of Nonconformity. The
convention of the set prayer is a coming together of the community:
'common prayer, which is the joint address of a whole congregation
with united voice, as well as heart'.[45] For to pray to a set form is to
join in the prayers of the whole Church of which this present
congregation is a part now standing for that whole and being
supported by it. On the other hand, when a man prays on his own he
has a terrible responsibility in which there is no time for the
modification of first by second thoughts and no place for all the
artifices of eloquence. 'The soul of man', says South, 'is but of a
limited nature in all its workings, and consequently cannot supply
two distinct faculties at the same time, to the same height of
operation': namely, the finding of words for prayer belongs to the
faculty of brain and invention; the finding of devotion to accompany
those expressions is the business of the heart.[46] Again, limitation
means the inability to be or to use more than one thing intensely at a
time.

It is clear that South stands to long extempore prayer as Johnson stands to religious poetry. Reading South, one can imagine why Johnson almost dreaded to mention the name of GOD, 'immovable', 'impassible' and (to Johnson perhaps most terrifyingly) 'void': 'how can ignorance inform omniscience!' Repentance can only tremble, says South, it has no leisure (as *Lycidas* regretably had, in Johnson's eyes) for 'cadences and epithets'. For the heart of prayer before God is to make Him 'the object of thy thoughts, who infinitely transcends them.'[47] At such times of realization the mind cannot properly think but only think that it is itself thought of: 'O Lord, thou hast searched me, and known me. Thou knowest my downsitting and mine uprising, thou understandest my thought afar off. . . . For there is not a word in my tongue, but, lo, O LORD, thou knowest it altogether' (Psalm 139). There is not a thought I think or word I say but Thou knowest it already – including this thought, this word. It is a strangely immediate and simultaneous doubleness: no sooner thought than known, known even before thought. And the set form of prayer makes it trebly thick, adding the presence of the human community in devotion and in trouble down all the ages, alike.

In the secular realm the writing that perhaps comes nearest to the vulnerable simultaneity of prayer is the writing of a letter, especially of confession. For a letter is writing at once very conscious of itself as being read, very aware that its subject is often also the autonomous person who will read it. We need to see what is at stake in saying that Johnson was a man of prayer rather than letter.

Here for example, then, is a letter of secular and individual confession made by Boswell in Holland at the age of twenty-five. He is writing of his unfitness to marry a girl; he is writing to the very father of that girl. Beneath the formal correctness of the procedure, the act of expressing doubts about the union to the very man who could authorize it seems to be as much incongruous as fitting:

> I must in all seriousness admit to you that these attacks of melancholy are sometimes so strong that it is well nigh impossible to support them, and at such times I am truly out of temper. To conclude, I have many faults; on my word, I mean what I say. My knowledge is very restricted. I have an excess of self-esteem. I cannot apply myself to study. I can nevertheless maintain my energy where my attention is interested. I have no sufficient zeal for life. I have the greatest imaginable difficulty in overcoming avarice . . . . I should require a prudent wife, a good housekeeper who would attend to everything and leave

me in peace. Judge, my worthy friend, if Zélide is capable of ever becoming such an one? Judge, I beg you, if she would not be happier with Monsieur de B—, who makes no such fastidious scrutiny, than with me who already have formed so severe a judgement of her.

I have at least this one consolation, that if my marriage with her were to prove unhappy, it could not be worse than I *fear*. It is equally true that matrimony is incapable of supplying greater felicity than I *hope* for from our union, which I sometimes contemplate with transports. I picture Zélide pious, prudent, kind, and tender, while retaining all her charms...[48]

As always with anything of Boswell's, the temptation is to resolve the difficulties of reading him into a dismissive criticism of his (undoubted) self-dramatization. But Boswell *used* his own fault of self-dramatization as a means of expressing all the human springs and malformations within himself that a more decorous and public literary account would not admit. This self-experiment was undertaken even at the risk and cost of the very means of dramatization disauthenticating everything that it revealed through the circular flaws of its own method. No wonder Boswell so hankered after Rousseau. So here, this letter is at once desperate, honest and scrupulous even in its doubts and fears, while also being self-congratulatory upon that very honesty and scruple, irresponsible even in its very sense of the responsibility to confess all this, anxious for rejection even in its sheer fair-mindedness and hope. It is as though one could read the letter straight for its content and ignore the machinery of consciousness that makes the confession possible; or one could read it with an eye on the form not as secondary means but as primary and self-damaging evidence, indirectly more revealing than its own internal confessions. There is no authority of one level over another here, only confusion between them. Boswell himself moves from one level to the other in a second: 'As a man of honour, I ask *you* to decide for *us*. I have set forth all my thoughts before you in a manner which *I am confident* will obtain *your praise*'; yet he also adds in postscript: 'Once for all, *I implore you* to take this letter in *good* part'; or again: 'All I ask of you, Sir, is to answer me *frankly*. I *deserve* it.'[49] To Boswell this confusion must have seemed productive of honesty, advertent and inadvertent alike, of life itself viewed as a leaky, untidy, undisciplinable thing. Perhaps no one in Johnson's acquaintance was more of an indicator of the approaching secular confusion of levels, categories and genres than Boswell. Johnson himself would surely have preferred the justly sharp replies that Zélide offered to the love letters of this middle-aged baby of a muddled twenty-five:

> You are *delighted* that I *blame* you for being too systematic; you are very well content to have, at twenty-five, the faults of a man of fifty. For my part, I am not clever enough to understand your felicity in this. Fault for fault, I like those of my own age, those which are natural to me, as well as any others.[50]

Johnson told Boswell, with mischievous good taste, 'I should have the Dutch lady'[51] – presumably for just that sort of ironic and lively intelligence which could so pointedly claim not to be 'clever enough' to be singular. Boswell (and one constantly must add: as he himself knew) always needed answering.

Johnson was always therefore a man of prayer, where Boswell was a man for a letter. Indeed, perhaps one reason for Johnson's admiration of Samuel Richardson's *Clarissa* lies in that novel's mixture of letter and prayer in the conflict of religious and secular, or sexual, ways of being. At any rate, it is in his formal prayers that we see Johnson private and alone, and these prayers are emphatically Anglican.

There was of course criticism of that formality in Johnson's own age. To a Nonconformist such as his contemporary John Wesley, the argument of the Church of England against extempore prayer and in favour of conformity to the *Book of Common Prayer* must have seemed a characteristic commitment to mere externals. After the Civil War in England, Martin Luther's call for justification by inner faith seemed to Wesley to have been stifled by a cautious and political conformity in works and practice. Of justification, sanctification and new birth the clergy of the Church of England, complained Wesley, speak 'as if it were an outward thing': 'I believe it is an inward thing'.[52]

But the purpose of the set forms of outwardness was both to sustain and to relieve the inward silence of the individual. We need to see the reality of this Anglican defence; what lies behind Johnson's saying that thanksgiving 'is to be *felt* rather than *expressed*'. These words do not belong to a tradition unconcerned with inward feeling. On 18 October 1767, aged fifty-eight, Johnson took his last leave of Catherine Chambers, the friend who herself had buried his father, brother and mother: she also was fifty-eight. It was, like Boswell's writing to Zélide's father 'you decide', another of those reflective situations in which the mind actively turns round upon its own passivity. For Johnson the natural result of such moments at the bounds of limitation, with consciousness conscious of its own status too in reflecting upon mortality, was prayer, or else madness. 'I desired all to withdraw, then told her that we were to part for ever; that as Christians, we should part with prayer; and that I would, if she was willing, say a short prayer beside her.' We are going to part for ever: the natural use of the world 'we' when beneath it 'you' and 'I' are actually going in different directions until I too die; the active formulation 'are going to part' ritualistically covering the passive sense of the truth; the unbelievable time when for once on earth we can say 'for ever' – these things have the same awesomeness at the bounds of sense as South's formulation that in prayer we make God the object of thoughts, even as He infinitely transcends and Himself thinks of them.

Johnson's prayer for Catherine, supported by such traditional simple mysteries, began thus:

> Almighty and most merciful Father, whose loving kindness is over all thy works, behold visit and relieve this thy servant, who is grieved with sickness. Grant that the sense of her weakness may add strength to her faith, and seriousness to her repentance.[53]

The first sentence seems to belong with the opening of the Anglican prayer for persons troubled in mind or in conscience: 'O Blessed Lord, the Father of mercies, and the God of all comforts; We beseech thee, look down in pity and compassion upon this thy afflicted servant'. The word 'this' in such prayers is that generalization at its most particular which Johnson himself would always have wished to approximate in his own writing: not just always set there for everyone but, activated, for anyone at any time, when the memory of human trouble takes flesh again. No one knows more about realization, that movement from words to their coming back to life, than Johnson. Similarly the second sentence – so much a Johnsonian mixture of pillar-to-post, yet with weakness at one level still creating the necessity for strength at another – is surely a memory of the prayer for a sick person, when there appeareth small hope of recovery: 'and the more the outward man decayeth, strengthen him, we beseech thee, so much the more continually with thy grace and holy Spirit in the inner man'. There is no talk of biographies now, of his being the same age as this woman, or of her having buried the rest of his family as he must now bury her. The prayer Johnson proposes in place of such unbearably silent, reflexive thoughts, but also in support of them, is 'a short prayer'.

It is a short prayer; for in South's words against long extempore prayer, 'all the usefulness of long speech, in human converse, is founded upon the defects and imperfections of human nature' – what was proper for *The Rambler* is improper now at the point where we all must put off the dressings of mortality:

> Nay, does not he present his Maker, not only with a more decent, but also with a more free and liberal oblation, who tenders him much in a little, and brings him his whole heart and soul wrapt up in three or four words, than he who, with full mouth and loud lungs, sends up whole volleys of articulate breath to the throne of grace?[54]

The way of much in little is more appropriate to our relative size. Moreover, the intense brevity of human limitation before Omnipotence, Infinity and Perfection is a thing founded not merely on an outward but an inner memory of *Common Prayer*; for in the same way, the sharing of language and trouble in *The Rambler* makes that work almost a lay version of the *Book of Common Prayer*. Tradition means something deeper to Johnson than the mere borrowing of a form of words in order to receive and revive their spirit for the sake of Catherine Chambers. 'Such a mutual communication of our thoughts being (as I may so speak) the next approach to intuition, and the nearest imitation of blessed spirits made perfect, that our condition in this world can possibly raise us to.'[55] The customary words become our moral intuition just as Burke argued that our prejudice made our virtues our habits, our duty our nature. Habit and the mysterious shaking down of the particular lessons of experience into a general second nature – these are for Johnson our fallen forms of intuition. More usually, as in *The Rambler*, the communication of thought is nothing like as immediate as it is in long-established set prayers: we have to work for Johnson's meaning in our own experience, just as he had had to work, through intelligence, for the words in which to express himself. There is always that gap between one person making sense and another realizing its meaning; a gap which writing and reading allow more time to attend to than do speaking and hearing.

In these moments of immediacy the English Church is at once so relative, to this particular tongue and custom, and so absolute, before God here. It is so temporary and also so lasting: in this place at this

time, look upon this thy servant – again and again but also always as
though for the first time, a living present. Burke was to find an
analogy in the idea of the nation itself:

> Our political system is placed in a just correspondence and
> symmetry with the order of the world, and with the mode of
> existence decreed to a permanent body composed of transitory
> parts; wherein, by the disposition of a stupendous wisdom,
> moulding together the great mysterious incorporation of the
> human race, the whole, at one time, is never old, or middle-
> aged, or young, but in a condition of unchangeable constancy,
> moves on through the varied tenour of perpetual decay, fall,
> renovation, and progression.[56]

Johnson would also have something bleaker to add, as in *The
Rambler*, 203:

> We know that the schemes of man are quickly at an end, that we
> must soon lie down in the grave with the forgotten multitudes of
> former ages, and yield our place to others, who, like us, shall be
> driven awhile, by hope or fear, about the surface of the earth,
> and then like us be lost in the shades of death.

Yet even as such, Tory Anglicanism in the eighteenth century is *that*
grand a vision of the one great, general human story; the species
incarnate in the individual, the individual a representative of the
mortal species, on and on in permanent transitoriness, 'mysterious'.
The Rambler is founded on that vision of strength and weakness, of
general particularity, of knowing how we do not know, of mortally
permanent transience as our lot.

Johnson was held down to earth by such paradoxes. There is a
silence which cuts his work short, a limitation which has to leave the
final things to the mystery of God. Yet that silence is partially picked
up again by his biographers, in their fear of waste and loss. For
Johnson's packed but short work is literature's loss as well as its
author's pain, and through the biographies there remains an almost
unspoken sense of human being, of essential residue valuably left as
unspeakable. No more than a part of Johnson belongs with Keats's
Men of Genius who were Poets, the men who dedicated their very
selves to literature. There is another part of him which, in the life,
made others write it down; a spiritual part which was in the man's
own written work, even behind it, but not entirely of it. As always
there is both success and failure in such facts, though we are too

limited, in truth, to see quite what they mean when existing simultaneously like this.

*

IV   Johnson's Anglicanism (ii): when Johnson said 'No' – beyond Negative Capability

In order to see what Johnson stood for deep in his spirit, I want to take two occasions on which he, (in Hutton's words) 'defending himself against the aggression of outer influences', virtually said 'no', reserving himself to the mystery of inner silence. These two occasions, both taken from Boswell but separated by nearly twenty years, between them suggest what it was to be – and remain being – Samuel Johnson.

In spring 1766 Boswell and Goldsmith began to talk to Johnson about his giving up writing for the theatre after the partial failure of his play *Irene*:

> BOSWELL. 'But, Sir, why don't you give us something in some other way?' GOLDSMITH. 'Ay, Sir, we have a claim upon you.' JOHNSON. 'No, Sir, I am not obliged to do any more. No man is obliged to do as much as he can do. A man is to have part of his life to himself. If a soldier has fought a good many campaigns, he is not to be blamed if he retires to ease and tranquillity. A physician, who has practised long in a great city, may be excused if he retires to a small town, and takes less practice. Now, Sir, the good I can do by my conversation bears the same proportion to the good I can do by my writings, that the practice of a physician, retired to a small town, does to his practice in a great city.' BOSWELL. 'But I wonder, Sir, you have not more pleasure in writing than in not writing.' JOHNSON. 'Sir, you may wonder.'[57]

Another refusal occurred on Friday 11 June 1784, during Johnson's last, farewell visit to Oxford and his old college. Talking about forms of prayer, Johnson confided to the Master:

> 'I have thought of getting together all the books of prayer which I could, selecting those which should appear to me the best, putting out some, inserting others, adding some prayers of my own, and prefixing a discourse on prayer.' We all now gathered about him, and two or three of us at a time joined in pressing

him to execute this plan. He seemed to be a little displeased at the manner of our importunity, and in great agitation called out, 'Do not talk thus of what is so aweful. I know not what time GOD will allow me in this world. There are many things which I wish to do.' Some of us persisted, and Dr Adams said, 'I never was more serious about any thing in my life.' JOHNSON. 'Let me alone, let me alone; I am over-powered.' And then he put his hands before his face, and reclined for some time upon the table.[58]

He died six months later, on 13 December 1784.

In this section I shall try to see how these two refusals go together in the man's way of being. First, I shall write a paragraph which I consider to be a false start, then try to say why it is.

In 1766 Johnson was saying, 'No man is obliged to do as much as he can do'. In 1784 he seems in agony about running out of time: 'There are many things which I wish to do'. Is 1784 the nemesis of 1766: the man who left off some of his work 'to have part of his life to himself' finds death not only taking that life but leaving its latter end filled with remorse for work undone? Johnson's private journal is full of notes like the following, made on 26 April 1772: 'On this day little has been done and this is now the last hour. In life little has been done, and life is very far advanced. Lord have mercy upon me.'[59] To a man obsessed with both time and limitation, the passing of a day – day after day – seemed emblematic of the passing of life itself in insidiously gradual, unheroic omissions. Is not this where the Social Man has to confront the Religious Man with his sense of wasted talents: 'Whatsoever thy hand findeth to do, do it with thy might; for there is no work, nor device, nor knowledge, nor wisdom, in the grave, whither thou goest'?[60] Even thus, Johnson as a lax youth had been confronted and 'over-matched' by the Hebraic austerities of high Anglicanism in William Law's *A Serious Call to a Devout and Holy Life*: 'As the whole world is God's, so the whole world is to act for God'; '[we are] beings that are to live above the world, all the time that they live in the world'; 'if, therefore, we are to live unto God at any time, or in any place, we are to live unto him at all times and in all places.'[61] In the meantime, since that early laxness, the Writer had preached against the Man: 'As he that lives longest lives but a little while, every man may be certain that he has no time to waste'.[62] And, to complete the vicious circle, perhaps that is why the Man had so often to cut the Writer out of his life in order to have (or was it waste?) part of his life to himself.

There may be some truth in the simplified account of failure I have just given, a truth that nags at the conscience which Johnson kept apart in his private and religious journals. But still I do not believe that the relation of 1766 to 1784 is thus essentially ironic and admonitory, any more than is *Rasselas*. The balances –between having a part of life to oneself and wasting time which should have been spent in work and works; between having to be something, a writer or a physician or a judge, and also simply being; between depressive sluggishness and periodic religious retreat and recollection – are finer that that; too fine for Johnson to be unwise enough to want them made verbally overexplicit. Traditionally enough, he refers to balance as the 'middle path'. In so doing he hides his particular difficulties – for example, with Law's 'there is no middle way to be taken, any more than there is a middle way betwixt pride and humility, or temperance and intemperance'[63] – within the form of a common term, even while restoring to that common term his implicit sense of uncommon difficulty involved in it: 'That there is a middle path which it is every man's duty to find, and to keep, is unaminously confessed; but it is likewise acknowledged that this middle path is so narrow, that it cannot easily be discovered, and so little beaten that there are no certain marks by which it can be followed' (*The Rambler*, 29). It is characteristic of Johnson thus to try to conceal one kind of mediocrity (his own need for balance) within the form of another (the commonness of the multitude): 'Happiness, as well as virtue, consists in mediocrity,' he writes in *The Rambler*, 38; 'the middle path is the road of security'; 'consider how much less is the calamity of not possessing great powers, than of not using them aright.' It was both a help and a rebuke to Johnson to write as though he were ordinary. Similarly the Anglican middle way was an easier way of holding in mind the difficulty of in-betweenness: 'In like manner Bernard: "Take away free will, and nothing is left to be saved: take away grace, and there is nothing left which can save." Therefore we must not so urge the liberty of the will as to be hostile to grace, nor so preach up grace as to take away free will.'[64] What Johnson's Anglicanism offered him, therefore, was the recognition – to use traditional language – that the way down could also turn out to be the way up: 'He delighted to express familiar thoughts in philosophical language; being in this the reverse of Socrates, who, it was said, reduced philosophy to the simplicity of common life.'[65] Johnson raised the common life to which he had descended even to the heights of philosophy. This is the two-in-one man he was – by a curious mixture of strategic duty, deviousness and grace.

'Perhaps, if we speak with rigorous exactness,' says Imlac in Chapter XLIV of *Rasselas*, 'no human mind is in its right state.' There is deviousness as well as prudence in Johnson; this he expected in himself and others alike: 'Human benevolence is mingled with vanity, interest, or some other motive'; 'To act from pure benevolence is not possible for finite beings'; 'If there are such [as do so act] under the earth, or in the clouds, I wish they would come up, or come down.'[66] But equally he also expected to pay a price for what was wrong in his mixed state.

Even so, the primary project of finding a middle path is not of itself a devious fudging. Think again of the 1766 refusal to write and the desire instead to live: 'No man is obliged to do as much as he can do.' We may imagine some amalgam of Boswell and Keats saying, 'I am surprised that you don't think writing to be your life': 'Sir, you *may* be'. Even more for such a Puritan as John Foster would there have seemed to be no choice in such a matter – or rather a choice so formulated and demanded as to leave no choice at all (which is perhaps why Foster himself went into mental paralysis):

> Some men seem to have been taken along by a succession of events, and, as it were, handed forward in helpless passiveness from one to another; having no determined principle in their own characters, by which they could constrain those events to serve a design formed antecedently to them, or apparently in defiance of them. The events seized them as neutral material, not they the events.[67]

The words become more and more violent: 'constrain', 'serve', 'defiance', 'seized'. Either character yields to time or time yields to character.

If we now put what we have learned in Chapters Three and Four together, we may see that the eighteenth century, at once so parochial and so cosmopolitan, had offered amidst a sense of limitation something also looser and more flexible, something more generous to ourselves in its idea of levels. William Warburton, Bishop of Gloucester, another Anglican humanist admired by Johnson, spoke for an age in which Man could be 'considered *under several Capacities*, as a *Religious*, a *Civil*, a *Rational* Animal, etc. And yet they all make but one and the same Man'.[68] For all Hutton's account of Johnson as a man aggressively defending himself against the world outside, it would be a mistake to take him simply as Foster's ideal of a strong character: to Boswell and Goldsmith, as they try to persuade him to further labour, Johnson seems paradoxically stronger than a man of single-minded principle who will always do his work without a 'no'. 'At different times,' said Boswell, 'he seemed a different man, in some respects': the shifting boundaries, the magistrate and the martyr.[69] Johnson's was the strength of a certain sort of looseness which he saw as the effect of time and practical experience working away at fixed principles.

Indeed, it was for this sort of strength that Johnson admired Richard Baxter (1615–91), the man in the midst of the era of Civil War whom the Roundheads took for a compromiser and the Cavaliers for a Puritan, and of whom an opponent said in exasperation: 'I would thou wert *either* hot or cold'.[70] One thing at a time, but there comes a time, after hot and after cold, which is made of both; such prudence is the beginning of that autonomy of character which Johnson himself loved in second-thought men like Baxter. For Baxter began in singularity, self-taught: 'so all those things were either new or great to me which were common and small to others'; but he aged into commonness: 'I knew much less than now, and yet was not half so much acquainted with my ignorance'. In age he knew more than he did when young; but what he knew was that he knew less for certain than the young man had supposed. The growth was also decay; that he now could not simply feel powerfully was both gain and loss, he knew. This secondary knowledge was for Johnson practical thought and a mark of character: 'Baxter, in the narrative of his own life, has enumerated several opinions which, though he thought them evident and incontestable at his first entrance into the world, time and experience disposed him to change' (*The Rambler*, 196). Thus Baxter confessed that now, as an older man, he was less interested in converting people: 'I find this effect mixed according to its causes, which are some *good* and some *bad*' – bad because of increasing impatience as well as decreasing surprise at human resistances and decaying physical vehemence-for-truth; good because of greater tolerance in respecting the general essentials in which men may conform and in not therefore working on them outside the terms in which they have their lives. This mixture, so deep as to feel like the settling down of the complexity of life into something beyond any one emotional expression, was pure Johnson too: so mixed a mixture as to be almost unspeakable, yet felt and registered at the level of the development of a whole character rather than a single feeling. To Johnson, Baxter's own character must have seemed that of an

Anglican misplaced by the forces of seventeenth-century history. For the Church of England was not to Johnson a dogma but the incarnation in this country, over much time, of a way of being.

Baxter, indeed, had called himself 'a mere Christian'. And such a man finds himself writing sentences like this: 'I now see more good and more evil in all men than heretofore I did' – the good are not so good, but the bad also not so bad as he had once thought.[71] This is the back-to-front immersion in the system of life that Johnson knew: 'As I know more of mankind I expect less of them,' he told Boswell, 'and am ready now to call a man *a good man*, upon easier terms that I was formerly.'[72] This is not in spite of practical knowledge but because of it. It is a magnificent *settling* for life, even though the sheer changeableness of mind and circumstances of itself allows no *rest*. Heaven was 'The Saint's Everlasting Rest' for Baxter: only there, he said, was there a cessation 'not of all action, but of that which hath the nature of a means, and implies the absence of the end'.[73] So much of practical thinking, the convolutions of so many sentences in *The Rambler*, has to nag away at means in the middle of things.

In virtually settling for being a writer part-time, by what he said to Boswell and Goldsmith in 1766, Johnson was giving an implicit sign. It was the sign of something beyond mere *means* of living, something which necessitated a flexible, provisional relation in him between being able to be anything and having to be something. As ever, such a relation was both for better –

JOHNSON. 'Mrs Thrale's mother said of me what flattered me much. A clergyman was complaining of want of society in the country where he lived; and said, "They talk of *runts*"; (that is, young cows). "Sir, (said Mrs Salusbury), Mr Johnson would learn to talk of runts": meaning that I was a man who would make the most of my situation, whatever it was.'[74]

– and for worse:

Sir William Scott . . . said to Johnson, 'What a pity it is, Sir, that you did not follow the profession of the law. You might have been Lord Chancellor of Great Britain, and attained to the dignity of the peerage; and now that the title of Lichfield, your native city, is extinct, you might have had it.' Johnson, upon this, seemed much agitated; and, in an angry tone, exclaimed, 'Why will you vex me by suggesting this, when it is too late?'[75]

Various are the modes by which a sense of potential is kept alive in a man's memory: Ambition, Disappointment, Temperance, Gusto, Propriety both as Adaptability and as Restraint. Yet beneath these ways of being reminded, there was in Johnson an underlying commitment which went deeper than any present form in which that commitment happened to manifest itself to him. Commitment to what, though? To a way of living and writing which in 1766 was expressed only negatively.

Nor is that way only that of the Tory gentleman in which Johnson liked (verbally!) to clothe himself – as when he told Mrs Thrale that 'it was the essence of a gentleman's character to bear the visible mark of no profession whatever'.[76] Behind his resolve not to give all his time to producing works of literature there was also Johnson's painful recognition of the limitation of mortal knowledge, a silence cutting work short. Yet from another centre of gravity within him, there was something almost the opposite of this: an intellectual pride and scorn in not being limited to one thing in life. Somewhere deep in Johnson, I have said, was the private desire to be a sort of Renaissance Universal Man, able to go anywhere into anything through sheer power of mind. 'He who is solicitous for his own improvement, must not be limited by local reputation, but select from every tribe of mortals their characteristical virtues, and constellate in himself the scattered graces which shine single in other men' (*The Rambler*, 201). Why else was he so liable to violent anger when it was lamented in his hearing that he had not been called to great office? Why did he devour or skim, rather than dutifully work through, so many books? This proud and voracious impulse was something Johnson could discipline or distract, but not destroy. Yet if the desire to be a Universal Man of Reason kept him out of the narrowness of specialization, the failure of the possibility of comprehensive knowledge kept him within a particular life – for his was, like Cowley's, 'a mind of large general powers, accidentally determined to some particular direction', yet still shooting up general thoughts out of that particular way.[77] Johnson had thus to hide his desire to be a Universal Man within the more chastened version of Representative Common Man:

> these scruples, if not too intricate, are of too extensive consideration for my present purpose, nor are they such as generally ocur in common life; and though casuistical knowledge be useful in proper hands, yet it ought by no means to be carelessly exposed, since most will use it rather to lull than awaken their own consciences; and the threads of reasoning, on

which truth is suspended, are frequently drawn to such
subtility, that common eyes cannot perceive, and common
sensibility cannot feel them. (*The Rambler*, 13)

In Johnson's mind, the modes of the social, the practical and the
sane thus came together. In writing *The Rambler* he was saved from his
more anguished 'scruples' by the idea of social duty. But just as his
own duty also served his turn, just so, reciprocally, the thoughts of the
nature of life that limited his writing, making him almost a part-time
writer, were themselves actually included within his writing. For this
is the alternative to Keats's way of giving one's life to be a Poet. There
are people who stop work at certain times or at certain levels – partly
because their work is about what stops them living fully (and indeed,
that can become a vicious circle); partly because of a sense of
priorities which the restarted work is then to embody. If they start
work for the sake of their lives, they may stop work not only for their
lives' sakes but for their work's sake too: 'As any action or posture
long continued, will distort and disfigure the limbs; so the mind
likewise is crippled and contracted by perpetual application to the
same act of ideas' (*The Rambler*,173). So much of Johnson's
character, making great what he does do, is about what he did not,
could not, would not do, and has to do instead. At the very least we
find in him the resistant raw material with which others have to
quarrel if they are to transmute it.

Yet this most authoritative of authors, when asked one day in 1784
for a final religious work in a mode that was essential to him – a book
of prayers – put his hands over his face and bowed his head on the
table, in full company. Did that expose to those outside, Johnson's
inner recognition that his life was in part a wasted, compromised one?
For all his achievements, large enough for most of us, a man still
lacking the major, self-justifying work of which he seemed
capable – his work being in fact in place of it?

Johnson's answer, for once, might well have been 'Yes' – but
without concession: this was what mortality was like, this was the
common end he had known about for so long and written of. 'And
Swift expires a Driv'ler and a Show.' The knowing of it, you may say,
is no defence. But for Johnson there *is* no defence in such matters; we
all end thinking, if think we still can, that we did not manage much,
with some truth. The fact that knowing this beforehand, even budget-
ing for it, makes only a little difference was for Johnson, however, no
simple irony but a sign that his sort of knowledge about life *was* life,
reality recognized on paper, confronted. Johnson's work, I have

argued, is always close to tautology or circularity, anticipating what still happens for all the anticipation.

So when we say: 'Doesn't it tell us something that a man who wanted time to himself finds, at the end of his life, that his time has run out?' the reply is, implicitly, yes, of course – but it tells us nothing we or he did not already know. 1766, 1784: different times, different needs; the need even for differences without the same pressure, freedom for a while; yet always the same pressure, beneath it all, forcing a person to dodge one way and another.'A man is to have part of his life to himself.' For not only did the wisdom of the writing threaten to 'cover' and anticipate the life, the wisdom of the writing was also to anticipate the very dangers of anticipation and dodge again:

> It is a maxim commonly received, that a wise man is never surprised ... But the truth is, that things to come, except when they approach very nearly, are equally hidden from men of all degrees of understanding; and if a wise man is not amazed at sudden occurrences, it is not that he has thought more, but less upon futurity. He never considered things not yet existing as the proper objects of his attention. (*The Rambler*, 29)

This turning of things round in themselves – like the fear of being too much afraid – becomes a shaking down of things, effecting out of all the turnings a courageous return to straightforwardness from a higher level. And this shaking down of one level inside another, of anticipation inside a knowledge of the dangers of anticipation, is the very opposite of Boswell's confused collapse of levels as we saw it in his confessional letter-writing. The truth is, Johnson needed his life to have a present tense free of his writing, as his writing itself could well understand. In the same way, for all the apparent opposition, he had needed to write in order not to live simply in the restrictions of the present: 'Whatever makes the past, the distant, or the future, predominate over the present, advances us in the dignity of thinking beings.'[78] Yet between the past and the future Johnson needed the room for a discretion and an ordinary sociability within the present; for if in this way he could, by another of those characteristics turns, fight for his right not always to have to be fighting, he need not feel himself to be merely slipping away or hanging round. The Stoic wise man had said, anti-Hebraically:

> Never confuse yourself by visions of an entire lifetime at once ... remember that it is not the weight of the future or the

past that is pressing upon you, but ever that of the present time.[79]

But Johnson could feel justified only in reclaiming such ordinariness through extraordinary efforts. Again, this was not merely ironical; he tested the claims of the ordinary even in his very acceptance of it, in order to distinguish it from the merely indifferent or laggardly. If he represents the basic raw material of an ordinary human life, he does so from the most sophisticated level.

When Johnson said in 1766 that he wanted time of his own away from the claims of work and the public, that he wanted to educate locally by speech without the hard definiteness of writing, all that was not the *cause* of the agony of 1784 when time ran out; for he knew that would come anyway. On the contrary, 1766 was paying tribute to 1784; it was already acknowledging how at the end we will fight for a few more minutes of precious life, by simply wanting those minutes earlier: pure being, room to breathe and talk, the thing itself not constantly to be used but also to be enjoyed.

But the Hebraic Enthusiast in Johnson cries: 'Is this the language of Religion?': 'Where are the painful toils of virtue, the mortifications of penitents, the self-denying exercises of saints and heroes?' And another voice answers: 'Suffering is no duty but where it is necessary to avoid guilt; nor pleasure a crime, but where it strengthens the influence of bad inclinations, or lessens the generous activity of virtue'; 'Society is the true sphere of human virtue ... a discipline of the human heart, useful to others, improving to itself' (*The Rambler*, 44). That other voice is vital to Johnson, and I shall continue to argue that it was to him the voice of the Church of England.

V Johnson's Anglicanism (iii): The ordinary mystery of the Church of England

Above all the Church of England was not – just as Johnson himself refused to be – specialized. Even the stringent William Law argued that the Christian way was not founded in the particular conditions and employments of this life, but (and this *was* its absolutism as well as its commonness) in the immutable nature of God and the general nature of man. In Law's language religious life has more to do with the adjective than the noun, with the spirit in which a thing is done rather than its particular embodiment:

> A man is not to be reasonable and holy, because he is a priest, or
> a father of a family; but he is to be a pious priest, and a good
> father, because piety and goodness are the laws of human
> nature.[80]

It is as though we cannot grasp 'piety and goodness' as nounal
absolutes in themselves; what we can do is practically apply and even
incarnate them within our ways and employments.

For this is the vision of a National Church – as Law magnificently
says, 'to redeem all orders of men into one holy society' and sustain a
'holiness of common life'.[81] Hooker had already distinguished a
society from a mere assembly: 'Men are assembled for performance
of public actions; which actions being ended, the assembly dissolveth
itself and is no longer in being, whereas the Church which was
assembled doth no less continue afterwards than before'.[82] Like life
itself, a society continued beyond its human ends and endings. Robert
South further refines that society's definition. For every man, he says,
may be considered under a double capacity or relation: as he is part of
the body politic with a particular station within the social community;
two, as he is a member of a spiritual and higher kingdom. The
temporal capacity is *not* to do with what is a man's own but with his
contribution to the public; the spiritual capacity is that a man should
pursue what is his own, the personal interest of his own salvation.
Where the two clash there is no doubt that temporal duty is to give
way to spiritual, but the ideal is to pursue the double capacity at once,
the one through the other, inside the other, like the soul within a
social body.[83] The stranger and pilgrim is to find temporary
accommodation in the ordinary life of England. Even so, to Bishop
Burnet the reconciliation of the two capacities was (he urged his
clergy) easiest for the clergy:

> The Clergy have one great advantage, beyond all the rest of the
> World, in this respect, besides all others, that whereas the
> particular Callings of Other Men, prove to them great
> Distractions, and lay many Temptations in their way, to divert
> them from minding their high and holy Calling of being
> Christians, it is quite otherwise with the Clergy, the more they
> follow their private Callings, they do the more certainly
> advance their general one: The better Priests they are, they
> become also the better Christians.[84]

Yet when Johnson was made tentative offers of a place among the
Clergy, what did he answer but 'No'! He refused, I believe, because he

felt he was not the man, as was Watts on the Dissenting side, to descend voluntarily and patiently to the mundane tasks of a parish priest among his people – and not a man willing to do less than that. There was still a bear there, as well as a laggard, a clubman and a high talker. But there was also, I suspect, a scruple of unwillingness to take advantage of the *special* way that Burnet's calling offered, to reconcile the temporal with the spiritual.

'Ever since the beginning of Christianity,' wrote Law, 'there hath been two orders or ranks of people amongst good Christians.' One 'feared and served God in the common offices and business of a secular worldly life'. The other 'raised above the ordinary state of nature' and 'renouncing the common business and common enjoyments of life', went into retirement; seeming 'dead to the life of this world, and having their bodies only upon earth', 'wholly separate and removed from ordinary conversation of common life'.[85] Though there remained a place for the second, retiring way within the Church of England, the drift of the idea of a national, Protestant priesthood was always towards bringing the second back within the life of the first, the common way. The more so, then, in a layman such as Johnson, to whom the voice of Religion said in *The Rambler,* 44:

> Return then with me from continual misery to moderate enjoyment, and grateful activity. Return from the contracted views of solitude to the proper duties of a relative and dependent being.

'I have thought of retiring, and have talked of it to a friend; but I find my vocation is rather to active life'; 'I said to the lady Abbess of a convent, "Madam, you are here, not for love of virtue, but the fear of vice."'[86] It was Johnson's vocation to *re-enter* the world, after knowing its vanity and predictability, rather than simply enter and remain without thought or experience. He re-entered the world because anyway you were always in it. 'For it is great to give up one's wish,' says Kierkegaard in *Fear and Trembling*, as another great Protestant, 'but is greater to hold it fast after having given it up, it is great to grasp the eternal, but it is greater to hold fast to the temporal after having given it up.'[87] Johnson's knowledge was, as we have seen, often circular, often consisting in a mere recognition at one level of knowledge's own limits or defeat at another. Even so, that paradox was a signal to him that this proud power which could recognize even its own powerlessness should 'return' to do what it could at a secondary level within the predicament it witnessed.

'Man knows the world only within himself,' said Goethe, and it was there, as a sort of microcosm, that Johnson was so powerful. But Goethe added, 'and he is aware of himself only within the world'.[88] For it was in the world, as a still 'relative and dependent being' for all that, that Johnson continued a more or less ordinary life, albeit from a different level of re-entry. He learned, from the Anglicanism of writers such as William Law, the subtlest rebounds. Law, for example, very much advocated the use of set, external habits of devotion because (as South also stresses) it is often so difficult for human beings to get themselves, of themselves, into the right spirit for prayer. Law therefore proposes a reversal: instead of working from inside-out, let us also work from outside-in: 'As the inward state of the mind produces outward actions suitable to it, so those outward actions have the like power of raising an inward state of mind suitable to them.' It is not as if, proudly and scrupulously, we cannot use the set words of fixed routine until we feel them innerly; we use the words and habits that we may, in using them, recover inner feeling through them. This flexibility, discretion, prudence is related to Law's sense of the union of soul and body, reciprocally acting upon each other, from within outwards, from without inwards. 'This union of our souls and bodies is the reason both why we have so little and so much power over ourselves.' *So little* 'because, outward objects act upon our bodies without our leave, so our bodies act upon our minds by the laws of the union of the soul and the body.' *So much* because

> as our souls, in a great measure, depend upon our bodies; and as we have great power over our bodies; as we can command our outward actions, and oblige ourselves to such habits of life as naturally produce habits in the soul ... so we have a great power over the inward state of our souls.[89]

The way to so much power is through the knowledge of so little power, that we may use our weaknesses as also our strengths. This almost devious use of our own ordinary condition – a deviousness toughly appropriate to a distrust of our own fallen inwardness – must have seemed a relief from the pressure for sudden, extraordinary inward spontaneity. Bishop Gibson had complained of the intolerable pressure which Enthusiasm put upon the individual; the Church of England would continue to teach that we were born again not instantaneously but 'by Degrees', lest good men should despair at once and not trust time; for the Christian religion 'is calculated for *common* life', 'suited for the *general* Situation and Circumstances of

Mankind'.[90] Johnson himself must have acknowledged the relief, as well as the humility, involved in working also from externals back inward. It was *like* him initially to keep the Knower inside him, as Mind, behind the outward man from whose experience, mistakes and feelings knowledge itself could be culled. But he had also to learn that the Knower could not simply stay inside his head, ready to be the author of *The Rambler*; the Knower had rather to get ahead also of the recalcitrant and dangerous man whose body he inhabited and work from outside-in, determining the situation in which that man was placed. It is a two-handed fight, the right often having to hide its working from the left.

Thus it was that Johnson could remain ultimately unshakeable in his principles even while using means to attain them which seemed momentarily to reverse his sense of priorities. That is to say, he could firmly believe in the subordination of external rituals to the internal spirit in which they were performed, just as he believed in the subordination of the body to the soul, and yet only begin to find the transcendence of that true inward spirit through the routine performance of religious practices in the first place.[91] Yet in Johnson the shaking down of things, what he called the *digestion* of them,[92] also meant that externals became part of his innermost mind: Boswell tells how he once hurried out of church without taking communion because, he later explained, he had not prepared himself for it. The mixture of inside and out sank down into something deeper than that opposition of terms from which it was first made up. The flexibility, the looseness, the shifting of boundaries and centres were themselves all still mixed with sober and stringent purpose.

In all this Johnson is the opposite of a Calvinist such as William Cowper. Or, perhaps more accurately, Cowper is like the inside of Johnson without either the resistance to or the support of externals. Here is Cowper describing the aftermath of his breakdown, living under the care of Dr Cotton, while still innerly convinced of his own damnation:

> I began to persuade myself, that while the execution of the sentence was suspended, it would be for my interest to indulge a less horrible train of ideas, than I had been accustomed to dwell upon. 'Eat, and drink, for to-morrow thou shalt be in hell,' was the maxim on which I proceeded. By this means, I entered into conversation with the Doctor, laughed at his stories, and told him some of my own to match them; still, however, carrying a sentence of irrevocable doom in my heart.

He observed the seeming alteration with pleasure. Believing, as well he might, that my smiles were sincere, he thought my recovery well nigh completed; but they were, in reality, like the green surface of a morass, pleasant to the eye, but a cover for nothing but rottenness and filth.[93]

To Cowper the ordinary is a surface, a cover, a seeming. If recovery is thus a deception for one who is damned, smiling distraction is likewise only a more outwardly sane form of madness: 'If, for a moment, a book or a companion stole away my attention from myself, a flash from hell seemed to be thrown into my mind immediately; and I said within myself, "What are these things to me, who am damned?" '[94] Time itself becomes only a distraction from eternity, the inward self horrified alike at both its own distance from and implicatedness in the external system of daily life on earth. The only reality is 'within', but that is also unbearable and unliveable-with; Cowper is therefore obliged, out of sheer exhaustion of 'attention', to live with an almost unbearably bearable 'normal' facade, eating, drinking, talking the while.

His friends tried to show Cowper from outside himself how cruelly wrong his internal self-diagnosis was. His mentor Newton got him to read of the case of Simon Browne. Browne was a dissenting minister who convinced himself of his own damnation and yet at the very height of his madness could still write utterly rational theological works – prefaced with a lucid account of what it was like to be without a mind. Browne's story was reprinted in the *Adventurer*, to which, of course, Johnson himself contributed: 'Of all the recorded delusions to which the human mind is subjected, none perhaps is more remarkable than this, which apparently could not be put into a form of words for description without demonstratively proving its fallacy'. It was a version of what the philosophers call the liar paradox: How could the man write so rationally of his own madness if he were indeed mad? Does the liar (Boswell?) speak true when he says he is an inveterate liar? Likewise, could not Cowper see that he only thought himself uniquely mad and uniquely damned, as Simon Browne had? Here is Cowper's answer:

I suppose no man would despair, if he did not apprehend something singular in the circumstances of his own story, something that discriminates it from that of every other man, and that induces despair as an inevitable consequence. You may encounter his unhappy persuasion with as many instances as you please, of persons who, like him, having renounced all hope, were yet restored; and may thence infer that he, like them, shall meet with a season of restoration; but it is in vain. Every such individual accounts himself an exception to all rules, and therefore the blessed reverse, that others have experienced, affords no ground of comfortable expectation to *him*. But you will say, it is reasonable to conclude that as all your predecessors in this vale of misery and horror have found themselves delightfully disappointed at last, so will you: – I grant the reasonableness of it; it would be sinful, perhaps, because uncharitable, to reason otherwise; but an argument, hypothetical in its nature, however rationally conducted, may lead to a false conclusion; and in this instance, so will yours.[95]

It is an impressively rational account of the limits of hypothetical reason and comparative probability, even though its rationality is by that very token self-dismissed as secondary. That there was something of Johnson in all this was a source of amazement of Boswell: 'Insanity, therefore, was the object of his most dismal apprehension; and he fancied himself seized by it, or approaching it, at the very time when he was giving proofs of a more than ordinary soundness and vigour of judgement.'[96] So sanely aware of the dangers of madness 'at the very time' he most feared it. In a curiously similar way, Hume the atheist – the man who could hardly understand how he could eat and drink after writing so sceptically about all existence – could use reason to argue against reason in what his critics claimed was thus a self-contradictory circle. Not at all, replied Hume to those accusers:

This patent (they say) has at first an authority proportion'd to the present and immediate authority of reason from which it is deriv'd. *But* as it is supposed to be contradictory to reason, it gradually diminishes the force of that governing power and its own at the same time; till at last they both vanish away into nothing by a regular and just diminution.[97]

In other words, the reason that attacks and the reason that is attacked mutually destroy each other in Hume. But Cowper takes that scepticism even into damnation: the room he makes for reason makes no difference to his despairing sense of his own half-madness as a punishment from God. Even thus he dismisses as no more than secondarily plausible one of the Rambler's central ideas – that the hardest, saddest but most important of life's lessons is the learning to shift from singular self-centredness to a more general, externalized perception of oneself as only one of many similar selves without privileged reality. To the sceptic of reason, as also to the fearer of madness and damnation, it must have seemed as though, however thorough your rational preparation, however elaborate your means, the resolution of whether finally you are right or saved rests on something perilously, inscrutably close to chance and risk. And Johnson had sufficient of the sceptic, the fearer and the religious enthusiast in him to know this feeling of sheer final chanciness beneath reason, choice and faith.

Yet far more than either Cowper or Hume, Johnson had a particularly intense interest in what seemed to make no difference. For one of the things he implicitly stands for is a complex strategy of playing safe and taking a chance at once, taking a chance on safety. It is hard to explain this, although we saw something of it in relation to Imlac at the end of our last chapter; but I shall try to show what is involved.

There was something in Johnson that loved the flexibly self-dissolving nature involved in the apparent protection of certain ways of being. Authors, for example, were never so much an object-lesson to other men as when they thought themselves separate from the ordinary run. There were also more positive examples. Johnson, for instance, must have relished Baxter's description of his moderate Presbyterian party – 'I am loth to call them a *party* because they were for Catholicism against parties'.[98] A party dissolving itself precisely by being against parties, restoring the old meaning of Catholicism against sectarianism and bringing itself back from 'party' to life: that too was for Johnson the implicit meaning of eighteenth-century Anglicanism, having shaking itself down into the nation's existence. It was like a man putting his extraordinariness into an ordinary life, without making authorship a special way of being. For it is as though Johnson had conceived of the supreme test of his Christianity and of himself to be a dissolving of his religion within an ordinariness that was almost representative of the nation – and then seeing, within a language of common sense, whether that religion survived incarnate; whether he, unlike a Cowper, could hold the spirtual within the temporal without any special name or sanction in so doing; whether there was a way in which it could be said that a religion both did and did not make a difference. For no one could ever quite know about such a project; by definition it was incarnate in the ordinary, the invisibility retained yet absorbed within the visible. Even when the projector *forgot* his project, even when the projector behaved ordinarily, he was carrying it out, in all the risks of apparently only safely falling away.

Indeed, in another sense this paradoxically special ordinariness or chancy safety was the very duty of Everyman, and included its own share of the mad audacity of the astronomer or the despair of Cowper. For Johnson often quoted William Law:

> Every man is to consider himself as a particular object of God's providence; under the same care and protection of God, as if the world had been made for him alone.

> You may fairly look upon yourself to be the greatest sinner that you know in the world... Because you know more of the folly of your own heart than you do of other people's.[99]

Johnson had to look upon himself as utterly alone, while also knowing that everyone else did so too: the social and the individual, like the martyr and the magistrate or like writing and living, were separate levels, each none the less maintained as such only by the thought of the other in it. The 'it makes no difference' irony – the irony that we are all the same both in wanting to be different and in not wanting to be alone – became conversely, for Johnson, the ground for an essentially religious project in which his own individuality was to be representative of our isolated sameness as individuals.

The strain of this could be immense, and it broke out at the thought of isolating death. Had the project failed? The hubris of being supremely ordinary? 'Shall I, who have been a teacher of others, myself be a castaway?' In characteristic double-bind – often the only way Johnson could find of holding things together – he cried out to those around him when his death was imminent:

> You all pretend to love me, but you do not love me so well as I myself do.[100]

Of course. Even when he cried out with such terrifying particularity, like the Cowper so long buried within him, it is still the voice of one also agonized to know that he is singular to himself only as others are to themselves. But for once the repression of silence is broken. To cry 'you do not love me as I myself do' was the cost, in life, of his managing the opposite, sanely, in his writing. Beneath the generic sanity Johnson had always to fear the expression of naked individuality as madness, but naked individuality in the end was precisely what God demanded, judged, sentenced to heaven or hell.

Yet up until that end Johnson kept individuality socially incarnate, amidst all men and women, an individual expressing himself most powerfully against mere individualism, until he had to deliver himself up singly, as all must. In the meantime Johnson's proud and humble contract was to be the lay spirit of the Church of England, religion translated into something almost no different from common sense. He knew what was at stake when he prayed, before starting *The Rambler:*

> Almighty God,... without whose grace all wisdom is folly, grant, I beseech Thee, that in this my undertaking thy Holy Spirit may not be withheld from me, but that I may promote thy glory, and the Salvation both of myself and others.[101]

To be so ordinarily religious as hardly to make the religion a visible difference; at the risk, furthermore, of a potentially damnable secularization which half-suited him anyway. This project of an unheroic, half-buried, lay mission seems almost vainglorious when put so nakedly. And Johnson himself never did spell it out: he could forget and still be in it, and he could see it as a common Christian duty, this project. But in a letter to Mrs Thrale (27 October 1777) he does speak of his own biographical interest in the private, secret simplicities that are both behind and absorbed into a person's increasingly complex schemes, until the person himself hardly remembers, or has to fully recall, the original idea. Sometimes in letters, he says, you can see it for all that: 'The original Idea is laid down in its simple purity, and all the supervenient conceptions are spread over it in stratum super stratum, as they happen to be formed.'[102] Johnson loved the simplicity of wholeheartedness, but knew one had to half-lose, half-commit it in the compromises of further complication. He himself has left few signs of his original Idea. But under the strata, by a sort of literary archaeology, we can discern the would-be Universal Man who found the ambitious task too much for a mortal and was forced, on second thought, into the ways of practice, supported not by absolute knowledge but by what Bishop Sanderson called the *via negationis* of relative experience: 'Look whatsoever thou findest in the creature, which savoureth of defect or imperfection, and know God is *not* such'.[103]

In this lay mission we have a clue to the way in which Imlac brought purposiveness and acquiescence into such a mutually self-dissolving relation, nameable only as what we call 'a life'. 'To me,' says the princess in the penultimate chapter of *Rasselas*, 'the choice of life is become less important.' There is something beyond that. But, like Imlac himself, Johnson's Anglicanism is neither specialized nor definitive. It can simply look vague. Yet, as neither specialized nor definitive, it precisely creates a greater, though freer, responsibility for practical moral discriminations in a life. Law himself warned of the narrow gap between a right and a wrong use and enjoyment of our estates in the world, for our specialist estates or habitual roles seem to define and protect us socially, even as they are luring and blinkering us into forgetfulness of a deeper function within them:

> What is more innocent than rest and retirement? And yet what more dangerous than sloth and idleness? What is more lawful than eating and drinking? And yet what more destructive of all virtue, what more fruitful of all vice, than sensuality and indulgence? How lawful and praiseworthy is the care of a family? And yet how certainly are many people rendered incapable of all virtue, by a wordly and solicitous temper.[104]

It all looks so definite in language and becomes so uncertain in practice. Johnson himself could forget his purposes, regret not being Lord Chancellor, let rest become sloth. 'We frequently fall into error and folly, not because the true principles of action are not known, but because, for a time, they are not remembered' (*The Rambler*, 175). Forgetting means that what at one level, from above, may be seen as a state of probation may be lived by us, down here, as ordinary day-to-day experience – and indeed, that is part of the test. We cannot bear always to remember, cannot live if we are ever remembering (even Law's is a 'Call' or reminder). And perhaps we have a right to that creaturely relief of forgetting and incarnating ourselves, precisely in so far as is consistent with our broader welfare and health of balance at other levels too. Nor can we always hold together in mind our own simultaneities of being: Johnson, for example, raising what is common even as he descends into it or both fearing and needing external habits. This looseness and complexity is both Christian freedom and the Christian burden. For although Anglicanism has to do with a people and a national destiny just as Judaism did, there is – as William Warburton pointed out – one crucial distinction:

> Both had in common, to be Political Societies by divine Appointment; but different in *this*, that God, for wise Ends, minutely prescribed the whole Mode of *Jewish* Policy; And *Christ*, on the contrary, with the same divine Wisdom, only

constituted the Church a Policied Society in *general;* and left the
Mode of it to human Discretion.[105]

The particulars have been left to us. For Johnson's God works not
now through direct, primary revelation and intervention but veiled
through secondary causes, such as illness or disappointment or relief.
He has to be inferred from indirect signs within the general structure
of things: as from the space left to discretion between the reciprocal
untrustworthiness of both hope and fear – between the two is the need
for faith. Even thus we may miss, or forget, the clues within the
ordinary.

To Johnson, therefore, the language of religion is no longer a
simple Rule or Prohibition but, more ordinarily and more widely, a
duty to a language of precision in what in our case had to be the
English tongue:

> To his lower faculties he must allow such gratifications as
> will, by refreshing him, invigorate his nobler pursuits ... He is
> intitled to a moderate share of whatever alleviating accom-
> modations this fair mansion of his merciful parent affords,
> consistent with his recovery. (*The Rambler,* 44)

It is that word 'consistent' that keeps faith between the temporal and
spiritual worlds. Morality is here to exercise itself upon the healthiest,
not the most starved, biological life of the human creature: that is its
biggest challenge, but also its best chance. Where Foster speaks
Puritanically of decision of character, Johnson the Anglican uses the
more sceptically possible word 'accommodation'. Accommodation
may look less heroic, as a way of ordinary compromise, but is in fact,
even by virtue of its near vagueness, a bigger thing: the challenge of
the fullest, least specific, way of a person's being none the less in line
with his potential and his duties. Least specific and defined in one
way; but most incarnated, personal and practical in another. The
healthiness of a creature's desire for happiness is an admission which
is part of the secret of Johnson's balance. In the sentences above we
can see him making room for it, as for 'recovery'.

*

VI Conclusion: A Religious Writer – his limits and endings

An Anglican such as South speaks sensibly of drawing 'the line nicely
between vice and virtue', for the case is, he admits, a difficult one

when general definitions 'come to subsist in particulars, and to be clothed and attended with several accidents and circumstances':

> Thus it is not always so obvious to distinguish between an act of liberality and an act of prodigality – between an act of courage and an act of rashness – an act of pusillanimity, and an act of great modesty or humility.[106].

But Johnson, starting even further inside the world, seeks not just to draw the line but make the sentence. And it is here, in refusing to allow the distinctions to be merely abstract and atomic, that by embedding them within a whole movement of mind he is truly and concretely a poet still. It is so with the man even when, in letters to friends during his last years, he is wretchedly prepared to have life state the terms, if only to hang on to it at all:

> it is culpable to murmur at the established order of the creation, as it is vain to oppose it. He that lives must grow old; and he that would rather grow old than die, has GOD to thank for the infirmities of old age.
>
> O! my friend, the approach of death is very dreadful. I am afraid to think on that which I know I cannot avoid.[107]

These sentences are signs of a great man: in the words of Isaac Watts, 'it is a sign of a large and capacious mind, if we can with one single view take in a variety of objects'.[108] Yet they also bespeak one who must see himself as 'a relative and dependent being'. It is Johnson's capacity to hold such things together, in the midst of his own sense of a limited ability to do so, that is so remarkable, as we have seen again and again. For these are characteristic Johnsonian sentences: at one centre of gravity, the man of emotion ('*I am afraid* to think . . .'); at another, the man of impersonal knowledge ('to think on that which *I know*); at another, the mortal man, whatever he thinks courageously or feels pusillanimously ('that which I know *I cannot avoid*'); while finally the writer has both to make and to watch the sentence by which he is sentenced, inside it and outside it at once. Indeed these letters, in contrast to Boswell's, are before men what South said prayer was before God: 'a man's passing sentence upon himself and his own condition'.[109] For such law-like sentences were to Johnson almost like the mortal condition itself: the content, with all its contradictions, held within a form which, on pain of a man's inner feelings, his own external knowledge had co-operated to make. Making sentences was

Johnson's achievement: the sentences self-subsistingly abiding in this place, like large heads full of different thoughts, centres, boundaries, turned within themselves into ways of carrying on and being:

> His mind resembled the vast amphitheatre, the Colisaeum at Rome. In the centre stood his judgement, which, like a mighty gladiator, combated those apprehensions that, like the wild beasts of the *Arena*, were all around in cells, ready to be let out upon him. After a conflict, he drove them back into their dens; but not killing them ... [110]

What Boswell describes there is the very arena of Johnson's syntax, the old man fighting at the centre of an established order in which he had also to acquiesce. 'He that lives must grow old; and he that would rather grow old than die, has GOD to *thank* for the infirmities of old age.' But the beasts of fear still circled him outside the writing. What writing did for Johnson was to give him room and time to get from one idea or centre to another, and to understand why he had to do so in the order of things: 'I am afraid to think/on that which I know/I cannot avoid'. The meaning of the whole seems just a fraction *beyond* the man who made up the sum of those parts: he cannot always quite hold it, except through the combination of the separate elements out of which it has come together. Such sentences mime the very experience of mind's existence in time, as Augustine himself realized:

> Not all the parts exist at once, but some must come as others go, and in this way together they make up the whole of which they are parts. Our speech follows the same rule, usings sounds to signify a meaning. For a sentence is not complete unless each word, once its syllables have been pronounced, gives way to make room for the next. ... In these things there is no place to rest, because they do not last. [111]

What writing does is make that transience permanently re-livable as transience; it is not God's true eternity. The characteristic Johnsonian sentence is curiously made up of the passing of its parts into itself. It divides the competition of thoughts in order to conquer human limitation, clause by clause: 'for the eye of the mind, like that of the body, can only extend its view to new objects, by losing sight of those which are before it' (*The Rambler*, 203). But in putting itself back together through the work of grammar, the sentence pushes the mind that made it almost beyond itself, as the nearest the eye of one part here below could get to God's-eye view above.

That is to say, the very working of the sentences, at the point of nearly breaking the bounds of human understanding, tacitly bespeaks the necessity for a God above all this to comprehend it. For consider a sentence from *The Rambler*, 189, on the feeble lies of people desperately trying to make themselves more important – the dividing marks are my own:

> But of the multitudes who struggle in vain for distinction
> and display their own merits
> only to feel more acutely the sting of neglect,
> a great part are wholly innocent of deceit,
> and are betrayed by infatuation and credulity
> to that scorn with which the universal love of praise incites us all
> to drive feeble competitors out of our way.

Hazlitt said of Johnson's writing that 'each sentence, revolving round its centre of gravity, is contained within itself like a couplet, and each paragraph forms itself into a stanza.'[112] But what is so marvellous is that this poetry of human integration works across several centres of gravity within a single sentence – and above it all, for this religious writer, is his thought of God, albeit unspoken. For that sentence from *The Rambler*, 189, would be a prayer were it not that, in Johnson, if God helps us at all, He helps (indirectly through second causes) those who help themselves – or rather, those who help themselves to help others. For the mind is here raised, from both 'neglect' by others and its own version of others' 'scorn', to a point of calmer understanding achieved via the ironies of 'only' in the third clause, 'innocent' in the fourth clause and 'betrayed' in the fifth; until 'feeble' is finally encountered not only by ludicrous competitiveness but by complex pity. The mind is thus obliged to make the transformation from parts to whole an imaginatively moral shift from competitiveness of part against part to a sheer magnanimity which we would normally consider beyond us. Yet we need that magnanimity for just those faults which so often prevent us exercising it in our turn, and the need for it in one part of us also makes us try to find it in another . We recognize this even in the midst of a sentence from the *Life of Savage* where Johnson is speaking of his friend's capacity to blame everything for his failures except himself:

> By Arts like these, *Arts which every man practices in some Degree*, and *to which too much of the little Tranquillity of Life is*

to be ascribed, Savage was always able to live at Peace with himself.[113]

Imlac's Being 'superior to time and place' here inserts itself in the *inferior* parts of that sentence, as emphasized: inserting itself partly like Imagination bursting through the limits, partly like Judgement presiding behind the life which can hardly face it, but most of all like Charity wrung out of the tight little spaces created by the pressures on all human lives, making even extraordinary behaviour part of our ordinary but now imaginative selves. This sympathetic yet tacit incorporation of himself into humiliating recognitions of shared weakness paradoxically makes Johnson larger, stronger and more elevated.

A sentence which preaches magnanimity still ends on the compulsion 'to drive feeble competitors out of our way'. Another, which describes a man's inability to live with himself, none the less ends with his being 'always able to live at Peace with himself'. That is to say, there is no real end to a typical Johnsonian sentence, in the midst of life. For all its apparent finality, the typical sentence customarily has its meaning in leading on or leaving behind thoughts which lie at the back of the mind, like those reflections of the mind upon the mind which the mind itself cannot wholly bear both to make and to receive at once. Where Augustine in his *Confessions* sought to hold open the mystery between the self that knows and the self that is known in the act of self-knowledge, Johnson hurries on below, keeping himself one, leaving the thing alone and silent.

Yet here is Johnson insisting on the importance of ending well:

> Whatever motive first incited action, has still greater force to stimulate perseverance; since he that might have lain still at first in blameless obscurity, cannot afterwards desist but with infamy and reproach. He, whom a doubtful promise of distant good, could encourage to set difficulties at defiance, ought not to remit his vigour, when he has almost obtained his recompence. To faint or loiter, when only the last efforts are required, is to steer the ship through tempests, and abandon it to the winds in sight of land; it is to break the ground and scatter the seed, and at last to neglect the harvest. (*The Rambler*, 207)

The passage seems to do what it describes: concretely *remember* in the very course of its formation the thought that originally prompted the man to write, and utterly bring that memory back to present, verbal life. To someone such as John Foster such writing might have seemed the very epitome of strength and finish:

> There is a great difficulty of what may be called *conclusive* writing and speaking. How seldom we feel at the end of the paragraph or discourse that something is *settled and done*. It lets our habit of thinking and feeling *just be as it was*. It rather carries on a parallel to the line of the mind, at a peaceful distance, than fires down a tangent to smite across it. The subject in question is still left afloat.... I want the speaker or writer ever and anon, as he ends a series of paragraphs, to *settle* some point irrevocably with a *vigorous knock* of persuasive decision, like an auctioneer, who with a rap of his hammer says, 'There! that's yours; I've done with it; now for the next.'[114]

Indeed, the difference between a sentence that runs parallel to the line of the mind and one that decisively cuts across it may be seen as a crucial distinction between Keats and Johnson. For where Keats so often seeks to release the mind – 'with a great poet the sense of Beauty overcomes every other consideration, or rather obliterates all consideration' – Johnson encouragingly rebukes the mind: 'to faint or loiter, when only the last efforts are required, is to steer the ship through tempests, and abandon it to the winds in sight of land.' In those sentences, 'or rather' is Keats's heightened parallelism; 'only' is Johnson's call for one more tolerable push. Those of us who need Johnson more than Keats need something more physical – the push of a word like 'only' – if they are ever to become more spiritual; more explicit if ever to become implicitly better.

And yet, for all the enlisting of such Hebraism against Negative Capability, there is something more to Johnson than that 'vigorous knock of persuasive decision' which Keats was to criticize in those who 'want to hammer their nail into you'. It is something which also doubts the complete capacity of a man to come to real, rather than self-deceptive, 'Peace with himself' while on earth. For beneath our passage from *The Rambler*, 207, on taking heart to realize at the end all that was implicitly at stake in the beginning, is the substance of Johnson's final *Idler*, 103, on the horror of the last, beyond all final human efforts:

> This secret horrour of the last is inseparable from a thinking being whose life is limited, and to whom death is dreadful. We always make a secret comparison between a part and the whole; the termination of any period of life reminds us that life itself has likewise its termination; when we have done any thing for

the last time, we involuntarily reflect that a part of the days allotted to us is past, and that as more is past there is less remaining.

It is very happily and kindly provided, that in every life there are certain pauses and interruptions, which force consideration upon the careless, and seriousness upon the light; points of time where one course of action ends and another begins; and by vicissitude of fortune, or alteration of employment, by change of place, or loss of friendship, we are forced to say of something, 'this is the last'.

An even and unvaried tenour of life always hides from our apprehension the approach of its end.... The uncertainty of our duration is impressed commonly by dissimilitude of condition; it is only by finding life changeable that we are reminded of its shortness.

As Johnson himself notes, this last *Idler* was itself written during Holy Week, the time which the Christian world sets apart for the review of life and the renewed consideration of its relation to religion. All this must have a strong bearing on Johnson's words to Boswell and Goldsmith in spring 1766 on the need to have time to be, to have part of his life left free from work's necessity, even with all the countervailing dangers of idling and wasting. Johnson was not to be driven always from pillar to post: 'there are certain pauses and interruptions'. 1766 was in effect a lay alternative to retirement within a holy order, just as Johnson's anxiety about doing his best at the end of his writings is a secular translation of what remains as a deeply religious concern. For the sheer strength of his apparent conclusiveness in his writing is no more the mere muscle of a practical he-man than it is a blanket disregard of all that Keats was to mean by Negative Capability. The end of anything, so far from being the bull's flourishing triumph, reminded Johnson of the final end of everything, including any of his last few words; religious needs were found in reason as well as in revelation; in the everyday as well as on the last day; on occasions when nothing is done as well as when something has to be done. For again there is a subtle balance: Johnson, feeling that 'secret horrour of the last', has to use that fear as also 'happily and kindly provided', not to end life but also to keep it going.

There is, that is to say, no real end to a typical Johnsonian sentence, because the sentences are about *keeping going* even when they seem to be most conclusively *ending*:

Thus men may be made inconstant by virtue and by vice, by too much or too little thought; yet inconstancy, however dignified by its motives, is always to be avoided, because life allows us but a small time for enquiry and experiment, and he that steadily endeavours at excellence, in whatever employment, will more benefit mankind than he that hesitates in choosing his part till he is called to the performance. The traveller that resolutely follows a rough and winding path, will sooner reach the end of his journey, than he that is always changing his direction and wastes the hours of daylight in looking for smoother ground, and shorter passages. (*The Rambler*, 63)

For the night cometh, when no man can work...

Reading such passages, it sometimes seems that if you *had* to risk putting into the hands of a person in despair the work of just one writer, you could trust Johnson not to let that person down. You can trust him always to pull himself together near the end, and us too; to support, encourage, urge continuance. And he can do this not by himself ending his essays with heroic exhortations but by even anticlimactic denials that all is over. That too is a sign of the man's essential faith, translated into common sense. In between sentences – as in between 'To faint and loiter, when only the last efforts are required, is to steer the ship through the tempests, and abandon it to the winds in sight of land' and 'it is to break the ground and scatter the seed, and at last to neglect the harvest' – we can sense this man, who felt he had scattered his own talents, feeling the responsibility to have another go, keep going, try again, himself too. For between those two big metaphors we can recognize, in small, one of those 'points of time where one course of action ends and another begins' – that point of momentary vacuum wherein the man secretly feels in himself the weight of life which the next moment he must again carry within it. 'We always make a secret comparison between a part and the whole', and even at their smallest Johnson's writings are parts that include that secret comparison within their still unashamedly mundane limitations.

*

We may conclude that at the very bounds of human being, Johnson is like on who stands, looks, and without ever quite ceasing to look up, still turns back to the matter at hand – any matter. For thus he stands at the end of his demolition of Soame Jenyns's Leibniz-inspired *A Free Inquiry into the Nature and Origin of Evil:*

> Our author, if I understand him right, pursues the argument thus: The religion of man produces evils, because the morality of man is imperfect; his morality is imperfect, that he may be justly a subject of punishment: he is made subject to punishment because the pain of part is necessary to the happiness of the whole; pain is necessary to happiness no mortal can tell why or how.
>
> Thus, after having clambered with great labour from one step of argumentation to another, instead of rising into the light of knowledge, we are devolved back into dark ignorance, and all our effort ends in belief that for the evils of life there is some good reason, and in confession, that the reason cannot be found. This is all that has been reproduced by the revival of *Chrysippus's* untractableness of matter, and the *Arabian* scale of existence. A system has been raised, which is so ready to fall to pieces of itself, that no great praise can be derived from its destruction. To object is always easy, and it has been well observed by a late writer, that *the hand which cannot build a hovel, may demolish a temple.*[115]

Like Wolsey trying to raise enormous weight on weak foundations, Jenyns collapses in the ruins of his own theory. Johnson, however, kept his head down: there was no difference between a man giving no reason and a man giving a reason which he said was inconceivable. Hence silence, while Johnson's modesty in the apparently final sentence bears relation also to his guilt. But the head down is still religious in being bowed, finite. For this was a man whose reach extended beyond his own grasp: he had to abide in a position necessarily short of consolidating that height from which he had looked down on his present position as inadequate and incomplete. Yet here I stand: character, belief.

Slipping back from the lure of the extraordinary, a man in his disappointment might find it difficult to continue to hold on to the ordinary, with its looseness. Johnson needed to remind himself, to remind himself not least of how and why the real challenge was in common life, because of its very undirectedness and indeterminacy. Sermon 15:

> Day rises after day, and one year follows another, and produces nothing, but resolutions without effect, and self-reproach

without reformation. The time destined for a new life lapses in silence; another time is fixed, and another lapses; but the same train of delusion still continues. He that sees his danger, doubts not his power of escaping it; and though he has deceived himself a thousand times, loses little of his confidence. The indignation excited by the past will, he thinks, secure him from any future failure. He retires to confirm his thoughts by meditation, and feels sentiments of piety powerful within him. He ventures again into the stream of life, and finds himself again carried away by the current.[116]

This is the writing which comes from the experience of years, at the apex of consciousness, built from below through time, not superimposed from above, as with Soame Jenyns. But 'nothing but *daily* experience could make it credible' that we behave as we do; thus, day rising after day:

EASTER DAY. APR. 7. 1765 ABOUT THREE IN THE MORNING. I purpose again to partake of the blessed Sacrament, yet when I consider how vainly I have hitherto resolved at this annual commemoration of my Saviour's death to regulate my life by his laws, I am almost afraid to renew my resolutions.

JUNE 1. 1770. Every Man naturally persuades himself that he can keep his resolutions... They therefore whom frequent failures have made desperate cease to form resolutions, and they who become cunning do not tell them. Those who do not make them, are very few, but of their effect little is perceived, for scarcely any man persists in a course of life planned by choice, but as he is restrained from deviation by some external power.

APR. 14 GOOD FRIDAY 1775... 10.30p.m.... When I find that so much of my life has stolen unprofitably away, and that I can descry by retrospection scarcely a few single days properly and vigorously employed, why do I yet try to resolve again? I try because Reformation is necessary and despair is criminal. I try in humble hope of the help of God.[117]

'Nothing, but resolutions without effect, and self-reproach without reformation.' Fifty-five, sixty, sixty-five... like Lawrence's Tom Brangwen in *The Rainbow*:

He was a man of forty-five. Forty-five! In five more years fifty,

Then sixty – then seventy – then it was finished. My God – and
one still was so unestablished! How did one grow old – how
could one become confident?...When did one come to an
end?... Did one never get old, never die. That was the clue. He
exulted strangely, with torture. He would go on with his wife, he
and she like two children camping in the plains.[118]

Only Johnson lost his own wife in 1752, when he was forty-three.
Instead his diaries, formed out of William Law's habits of devotion,
exist like children on the plains, beneath the lofty sermon which
seemed so much older, settled. Johnson was Moses to his own
childishness of Israel. It was his fate to see 'an end', write backwards
from it, and still have to go back and struggle within his own life
towards it. We can feel in those diary entries the knower and the seer
locked up within an errant body: he had returned to life, incarnated
himself, and now feared that, ironically, the incarnation was a form
of forgetful imprisonment on earth. The writer still struggles within
all that, making (with precision in language) 'some atonement for his
faults, if he warns others against his own failings', honestly
recommending 'to others, those attempts which he neglects himself'
(*The Rambler*, 14). It even made *him* carry on the attempts, his own
pupil inside-out.

   Johnson knew the 'cunning', as he calls it, of not telling. He told
Mrs Thrale that he was amazed that people let out their secrets as they
did, and often we can only see Johnson's back as he preaches from the
book of his own errors or prays in brevity to Him who is 'better able
to understand than he himself can be to express his own case'. When
Johnson prays to God, 'to enable me to drive from me all such
unquiet and perplexing thoughts as may mislead or hinder me in the
practice of those duties which Thou hast required', his language is
once again at the very bounds of human being, beyond the point at
which there is a need to particularize to One who already knows those
'unquiet and perplexing thoughts'. That double 'me' – 'enable me to
drive from me' – bespeaks one long used to shift centres and levels,
thought turning himself upon himself. It is also, magnificently, the
grammar of a man who knows, with Robert South, that God Who is
the object of these thoughts already knows and transcends them; that
the God *of* Whom the words speak is the God *to* Whom they are
spoken and the God *for* Whose help they pray, the God for Whom
they are ofered as worship and acknowledgement.[119] This is at the
very limits of human vulnerability and imagination, beyond even
poetry as far as Johnson was concerned; the prayer itself almost

above and beyond the man praying beneath it. 'And this is properly', says South, 'that which men call *to depend.*'[120]

Only once, I think, in his public work is Johnson ever so near the edge and almost beyond the bounds of mortality within which he resolved to live, and then it is a work which he wrote biographically outside himself, as it were, for someone else. It is a sermon written for William Dodd, a clergyman sentenced to death for forgery. But at some level Johnson must have felt himself akin to the forger-hypocrite, amidst all those vicious circles of writing better than he lived and the perpetual resolutions to live better yet: 'when I consider how vainly I have hitherto resolved at this annual commemoration of my Saviour's death to regulate my life by his laws, I am almost afraid to renew my resolution'. In charity, Johnson wrote the sermon of repentance for Dodd which the man could hardly write for himself – to be delivered before his similarly condemned fellow-prisoners:

> We must not allow ourselves to repine at those miseries which have followed our offences, but suffer, with silent humility and resigned patience, the punishment which we deserve; remembering that, according to the Apostle's decision, no praise is due to them who bear with 'patience to be buffeted for their faults'.... The shortness of the time which is before us, gives little power, even to ourselves, of distinguishing the effects of terrour from those of conviction; of deciding, whether our present sorrow for sin proceeds from abhorrence of guilt, or dread of punishment; whether the violence of our inordinate passions be totally subdued by fear of God, or only crushed and restrained by the temporary force of present calamity.[121]

'We' here are specifically those due to be executed, without time left in which to test, 'even to ourselves', the lastingness of our contrition. Johnson must have felt himself similarly, if less dramatically, double-bound when what he wrote as a philosopher comprehended the limitations he would still suffer from and live out of a minute later, in fear and trembling. – We do not know if we mean it; we would be *bound* to think we did mean it, of course; we say therefore we do not know if we mean it or we explain how people would delude themselves into it; and all the time amidst the infinite regressions, level of thought upon level of thought, it makes no difference – we are simply going to die, and there is somewhere the truth of what we are and mean, and it is a truth we are then going to be faced with, judged upon. Every man, said William Law, is to himself the greatest sinner in the world; he has to see that and then leave himself depending upon God.

A man like Dodd would be near tongue-tied with circularity: our sense of our individual uniqueness being plausibly so like everybody else's, our sense of the truth being so implicated in what we merely want it to be. Dodd looks as though he were defeated twice over: made to repent; but, by that very token of being *made*, thus also made to doubt the very value of such a repentance. Yet through Samuel Johnson, Dodd, like a fallen Adam, is given language that such a double defeat might not be silence deprived of repentance but the true voice of repentance even in that, praying for its very possibility against itself. 'Lord, I believe; help thou mine unbelief.' In the face of such a double defeat, to find words is an act of human faith, beyond any faith in one's own innocence, and under the very threat of death and damnation. Robert South urged brevity before God: 'let a man contract his expression where he cannot enlarge his affection'. But the miracle in this case lies in the perseverance with a few extra words, knowing as the preacher does that 'Death makes short work when it comes, and will teach him who would prevent it to make shorter'.[122]

Although Johnson saw the circles and regressions of irony, he wanted to resist the mechanisms of pre-emptive self-cancellation: I mean, for example, the way that the failure of resolution might seem to demand the cessation of the very right to resolve any more. 'I am almost afraid to renew my regulations' – but he does renew them, again and again, and it is not simply ironical or fraudulent that in being the continual object-lesson of his own sermon, Johnson was still trying to learn from it. 'I try because Reformation is necessary and despair is criminal. I try in humble hope of the help of God.' That is why 'I' do it: he tells himself why he does it, in *retrospective* explanation of the compulsion – and that is much greater than if he had told himself why he *should* do it; more self-baffled than a sermon; at that deep, real level of the self when it is a soul rooted in beliefs. Johnson continued to resolve, to write, to be kind, even when the very activities themselves seemed to point up their own deficiencies. For the circles of contradiction may also gear the circles of charity. The way we learn from our own mistakes, hints Johnson, may be in learning that we all continue to make them. That is how vicious circles can also become virtuous ones.

If we give it a chance. But where to Johnson-the-Anglican 'despair is criminal', Byron-the-Calvinist almost went so far as to seek self-punishment and imaginative criminality as a last resort. Johnson always lived under a tradition, a memory of Truth even if half-forgotten or mistranslated here below; he lived under the mind of his own writings as it looked down on him like divinely mandated conscience. He lived under the necessity. But Byron, in *Cain* and in *Manfred*, does not allow such a memory of the human disposition to hang above his physical life; he pulls it down *into* that life as a fate or a fake, using his own existence as an experiment to see if Truth was true. The one man under memory, with the bounds of the ordinary about him; the other with the memory working itself out within his acts, in a sort of extraordinarily individual race against life. They are two very different projects and purposes, from perhaps the two greatest characters in our literature. But Johnson's way gave him the complex freedom (as in the parable of the Magistrate and the Martyr) also to tell Boswell that he had not wished to make Dodd a saint; that his petition for the man's pardon was entirely at one with his judgement of him as guilty.

The Church of England, claiming continuity with the primitive church and the apostolic succession, vowed to maintain its national purpose incarnate, amidst all the differences, within its own country, under whatever was the established rule. In carrying on Johnson was like his Church which, at a different level, resolved (as South put it) 'while it parts with every thing else, to hold fast its integrity'.[123] Johnson was of course only one man, a lay figure always committed to being *in* the world and sometimes (for good and for ill) *of* it too. But I believe he almost thought he was a chosen man, a man of enormous God given talents; though, terrifyingly to himself, he could not be sure of the difference between thinking that and its mundane translation as egoism or madness such as *Rasselas*'s astronomer suffered.

This man of enormous talents could not be sure, that is to say, whether he had not let God down through his own inadequacies; *or* whether even in that it was not his chosenness to be a *great* failure, to write successfully about failure as another incarnate sufferer, a man chosen to represent human limitation to itself by another of God's strange ways of sacrifice. Johnson was utterly silent about this final transcendent idea – because in one way it made no difference. Either way he had to remain a failure and a struggler against failure, if he were either fulfilling or letting down some plan of God's. There may be a plan or there may be only his own consoling imagination of it; whichever it is, or whether there is or is not a vital difference between the two, these are thoughts which, in our limitation, we cannot really think. The shame is 'to think that there is any difference between him that gives no reason, and him that gives a reason which by his own confession cannot be conceived'. So Johnson kept silent, committed not to Calvinist self-cancellations but to the self-dissolving nature of Anglicanism as a lay mission apparently no different from living an ordinary life. It is the same double-bind as that by which he is *unlike* others most of all in thinking himself all too like them (as George Eliot says of Farebrother, the Vicar in *Middlemarch*). Johnson's final letter to Dodd on the eve of execution started, 'That which is appointed to *all* men is now coming upon you', and ended, 'let me beg that you make in your devotions one petition for *my* eternal welfare'.[125] Had Johnson been able to lift up his head and see the difference between himself and Dodd, it would have ceased to exist in its true spirit.

He stayed bowed instead, but without judging Dodd innocent either. After all the work of human judgement and all the distinctions of reason, to discover the limitations of both and yet cancel neither was for Johnson still to go on beyond or beneath (which was it?) the pair of them – in emotion, pity, charity, art, religious resignation. I love the memory of the people who use writing not only, in the first place, to make a strenuous criticism of life but also, in the second, to smudge their own fine print and return, even through their writing, to living again.

In Ford Madox Ford's *Parade's End*, Christopher Tietjens's General says to him: 'How do you define Anglican sainthood? The other fellows have canonizations, all shipshape like Sandhurst examinations. But us Anglicans ... I've heard fifty persons say your mother was a saint. She was. But why?'[125] Perhaps Anglican sainthood looks something like Johnson precisely in being unwilling and unable to call himself a saint. 'Taylor justly blames some pious persons, who indulge their fancies too much, set themselves, by the force of imagination, in the place of the ancient martyrs and confessors ... It is, says he, sufficient that you are able to encounter the temptations which now assault you.' 'I am ready now,' said Johnson, 'to call a man *a good man*, upon easier terms than I was formerly.' We may judge it 'sufficient' to call Johnson at least *that*, a good man – not least for being able to speak in that way.

CHAPTER SIX

'In which Nothing is Concluded'?

I 'He runs the great circle, and is still at home'?

Trying to write because afraid of not working, whilst frightened too
that writing was a way of not living, Dubin the biographer sat with
depression, still in his own vicious circle. 'Samuel Johnson', Dubin
remembers, 'sat on a three-legged stool in a tiny room, gazing into a
vile abyss. He prayed to God and it came back nought: "My memory
grows confused, and I know not how the days pass over me".'
Malamud's literary man is in trouble, an ageing man unable to get a
young girl out of his mind, unable to write of Lawrence and love; he is
getting nowhere:

> From his bookshelves he plucked an armful of lives and letters
> he knew well. Dubin thumbed through lives of Jung, Freud,
> Swift, Samuel Johnson, Chekhov, Goya, Montaigne, Ruskin,
> Darwin, Hardy, Mahler, Virginia Woolf. On August 21, 1581,
> Montaigne, after a night of torment, had passed a stone,
> 'having, to tell the truth, exactly the shape of a prick'. 'My
> thoughts have been clouded with sensuality . . .' Johnson
> lamented. 'A strange oblivion has overspread me.' 'I wind
> round and round in my present memories the spirals of my
> errors': Augustine. 'Why is it so dull here?' asks Chekhov. 'It is
> snowing, a blizzard, there is a draft from the windows, the stove
> is sizzling hot, I had the thought of writing, and am not writing
> anything.' 'I am sometimes so agitated that I can no longer
> stand myself,' Goya told a friend. 'I lack force and work little.'
> Freud devastated Dubin: 'Anyone turning biographer has
> committed himself to lies, to concealment, to hypocrisy, to
> flattery, and even to hiding his own lack of understanding: for
> biographical truth is not to be had, and even if it were it couldn't
> be useful.' 'I shall be like that tree,' said Swift, 'I shall die first at

the top.' 'But really, for me,' Lawrence wrote in a letter, 'it's been a devilish time ever since I was born. But for the fact that when one's got a job on, one ought to go through with it, I'd prefer to be dead any minute.' Dubin read to learn what he didn't know or might have forgotten. He sought insights as if hunting for burning bushes on Sinai: how men hold themselves together. But the biographies reminded him of the life he wasn't writing; the life he wasn't living.[1]

Seriousness in Malamud is always at the risk of making a fool of itself: the earnest man scrabbling among the shelves for dear life. And yet what was Johnson doing, what was in his mind, as he wrote, with what must now seem to us a much greater dignity, *The Vanity of Human Wishes*?

> There mark what Ills the Scholar's Life assail,
> Toil, Envy, Want, the Garret, and the Jail.
> See Nations slowly wise, and meanly just,
> To buried Merit raise the tardy Bust.
> If Dreams yet flatter, once again attend,
> Hear Lydiat's Life, and Galileo's End.
>
> ...
>
> From Lydia's Monarch should the Search descend,
> By Solon caution'd to regard his End,
> In Life's last Scene what Prodigies surprise,
> Fears of the Brave, and Follies of the Wise?
> From Marlb'rough's Eyes the Streams of Dotage flow,
> And Swift expires a Driv'ler and a Show.

Johnson's men are not only artists and intellectuals, and unlike Dubin Johnson, for all the ills of his own life as a scholar, is not lamed by self-consciousness. Nor is he in quite such danger of treating life as a part of art but, still, treats art as part of living. Yet, for all the difference between Malamud's novel and Johnson's poem, 'There mark', 'see', 'attend', 'hear', 'search', 'regard' – Johnson himself ransacks the lives of the great in despair of vanity, directing people such as both Rasselas and Dubin to the experience of mankind left on the shelves as well as in the heart.

Books, says Johnson in *The Rambler*, 87, are dead counsellors to whom we may attend when sheer pride prevents our listening to the advice of the living. Yet even the consultation that reading constitutes is still part of our flawed and partial way of being:

We are not unwilling to believe that man wiser than ourselves, from whose abilities we may receive advantage, without any danger of rivalry or opposition, and who affords us the light of his experience, without hurting our eyes by flashes of insolence...Yet so prevalent is the habit of comparing ourselves with others, while they remain within the reach of our passions, that books are seldom read with complete impartiality, but by those from whom the writer is placed at such a distance that his life or death is indifferent.

Perhaps not even then. For some good as well as some bad reasons, Dubin is not completely impartial in his reading of Johnson. And his best reason for being partial is the reason that Johnson himself probably would have disapproved of least: Dubin wants to apply what Johnson wrote to his own life. For indeed, this is what I am finally concerned with in this book: the question of how properly to use Johnson in practice – given that his writings so forcibly demand a living context which they themselves, in their linguistic abstraction, so austerely refuse to particularize.

Dubin, again:

Work generally pulls me out of the clutch of the subjective self; but since I'm not working well I have to spring myself another way, if I know another way. S. Johnson, unable to work, would walk twenty-six miles to Birmingham, to shake himself into shape. Dubin was not prodigal with miles, limited himself to four or five each day. 'The safe and general antidote against sorrow is employment,' Johnson said. Dubin hopes to find an antidote growing in nature.[2]

'Nothing like a little "agitation", Johnson had said, to escape misery': so the biographer sets himself daily, in the midst of winter and a writer's block, either a short or a long run from home and back.[3] 'He fought winter as if it were the true enemy', as if it were his depression and his block as well as outside those things, and so Dubin gradually forms for himself, outside-in, that crucial but ambiguous thing in Johnson – namely, a habit:[4]

He had fitted himself for the task: you did it daily and therefore could do it. The experience proved you could. He was compelling a willed experience to contend with another, unwilled, that lingered. But as soon as it became easier to do, the wind, freezing cold, and the icy earth, made it harder to do.

> If you stopped for a single day, much you had accomplished – at least got used to – you had to accomplish again.[5]

For the formation of habit in Johnson's work can kill or cure, is both gain and loss even at best. You lose the freedom – which perhaps you had only to feel worse. Or, the new order, the fresh start becomes the same old beginning again or even, in time, another confinement. It is of course defiantly marvellous that Johnson dare end so many of his moral essays short of revelation, on the very verge of anticlimax: *The Rambler*, 47, on the death of loved ones, from which Dubin himself quotes, merely concludes: 'Sorrow is a kind of rust of the soul, which every new idea contributes in its passage to scour away. It is the putrefaction of stagnant life, and is remedied by exercise and motion.' The mimetic lameness of such an ending short of death is actually a deliberate, sober challenge: that is it, stumbling and walking on, all that's on offer, get on and make do with what we have to. *But*, equally, Dubin has to carry on like this after *The Rambler* leaves off. Let us follow him in his course just a little further:

> There were times he turned back at the wooden bridge: temporary cure: felt he could get into writing if he tried. Dubin turned back rarely. He went on if when he thought of himself it touched pain. The trick was to get into the winter world and out of within – shift the weight of inner conflict to outside. The cock's tail turns where the cock's head had been . . . Segments of the road he had once thought level, he realized, were pitched up from five to ten degrees. He tried not to stop on the walk up; it was hard to get started again. Ravenous for summer, for an end to the barren season, he hurried on thinking of the next rise or bend. He felt with each step resistance of the long walk-run, monotony of self-inflicted cure. Climbing is not ascending. My will is my enemy. It restoreth not my soul. Yet he stayed with it . . .[6]

It is terrifying, almost to the point of a maddening confusion, to see this driven man thus running away from his trouble and struggling with it at virtually the same time. As day after day he takes the circular road from desk and back again, to get *out* of his own head, even in so doing is he not back *in* it? 'How can I keep from walking in circles? You can't if you live in them.'[7] He stays with it, but 'it' – as Johnson himself sees near the very beginning of *The Vanity of Human Wishes* – is both inside and outside him, and both of them against him:

> Then say how Hope and Fear, Desire and Hate,
> O'erspread with Snares the clouded Maze of Fate,
> Where wav'ring Man, betray'd by vent'rous Pride,
> To tread the dreary Paths without a Guide;
> As treach'rous Phantoms in the Mist delude,
> Shuns fancied Ills, or chases airy Good.

Really, more than just physically, Dubin is getting nowhere, wavering and venturing as from pillar to post. 'Climbing is not ascending.'

Yet talking of getting nowhere, let us take the road back to Johnson. Specifically, to the following from Chapter xxxv of *Rasselas*, where Imlac is faced with a princess who seems resolved never to get over the death of Pekuah, her lady-in-waiting:

> The state of a mind oppressed with a sudden calamity, said Imlac, is like that of the fabulous inhabitants of the new created earth, who, when the first night came upon them, supposed that day would never return. When the clouds of sorrow gather over us, we see nothing beyond them, nor can imagine how they will be dispelled: yet a new day succeeded to the night, and sorrow is never long without a dawn of ease. But they who restrain themselves from receiving comfort, do as the savages would have done, had they put out their eyes when it was dark. Our minds, like our bodies, are in continual flux: something is hourly lost, and something acquired. To lose much at once is inconvenient to either, but while the vital powers remain uninjured, nature will find the means of reparation. Distance has the same effect on the mind as on the eye, and while we glide along the stream of time, whatever we leave behind us is always lessening, and that which we approach increasing in magnitude. Do not suffer life to stagnate; it will grow muddy for want of motion: commit yourself again to the current of the world; Pekuah will vanish by degrees; you will meet in your way some other favourite, or learn to diffuse yourself in general conversation.

You will have to replace her either by particular concentration upon one other or by general diffusion among several. For Imlac, that is the economy of the sort of creature we are: Dubin has to fill up the space left by loss (of a desirable girl, of the ability to write) through his daily trial by running. 'Our minds, like our bodies': we switch from one to the other to dodge the trouble, fill the vacuum. Yet this almost seems to be the Outsider's view of ourselves that Johnson himself abhorred:

one quantity of love, or distraction, replaces the loss of a similar amount; what is close or approaching counts for more than what is distant and receding, almost automatically. This may not quite be the Stoic's all too human wish to be almost inhuman, as Seneca would have it:

> Even a person who has not deliberately put an end to his grief finds an end to it in the passing of time. And merely growing weary of sorrowing is quite shameful as a means of curing sorrow in the case of an enlightened man. I should prefer to see you abandoning grief than it abandoning you.[8]

But the difference is that Imlac prefers *time* to dignity and trusts that 'nature will find the means of reparation' more gently and safely than can the human will, unless it waits for time. In time, then, 'commit yourself again to the current of the world': if the would-be hero thinks the most important word in that phrase to be 'commit', any depressive will tell you that it is really 'again'. Not again: yes, again and again and again, stumbling but walking on. It is only the repetitions which Johnson puts him through that teach Rasselas anything about life. Yet the charge against Johnson and against Imlac which must have occurred to Dubin is simply this: that all the keeping going, the circling and returning, the calls for recommitment, are really still getting us nowhere. It is not as if Johnson's physcial realism of mind would allow him to say to us, as he might like to, '*Do not suffer*'. His predicament is both that he could not go so far as to say that and yet had also therefore to go further: 'Do not suffer *life to stagnate*; it will grow muddy for want of motion: commit yourself again . . .'. Again? Even if it gets us nowhere?

But who could think it right to let people, in one way or another, kill themselves through grief or despair? It drove Johnson into a fury that that very question was coming to be seen as something other than merely rhetorical. David Hume admired the Stoics for knowing themselves always free to commit suicide. Who or what is to stop them? is his new rhetorical question. And Johnson hated that sort of intelligence for being grounded, like a Stoic's, upon nothing, nothing but its own free operation. For our minds are to Johnson grounded, rooted in our bodies; and death itself, with banal and masterly regularity, shows that there is something more in our condition than intelligence, something which intelligence cannot merely play with but to which it must submit. That other great stoical anti-Stoic of the eighteenth century, Immanuel Kant, is equally firm in his own way:

The Stoic therefore considered it a prerogative of his personality as a wise man to walk out of this life with an undisturbed mind whenever he liked (as out of a smoke-filled room), not because he was afflicted by actual or anticipated ills, but simply because he could make use of nothing more in this life. And yet this very courage, this strength of mind – of not fearing death and of knowing of something which man can prize more highly than his life – ought to have been an ever so much greater motive for him not to destroy himself, a being having such authoritative superiority over the strongest sensible incentives; consequently, it ought to have been a motive for him not to deprive himself of life.[9]

What Kant offers here is an almost Johnsonian power of practical reason, but with Johnson's characteristic second thoughts now raised to the level of formal metaphysics: a man who has the power to commit suicide has even in that the reason not to; our despair is only the descendant of a prior grounding hope on which it is based – in itself it is nothing. The despair by which Johnson himself was sometimes plagued was also like suffering, equivocally, from nothing. At such moments he had to keep forcing himself round his mental circle in order to believe again, at the very bounds of sense, that this nothing *was* nothing, was not really there (in the sense that Samuel Beckett thinks it *is*). Our lives are grounded upon principles within us which we ourselves have not merely made up to fill a void and which are not merely our own to do with as we like: that is Johnson's belief. But the fear that Imlac's advice about keeping busy, keeping going, merely covers over an abyss beneath it is very strong still.

Yet perhaps what is at stake here ought finally to be put less formally, in a sort of novelist's story or modern parable. 'I love anecdotes,' Johnson told Boswell – and he went on to say that he thought books of the future might be made up just of short, interim anecdotes, their connections left implicit or awaiting realization: a body of raw material in lieu of the big system-making books. 'If a man is to wait till he weaves anecdotes into a system, we may be long in getting them, and get but a few, in comparison of what we might get.'[10]

A seventy-year-old man, John Bainbridge, remembers this: that one beautiful spring morning, over thirty years ago, he had bumped into a former schoolmaster of his, part-time poet, now retired. In retirement Potter had spent his time walking about in the mornings, writing in the afternoons: he must have been, Bainbridge recalls, much the same age as I am now. At any rate, Bainbridge remembers Potter telling him that his whole life seemed to him to have consisted, in essence, 'of a series of walks, short journeys taken years ago'. Is not this man Potter also Malamud's Dubin a few more years on, thinking of old Johnson too on a three-legged stool in a tiny room gazing into a vile abyss:

'I'm walking on an Easter Sunday morning in the village street where I was born to church. Early communion. I'm sixteen. Or I'm on my way to the library in the lunch hour from school. All this mainly in adolescence. Small trips with expectation. I never think about the arrival. That doesn't matter. It would be a disappointment, anyway. I don't know whether I'm thinking about real walks, or some composite figment of imagination. But on mornings like this these snatches, these bits of, hm, pedestrianism, make up an exact picture of my life. What do you think about that?...'

'You don't get anywhere, you say. And you don't include your later life, your maturity...You concentrate on what you haven't quite got rather than on what you have.'

'That's so...I tell you this, Bainbridge. If I could express this sense of travel, of going towards some good thing nonexistent as that may be, in a poem, that would be a sufficient justification for my life. I think this sense of intense purposive activity, the walk, leading generally nowhere, is typical of the human condition, or Western European/North American life. I would also claim that this applies equally, if not strongly, to people of the highest genius, because their objectives or expectations are so much greater.'

'What about religious people?'

'In theory, it should not apply. In fact it is just as apparent because their apprehension of God is so limited...the greater part of our lives is spent in a moderate, bearable muddle of pleasure and pain.'

'Have you tried to put this into verse?'

'Many times.'

'And failed?'

'And failed. It appears, as it must appear to you now, either banal or pretentious.'

'And yet it's the truth?'

'It is my truth.'

These are the 'cold gradations' that Dr Levet escaped.[11] What Potter helps to show is that those gradations are not only personal, with their memories of 'bearable muddle' and decay after first youth, but also carry more-than-personal resonances of 'Western European/ North American life'. For they are also the gradations that mark, for example, the descent from Bunyan's *The Pilgrim's Progress*, so strong of faith in getting somewhere, so much a favourite work of Johnson's, to the state of a man such as Thomas Hardy, hopelessly repeating his deadlock within imprisoningly short verses:

> Thus I; faltering forward,
> Leaves around me falling,
> Wind oozing thin through the thorn from norward
> And the women calling.　　　　('The Voice')

Situated as he is, chronologically and experientially, in between John Bunyan and Thomas Hardy, in between struggling faith and struggling doubt, can Johnson and the memory of Johnson do anything other now than succumb to the position of Hardy, Dubin, Potter – the men who, more or less, *want* to believe in a higher purpose but see the desire as more real, and less valuable, than the belief? Has Johnson not enough in him to help such people, because his way leads towards their impasse?

For these people are kin to, descendants from, Samuel Johnson. 'If I could express this sense of travel, of going towards some good thing, nonexistent as that may be, in a poem . . .'. Likewise Johnson himself admired, and wished he had written, these lines from Pope's 'An Essay on Criticism':

> In fearless youth we tempt the heights of arts,
> While from the bounded level of our mind,
> Short views we take, nor see the lengths behind,
> But more advanced, behold with strange surprise
> New, distant scenes of endless science rise!
> So pleased at first, the towering Alps we try,
> Mount o'er the vales, and seem to tread the sky;
> The eternal snows appear already past,
> And the first clouds and mountains seem the last:
> But those attained, we tremble to survey
> The growing labours of the lengthened way,
> The increasing prospect tires our wandering eyes,
> Hills peep o'er hills, and Alps on Alps arise! (220–32)

Montaigne said that the virtue of the soul did not consist in flying
high but in walking orderly.[12] In *Rasselas* the artist who would fly
'waved his pinions a while to gather air, then leaped from his stand,
and in an instant dropped into the lake': the wings 'which were of no
use in the air, sustained him in the water'.[13] The whole work ends with
a conclusion in which nothing is concluded, the prince full circle back
in Abissinia resolving to rule well a little kingdom but incorrigibly
never quite able to fix its limits. Quoting Cowper, Hazlitt complained
of Johnson: ' "He runs the great circle, and is still at home." No
advance is made by his writings in any sentiment, or mode of
reasoning.'[14] But it was crucial to Johnson's Anglican balance of
enjoying as well as using the world that he should resist, in Rasselas
himself, the self-harassing human obsession with purpose as if it were
synonomous with progress, with continual advance – and resist it
without falling into the opposite snare of depressive stagnation in
vacuity. Faced with a metaphysical Alps, was it not virtue of soul that
made Johnson a walker rather than a flyer, a survivor rather than a
seeker of transcendence – or was it something missing in him, which
thereafter made his way essentially and self-defeatingly *prosaic*?
Potter failed to write the poem about human failure, and just possibly
there was a logic in that: either because it was not true (save for him)
or because even he could not bear fully to realize its truth while
suffering under it. Our final task in this book, then, is another
thought-experiment: to try to test the use, the truth, the deficiencies of
Johnson – what Mudford called his moral utility – if the predicament
of the Dubins, Potters, Thomas Hardys and finally Samuel Becketts is
not to be a final judgement on him – or on life. As Johnson puts it
towards the close of the sort of poem Potter might have wished to
write, *The Vanity of Human Wishes*:

> Must helpless Man, in Ignorance sedate,
> Swim darkling down the Current of his Fate?
> Must no Dislike alarm, no Wishes rise,
> No Cries attempt the Mercies of the Skies?

*

II   'What about religious people?' – *Johnson* and the Essay on Man

Even people of the highest genius, Potter had said, feel this sense of
'intense purposive activity, leading generally nowhere' – perhaps

even feel it more powerfully, 'because their objectives or expectations are so much greater'.

'What about religious people?' Bainbridge had countered.

'In theory, it should not apply. In fact it is just as apparent because their apprehension of God is so limited.'

– And Johnson, said Dubin, prayed to God and it came back nought: 'My memory grows confused, and I know not how the days pass over me'. On this (flawed) Doctor's advice, Dubin takes his daily run, struggles on. But 'climbing is not ascending. My will is my enemy. It restoreth not my soul'. What can?

One of the books to which Dubin turned was Augustine's *Confessions*. But Johnson's religion seems always less than that; he does not seem to be one of the big old men of faith such as Augustine made himself into. Indeed, Johnson, I think, was relieved and comforted that Baxter, a man whom assuredly one would call a religious man, could still write in this strain:

> I am not so foolish as to pretend my certainty to be greater than it is merely because it is a dishonour to be less certain...My certainty that I am a man is before my certainty that there is a God...my certainty that there is a God is greater than my certainty that he requireth love and holiness of his creature; my certainty of *this* is greater than my certainty of the life of reward and punishment hereafter; my certainty of that is greater than my certainty of the endless duration of it and of the immortality of individuate souls; my certainty of the Deity is greater than my certainty of the Christian Faith; my certainty of the Christian Faith in its essentials is greater than my certainty of the perfection and infallibility of all the Holy Scriptures...[15]

Subjective certainty cannot go beyond the objective evidence. It supports my faith, says Baxter, that faith is thus consonant with the law of nature. Naturally I can only go thus far, and yet the gradations of relative certainty carry him further than you might expect of honest inadequacy. We creatures of limitation work backwards: not more certain in affirming, but more uncertain in denying as the issue rises in importance. Baxter would be more certain of the existence of God than that his own belief in Him would actually get him anywhere; more certain that it would get him somewhere than that disbelief would do better: 'And they that have attained to greater perfection and a higher degree of certainty than I should pity me and produce their evidence to help me.' Notice that second, tough 'and': evidence.

Johnson was a man who in many ways started from the bottom, not the top: 'My certainty that I am a man is before my certainty that there is a God.' But if Johnson's realism did mean thus beginning at the bottom, none the less that did not mean that he imprisoned himself in thinking that the lowest interpretation was therefore necessarily the most plausible. He had read Mandeville's *The Fable of the Bees* as a very young man and found that Mandeville's scepticism about idealistic, self-disinterested virtue had 'opened my views into real life very much'.[16] Johnson must have relished Mandeville's ripping open of the secret workings of human artifice, as though the play of levels within consciousness could get away from nature! 'The man of sense and education never exults more in his pride than when he hides it with the greatest dexterity, and in feasting on the applause which he is sure all good judges will pay to his behaviour.'[17] But Mandeville also argued, notoriously, that there was no true virtue in saving an innocent babe ready to drop into the fire: 'we only obliged ourselves; for to have seen it fall, and not strove to hinder it, would have caused a pain, which self-preservation compelled us to prevent.'[18] To Johnson this was indeed reductive, since it left true virtue defined as only that by which man helped others '*contrary* to the impulse of nature', in utter self-denial.[19] Mandeville, said Johnson, 'takes the narrowest system of morality, monastick morality, which holds pleasure itself to be a vice, such as eating salt with our fish, because it makes it taste better.'[20] Is it no virtue to help my own child because it also gives me pleasure to do so? In fact Mandeville plays the same sort of trick as the proud man who is proud of not seeming so: his low interpretations are created as such by artificially *raising* the definition of virtue above anything agreeable to nature. His cynicism is parasitic upon an idealism of his own devious creation. And although Johnson is deeply sceptical of arguments in favour of our living according to nature, whatever that is, he is even *more* sceptical of a morality or (like Baxter) a faith necessarily and invariably *opposed* to the ordinary limitations of what seems to be our general nature. Being more sceptical of one thing than another is the pessimistic equivalent of Baxter's practical series of relative gradations of certainty. 'Monastick morality' in its more narrowly absolute certainty was unacceptable to the Anglican search for a morality and a religion which, though undiluted, were none the less at home within our ordinary human possibilities.

There was therefore some careful way in which Johnson was prepared to start only from the bottom line of reality, feet on the ground. When Soame Jenyns, apologist for evil and suffering, tries to offer comfort like this:

> The sufferings of the sick are greatly relieved by many trifling gratifications imperceptible to others, and sometimes almost repaid by the inconceivable transports occasioned by the return of health and vigour

downright Johnson sweeps aside that 'sometimes almost' with his basic 'no':

> the compensations of sickness I have never found near to equivalence, and the transports of recovery only prove the intenseness of the pain.[21]

The joy of the release 'only proves' the pain of the imprisonment: Johnson will not have it turned round, from earth to heaven, even at the risk of seeming pessimistic, ungrateful, dissident or restrictive with his deliberate 'only'. Yet this is not a man who simply believes that we know best where the shoe pinches or that physical reality is invariably the basic and best purchase that we have upon the truth. For on the other hand, he can write this in *The Rambler*, 7:

> The senses have not only that advantage over conscience which things necessary must have over things chosen, but they have likewise a kind of prescription in their favour. We feared pain much earlier than we apprehended guilt, and were delighted with the sensations of pleasure, before we had capacities to be charmed with the beauty of rectitude. To this power, thus early established, and incessantly increasing, it must be remembered, that almost every man has, in some part of his life, added new strength by a voluntary or negligent subjection of himself...
>
> From the necessity of dispossessing the sensitive faculties of the influence which they must naturally gain by this preoccupation of the soul, arises that conflict between opposite desires, in the first endeavours after a religious life.

Thus what forced Johnson up to a higher level than that of the senses was, as by the logic of Baxter, the still lower thought, or fear, that the senses would enthral and ruin a man. It is entirely consistent with Johnson's refusing to trust 'the transports of recovery' that his empiricism is thus of a *mental relation* to physical reality rather than a simply bodily reaction. He was more certain of always feeling pain than of always feeling guilt; but he was more certain of the necessity mentally to check up on the evidence of the senses than he was of unthinkingly trusting them altogether. And again, if he was certain that it was not in reason for a morality or a religion to be utterly opposed to the bent of human nature, he was equally certain that no morality or religion would result from simply following the dictates of our nature as physically given: for the influence of the senses 'must *naturally* gain' from our original, immediate, low and close dependence upon them.

Looking thus at what physical Johnson retorted to Soame Jenyns alongside what religious Johnson warned in *The Rambler*, 7, we notice something very characteristic of the man: not a division or a contradiction so much as a recognition of the (paradoxical) human *necessity* to be *free* enough to say different things at different times according to different circumstances. In the eye of eternity two or more things may be true *at the same time.* But for a human being (for what Johnson in *The Rambler*, 110, called an 'incorporated mind') Time, with its specific and peremptory occasions, is both a rescue from the necessity of the whole eternal truth and a prevention of its possibility. Thus Johnson has to think at two levels: at the lowest he must think, practically, 'one thing at a time' in order to cope; at another, even so, he must recognize that there never is one thing at a time, that the experience of it at other times (never wholly the same but never utterly different) either is missed and wanted or obtrudes and complicates.[22] We build *up* from *below* in Johnson, we get Experience from experiences, something general from the accumulation and the shaking down of particulars:

> Great thoughts are always general, and consist in positions not limited by exceptions, and in descriptions not descending to minuteness.[23]

But this middle-order greatness is always almost self-dissolvingly turned back in Johnson, recommitted to the study of those particulars from which it was gained, or refinding at its own level that even the general is only one particular aspect of something ever greater rising like more Alps:

> As a question becomes more complicated and involved, and extends to a greater number of relations, disagreement of opinion will always be multiplied, not because we are irrational, but because we are finite beings, furnished with different kinds of knowledge, exerting different degrees of attention, one discovering consequences which escape another, none taking in

the whole concatenation of causes and effects, and most comprehending but a very small part; each comparing what he observes with a different criterion, and each referring it to a different purpose...

We have less reason to be surprised or offended when we find others differ from us in opinion, because we very often differ from ourselves...(*The Adventurer*, 107)

Thus there are always *at least* two differently facing thoughts at any one time for Johnson and some single resolution or priority temporarily required. The other aspect or aspects of the truth will be remembered later, elsewhere, as though in general storage for particular spontaneous recollection. That is why *The Rambler* as a whole counts for more than the sum of its particular essays: for as one part of an essay unpremeditatedly connects with or depends for its fuller, qualified meaning upon another, so we participatingly witness the supple living wholeness of one human being dividing and reconstituting himself spontaneously in the written equivalent of a life of differing days, thoughts and occasions. Yet this also means that at any particular time Johnson seems very tucked-up in himself, for having to think too many potential thoughts at once. In *The Rambler*, 25, to give a brief example, he writes with typically fused ambivalence that 'It is *natural* for those who have raised a Reputation by any Science, to exalt themselves as endowed by Heaven with peculiar Powers': natural, but not to be believed – for the lowering thought that there are no special gifts from above is kept within the encouragement that we all have but to try our human best. The two or more thoughts are compressed into one, for a specific local purpose, and may be reassembled differently for another; but always it seems, at such individual moments, that Johnson's mind is nearly too big for himself or for what he finds himself in.

Could a life be bigger and less knotted? What *about* the religious people, the bigger ones than even Baxter and Johnson? Dubin quoted Augustine's sense of equivalent dilemma: 'I wind round and round in my present memories the spirals of my errors'. But to Augustine, the state of being prepared to start only from the bottom, with whatever complicated qualifications and manoeuvres, was *the* error. For perhaps nowhere is there a more powerful example than Augustine of a person convinced of the sin of living the wrong way round – inside-out, upside-down, back-to-front – and struggling even from within to get out of himself at the very risk of simply turning yet another vicious circle. 'While I fled from it,' Augustine says of his own journey to faith, 'I still searched for it.'[24] For so long the solution, if there was one, had seemed to him to lie behind his own back, while his whole life was a symptom of moving away from it. All he had to go on was all he had to get away from, but that was also all he had. He cries to God:

if I exist in you, how can I call upon you to come to me?[25]

How do I get the right way round? How can I deduce my way back from thinking myself whole and yet inadequate to seeing myself as but a part of a whole universe? As Pope put it in his *Essay on Man*:

> God loves from whole to parts: but human soul
> Must rise from individual to the whole. (IV, 361–2)

If a human life cannot turn round within itself in that way, then it suffers from the truth which it does not have but which, rather, has it: 'for it cannot conceal itself from the truth, but truth remains hidden from it'.[26]

A part of Johnson always feared that he was not fully converted: that he had played a dangerously safe game, tucking himself up within his very own warnings against thus playing safe *and* against its rash opposites. Moreover, there had been one Augustan poet who seemed to be able to go further than Johnson and whom Johnson therefore read, still on edge between scepticism and self-doubt, as though in a test. The poet was Pope, the poem *An Essay on Man*. For the very opening of the second epistle must have reminded Johnson, oddly, of himself:

> Know then thyself, presume not God to scan;
> The proper study of mankind is Man.
> Placed on this isthmus of a middle state,
> A being darkly wise, and rudely great:
> With too much knowledge for the Sceptic side,
> With too much weakness for the Stoic's pride,
> He hangs between; in doubt to act, or rest,
> In doubt to deem himself a God, or Beast;
> In doubt his Mind or Body to prefer,
> Born but to die, and reas'ning but to err;
> Alike in ignorance, his reason such,
> Whether he thinks too little, or too much:
> Chaos of Thought and Passion, all confus'd (II, 1–13)

For what could be more like Johnson's own view of Man? The same stress on limitation on earth ('presume not God to scan'), on in-betweenness ('He hangs between', 'Whether he thinks too little, or too much'), on a pillar-to-post existence ('With too much knowledge ... With too much weakness'). Above all, the very lack of definition is the 'proper' definition of Man, by a sort of circle; so that 'in doubt to act', for example, has us constantly rebounding between being doubtful about acting and having to act in the midst of and because of the doubt itself. Nor does it help to turn the other way: we are also doubtful about resting and so rest doubtfully even when we resolve to do so. This dividedness is also, paradoxically, our whole life: the lines show our uncertainty to be so certain as to make this 'Chaos' simultaneously our Order, through our very doubts.

'Uncertainty and imperfection is the lot which our Creator has appointed for us' – that is what Johnson himself says.[27] We are stuck in the chaos of our situation on earth *and yet* we can also see, from a mental meta-level still embodied in it all, something of the pattern of that chaos. All his life Johnson laboured to make that distinction other than ironic or tragic or irrelevant: he wanted to bring the general patterns of reason to the aid of particular difficulties rather than leave a mere gap for speculation to preside over practice in mutually damaging relation.

In Pope, correspondingly, there is the predicament of the man, caught inside the tightness of the lines, and the mastery of the poet, almost simultaneously looking down on his own troubled human content and, as though above and outside it, resolving it into the form of the whole –saying, in effect:

> All Nature is but Art, unknown to thee;
> All Chance, Direction, which thou canst not see;
> All Discord, Harmony, not understood;
> All partial Evil, universal Good:
> And, spite of Pride, in erring Reason's spite,
> One truth is clear, 'Whatever IS, is RIGHT.' (I, 289–94)

Eighteenth-century man was the first, not to know, but to realize fully and completely the truth revealed by Copernicus and Galileo: that this earth is not the centre of the universe but a grain of sand amidst countless others. 'What did this really apocalyptic revolution in his picture of the universe mean for man?' asks the theologian Karl Barth. 'An unprecedented and boundless humiliation of man? No, said the man of the eighteenth century ... no, man is all the greater for this, man is in the centre of all things, in a quite different sense, too, for he was able to discover this revolutionary truth by his own resources and think it abstractly.'[28] In the same way, what Johnson precisely feared about Pope, I think, was that Pope had turned humility into pride and produced a trick, where Johnson himself was still stuck in a dilemma.

Of course, Johnson saw, Pope had covered his tracks by himself warning against presumption – take even a Newton, he had said:

> Could he, whose rules the rapid comet bind,
> Describe or fix one movement of his mind?
> Who saw its fires here rise, and there descend,
> Explain his own beginning, or his end? (II, 35–8)

The mind of Newton, like that of Copernicus or Galileo, may be said to 'bind' the comet, as though in control of it, but equally the comet – and much more, the Force behind the comet – binds the mind of Newton. Yet Pope himself virtually tried to look at his own *mind* even as Newton traced the *comet*. For it is as though Pope's consciousness of his own mind being bound in an ordered chaos was like Newton simultaneously realizing, and even thus momentarily transcending, the necessary limitation of his own understanding. It was this revelation – the simultaneity of knowing-you-do-not-know still proving to be knowledge – that Johnson suspected to be fast, verbal trickery:

> This *Essay* affords an egregious instance of the predominance of genius, the dazzling splendour of imagery, and the seductive powers of eloquence. Never were penury of knowledge and vulgarity of sentiment so happily disguised. The reader feels his mind full, though he learns nothing.[29]

To factual, empirical Dictionary Johnson, to know that we do not know is, thus, *not* to know; except to poetry's spurious genius, limitation means limitation.

'When these wonderful sounds sink into sense,' says Johnson, 'and the doctrine of the *Essay*, disrobed of its ornaments, is left to the powers of its naked excellence, what shall we discover?'[30] We shall discover, as far as Johnson sees, Soame Jenyns's *A Free Inquiry into the Nature and Origin of Evil* – Pope and (prosaic) water. For there, in reviewing Jenyns's version of 'whatever is, is right', Johnson finds a retort to those tempted to think that his own line – limitation means limitation – gets us nowhere. Where does Soame Jenyns get us? Says Johnson:

> I do not mean to reproach the author for not knowing what is

equally hidden from learning and from ignorance. The shame is to impose words for ideas upon ourselves or others. To imagine that we are going forward when we are only turning round. To think that there is a difference between him that gives no reason, and him that gives a reason, which by his own confession cannot be conceived.[31]

It was precisely because Johnson so wanted to find, and to give, hope and faith that the offer of what seemed to him a false version of them so exasperated and offended him.

We all go round in circles, thought Johnson, but what Pope was doing was pretending that that was the way forward:

> Presumptuous man!, the reason wouldst thou find,
> Why formed so weak, so little, and so blind!
> First, if thou canst, the harder reason guess,
> Why formed no weaker, blinder, and no less! (I, 35–8)

> The bliss of Man (could Pride that blessing find)
> Is not to act or think beyond mankind;
> No powers of body or of soul to share,
> But what his nature and his state can bear.
> Why has not Man a microscopic eye?

> For this plain reason, Man is not a Fly. (I, 189–94)
> Respecting Man, whatever wrong we call,
> May, must be right, as relative to all. (I, 51–2)

To all this Johnson would have had to retort as he did to Soame Jenyns: 'We are ... little enlightened by a writer who tells us that any being in the state of man must suffer what man suffers, when the only question is, Why any being is in this state?' Or again: 'whether evil can be wholly separated from good or not, it is plain that they may be mixed in various degrees, and as far as human eyes can judge, the degree of evil might have been less without any impediment to good.'[32] Why any being in this state? Why this degree of wrong for our own good? Pope himself might well have picked up this 'as far as human eyes can judge' of Johnson's and say that that was precisely the point: that does not go *far* enough. But downright Johnson, like a sort of latter-day Job, would still stick with such judgement as we have:

> Though he slay me, yet will I trust in him, but I will maintain
> mine own ways before him. (Job 13: 15)

In contrast to that stubborn Hebraism of Johnson's, the ambiguity of

Pope's 'whatever wrong we call' slides easily over a distinction crucial 'as far as human eyes can judge': that between our *calling* something wrong when it is not at all, and *our* calling something wrong when it is so but only relative to us. From Pope's height it comes to the same thing, just as 'may' is forced into 'must be right'.

Yet, again, what is so curious in all this is how close to Pope's, Johnson's 'own ways' may often at least *appear* to be. We have seen him virtually saying to Boswell: it is as it is, such is the system of life, such seem to be the laws of man's condition – we can turn up such things almost at random among the essays:

> friendship between mortals can be contracted on no other terms, than that one must sometimes mourn for the other's death.

> it is by affliction chiefly that the heart of man is purified, and that the thoughts are fixed upon a better state.

> There is indeed nothing more unsuitable to the nature of man in any calamity than rage and turbulence, which, without examining whether they are not sometimes impious, are at least always offensive, and incline others rather to hate and despise than to pity and assist us.[33]

Just as surely as in Pope, and as if from above, the writer sentences what the man suffers from and balances the imbalances into a pattern:

> we do not always suffer by our crimes; we are not always protected by our innocence.[34]

And Johnson, too, seeks a way to see weakness as also strength or bad news as transmutable also into good, at another level. It is bad and good that the princess will get over Pekuah's death through simply having to forget her bit by bit: Imlac is pessimistic and encouraging, almost at once cynical and yet life-loving in his speech. And with Johnson himself we remember that, on second thought, to feel sorrow is also to be human, and that relative unimportance need only make the individual more truly one with his fellow-men. Thus he ends *The Rambler*, 32:

> A settled conviction of the tendency of every thing to our good, and of the possibility of turning miseries into happiness, by receiving them rightly, will incline us to 'bless the name of the Lord, whether he gives or takes away'.

That last is, again, the voice of Job struggling to keep faith, from below.

If faith is kept, is there, after all, so very much difference between Johnson's Christianity and Soame Jenyns's or Pope's? Is not the difference only this: that what Johnson acquiesced in – as though muttering inside himself 'whatever is, is' – Pope celebrated hugely, cosmically, driving faith out into the open to admit its essential risk: 'Whatever IS, is RIGHT'. But this was precisely Johnson's trouble – what to the eye may appear from outside to be a small difference between him and Pope, as we compare quotations, to Johnson's own heart was huge; for Johnson, the huge is always contained within the small. Thus although it is possible to see *The Rambler* and *An Essay on Man* working in similar ways at different levels, it is crucial that Pope's task is offered as primary, to 'vindicate the ways of God to man', while Johnson's is deliberately secondary: 'The cure for the greatest part of human miseries is not radical, but palliative'.[35] For a man to rage at calamity is bad even in human terms, says down-to-earth Johnson, temporarily leaving aside the higher question of whether it is also 'not sometimes impious'.

In *The Rambler* Johnson is clearly not concerned with trying to justify God's ways, as is Pope, or condemning their injustice, as the sight of Soame Jenyns's extenuations almost forces him to in his *Review*. He is simply concerned with the encouragement of man's efforts at amelioration of his own position – in the meantime, through perseverance, hope and kindness – without his wasting his limited resources on useless complaint or fictive speculation. 'The only end of writing is to enable the readers better to enjoy life, or better to endure it.'[36] It would be easy to take Johnson at his own word and dismiss his aim as merely second-order prudence; for it is Johnson, more than Pope, who is saying: 'The proper study of mankind is Man'. But actually Johnson's objections to Pope are themselves religious as well as prudential, though as ever the religion is translated within the terms of the smaller thing, the prudence. For Johnson, I think, believed that Pope had taken faith out of its proper, incorporated place in human beings, at the very back and basis of their minds, and turned it out above them by his art. Pascal, one of Pope's mentors, describes how such a movement may take place: 'In a word man knows he is wretched. Thus he is wretched because he is so, but he is truly great because he knows it'; 'Man transcends man.'[37] And, as we would expect of Pascal, that is pure Augustine: a working backwards which turns round upon itself; a poetry raised from below to look down on itself from above; the very thought that limitation is proper

to man raises man to imagination of the system that 'may, must'
make it so. Yet is not that, Johnson would say, the very act of
presumption? The proudest use of humility?

For Pope, man's is a dynamically double nature. We find what is
proper to us only by going beyond or out of it and having to return.
We work dialectically – outwards: 'Why has not Man a microscopic
eye?' and back inwards: 'For this plain reason, Man is not a Fly'. And
we no sooner return to what is proper to us than we are off again
imagining from within *what* makes it proper from without. By
another swift turn Pope makes that *lack* of true stability into what is
proper to us. In just the same way he makes the incomprehensible
into a way of comprehending God's Order. Or he makes human
doubt, holding us uncertainly between God and Beast, Mind and
Body, Acting and Resting, a point of paradoxical balance in the
equilibrium of the whole. When we do not thus see content in terms of
its form, we complain about our doubt and lack of comprehension; to
such complaints Pope says:

> Cease then, nor ORDER imperfection name:
> Our proper bliss depends on what we blame. (I, 281–2)

And so it must have seemed to Samuel Johnson a seductively
magnificent reassurance that incomprehension might be a way of
comprehending, that not knowing might be a way to knowledge, that
doubt might be the path to faith. Yet what was all this but 'to impose
words for ideas upon ourselves or others'?, to pretend that there is a
real difference between 'him that gives no reason, and him that gives a
reason, which by his own confession cannot be conceived'? It is
agonizing to imagine Johnson having to give up the reassurance,
remain him that gives no reason (it is as it is), and moreover do so in
the very name of religion itself, in faithful, doubtful steadfastness.
For he could not even say that that doubt was a form of faith, as Pope
would say for him, for fear of fictively removing it, however much he
also hated its pain.

Johnson's reaction to knowing that we do not know was always
uncomfortably equivocal. Something of Job in him, with his great cry
'Wherefore is light given to him that is in misery?', tempted Johnson
towards Soame Jenyns's view that the insensibility of ignorance
might be a compensating opiate for the unfortunate, for would it not
be better not to know at all? Yet again however, morality, with its
insistence on the continuance of hard thought amidst the many, tiny
but significant complications of human life, draws Johnson back

down from the larger gestures and into qualification: 'Whatever knowledge is superfluous, in irremediable poverty, is hurtful, but the difficulty is to determine *when* poverty is irremediable, and *at what point* superfluity begins.'[38] Always he is pulled back from the verge of complaining that it is a cosmic injustice that human beings alone have been given consciousness without relief – 'Imperfection may imply privative evil, or the absence of some good, but this privation produces no suffering, but by the help of knowledge.'[39] Some help! Yet Johnson is still pulled back from complaint against that consciousness by the very consciousness itself – as Imlac would put it, to lose our reason would be to do 'as the savages would have done, had they put out their eyes when it was dark'.

Thus in all his double-binds Johnson had almost ironically to reject the very poet, Pope, who might have told him that his difficulties were intrinsic to the scheme of his salvation. Yet to this Anglican, to say it would have been to undo it, even were it true. What Johnson was rejecting, moreover, was Pope's use of poetry to occupy a position ordinarily impossible to man and actually only God's. Like a more flawed Milton, Pope was another of those vain men guilty of

> the absurdity of stretching out our arms incessantly to grasp that which we cannot keep, and wearing out our lives in endeavours to add new turrets to the fabrick of ambition, when the foundation itself is shaking, and the ground on which it stands is mouldering away. (*The Rambler*, 17)

If it was not absurd, it would be blasphemous. 'All Chance, Direction, which thou canst not see': if Pope had writted 'I' instead of 'thou', as Johnson might think he ought to have, *An Essay on Man* would not have been written. And to Johnson it could not have been written; he wrote no such major work.

*

III *Transmutations: not Pope but Butler*

Perhaps now we could give up this attempt to work Johnson out of himself and come instead to some final reckoning of the gains and losses of his position – were it not that the sight of Johnson himself, having to settle so short of what he so needs, compels one last effort, even by him. Miss Reynolds reports:

> Dr Johnson commonly read with amazing rapidity, glancing

his eye from the top to the bottom of the page in an instant. If he made any pause, it was a compliment to the work; and, after seesawing over it a few minutes, generally repeated the passage, especially if it was poetry. One day, on taking up Pope's *Essay on Man*, a particular passage seem'd more than ordinarily to engage his attention; and so much, indeed, that, contrary to his usual custom, after he had left the Book and the place where he was sitting, he return'd to revise it, turning over the pages with anxiety to find it, and then repeated –

> Passions, tho' selfish, if their means be fair
> List under Reason, and deserve her care;
> Those that, imparted, court a nobler aim,
> Exalt their kind, and take some virtue's name.[40]

Always, in reading Pope's *Essay*, Johnson suspected that the lines on the page would not carry over into any possible life off it. That is why, similarly, he rebuked Soame Jenyns for an artificial explaining away of what remained as real experience: 'Life must be *seen before* it can be *known*'.[41] Johnson was the sort of literary man who could still look at a book and ask, 'Isn't this only writing, merely words?' 'The shame is to impose words for ideas.' Yet clearly something in that passage from Epistle II gave Johnson pause as he tried to see if the words would translate into his own experience of life. And what must have struck him, I believe, was Pope's offer, in such passages, of a form of wholeness in human beings that also included transmutation. For what Pope offered was in opposition to those whom he called 'More studious to divide than to unite' – such as even Johnson must have felt himself forced to be. For Pope, that is to say, passion and reason need not be in divisive conflict: a person could hold himself together and find one thing dynamically becoming another if passion, via reason, could be virtue:

> In lazy apathy let Stoics boast
> Their virtue fixed; 'tis fixed as in a frost,
> Contracted all, retiring to the breast;
> But strength of mind is Exercise, not Rest:
> The rising tempest puts in act the soul,
> Parts it may ravage, but preserves the whole.
> On life's vast ocean diversely we sail,
> Reason the card, but Passion is the gale...
>
> Yes, Nature's road must ever be preferred;

Reason is here no guide, but still a guard:
'Tis here to rectify, not overthrow,
And treat this passion more as friend than foe...

The surest virtues thus from passions shoot,
Wild Nature's vigour working at the root...

Thus Nature gives us (let it check our pride)
The virtue nearest to our vice allied;
Reason the bias turns to good from ill.

(II, 101–8; 161–8; 183–4; 195–7)

What a basis it would give if we could work *through* our nature, rather than merely *against* it with Reason aways saying 'Thou Shalt Not' to the passions. A transformation of our raw emotional material into a finished product that was also moral would be like a renewal of prelapsarian integrity. For though Reason would still have to be on guard, the nearness of a virtue to a vice, the very closeness of the two within our raw emotive energy makes morality not something 'fixed as in a frost' but the very transformation of our lives.[42] The essence of what is at stake here may be illustrated by some words of John Ruskin's on what human beings need:

First, that the affections be vivid, and honestly shown; secondly, that they be fixed on the right things.

You think, perhaps, I have put the requirements in the wrong order. Logically I have; practically I have not: for it is necessary first to teach men to speak out, and say what they like, truly; and, in the second place, to teach them which of their likings are ill set, and which justly.[43]

You start with what you are; with the passions, rather than formal moral principles, at the root – not least because those moral principles will never be a true – integrated part of you unless the passions grow through to them rather than take them as a grafting. 'Wild Nature's vigour working at the root.' Again, as with faith's 'Whatever IS, is RIGHT', so here with true virtue, Pope makes risk the revelation of what is really involved.

For all Pope's avowal of good sense, therefore, Johnson, with ambivalent feelings, recognized in Pope something beyond that 'sedate and quiescent quality which manages its possessions well but does not increase them', for Pope had genius:

in its widest searches still longing to go forward, in its highest
flights still wishing to be higher, always imagining something
greater than it knows, always endeavouring more than it can
do.[44]

Thus it is painful to see Johnson pausing over the idea of using yet
transmuting the wild selfish primal passions, and still having to reject
this larger adventurousness for lack of trust. And the pain is also
Johnson's. Yet he does reject faith in one's own passions, as what we
have first to go on, just as surely as he rejects Pope's belief in every
man having a particular master passion in his life – and for the same
reason in both cases. For Johnson fears the tendency of such views
towards a kind of moral predestination, if we can indeed work only
on the basis of the authoritative power of such emotions as we are
given in our individual make-up. Pope said, for example, that out of
lust could come love: we can work upwards from beneath, we are
creatures who can find high values arising out of our very biology. All
this might well have appealed to Johnson's physical common sense,
were it not that he also felt that lust, in practice, was far more likely to
destroy the possibility of love; that it was dangerous and wrong to
suggest that vice could be a way out of vice. Mrs Thrale said that
Johnson's incredulity or distrust amounted to a virtual disease, and
certainly in the case of Pope Johnson was all too likely entirely to
cancel the meaning that any large but flawed proposition was still
aiming at. For he was not simply frightened at what went on in
human society, he was most particularly afraid of what went on in the
solitude of the individual mind – including his own:

> we are easily shocked by crimes which appear at once in their
> full magnitude, but the gradual growth of our own wickedness,
> endeared by interest, and palliated by all the artifices of self-
> deceit, give us time to form distinctions in our own favour, and
> reason by degrees submits to absurdity, as the eye is in time
> accommodated to darkness. (*The Rambler*, 8)

Reason, too often, neither guides nor guards but submits – and
submits so gradually that it becomes the very voice and tool of the
passions without even knowing it. Johnson's disease, if such it be, was
to believe that we are indeed fallen and especially untrustworthy to
ourselves in the secret courses of time. Even when we think we are
starting most securely from the bottom, there is something below us,
in our unconscious nature, threatening to undermine even that
cautious level of trust. The stakes are high in Pope's poem:

> If then to all men Happiness was meant,
> God in externals could not place content. (IV, 65–6)

A reader such as Johnson cannot undertake the full imaginative experiment because he has to stop short at that 'If'.

It is easy to see how Johnson's use of fear or distrust as a balancing second thought to combat evil could overtopple into a merely repressive belittling of life. But that is not what Johnson lets it simply become. For look what happens to the distrust of self-interest, when he responds to Soame Jenyns's idea that the irremediable poor should not be educated out of their only compensation – insensibility:

> I am always afraid of determining on the side of envy or cruelty. The privileges of education may sometimes be improperly bestowed, but I shall always fear to withhold them, lest I should be yielding to the suggestions of pride, while I persuade myself that I am following the maxims of policy; and under the appearance of salutary restraints, should be indulging the lust of dominion, and that malevolence which delights in seeing others depressed.[45]

'I am always afraid' becomes also, unashamedly, 'I shall always fear'. The negative inhibition begins to turn into something positive and be embraced as a commitment: 'always'. It is better, in Johnson's view, not to carry through your own emotional purposes, however dynamic, but to relearn what our general human purposes were meant to be: we must endeavour, he writes in *The Rambler*, 8, not to be led by our own feelings but 'to excite in ourselves those sentiments which the great author of nature has decreed the concomitants or followers of good or bad actions'. And it is not as if this simply leaves Johnson 'always afraid': the emotion learnt from distrust and raised to a principle becomes again transformed in the course of experience. For what is wonderful in Johnson is his ability to recover a rule out of an obstacle, and better still, as that rule sinks in, to recover feeling from the rule:

> Before we permit our severity to break loose upon any fault or error, we ought surely to consider how much we have countenanced or promoted it.
>
> It may likewise contribute to soften that resentment, which pride naturally raises against opposition, if we consider, that he, who differs from us, does not always contradict us.[46]

Here, as in response to Jenyns on the education of the poor, an emotion is recovered as a value: the emotion of kindness from the principle of charity, the principle of charity from the fear of error, the fear of error from a recognition of the problems of knowledge. Just as surely as in Pope, but from Johnson's point of view more really, fear has been transmuted into generosity, generosity on the other side of fear as things shake down within human nature in time. Unlike Pope, Johnson cannot say much about what he has done, for fear of undoing it again, but he knows for sure that the effort which gives way to right feeling *is* an achievement, when he writes thus:

> Of him that hopes to be forgiven it is indispensably required, that he forgive. It is therefore superfluous to urge any other motive. On this great duty eternity is suspended, and to him that refuses to practise it, the throne of mercy is inaccessible, and the Saviour of the world has been born in vain. (*The Rambler*, 185)

Those are, properly, the last words of that essay. What we do at one level, even out of fear first, is the lower equivalent of what Christ himself did, out of the higher love incarnate. Yet, for a moment, it is as though we not only help ourselves and each other but also, by repeating his presence in ourselves, help *Him* by the very act of forgiving – repaying something by making it that the Saviour has *not* been born in vain again. The issue of eternal life or death waits on the result and, in that suspense, Christ is not lost to ordinary time nor eternity itself predestined and irrevocable. That is a huge thing, for even eternity is suspended for a moment to witness that redemption from below.

*

At the close of some of the moral essays like this one, Advice to us virtually becomes Prayer for us, yet as though Johnson were praying to *us* for ourselves. If it is almost like that at the end of *The Rambler*, 185, so it is at the close of *The Adventurer*, 120:

> While affliction thus prepares us for felicity, we may console ourselves under its pressures, by remembering, that they are no particular marks of divine displeasure; since all the distresses of persecution have been suffered by those, 'of whom the world was not worthy'; and the Redeemer of mankind himself was 'a man of sorrows and acquainted with grief'.

Of course Johnson is always *thoughtful* in this way, always properly afraid of people taking his words too particularly and too gloomily to themselves and going one way, to despair, when he meant them to try to go the other. In *The Rambler*, 8, in the midst of warning us against allowing ourselves to indulge in irregular and tempting thoughts, Johnson interrupts himself thoughtfully: 'I cannot forbear, under this head, to caution pious and tender minds, that are disturbed by the irruptions of wicked imaginations, against too great dejection, and too anxious alarms; for thoughts are only criminal, when they are first chosen, and then voluntarily continued.' Whatever there was to be said on one side, there was also almost simultaneously something to be thought on the other: in *The Rambler* Johnson saved himself from mere self-harassment by knowing that these different *thoughts* in this context stood for real and different types of *people*. Going one way, he remembers also to turn another for the sake of 'pious and tender minds'. This thoughtful *kind-ness* in Johnson results from his knowing, even microcosmically within himself, the differing varieties, pressures and temperamental dispositions within our kind. His sheer imagination will include you just when he anticipates your taking his words out of their general context and back into particular lonely troubles which you can barely help exacerbating on your own. Remember, says Johnson at the end of *The Adventurer*, 120, what you are suffering on your own is not what you alone are suffering, is not (as a Calvinist such as Cowper might fear) a particular mark of divine displeasure towards you especially. Under this general affliction, still look after yourselves – that seems to be Johnson's prayer.

It gives sustenance to see Johnson, like God's middleman, giving and also urging kindness to ourselves and others even while God Himself seems to be so unkind, above it all. It is truly lovely to see Johnson, in the midst of a sentence about eternity or universal affliction, work below all that to gather bits of human consolation from lying beaten on the ground. The underpresence at times of a sort of comedy – as though to say to God's sufferers: 'He isn't just getting at you especially, you know' – is a tacit admission that the consolation is small, ruefully plucky, that of mere creatures. But it gives us some remembrance of what Christ has meant in ordinary human life when we recognize how Johnson, without the blasphemy of explicit imitation, sees Christ as himself the highest mediator; not coming down from the cross like a transcendent god but staying there even in affliction. In that context Johnson's few pieces of practical consolation and mediating encouragement seem both poignantly, resolutely little and yet, though far below him, still a Christian's naturally human understanding of following Christ. 'Of him that hopes to be forgiven it is indispensably required, that he forgive.' This is not merely a case of do-down-here-as-you-would-be-done-by-up-there, of humans almost making up for God or prudence merely standing in place of virtue. But neither does Johnson scorn these almost primitive, if not crude, thoughts. A little so often has to stand in place of a lot. That is the end we start from.

I think I have to say, at this final stage, that I admire this and yet am not a Christian. In a chapter concerned with the threat of getting nowhere, and looking for the possibility of any proper conclusion which is not merely fictive, to say as much may not be out of place this time. For what, it may be asked, is the use of admiring the man without believing his belief, when what he believes is so essential to what he is? Such admiration might seem – what Johnson himself surely would have condemned – a fictional, aesthetic emotion, a luxury of reading rather than a matter of living. While we praise Handel, said the poet Cowper, we forget the Messiah.

'It is a suspicious circumstance,' says Kierkegaard, 'when a man, instead of getting out of a tension by resolution and action, becomes literarily productive about his situation in the tension.'[47] Would it not be cleaner to admit either Pope's faith as a whole, 'whatever IS, is RIGHT', or Hume's utter atheism, rather than let second-hand admiration for Johnson fudge the issues?

Hume's *Dialogues Concerning Natural Religion*, published post-humously in 1779 but written during the 1760s, the decade after *The Rambler*, could clear our way forward to a more 'modern' position. When God does not seem to give kindly, you give kindness for Him; when He does not seem to provide stamina, you find it for yourself: to Johnson such are themselves the ways and laws of God – but what do they prove, atheist Hume might say, but the want of even *human* goodness in the alleged Deity? We make sacrifices for Him out of our own (afflicted) goodness; forgiving in order to be forgiven, we frighten ourselves into a prudence which we then call virtue, when virtue itself might come more naturally without all the primitive wrenchings. Johnson, committed neither to complain of nor to justify human suffering, may be seen in retrospect as having to stand in between David Hume and Soame Jenyns, as between the Devil and the deep blue sea. But to Hume, even so, Johnson would have seemed like a superior version of Jenyns: an apologist for God, who made things worse for us. If away with God, away with such men, for our own sake.

Yet what happens if we are not as optimistic as Hume about enlightened human virtue? This sort of question, we may recall, was just what was going through Boswell's mind as he felt himself torn between two mentors, Johnson and Hume. We may want to think – as William James was to think – that although religion may not be true, a belief in it may do good. Indeed, that has been the hapless state of many, many people throughout the nineteenth and twentieth centuries, as I tried to indicate at the beginning of this chapter. Yet it still does credit to the memory of the meaning of religion for Thomas Hardy, for example, that he emphatically rejected the possibility of coherently sustaining William James's position. Utility without a grounding truth was for Hardy neither gift nor adventure but torment: not for him a possible illusion consciously maintained for the mileage it gave! Better to get nowhere – that was the religious need and integrity buried within Hardy's pessimism. There is something powerfully Johnsonian in his downright response to reading William James's dictum 'Truth is what will work'. Said Hardy: 'A worse corruption of language was never perpetrated'.[48] Words were imposed for things: No, Sir, Truth is not synonymous with, dependent upon or proved by Success; what is more, it is often to do with what does not wrok and why not.

It is crucial that Johnson's practicality, for all his concern with survival and what will work, is not the same as James's pragmatism. Johnson is not Soame Jenyns; truth does not always work; there are uncertainties and tragedies and injustices as well as immoral successes. Even the best of what works is far below the lofty level of Truth. That is the force of Johnson's pessimism: not to depress but to caution and to balance against both presumption and injustice. Yet even from so far down as the level of human practice, there is, as we have just been seeing, a relationship to Truth: forgiveness here taught by and itself calling down forgiveness above. This brings me to why, finally, I think we still need *The Rambler*: because of what it does with practicality not merely in replacement of a higher Truth but in translation of it, within our limits.

That is to say, *The Rambler* exists to affirm that the language of religion may be translated into the language of ordinary living not simply for the purposes of persuasive convenience but because the experienced constitution of the world and what religion offers as truths are consonant with one another as one life. This is the hidden dynamic of the enterprise, and in order to show that it is I need to refer to what seems to me the only other eighteenth-century work to point in the same direction: another Anglican work, Bishop Butler's

The Analogy of Religion, Natural and Revealed, to the Constitution of Nature (1736):

> From analogical reasoning, Origen has . . . observed, that *he who believes the Scripture to have proceeded from him who is the Author of Nature, may well expect to find the same sort of difficulties in it as are found in the constitution of Nature.* And in a like way of reflection it may be added, . . . if there be an analogy or likeness between that system of things and dispensation of Providence, which revelation informs us of, and that system of things and dispensation of Providence which Experience together with Reason informs us of, i.e., the known course of Nature; this is a presumption that they both have the same author and cause.[49]

Analogy is the view from below, the deduction that works backwards: for the repetition of the same general configurations and difficulties in different spheres and levels gives us from below an intimation of the whole scheme of things above our heads. 'We are placed, as one may speak, in the middle of a scheme, not a fixed but a progressive one, every way incomprehensible': Butler's *Analogy* itself stands in between Pope's *Essay* optimistically proclaiming the scheme of things and Johnson's *Rambler* struggling silently within it.

In his *Journal of a Tour to the Hebrides* Boswell gives evidence of Johnson's characteristic ability to gut a book:

> Dr Blacklock spoke of scepticism in morals and religion, with apparent uneasiness, as if he wished for more certainty. Dr Johnson, who had thought it all over, and whose vigorous understanding was fortified by much experience, thus encouraged the blind bard to apply to higher speculations what we willingly submit to in common life: in short, he gave him more familiarly the able and fair reasoning of Butler's *Analogy*: 'Why, sir, the greatest concern we have in this world, the choice of our profession, must be determined without demonstrative reasoning. Human life is not yet so well known, as that we can have it. And take the case of a man who is ill. I call two physicians: they differ in opinion. I am not to lie down, and die between them: I must do something.'[50]

Butler's *Analogy* was one of the books Boswell was reading in 1763 to buttress the influence of Johnson upon him. We can well imagine 'the able and fair reasoning' Johnson's vigorous familiarity served to translate and recall to Boswell:

It hath always been allowed to argue from what is acknowledged, to what is disputed. And it is in no other sense a poor thing to argue from natural religion to revealed, in the manner found fault with, than it is to argue in numberless other ways of probable deduction and inference, in matters of conduct, which we are continually reduced to the necessity of doing. Indeed the epithet *poor* may be applied, I fear as properly, to great part or the whole of human life, as it is to the things mentioned in the objection. Is it not a poor thing, for a physician to have so little knowledge in the cure of diseases, as even the most eminent have? To act upon conjecture and guess, where the life of man is concerned? Undoubtedly it is: but not in comparison of having no skill at all in that useful art, and being obliged to act wholly in the dark.[51]

'They who restrain themselves from receiving comfort', said Imlac, 'do as the savages would have done, had they put out their eyes when it was dark.' 'All human excellence is comparative,' writes Johnson in *The Rambler*, 127, 'no man performs much but in proportion to what others accomplish.' Not much but not blind nothing; a pessimistic Anglican's precious little. For want of high certainty, the accumulation of many small details from the lower degrees of evidence has to serve to build up an experienced, habitual, even if 'poor' *intuition*. 'It may be hard to explain the faculty', says Butler; it is one 'not given by nature, but which nature directs us to acquire.'[52]

Thus the man of experience must, in Johnson's words, 'apply to higher speculations what we willingly submit to in common life'. That is still submission, at a higher level, not the confidence of a merely bluff common sense. There is, as Butler helps to show, a subdued metaphysic within its realism, and that metaphysic has to do with analogy: always the same thing working at different levels in what remains throughout, up and down, one whole system of life.

Consider the nature of prudence: perhaps uncomfortably close, as we have seen, to the mere utility of forgiving in order to be forgiven. Butler points out, obviously enough, that on some occasions our passions may tempt us towards some present gratification which none the less in the long run goes against even our temporal interests. On such occasions prudence is necessary in order to hold off temptation for the sake of a more distant end. 'This is a description of our state of trial in our temporal capacity,' concludes Butler, and then he offers this rule of translation:

Substitute now the word *future* for *temporal*, and *virtue* for
prudence; and it will be just as proper a description of our state
of trial in our religious capacity, so analogous are they to each
other.[53]

It is not that prudence is *the same* as virtue, any more than what works
is the same as truth; it is that they work in an analogous way. Butler
would no more believe them the same than would Johnson, for Butler
is the enemy of Hobbes and ideas of the dominance of sheer self-
interst, just as Johnson finally opposes Mandeville. Indeed, one of the
few points that Johnson praises in Soame Jenyns's work is the
distinction drawn between morality and religion. They are very
different in Johnson's eyes. For morality induces men to embrace
virtue, as Soame Jenyns says, 'from prudential considerations' – considerations to do with the balancing out of general happiness when a
person lives in a society of other people too, all of them bearing and
responding to the consequences of each other's actions. But religion
goes beyond utilitarianism in urging men to do right not merely for
the sake of a gain in happiness but out of blind gratitude and
obedience to God in our state of probation, even if (adds Johnson) we
in our limitation cannot see the immediate good of what He
commands.[54] None the less, if religion is not at all the same as
morality, what brings us back to Butler is this: that the religious act,
precisely for eschewing immediate happiness or satisfaction, stands
to our hope of making a success of our probation even as our moral
behaviour is more directly related to our motive of securing more
good or less harm. That is to say, the higher level both eschews and
restores to its original form the fallen lower copy. At any rate that is
how it seems given us to be understood, so that we may be 'allowed to
argue from what is acknowledged, to what is disputed'. Doubtless
Johnson would be bound to have sceptical reservations here, lest, like
Soame Jenyns, we insist that God operates according to our reasons;
but equally it is no part of Johnson's careful balance to be guilty of
the opposite blasphemy of rejecting the gift of reason as the trick of an
unreasonable God.

The economy of Butler's universe is severe. There are no special
extras that raise a human being from prudence to virtue or from a
secular to a religious life: the human faculties at the higher level are
the same *general* faculties as at the lower, only working harder. When
we trust as God-given the terms in which we work and so try to
proceed even at the highest levels of meaning on a basis analogous to
that on which we rely in common life, there is still, of course, a risk. It

is terrifying to think that the universe operates on a principle quite *unanalogous* to what we hope and know as human beings in it. But to risk working on the basis that it *is* consonant with our own experience is – argues Butler – precisely, by analogy, the risk one might expect at this level:

> Indeed if mankind, considered in their natural capacity as inhabitants of this world only, found themselves from their birth to their death in a settled state of security and happiness, without any solicitude or thought of their own, or if they were in no danger of being brought into inconveniences, and distress by carelessness, or the folly of passion, through bad example, the treachery of others, or the deceitful appearances of things; were this our natural condition, then it might seem strange and be some presumption against the truth of Religion that it represents our future and more general interest, as not secure of course, but as depending upon our behaviour, and requiring recollection and self-government to obtain it.[55]

But it does not seem strange – save to those who expect the religious way to be easier than the secular. Internal doubts, in Butler's view, are analogous to external temptations: as tests of virtue, 'speculative difficulties are, in this respect, of the very same nature with these external temptations'.[56] And that sort of equivocal comfort, not making one thing better but making it seem to be in the same boat as all the other troubles, is the essence of *The Rambler*. As Imlac said, using analogy, 'Our minds, like our bodies, are in continual flux: something is hourly lost, and something acquired.... Distance has the same effect on the mind as on the eye, and while we glide along the stream of time, whatever we leave behind us is always lessening.' Words in *The Rambler* are mental analogues to physical reality, substantiating mental problems and making them no less and no more real in their way than external harassments – even thus in Number 32:

> Patience and submission are very carefully to be distinguished from cowardice and indolence. We are not to repine, but we may lawfully struggle; for the calamities of life, like the necessities of nature, are calls to labour, and exercises of diligence. When we feel any pressure of distress, we are not to conclude that we can only obey the will of heaven by languishing under it, any more than when we perceive the pain of thirst we are to imagine that water is prohibited. Of

misfortune it never can be certainly known whether as proceeding from the hand of God, it is an act of favour, or of punishment: but since all the ordinary dispensations of providence are to be interpreted according to the general analogy of things, we may conclude, that we have a right to remove one inconvenience as well as another; that we are only to take care lest we purchase ease with guilt; and that our Maker's purpose, whether of reward or severity, will be answered by the labours which he lays us under the necessity of performing.

Just as 'the calamities of life' are like 'the necessities of nature', so problems of the mind can be expressed, for good and for bad, in physical terms. For we begin physically to feel here the mental difference between 'submission' and 'indolence' and feel, too, how to 'obey' and to 'struggle' need not be in conflict but in a precise and careful union, albeit less optimistically than in Pope's harmonies. For crucially, this union in 'the general analogy of things' is double, inside and out. Outside we are to see that 'the calamities of life' are 'like the necessities of nature': the pain of distress, like the pain of thirst, calls for efforts at relief, but both are pain. Inside there is no oversimplifying tragic tension between 'patience' and 'labour', or between reason and desire, or between duty and self-interest. It is here as it is in Butler's *Dissertation of the Nature of Virtue* when he speaks of moral conscience as both 'a sentiment of the understanding' and 'a perception of the heart'.[57] Or again, it is as it is with Aristotle, in the book that Butler drew on and Johnson once proposed to translate – *The Nicomachean Ethics*: when Aristotle speaks of choice as desiderative reason or rational choice.[58] That is to say, the symmetries and analogies reveal man as essentially not a torn but a composite being, maintaining his unity of nature even through the distinction of different levels and areas, in mind and body. This is much the same flexibility as that which is manifested in Johnson's own exercise of a strong general mentality upon a diversity of particular problems: an economical flexibility. For although Johnson would be the first to point out the often painful distinctions between, say, theory and practice in human beings, that distinction is itself analogous to others in our nature – mind and body, truth and action, denial and avoidance: the very parallelism of analogous distinctions at different levels implies an order in human nature even through those very differences.

'When we feel any pressure of distress, we are not to conclude that we can only obey the will of heaven by languishing under it'; 'for the

calamities of life, like the necessities of nature, are calls to labour.'
Magnificently, it is not the case that the religious life is simply
different from the ordinary or offering a way out of it. What we do in
thirst we should do in trouble: it is the same nature at different levels.
But what, then, does religion add? Does it not just leave us in the same
boat, heading for trouble? The answer, of course, is this: it adds the
conviction that not only are things as they are, but they are as they are
somehow *meant* to be.

That such a belief in a divine scheme still partakes of a risk is itself
for Butler, as we have already seen, part of the very nature of that
scheme. But that is not quite how Johnson works. For fear of
appearing (even to himself) to *make* life into a scheme by a mental
tour de force, Johnson retains in his short essays that life which,
scheme or no, still goes on around, above and after his writing. The
Johnson whose scepticism could so completely dissolve Pope's bold
speculations had to keep his own principles half-buried. If he was
wrong, at least some reader's correcting disagreement might rescue
from his own misinterpretation the life and thought which he none
the less describes. And even if the tacit theory behind it all was faulty
(as all were), at least the practice that results from it may be
sometimes better than the theory itself, either by a lovely mistake or
by the sheer force of life over mind. One of Johnson's most crucial
sentences is this: 'And though perhaps he misses his end, he
nevertheless obtains some collateral good'.[59]

Although Johnson tried to keep his eye steadily on the centre of
life's troubles, the good that comes from his view often has to be
collateral. For the good often comes from the personal way he copes,
rather than in anything he fundamentally changes. About God, the
centre and cause of everything, Johnson can only be silent. And
indeed, Johnson's *Review* of Soame Jenyns is perhaps his greatest
and, moreover, his most religious work in so far as it establishes the
necessity for human silence about God the Unknowable. It is that
sense of gap between man and God which leaves Johnson using
analogy only as probability, only as the human terms for guessing at
understanding. With reservations, therefore, I am suggesting that
Butler the Anglican takes us further into Johnson than does Pope the
Deist/Catholic. Butler takes us further not least because through the
Analogy we gain a more open admission: through Butler we can see
that to treat religion as part of human ordinariness with rationality,
probability and, even after that, still risk is not simply the death of the
extraordinary religious spirit of English literature in the seventeenth
century but is itself another form for obscure feeling and intimation

sensibly translated. As when reading Pope, Johnson still has great fears lest, for all his words to Dr Blacklock, to reason from human to divine should none the less partake of presumption. But in *The Adventurer*, 125 we may finally see him just about sustaining a position like Butler's – if only for fear of the evil opposite to that of presumption, namely the evil of doubting God's goodness:

> The miseries of life, *may, perhaps,* afford *some* proof of a future state, compared as well with the mercy as the justice of God. It is *scarcely* to be imagined, that Infinite Benevolence would create a being capable of enjoying so much more than is here to be enjoyed, and qualified by nature to prolong pain by remembrance and anticipate it by terror, if he was not designed for *something* nobler and better than a state, in which many of his faculties can serve only for his torment, in which he is to be importuned by desires that never can be satisfied, to feel many evils which he had no power to avoid, and to fear many which he shall never feel: there will *surely* come a time, when every capacity of happiness shall be filled, and none shall be wretched but by his own fault.
> *In the mean time . . .* [60]

I think Butler would say of this shaking passage that it was just like the human relation to both life and religion: 'our being incompetent judges of one, must render it credible that we may be incompetent judges of the other'.[61] A *doubtful* faith? A doubtful *faith*?

*

IV *King Lear and After*

'It is scarcely to be imagined' – that Infinite Benevolence would create a being at once 'capable of enjoying so much more than is here to be enjoyed' and 'qualified by nature to prolong pain by remembrance and anticipate it by terror'; a being in a state, Johnson has to go on and on saying, 'in which many of his faculties can serve only for his torment, in which he is to be importuned by desires that never can be satisfied, to feel many evils which he had no power to avoid, and to fear many which he shall never feel'. Johnson can hardly stop himself still assembling one of the very greatest catalogues of woe, as though giving Lawrence's 'great kick at human misery':

The pangs of disprized love, the law's delay,
The insolence of office, and the spurns
That patient merit of th' unworthy takes (*Hamlet*, III, i, 72–4)

'Look round this universe,' said David Hume in his *Dialogues:* an atheist such as he could hardly have composed a more pained indictment that does this Johnson of doubtful faith. 'There seem', writes Hume, 'to be *four* circumstances on which depend all or the greatest part of the ills that molest sensible creatures.' All four are questionable, in the name of justice. One: Why did God make pain a necessary part of our motivation when rationally He could have made the pleasure principle sufficient? Two: Why is the world conducted by general laws without particular intervention by the Deity to make the world happier? Three: Why is this inconceivably powerful Author of Nature so rigid a master as to allow His creatures only such limited and yet frustrated powers and faculties? Four: Why is this workmanship of the universe so apparently inefficient as to allow chance disasters? There may be good reasons for all this, says Hume, 'but they are unknown to us':

> and though the mere supposition that such reasons exist may be sufficient to *save* the conclusion concerning the divine attributes [as just], yet surely it can never be sufficient to *establish* that conclusion.[62]

Why should we 'save' the idea of God and Justice as one?

'It is *scarcely* to be imagined' – a universe centred on a principle alien to human reason and inimical to human fate and feeling. But the atheist does imagine it and, what is more, the orthodox apologist for such a universe, in the person of Soame Jenyns, ironically forces Johnson himself towards the unbearable image. For Soame Jenyns, notes Johnson:

> imagines that as we have not only animals for food, but choose some for our diversion, the same privilege may be allowed to some beings above us, *who may deceive, torment, or destroy us for the ends only of their own pleasure or utility.* This he again finds impossible to be conceived, *but that impossibility lessens not the probability of the conjecture, which by analogy is so strongly confirmed.*

'When I was boy,' Johnson recalled, 'I used always to choose the wrong side of a debate.'[63] For satirical purposes, this time, he begins to take and blow up Jenyns's side; but even as he does so, Jenyns has

him shaking away at Butler's principle of analogy as a defence of
religion:

> I cannot resist the temptation of contemplating this analogy,
> which I think he might have carried further very much to the
> advantage of his argument. He might have shewn that these
> *hunters whose game is man* have many sports analogous to our
> own. As we drown whelps and kittens, they amuse themselves
> now and then with sinking a ship, and stand around the fields of
> *Blenheim* or *Prague*, as we encircle a cock-pit. As we shoot a
> bird flying, they take a man in the midst of his business or
> pleasure, and knock him down with an apoplexy. Some of
> them, perhaps are virtuosi, and delight in the operations of an
> asthma, as a human philosopher in the effects of the air pump.
> To swell a man with a tympany is as good sport as to blow a
> frog. Many a merry bout have these frolic beings at the
> vicissitudes of an ague, and good sport it is to see a man tumble
> with an epilepsy, and revive and tumble again, and all this he
> knows not why.[64]

Somewhere this wickedly ironic fancy ceases to be funny and
becomes angry – angry not only at Soame Jenyns but also at the
wickedness of human suffering itself – with a suddenly reviving
soreness, 'and all this he knows not why'. Why? Johnson is just one
stop from being made to see 'these *hunters*' as his God:

> As flies to wanton boys, are we to th' Gods;
> They kill us for their sport.

As Johnson makes Soame Jenyns's defence increasingly indefensible,
there comes through from behind the *Review* a memory of *King Lear*,
whether Johnson will or no; a play that in the history of human
feeling exists to imagine precisely what 'is scarcely to be imagined'.
We know its deep effect within Johnson, even as though the tragedy
were a revenge upon that principle of 'Whatever IS, is RIGHT' which
Johnson himself had so painfully to doubt:

> Shakespeare has suffered the virtue of Cordelia to perish in a
> just cause, contrary to the natural ideas of justice, to the hope of
> the reader, and, what is yet more strange, to the faith of
> chronicles... A play in which the wicked prosper and the
> virtuous miscarry may doubtless be good, because it is a just
> representation of the common events of human life; but since
> all reasonable beings naturally love justice, I cannot easily be

persuaded that the observation of justice makes a play worse.[65]

Johnson's language here may seem confused, but it is precise. For nothing comes closer to the almost literally maddening paradox at the heart of *King Lear* than Johnson's recognition that the play is 'good' and yet about evil, as though this were a contest not only between aesthetic and moral criteria but, more than that, between the claims of power and the claims of justice. *King Lear*, says Johnson, is a 'just' representation of the want of justice. Its author, like some unjust god, has 'suffered' Cordelia to suffer, to die 'in a just cause'. This is precisely the way in which the play pulls itself apart, even in its very language:

> Blow, winds, and crack your cheeks! rage! blow!
> You cataracts and hurricanoes, spout
> Till you have drench'd our steeples, drown'd the cocks!
> You sulph'rous and thought-executing fires,
> Vaunt-couriers of oak-cleaving thunderbolts,
> Singe my white head! (III, ii, 1–5)

This is at once Lear opposing the storm and the storm itself speaking through him, as though even in opposition the two powers were also self-destructively one. Out-storming the storm in the very tempest of his own mind, Lear also uses the storm as a power against himself in his own head. The result is a simultaneous microcosmic implosion. And the whole play is like that: as Lear faces the storm, so Shakespeare confronts the chaos of unjust suffering and in each case the force begins to take over the mind which grasps it. *'Thought-executing* fires' are a precise image of this tragic process even in Shakespeare's own mind: for the fire of energy simultaneously *carries out* the preconceived thought and *burns* that thought *up* even so in the white heat of writing without blotting. It was this simultaneous creative destruction that must have seemed to Johnson almost madness itself in the face of an even madder order in the universe. It was like Johnson *seeing* Gloucester's *blinding*, 'an act too horrible to be endured in dramatic exhibition': a human faculty subjected to the very spectacle which turns our power against itself, makes us want to close our eyes. In the same way, our very capacity to say: 'This is the worst' means that it is not. Johnson is used to good-and-bad news, is used to the idea that one's strengths are also one's weaknesses, one's weaknesses also one's strengths. But what is so unbearable for him is that Shakespeare makes this a tragic rather than a modifying thought: 'the worst is not so long as we can say this is the worst' is no sooner a comfort than it becomes a threat, and such thoughts may destroy the person capable of conceiving them. 'O let me not be mad, not mad, sweet heaven.' Gloucester's heart is torn apart in the mixed grief and joy of regaining Edgar: there is implosion rather than in-betweenness.

Johnson does not use many words to describe *King Lear*. But so deep in him is the memory of all the play stands for that when he writes: 'Shakespeare has suffered the virtue of Cordelia to perish in a just cause', the word 'suffered' (meaning first of all, of course, 'allowed'), comes from something in him deeper than even anger at what Shakespeare has done, in his unsympathetic sufferance of suffering. It comes from the play itself, using language quite as bitter as Johnson's 'suffered': 'O! our lives' sweetness,/That we the pain of death would hourly die/Rather than die at once!' (V, iii, 183–5): 'sweetness' is sourly relative; only the more awful taste of instant death could force us to swallow the description. At all levels the play tears itself apart, even in bringing Lear and Gloucester together on the heath, and kills what is killing it too. For all Edgar's strictures against suicide, the play is a form of what Johnson most feared and abhorred – self-destructiveness as a response to a sense of cosmic injustice.

This should help us to see why *King Lear* is a deep and threatening memory behind Johnson's angry criticism of Soame Jenyns's account of justice in the universe. We do not want to watch Gloucester on Dover Cliff as Johnson says Soame Jenyns's higher beings watch us: 'and good sport it is to see a man tumble with an epilepsy, and revive and tumble again'. For if we see it from Johnson's point of view, we do not say with the moralist, as Soame Jenyns would:

> Stand up man; it cannot hurte thee if thou beest a man.[66]

For Johnson knew, surely, that Shakespeare was almost right to reply thus with Gloucester:

> The King is mad: how stiff is my vile sense
> That I stand up, and have ingenious feeling
> Of my huge sorrows! Better I were distract:
> So should my thoughts be sever'd from my griefs,
> And woes by wrong imaginations lose
> The knowledge of themselves. (IV, vi, 276–81)

That is to say, as Johnson himself might well have: Stand up, man; it will hurt you the more if you are a man; but stand up. Here is the force of thoughts *not* being severed from griefs, for here to know oneself is not to stand above oneself by that knowledge but to be all the more recommittedly bound to oneself, in all the additional effort of sanity. But what Shakespeare then does with that realistic non-transcendence which Johnson must so much have admired, is finally the thing for which Johnson never forgives him: he smashes Gloucester and Lear, most of all through Cordelia. All that, for nothing.

In a way Johnson's response to the play is not fundamentally different from Lear's within it. If the world is like this, its madness will drive us mad–if only to show that world to itself through ourselves. If Johnson had accepted the vision of *King Lear*, he would have had to regard the heavens at the level of justice as Lear regarded his daughters at the level of gratitude. For it is the perception of ingratitude, the human form of injustice in the feelings, that drives Lear mad, and it was madness that Johnson feared most of all. 'No man can live only for others,' wrote Johnson, 'unless he can persuade others to live only for him', and that 'unless' is the option that will not be given and cannot be enforced.[67] What Johnson knows human beings need at that moment when 'unless' gives way as a saving possibility is the assurance of a just God, a Maker distinct from the world He has made.[68] Again, Johnson's *Review* of Soame Jenyns makes clear what is at stake in his own reading of *Lear*:

> no man can be obliged by nature to prefer ultimately the happiness of others to his own. Therefore, to the instructions of infinite wisdom it was necessary that infinite power should add penal sanctions. That every man to whom those instructions shall be imparted may know, that he can never ultimately injure himself by benefiting others, or ultimately by injuring others benefit himself; but that however the lot of the good and bad may be huddled together in the seeming confusion of our present state, the time shall undoubtedly come, when the most virtuous will be the most happy.[69]

Hume would ask why nature was not made to oblige or allow men to be unselfish in the first place. But to Johnson it is the essence of God that the Revealed should be separate from the Natural which It has created, even while the Natural, by analogy from the deficiencies of its own situation, prays to and for the completion of Revelation. Yet Johnson will eschew as evil temptation what Soame Jenyns virtually asserts: that that is why the deficiencies are put there, to reveal God. For Johnson's ordinary world cries out for a distinct and just God, because if indeed the whole scheme of the world seems to call for a higher corrective and tragically receives no response, that way madness lies. Yet Shakespeare's promised end in *King Lear* is precisely not that ultimate time when the most virtuous will be the most happy, when 'pleasure and virtue will be perfectly consistent';[70] rather, it is the finality of the death of Cordelia:

> ...No, no, no life!
> Why should a dog, a horse, a rat, have life,
> And thou no breath at all? Thou'lt come no more
> Never, never, never, never, never! (V, iii, 304–7)

Nowhere is Johnson closer to the play's own spirit than when he pays it the tribute of his hatred, pain and fear. It reveals the very nature of his incarnation of religion deeply within his ordinary self that whenever he is driven explicitly to the question of Belief, he becomes personal and releases his feelings:

> And if my sensations could add anything to the general suffrage, I might relate that I was many years ago so shocked by Cordelia's death that I know not whether I ever endured to read again the last scenes of the play till I undertook to revise them as an editor.[71]

It is not merely that sanity, like editorship, is a strategy Johnson uses to protect himself from anguish; sanity is, rather, for him finally rooted in a belief that anguish is not – but justice is – the ultimate reality. This is the only risk he can make which remains compatible with ordinary living – the risk of so deep a commitment to the meaning of sanity; for compatibility is always, in Johnson's ordinary faith, the barely visible test of a religion that can be lived out. But it *is* a risk and a commitment, that thus can give madness a possible status as not only a nervous threat but a personal human judgement to end all judgement. It is both awesome and ordinary that Johnson, at his level, staked his sanity on God and the nature of God's justice, at the highest level, without knowing either.

*

'I know not whether I ever endured to read again the last scenes of the play.' But over the body of Cordelia, Lear cries: 'Look there, look there!' Was Johnson always looking away from the big thing?

Once again encouraged by a novel, I take a final imaginative liberty to see what is the good of Johnson. The scene is as follows. A university lecturer, Edwin Fisher, is taking a tutorial, but even as he is teaching, he is waiting to go back to the hospital where his young son is desperately ill after what has at first seemed no more than a bad chill. Meanwhile the three young students in the class fall into powerfully felt, yet nugatory, disagreement before their lecturer's eyes:

> The flurry of words, the spilling of text-book jargon, the spattering of non-supporting circumstance, even the clenched fists and the raised voices made no impact. It is true he spoke ... but in reality he concentrated, was concentrated, on a sentence his wife had 'phoned him at one-thirty. 'There's no hope. He'll die in a few hours.'

By the time the father arrives at the hospital, the little boy has been dead for half an hour. He is met by his wife. 'Can I see him?' he asks the nurse:

> The sister scraped the curtain along, ushered them forward, lined up with them in the part-darkened space. The child lay straight, in a white gown, his fair hair brushed neatly flat, his small lips pursed tight, taut as if he were about to resist some demand; death, perhaps. The little face had about it a kind of obstinacy, or purpose, that should have been accompanied by a puckering of the brows, but the forehead was clear, unmarked, perfect. One could see. Look there, look there.
>
> Fisher was most aware of the other two with him, their stiffness, their silence. In their ordeal, they did not want anything from him, nor observe him, only waited on the little face, the carefully combed and parted hair, knowing nothing but that small beauty, the delicacy of nostril. Then the father wished, suddenly, without reason, that he could see the hands.[72]

Quietly the last words of that first paragraph remind us that this is *King Lear* translated into terms that Wordsworth provides in 'The Ruined Cottage':

> ... 'Tis a common tale,
> An ordinary sorrow of man's life,
> A tale of silent suffering, hardly clothed
> In bodily form. –

Yet Fisher has to see, and touch, that bodily form.

Who dares to speak after *King Lear* has ended? Yet terrible as is

King Lear, Edwin Fisher, university lecturer, father, will not be thinking of it compared to the reality of this 'ordinary sorrow of man's life'. What speaks to that?

For what it is worth, *whatever* that is, Johnson still does manage to speak, after all: 'We see a little, very little', 'every individual is a very little being... a little more than nothing is as much as can be expected'; 'I do not regret the hours which I have laid out on these little compositions.'[73] It is not that Johnson rises to speak loftily, not knowing what it is to be utterly diminished by the sight and fact of death:

> The most indifferent or negligent spectator can indeed scarcely retire without heaviness of heart, from a view of the last scenes of the tragedy of life, in which he finds those who, in the former parts of the drama, were distinguished by opposition of conduct, contrariety of designs, and dissimilitude of personal qualities, all involved in one common distress, and all struggling with affliction which they cannot hope to overcome. (*The Rambler*, 69)

The sentence, pulling 'distinguished' back down to 'common', closes up in that final clause the verbs of life – 'struggling', 'they hope to overcome' – and clears them away within the condition of 'affliction' itself: 'The little face had about it a kind of obstinacy, or purpose, that should have been accompanied by a puckering of the brows, but the forehead was clear... One could see.'

But he who is more than an indifferent spectator of the tragedy of life has most of all to see what 'Thou'lt come no more' really means and feels like:

> The loss of a friend upon whom the heart was fixed, to whom every wish and endeavour tended, is a state of dreary desolation in which the mind looks abroad impatient of itself, and finds nothing but emptiness and horror. The blameless life, the artless tenderness, the pious simplicity, the modest resignation, the patient sickness, and the quiet death, are remembered only to add value to the loss, to aggravate regret for what cannot be amended, to deepen sorrow for what cannot be recalled.
>
> These are the calamities by which Providence gradually disengages us from the love of life. Other evils fortitude may expect, or hope may mitigate; but irreparable privation leaves nothing to exercise resolution or flatter expectation. The dead cannot return, and nothing is left us here but languishment and grief. (*The Idler*, 41)

All those words and sentences are themselves 'only to add value to the loss' – that is to say, are raised only to support with the dignity of human care their fall into 'finds nothing', 'leaves nothing', 'nothing is left'. 'Never, never, never, never, never!' – the words of a 'life stripped of those ornaments which make it glitter on the stage, and exposed in its natural meanness, impotence and nakedness'.[74] The thing itself, 'nothing'. For sorrow there is no remedy:

> it requires what it cannot hope, that the laws of the universe should be repealed; that the dead should return, or the past should be recalled. . . . Sorrow is properly that state of mind in which our desires are fixed upon the past, without looking forward to the future, an incessant wish that something were otherwise than it has been, a tormenting and harassing want of some enjoyment or possession which we have lost, and which no endeavours can possibly regain. (*The Rambler*, 47)

The binding of words in Johnson is a creativity that often feels more like imprisonment within 'the laws of the universe': 'want . . . lost . . . no . . . possibly regain'. On the other side of the formal discipline of the sentencing we can hear a sort of private, shrieked telegraphese between heart and brain, brain and heart. The 'incessant' wish – the wish that is always, always, the same now – is that something were 'otherwise' – different, always different. There is just the same conscious self-defeatingness, resulting from the different centres of being, in that deadlock by which sorrow still 'requires' what even so it knows, to its sorrow, it cannot 'hope'. These are not mere words, or rather these mere words are as imaginative of the feelings of the desperately bereaved as is any novel. Yet to praise the creative poetry of this language would be to invite from its own maker precisely the *King Lear* protest that he himself makes in response to Soame Jenyns's claim that poverty at least saves the poor from the subtler mental pains of the more physically comfortable:

> this happiness is like that of a malefactor who ceases to feel the cords that bind him when the pincers are tearing his flesh.[75]

Johnson does not write of sorrow: 'it requires what it cannot *have*', like any knowing-better moralist; sorrow already *knows* that, which is why it *is* sorrowful; he writes: 'it requires what it cannot *hope*', a double loss, and the fine binding of the sentence in no way compensates for the inner tearing.

'The dead cannot return, and nothing is left us here.' If Johnson stops there and does not go on, what could he expect the bereaved to do? Reluctant writer as he is, he knows his vicarious responsibility, and best exercises it through his capacity to revive the heart by turning back from last to first again:

> Against the instillations of this frigid opiate, the heart should be secured by all the considerations which once concurred to kindle the ardour of enterprize. Whatever motive first incited action, has still greater force to stimulate perseverance ... To faint or loiter, when only the last efforts are required, is to steer the ship through tempests, and abandon it to the winds in sight of land; it is to break the ground and scatter the seed, and at last to neglect the harvest. (*The Rambler,* 207)

When Conrad's sea-captain in 'Typhoon' tells the young mate, 'Keep facing it', steer the ship through tempests, that is also what Conrad is simultaneously telling himself, pen-pushing. Edwin Fisher, looking at his dead boy, wants to put his finger into the small palm as he did on the child's first day of life. 'All the considerations which once concurred to kindle the ardour.'

But now Johnson, this land-bound Conrad, has to speak to such as Fisher. What 'last efforts' are possible when the last seems already to have occurred and nothing seems left? The 'harvest' is ruined. Wordsworth's Michael leaves the sheepfold on which he had worked with his son unfinished, when the son has died – 'and 'tis believed by all':

> That many and many a day he thither went,
> And never lifted up a single stone. ('Michael', 456–7)

Never, never, never, never, never! And Fisher's lost child is only a little boy.

Johnson had no children. On hearing of the sudden death of Mr Thrale's only son, he said to Boswell that it was one of the most dreadful things that had happened in his time, but: 'Sir, it is affectation to pretend to feel the distress of others, as much as they do themselves. It is equally so, as if one should pretend to feel as much pain while a friend's leg is cutting off, as he does.' Yet he also added: 'I would have gone to the extremity of the earth to have preserved this boy.'[76]

But Johnson, this complex man, had had a wife. She seems to have ended as a drunkard, and the apparently strained marriage to the fat older woman who would have him seems to have been laughable to outsiders. But the loss of his wife was terrible to Johnson, as is clear from the sermon he wrote for her funeral – which a friend refused to deliver on the grounds that it too lavishly, or gullibly, praised the deceased[77]:

> The whole mind becomes a gloomy vacuity, without any image or form of pleasure, a chaos of confused wishes, directed to no particular end, or to that which, while we wish, we cannot hope to obtain; for the dead will not revive; those whom God has called away from the present state of existence, can be seen no more in it; we must go to them; but they cannot return to us.[78]

Tetty Johnson died on 17 March 1752. She had told her husband as *The Rambler* began to appear, 'I thought very well of you before; but I did not imagine you could have written any thing equal to this', and we can see how much of this sermon is taken from *The Rambler*, 47, 28 August 1750.[79] What is added in the extract above, however, is the biblical quotation from 2 Samuel 23:

> Then said his servants unto him, What thing is this that thou hast done? thou didst fast and weep for the child, while it was alive; but when the child was dead, thou didst rise and eat bread.
>
> And he said, While the child was yet alive, I fasted and wept: for I said, Who can tell whether GOD will be gracious to me, that the child may live?
>
> But now he is dead, wherefore should I fast? can I bring him back again? I shall go to him, but he shall not return to me.

There is, as Arnold knew, something Hebraic in Johnson. Two of his most powerful sermons begin with quotations from Job which precisely show the two sides of himself that a man such as Job had to fight to reconcile: 'Man that is born of woman, is of few days, and full of trouble'; 'In all this Job sinned not, nor charged God foolishly.'[80] What is marvellous is that it is precisely a Job-like dogged plainness in Johnson that greets the Messiah bearing the transcendent promise of life after death:

> it is plain, that the constitution of mankind is such, that abstruse and intellectual truths can be taught no otherwise than by positive assertion, supported by some sensible evidence.[81]

'Sensible evidence', in the spirit that Baxter required it, is what Christ was. God willing to be, in every sense, *sensible* at our level.

Johnson is a Christian most of all in wanting to offer a translated equivalent to that sensible demonstration, at the lower level of his own moral essays. 'Whatever motive first incited action, has still greater force to stimulate perseverance.' That was his motive: to incarnate Christianity again within the daily world as a fully human way of being, and that is why formal sermons did not sufficiently fulfil his purpose. For he had also to try to remember for us what at the prime basis of an ordinary life made it still sustainable in the face of losses and pains. To carry on with and complete an essay, itself struggling to sustain the endurance of trouble, was for Johnson a representative and analogical act: managing down here on the page what has to be done off it, what God might want above it. 'Nothing is left us here but languishment and grief' seems conclusively to end the paragraph from *The Idler*, 41; but another begins:

> Yet such is the course of nature, that whoever lives long must outlive those whom he loves and honours. Such is the condition of our present existence, that life must one time lose its associations, and every inhabitant of the earth must walk downward to the grave alone and unregarded, without any partner of his joy or grief, without any interested witness of his misfortunes or success.

'Must... must... must...' At such moments Johnson's eye is so intently on the *facts* as actually to release, as no more or less than natural, those *feelings* which he does have but believes he should not primarily regard. What Johnson has done is turn from one particular death, the death of someone close and dear, to Death itself as the basic fact for all mortals. It must always seem like double vision for him to see both the simplicity of the few, general elemental facts that generate the scheme of things and the particular complexities that emerge out of them as precariously diverse compounds. 'It has been discovered by Sir Isaac Newton', notes Johnson in *The Adventurer*, 95, 'that the distinct and primogenial colours are only seven; but every eye can witness, that from various mixtures in various proportions, infinite diversifications of tints may be produced.' There is, science suggests, a natural economy, using the few basics again and again in almost infinite transmutations. That is how Johnson, so particular a generalizer, also tries to work, in writing from his store of basic, general elements: that is what makes him always the same yet always flexible. Life and lives, Death and deaths. But the question remains: What happens to the feelings, those natural indicators of commitment to one particular life, while he is directing all attention to the general facts, the basic condition?

> life must one time lose its associations, and every inhabitant of

the earth must walk downward to the grave alone and unregarded, without any partner of his joy or grief.

Johnson's move here is from a life losing friends to a life losing itself in even greater loneliness. It is not a logical so much as a chronological transition; for the mind itself, whatever its subtleties, will be overcome by time and death. But the effect that this move has upon the feelings – the very things he seems to be subsuming in looking at the primogenial facts that pre-empt them – is tremendous. For what is happening in these few paragraphs from a no more than typical essay is this: the sorrow of mourning, with which we started and which seemed to be the finish, is confronted with a sudden widening of loss and loneliness that turns the mourner's depressively emotive identification with the condition of the deceased into an imaginative but factual sharing of it, in the future and alone:

> every inhabitant of the earth must walk downward to the grave alone and unregarded, without any partner of his joy or grief . . .

Sorrow becomes fear. You have lost your partner, you would have been a partner to him or her still if you could; but you too will die, like the one you mourn, not only missing someone in particular, as now, but anyone at all. The same elements have been transmuted into a new compound – and then into another. For the fear is itself also converted to pity – sorrow over the bereaved becomes fear for oneself becomes pity for the race ('every inhabitant'), all together alone finally. It is as though the feelings about death were as much a part of our mortal nature as is death itself. Moreover, that which I fear alone, I also feel sorry that anyone *should* fear alone, on account of the nature we all so separately share. By writing Johnson gives us the chance to see what our self-pity, either in mourning or in fear of death, can elementally stand for *outside* those individual selves wherein it is trapped precisely by loss or lack of external partners. To see us all trying to understand our condition even from inside it also makes us feel sorry inside for each other. But Johnson's last move is still to keep the transmuted feeling *inside* ourselves, because finally, in place of self-pity, the pity we would exercise for others like ourselves is retained within as a life-force to do for the species in yourself what you cannot do for it otherwise. If you feel sorry for others like yourself, feel sorry for yourself in a way that transmutes the earlier self-pity into a caring for your own life, the life in you, precisely because another life has been recently lost to you.

To see the elements combining and recombining in this way, to see something higher come out of something lower and still be committed back into sustaining what is lower, is to know something very deep about what passes for ordinary sympathy in Johnson:

> The highest flights of the soul soar not beyond the clouds and vapours of the earth; the greatest attainments are very imperfect; and he who is most advanced in excellence was once in a lower state, and in that lower state was yet worthy of love and reverence.[82]

To move between higher and lower states, as here, has an analogy with turning back to first motives in order to carry on to the end; and both, at their different levels, work on the same pattern as that which seems to make up the general blueprint for the whole scheme of things: the few simple basics allowing complex combinations to be raised out of them.

> Such is the general heap out of which every man is to cull his own condition: for, as the chemists tell us, that all bodies are resolvable into the same elements, and that the boundless variety of things arises from the different proportions of very few ingredients; so a few pains, and a few pleasures are all the materials of human life, and of these the proportions are partly allotted by providence, and partly left to the arrangement of reason and of choice. (*The Rambler*, 68)

No one moves about within human limitations more marvellously than Johnson, making one thing serve for another within the tight yet flexible organization of himself, like a microcosm.

Yet although he could morally convert self-pity into fear and fear into sympathy, he always knew, through his self-distrust, that the fear would keep coming back, along with the selfishness and the languishing depression. On the day of his mother's funeral he makes a prayer to God: 'Forgive me whatever I have done unkindly to my Mother, and whatever I have omitted to do kindly. Make me remember her good precepts, and good example . . . I am sorrowful, O Lord, let not my sorrow be without fruit.' 'Remember her good precepts': when Johnson had talked to Mrs Thrale of his mother, he had remembered that she had only offered him 'general rules', saying he should learn 'behaviour', should learn (somehow) 'to behave'. It was cant, said Johnson; I told her 'she ought to tell me what to do, and what to avoid'. For that was what that far more specific generalizer, the Rambler, was to try to do. Even as a verbally adroit child he had turned his mother's calling him a puppy into his asking

her 'if she knew what they called a puppy's mother'.[83] Boswell adds to
all this a clumsily tactful account of the last years:

> I have been told that he regretted much his not having gone to
> visit his mother for several years, previous to her death. But he
> was constantly engaged in literary labours which confined him
> to London; and though he had not the comfort of seeing his
> aged parent, he contributed liberally to her support...[84]

The comfort or the silly bitch? Just at the point, therefore, when
Johnson seems to have ended his prayer on the day of her funeral and
has actually written 'for Jesus Christ's sake. Amen.', he begins again:

> And, O Lord, grant unto me that am now about to return to the
> common comforts and business of the world such moderation
> in all enjoyments, such diligence in honest labour, and such
> purity of mind, that amidst the changes, miseries, or pleasures
> of life, I may keep my mind fixed upon thee, and improve every
> day in grace, till I shall be received into thy kingdom of eternal
> happiness.[85]

He thanks God again for his mother's good example, asks pardon for
neglecting it; thanks God for the alleviation of this sorrow; notes a
dream of his dead brother – who, it is now thought, committed
suicide and whose one surviving letter complains of harsh treatment
from Samuel. If Johnson ever thought of charging God with
injustice, he was unmanned by the thought of what God's Judgement
of him at death would be. '*Improve* every day in grace.'

But what is crucial here is that 'me that am about to *return* to the
common comforts and business of the world'. The mistakes, habits,
vices may well alike return, but still Johnson also returns for another
effort in the ordinary world that is his proper test. 'Because a man
cannot be right in all things, is he to be right in nothing?': go back,
remember what for, try again.[86] Similarly the fear will often,
doubtless, come back upon the pity when he thinks 'every inhabitant
must walk downward to the grave alone and unregarded'. *Walk*,
though you would want to run away. But when the fear oscillates with
the pity, it is much the same for Johnson as it is when sorrow 'requires
what it cannot hope'. At those moments of double vision or
alternating feelings, Johnson stares steadily and obstinately at the
fact or law or sentence and lets the feelings about it, like those of a
mere creature even to himself, go on behind his gaze. He will not
count the suffering in himself which he cannot lessen; yet on the other
hand he leaves it, even so, as no more and no less than human beneath

God. 'Though he slay me, yet will I trust in him: but I will maintain mine own ways before him.' 'Though', 'yet', 'but': like Job, Johnson makes integrity have to include the whole of himself, even though he himself (let alone God) would not want some parts to exist. That tough, wry poise of being is, like an incarnate prayer, the creature's equivocal offering of himself to his Creator. No wonder Malamud's literary man looked to Johnson in his trouble: 'He sought insights as if hunting for burning bushes on Sinai: how men hold themselves together'. I am not saying that Johnson performs miracles, but he helps the holding together.

*

V *Conclusion*

'How men hold themselves together.' To what Seneca had thought –

> Unless above himself he can
> Erect himself, how poor a thing is Man

– Montaigne said this: 'Observe here a notable speech and a profitable desire; but likewise absurd':

> For to make the handfull greater than the hand, and the embraced greater than the arms, and to hope to straddle more than our legs length, is impossible and monstrous: nor that man should mount over and above himself or humanity.[87]

Holding himself between these two, Johnson *is* one of the human non-transcendentalists, and that (since the paradox is only apparent) is part of his *religion*. 'How poor a thing,' they might have said to Bishop Butler of his faith: 'Undoubtedly it is,' he replied; but, he went on, this which is all we have is still not nothing. Like a middleman, Johnson will not let himself sink, but he will not try to get above himself. He will not make more of it all, as the idea of a more freely imaginative literature seems to urge; for this our most *implicit* of authors, in whom so many moral changes seem to go on within what remains the same self, always seems to be about to *return* his writing to the living in which it essentially takes place. Missing that hidden subtlety means taking the achievement of Johnson the Rambler to be merely one of 'character' or 'common sense' rather than 'art'. Yet to do so would be to mistake just how seriously Johnson took the act of writing, in not wanting it to be – like Soame Jenyns's comforts – an irresponsible and unselfconscious fiction. If, as Jenyns says, memory is the comfort of age, then:

I will venture to admonish him, since the chief comfort of the old is the recollection of the past, so to employ his time and his thoughts, that when the imbecility of age shall come upon him, he may be able to recreate its languors by the remembrance of hours spent, not in presumptuous decisions, but modest enquiries, not in dogmatical limitations of omnipotence, but in humble acquiescence and fervent adoration. Old age will shew him that much of the book now before us has no other use than to perplex the scrupulous, and to shake the weak, to encourage impious presumption, or stimulate idle curiosity.[88]

Johnson's criticism only does externally what he feels Jenyns's conscience should have done in the first place: make it impossible for Jenyns to live with having written such a book. If people took writing as seriously as did Johnson, their pens (and, I fear, my own) would be more *still* before matters of the highest seriousness, and it has to be said that such a demand stilled Johnson's own pen, perhaps too often. Yet *The Rambler* emerged from that tension: what Johnson the Rambler offers is a challenge to the idea of 'art' as a thing essentially autonomous and superhumanly transcendent. He starts lower than that, in order to be real. He deliberately offers something challengingly smaller and more ordinarily supportive than the genius of *King Lear* or *Paradise Lost*, though his opposition to both is honourably troubled and more than respectful. Speaking like a man restarting at his own level, he hints, in *The Adventurer*, 137, that there is room to hope 'that pigmies should conquer where heroes have been defeated'.

That challenge to literature and the sight of Johnson himself stopping short must provoke others to assert the necessity of trying to go further in their writing, for a sense of reality, than did he. For as we have seen, there is an honestly acknowledged cost in the achievement of the Rambler, a sense in Johnson himself of loss as well as gain, a feeling of something short of the realization of the fullest potential in the face of his own demands. Living with that, none the less, is Johnson's circular subject matter, as it is for many human beings feeling that they are stuck in between what they have done and what they might have done. I do not write this book to say that Johnson's is always the last word. Byron in *Don Juan* takes Johnson's dilemma, I believe, as one of his own implicit starting points and sees in its deadlocks a sanction for the casualness of apparent irresponsibility, present process and invention, for the sake of something more experimental than fixedly looking at life full on and in sum. The whole risk and point of Wordsworth's career, it seems to me, rests on the possibility that there may be some difference to be more gently intimated between 'him that gives no reason, and him that gives a reason, which by his own confession cannot be conceived' – more gently, that is, than Johnson can allow. But then, Johnson is precisely the measure and the test of the achievement of such poets' efforts. I have written this book because, I think, he remains in our memories as the Representative of the basic, the ordinary, the normal, the sane, the surviving, to fall back on and not fall.

For Johnson does remain like a memory standing for something. When he leaves, rather than either encourages or seeks to transcend, his feelings and his doubts, it is at once his strength and his weakness thus to bequeath us a bigger view of what still seems ordinary. For a reader such as Dubin, the challenge of many works and many writers lies in the question that follows upon intense appreciation: What does this mean? What does it stand for? How can I use its wisdom even to get away from the idea of use? But Johnson is the author who seems to have already anticipated those ordinary questions of the common reader, standing as he does like a middleman between writers and readers, between normal and poetic consciousness. Dubin believed that the genius of some great writers 'made their humanity more clearly apparent. One learns easily from their ordinary lives'.[89] Johnson, at any rate, mediates for us, and that too is a mark of his form of Christianity.

For just as writing is returned to the ordinary world, so too in him is religion. Martin Buber, confessing that 'in my earlier years the "religious" was for me the exception. There were hours that were taken out of the course of things', tells the story of how he came to alter his view. One day, after a morning of rare religious enthusiasm, he was visited by an unknown young man. The meeting seemed to go well, to be friendly. But not long after, the young man was dead. Buber learned that the young man had come to him in despair, looking for the word of the religious man. 'I omitted to guess the questions which he did not put ... Since then I have given up the "religious" which is nothing but the exception ... or it has give me up.'[90] There are, says Johnson, desperate moments in life when we find through sheer necessity a power within ourselves that overcomes what in cold blood would seem an insurmountable difficulty:

> But whatever pleasure may be found in the review of distresses
> when art or courage has surmounted them, few will be

persuaded to wish that they may be awakened by want or terror to the conviction of their own abilities. Every one should therefore endeavour to invigorate himself by reason and reflection, and determine to exert the latent force that nature may have reposited in him before the hour of exigence comes upon him, and compulsion shall torture him to diligence. It is below the dignity of a reasonable being to owe that strength to necessity which ought always to act at the call of choice, or to need any other motive to industry than the desire of performing his duty. (*The Rambler*, 129)

That he may raise us up he first casts down: it is that word 'dignity' that calls for the extraordinary and the religious not to be above life but in it, all the time down here. That dissolving or cancelling into life is, in Johnson's revaluation of words as things, real implicit dignity, for all the kicks to pride. Johnson is essentially concerned neither with reduction nor with transcendence, but with the analogy of incarnation. And nowhere perhaps is this shown more powerfully than in that sentence from *The Rambler*, 32, which Boswell said he could never read without feeling a physical thrill of his frame:

I think there is some reason for questioning whether the body and mind are not so proportioned, that the one can bear all which can be afflicted on the other; whether virtue cannot stand its ground as long as life, and whether a soul well principled will not be sooner separated than subdued.

Even admidst the syntax of caution and doubt, Johnson's language is like a fist clenching and embodying an inner force of belief incarnate. The thrill in Boswell's frame was like the mind and heart and soul in Johnson's, as for a moment once again the wavering Boswell could believe that the inner things were as real and as persevering, at their own level, as the outer in which they belonged. The wholeness of a Protestant, an Anglican belief in incarnation 'stands its ground', body and soul together, and religion and life in one. If we want to know in ordinary terms what is the felt meaning of a religious life on earth, what it feels like to have a belief thoroughly incarnate in life, then Johnson is one of those who holds on to it for us.

'He will be seen in this work more completely than any man who has ever yet lived.'[91] It is remarkable that Boswell's huge boast about doing for Johnson in his *Life* what Rousseau had claimed to have done for himself in his *Confessions* is so nearly just and true. Yet more than to Boswell's dedication even, to say as much is a tribute to the survival power of Johnson's abidingly physical presence as a human spirit. 'He has long outlived his century,' as Johnson himself said of Shakespeare, 'the term commonly fixed as the test of literary merit.'[92] It is indeed just, that one who believed so strongly in perseverance and survival should so have lasted. At the least, Johnson's presence reminds us that there have been ways to and from, translations between, *good sense* and *religion*, and it is that translation within the survival, as much as the survival itself, that is important for making it all possible. By putting and leaving his faith and its difficulties in ordinary terms, Johnson the Rambler leaves us a store of experience that cannot be easily discounted even by those who would think to see religion as a disposable extra. There is 'something *in* it', kept deeply and implicitly in it, that, in Johnson's hands, refuses to drop out or be given up. He will not let it let go.

Like Butler, Johnson does not translate religion into the ordinarily real so as then to make religion unnecessary. On the contrary, although life may turn out to be something other than it appears to be down here, it will not be *unless* we now treat what we have here as real. That is the two-in-one nature of Johnson's religion. It is as if we now, even in our century, could still fight at our own level for the presence of what may be above it, as soon as we begin to recognize all that secular common sense may itself be a forgotten translation of. Saul Bellow's Mr Sammler is the sort of descendent of Johnson that I have in mind for the sake of our future:

> And what is 'common' about 'the common life'? What if some genius were to do with 'common life' what Einstein did with 'matter'? Finding its energetics, uncovering its radiance. But at the present level of crude vision, agitated spirits fled from the oppressiveness of 'the common life', separating themselves from the rest of their species, from the life of their species, hoping perhaps to get away (in some peculiar sense) from the death of their species. To perform higher actions, to serve the imagination with special distinction, it seems essential to be histrionic. This, too, is a brand of madness.[93]

From this point of view, Johnson, sanely refusing to flee from the ordinary, is like a Newton awaiting an Einstein, holding open the material on which some future poet, or novelist, or discursive prose-writer will have to work again. Mr Sammler is one who might recognize how what we now call the mid-life crisis, for example, would have been called – and been – a religious crisis in other ages; though the two are at least analogous. Probably we would stress the differences between the two, these days, in a historical light; repressing the thought that there may be 'something' more general and common behind both of them, translating itself through them; repressing that thought because it is not a thought we can really think. 'Something'? But thoughts we cannot really think mark the human limits.

To some readers it will seem as if it is with Johnson as we saw with Imlac's knowledge in Chapter Four or with Anglicanism itself in Chapter Five: that he does not make much or sufficient difference after all. But if that is so, it is true only as it is for that other Representative Man, Levin, at the very end of *Anna Karenina*. What difference does Levin's religious vision make? 'This new feeling has not changed me, has not rendered me happy, nor suddenly illuminated me as I dreamt it would':

> I shall still get angry with Ivan the coachman in the same way, shall inopportunely express my thoughts; there will still be a wall between my soul's holy of holies and other people; even my wife I shall still blame for my own fears and shall repent of it. My reason will still not understand why I pray, but I shall still pray, but my life, my whole life, independently of anything that may happen to me, is every moment of it no longer meaningless as it was before, but has an unquestionable meaning of goodness with which I have the power to invest it.[94]

'Why do I yet try to resolve again?' cries Johnson in his journal, making the same mistakes and the same attempts. Yet the difference that Johnson makes, though perhaps even more chastened, is none the less essentially similar to that which Levin finds: neither Levin nor Johnson invents or discovers something, or even fundamentally changes himself or the world in which he lives. Yet the difference is all the deeper – and the more religiously intrinsic to the very nature of human creatures in the structure of the creation – for the very lack of apparent difference it makes.

At the end of his *Review* of Soame Jenyns, when Johnson stands on the verge of that unknown which is known to him only as God, his Job-like refusal of a comforter's rationalized faith is itself, at the human limits, truly religious. For as he draws back from explanation, Johnson simultaneously pushes agnosticism back into a silent, ancient acknowledgement of its own hidden faith. And he ends as though Jenyns's inadequacy reminded him finally only of his own at a different level:

A system has been raised, which is so ready to fall to pieces of itself, that no great praise can be derived from its destruction. To object is always easy, and it has been well observed by a late writer, that *the hand which cannot build a hovel, may demolish a temple.*[95]

The power to reject, Johnson knew in his balance, is also too often the other side of the inability to find. The temple of belief may rock in that silence. But he does not demolish the temple, along with Soame Jenyns's hovel, and steadingly warns against doing so. For the short, packed essays that make up *The Rambler* are actually his building bricks. In Imlac's words:

Great works are performed, not by strength, but perseverance: yonder palace was raised by single stones, yet you see its height and spaciousness.[96]

That is what we have been looking at: the raising of a temple of faith and a palace of wisdom within an ordinary shelter called *The Rambler*.

Endnotes

Chapter One

1. *Johnsonian Miscellanies*, ed. G.B. Hill, 2 vols (Oxford, 1897), vol. 2, p. 247 (Miss Reynolds's Recollections of Dr Johnson). In writing this book I have found help in Iain McGilchrist, *Against Criticism* (London, 1982) and John Wain, *Samuel Johnson* (London, 1974).
2. Ibid., vol. 2, p. 216 (Anecdotes and Remarks by Bishop Percy).
3. Boswell, *Life of Johnson*, ed. R.W. Chapman, rev. J.D. Fleeman (Oxford, 1970), p. 105.
4. W. Jackson Bate, *Samuel Johnson* (London, 1978), pp. 454–5.
5. *Johnsonian Miscellanies*, vol. 2, p. 231.
6. Ibid., pp. 231, 227.
7. Sir Joshua Reynolds, *Discourses on Art*, ed. R.R. Wark (New Haven and London, 1975), pp. 98, 102.
8. Boswell, op. cit., p. 1312.
9. Reynolds, op. cit., p. 94; Johnson, *The Rambler*, 137.
10. Johnson, *Lives of the Poets*, 2 vols, World's Classics (Oxford, 1972), vol. 2, p. 31.
11. Ibid., p. 464.
12. Reynolds, op. cit., p. 104.
13. Ibid., pp. 124, 127, 83. I am indebted to T.R. Langley.
14. Ibid., p. 134; cf. Johnson, *Preface to Shakespeare:* 'The pleasures of sudden wonder are soon exhausted, and the mind can only repose on the stability of truth.'
15. Boswell, op. cit., p. 321.
16. *Lives of the Poets,* vol. 1, p. 14.
17. Ibid., pp. 323–4.
18. Reynolds, op. cit., p. 83.
19. See my *Memory and Writing* (Liverpool, 1983), pp. 54–69.
20. Boswell, op. cit., pp. 447–8.
21. Ibid., p. 1098.
22. *Lives of the Poets,* vol. 2, p. 464.
23. Boswell, op. cit. p. 295.

24. Bate, op. cit., pp. 243–4.
25. *Johnsonian Miscellanies,* vol. 2, p. 223.
26. Boswell, op. cit., p. 188.
27. Hester Lynch Piozzi, *Anecdotes of Samuel Johnson* (with William Shaw, *Memoirs of Dr Johnson),* ed. A. Sherbo (Oxford, 1974), p. 89.
28. Doris Lessing, *The Sirian Experiments* (London, 1981), pp. 241–2.
29. Sir John Hawkins, *The Life of Samuel Johnson LLD,* ed. Bertram H. Davis (London, 1962), p. 257.
30. Boswell, op. cit., p. 1159.
31. Johnson, *Sermons,* ed. J.H. Hagstrum and J. Gray (Yale, 1978), pp. 86–7.
32. Piozzi, op. cit., p. 106.
33. Boswell, op. cit., p. 1357.
34. Johnson, *Diaries, Prayers and Annals,* ed. E.L. McAdam, Jr with D. and M. Hyde (Yale, 1958), p. 152.
35. *Sermons,* pp. 86, 166.
36. Ibid., p. 120.
37. *Samuel Johnson,* ed. Donald Greene, The Oxford Authors (Oxford, 1984), p. 534.
38. Boswell, op. cit., p. 946.
39. Hawkins, op. cit., pp. 172–3.
40. *Sermons,* p. 297.
41. Boswell, op. cit., p. 281.
42. *Johnsonian Miscellanies,* vol. 2, pp. 393, 113.
43. Boswell, op. cit., p. 1151.

Chapter Two

1. *Johnson: The Critical Heritage,* ed. J.T. Boulton (London, 1971), pp. 444–5; Boswell, *Life of Johnson,* p. 400.
2. Hester Lynch Piozzi, *Anecdotes of Samuel Johnson,* p. 109.
3. Ibid., pp. 96–7.
4. Ibid., p. 11.
5. Boswell, *Life of Johnson,* p. 1294.
6. Havelock Ellis, *Selected Essays* (London, 1940), p. 75.
7. *Johnson: The Critical Heritage,* p. 76.
8. Ford Madox Ford, *Parade's End* (Harmondsworth, Middlesex, 1982), pp. 151, 761.
9. Piozzi, op. cit., p. 156.
10. Ibid., pp. 55, 27.
11. Ibid., p. 84.
12. *Diaries, Prayers and Annals,* p. 338; Boswell, *Life of Johnson,* pp. 1190–1.
13. *Johnson: The Critical Heritage,* pp. 87.
14. Ellis, op. cit., pp. 76–7.
15. Ford Madox Ford, op. cit., p. 45.

16. Boswell, *The Journal of a Tour to the Hebrides* (reprinted with Johnson, *A Journey to the Western Islands*) (Harmondsworth, Middlesex, 1984), p. 283.

17. Ford Madox Ford, op. cit., p. 18.

18. Piozzi, op. cit., pp. 92–3.

19. Boswell, *Life of Johnson,* p. 176.

20. Ibid., p. 45.

21. Jane Austen, *Persuasion* (Harmondsworth, Middlesex, 1979), p. 58 (ch. IV).

22. Piozzi, op. cit., p. 93.

23. Boswell, *Life of Johnson,* p. 1048.

24. Ibid., pp. 1277–8.

25. Piozzi, op. cit., p. 134.

26. Boswell, *The Journal of a Tour to the Hebrides,* p. 349.

27. *The Rambler,* 155.

28. Boswell, *Life of Johnson,* p. 173.

29. Adam Smith, *The Theory of Moral Sentiments,* ed. D.D. Raphael and A.L. MacFie (Oxford, 1976), pp. 22, 27; see also pp. 47–8.

30. Boswell, *Life of Johnson,* p. 670.

31. Ibid., p. 857; see also p. 870.

32. William B. Todd, Cowper's Commentary on the *Life of Johnson, Times Literary* Supplement, 15 March 1957.

33. Boswell, *Life of Johnson,* p. 1309.

34. Jane Austen, *Mansfield Park* (Harmondsworth, Middlesex, 1971), p. 116 (ch. IX).

35. Boswell, *Life of Johnson,* p. 1038.

36. *Johnson: Selected Prose and Poetry,* ed. Mona Wilson, The Reynard Library (London, 1969), p. 105.

37. Ford Madox Ford, op. cit., p. 127.

38. Quoted in W. Jackson Bate, *Samuel Johnson,* p. 196.

39. *Johnson: Selected Prose and Poetry,* pp. 76–7.

40. *The Rambler,* 185; Piozzi, op. cit., p. 102; Boswell, *Life of Johnson,* p. 1140.

41. *Johnson: Selected Prose and Poetry,* pp. 115, 95.

42. Piozzi, op. cit, p. 141; Boswell, *Life of Johnson,* p. 972.

43. Boswell, *Life of Johnson,* p. 1235.

44. *Johnson: Selected Prose and Poetry,* pp. 71, 93.

45. Ibid., p. 116.

46. F. Nietzsche, *Beyond Good and Evil,* trans. R.J. Hollingdale (Harmondsworth, Middlesex, 1973), p. 136.

47. Boswell, *Life of Johnson,* p. 1282.

48. Ibid., p. 1358.

49. W. Jackson Bate, op. cit., p. 587.

50. D.H. Lawrence, *Phoenix: the Posthumous Papers,* ed. E.D. McDonald (London, 1970), pp. 540–1.

51. *Johnson: The Critical Heritage,* p. 76.

52. Piozzi, op. cit., p. 90.
53. Sir Joshua Reynolds, *Discourses on Art,* pp. 230–1.
54. Leslie Stephen, *History of English Thought in the Eighteenth Century,* 2nd edn, 2 vols (London, 1881), vol. 1, p. 59. See also Boswell, *Life of Johnson* p. 314.
55. Hume, *A Treatise of Human Nature,* ed. E.C. Mossner (Harmondsworth, Middlesex, 1969), pp. 311–2, 316.
56. Ibid., p. 300.
57. Ibid., p. 267.
58. Ibid., pp. 316–7.
59. David Hume, *Dialogues Concerning Natural Religion,* ed. H.D. Aiken (New York, 1959), p. 31.
60. Ibid., p. 80.
61. See Hume's letter of 17 September 1739 to Hutcheson (quoted in W.R. Scott, *Frances Hutcheson* [Cambridge, 1900], p. 117): 'There are different ways of examining the mind as well as the body. One may consider it either as an anatomist or as a painter: either to discover its most secret springs and principles, or to describe the grace and beauty of its actions. I imagine it impossible to combine these two views.'
62. Boswell, *Life of Johnson,* p. 314.
63. *The Philosophical Works of David Hume,* 4 vols (Edinburgh, 1854), vol. 4, p. 543.
64. Ibid., p. 551.
65. Johnson, *Sermons,* p. 239 (Sermon 23).
66. William Tyndale, *The True Obedience of a Christian Man,* ed. Richard Lovett, Religious Tract Society, Christian Classics Series No. 5, p. 135.
67. F. Nietzsche, *Untimely Meditations,* trans. R.J. Hollingdale (Cambridge, 1983), p. 63 ('Of the uses and disadvantages of history for life').
68. *The Prose Works of William Wordsworth,* ed. W.J.B. Owen and J.W. Smyser, 3 vols (Oxford, 1974), vol. 2, p. 17.
69. Ibid., p. 16; see also my *Memory and Writing: from Wordsworth to Lawrence* for an account of Wordsworth's own back-to-frontedness.

Chapter Three

1. Johnson, *A Journey to the Western Islands,* p. 97.
2. *Boswell's London Journal,* ed. F.A. Pottle (London, 1951), pp. 78–9.
3. Ibid., p. 47.
4. See above, p. 14.
5. Boswell, *Life of Johnson,* p. 426.
6. Quoted in E.C. Mossner, *The Life of David Hume,* 2nd edn (Oxford, 1980), pp. 597–8.
7. Hester Lynch Piozzi, *Anecdotes of Samuel Johnson,* p. 143.
8. Edmund Burke, *Reflections on the Revolution in France,* ed. Conor Cruise O'Brien (Harmondsworth, Middlesex, 1978), p. 188.

9. *History of Rasselas, Prince of Abissinia,* chs xxx, iv.

10. Ibid., ch. viii.

11. Ibid., ch. iii.

12. See Thomas Nagel, *Mortal Questions* (Cambridge, 1978), particularly his chapter on 'The Absurd'; also my 'On the Strength of Limitation', *Stand Magazine,* Autumn 1983, pp. 34–45.

13. *Butler's Analogy and Sermons* (London, 1898), p. 532.

14. Ibid., p. 179.

15. Ibid., p. 398.

16. *Montaigne's Essayes,* trans. John Florio, 3 vols (London, 1980), vol. 3, pp. 253–4, 262.

17. St Augustine, *The City of God,* trans. H. Bettenson (Harmondsworth, Middlesex), p. 349.

18. Ibid., p. 564.

19. *The Rambler,* 89, 108, 63.

20. Piozzi, op. cit., p. 68.

21. Ibid., p. 111.

22. Boswell, op. cit., p. 848.

23. *The Rambler,* 2.

24. Boswell, op. cit., p. 757.

25. *Samuel Johnson,* ed. Donald Greene, Oxford Authors (Oxford, 1984), p. 327.

26. Matthew Arnold, *Essays, Religious and Mixed,* ed. R.H. Super (Michigan, 1972), p. 319.

27. Ibid., p. 174.

28. Burke, op. cit., p. 183.

29. See *The Rambler,* 176, 180, 96, for warnings against *un*just prejudice.

30. Piozzi, op. cit., p. 96.

31. *Sermons,* p. 10 (Sermon 1).

32. 1 Corinthians 7: 1–10.

33. *Rasselas,* ch. viii.

34. Ibid., ch. xxix.

Chapter Four

1. *Autobiography and Memoirs of Benjamin Robert Haydon,* ed. Tom Taylor, 2 vols (London, 1926), vol. 1, p. 81.

2. Ibid., p. 71.

3. *Lives of the Poets,* vol. 1, p. 120.

4. Ibid., p. 118. I am indebted on Milton to Dr. M. Stocker.

5. *Rasselas*, ch. xliv.

6. *Sermons,* pp. 132, 157 (Sermons 12, 14).

7. *The Collected Works of William Hazlitt,* ed. A.R. Waller and A. Glover, 12 vols (London, 1904), vol. 11, pp. 131, 128.

8. David Hume, *Dialogues Concerning Natural Religion*, p. 80.

9. David Hume, *A Treatise of Human Nature*, pp. 454–5.

10. *The Rambler*, 194, 175.

11. *The Rambler*, 184.

12. *The Rambler*, 166, 156, 158.

13. *Diaries, Prayers and Annals*, pp. 77, 81, 49.

14. *Sermons*, p. 160 (Sermon 15).

15. *Lives of the Poets*, vol. 2, p. 290.

16. Burke, *Reflections on the Revolution in France*, p. 152.

17. *Montaigne's Essayes*, vol. 3, p. 376.

18. *The Rambler*, 41.

19. Burke, op. cit., p. 285.

20. Tolstoy, *The Cossacks*, trans. Rosemary Edmonds (Harmondsworth, Middlesex, 1978), pp. 250–1 (ch. 20).

21. *Johnson: The Critical Heritage*, p. 149.

22. Daniel Defoe, *The Life and Adventures of Robinson Crusoe*, ed. A. Ross (Harmondsworth, Middlesex, 1982), p. 149.

23. Edmund Gibson, fourth *Pastoral Letter* (London, 1739), pp. 19–20.

24. Johnson, *Journey to the Western Islands*, p. 136.

25. *Butler's Analogy and Sermons*, p. 499; Burke, op. cit., p. 135.

26. *Robinson Crusoe*, p. 124.

27. Ibid., p. 100.

28. Ibid., p. 182.

29. *Journey to the Western Islands*, p. 61.

30. Jeremy Taylor, *Works*, 3 vols (London, 1862), vol. 1, p. 496: *Holy Living*, ch. IV, sect. IX ('Of Repentance').

31. Sir John Hawkins, *The Life of Samuel Johnson LLD*, p. 156.

32. *Rasselas*, chs XXX, XXIX.

Chapter Five

1. Boswell, *Life of Johnson*, p. 999.

2. *Lives of the Poets*, vol. 2, pp. 364–5.

3. Gilbert Burnet, *A Discourse of the Pastoral Care* (London, 1692), pp. 149–50.

4. *Johnsonian Miscellanies*, vol. 2, pp. 53–4.

5. *Lives of the Poets*, vol. 2, p. 366.

6. Boswell, op. cit., p. 222.

7. *Samuel Johnson*, ed. D. Greene, pp. 62, 68, 66.

8. *Johnson: Selected Prose and Poetry*, pp. 67, 118 (emphasis added), 71.

9. *Robinson Crusoe*, p. 126.

10. Hawkins, *The Life of Samuel Johnson LLD*, p. 70.

11. Boswell, op. cit., p. 1296.

12. *Samuel Johnson*, pp. 28–9 (translation by John Wain).

13. R.H. Hutton, *Contemporary Thought and Thinkers*, 2 vols (London, 1894), vol. 1, pp. 164–5.

14. *Biographia Literaria,* ch. xv.

15. Doris Lessing, *Shikasta* (London, 1979), pp. 75, 78.

16. *Autobiography and Memoirs of Benjamin Robert Haydon,* vol. 1, p. 126.

17. John Foster, *Essays in a Series of Letters,* 11th edn (London, 1835), p. 123.

18. Keats, *Letters,* 17–27 September 1819.

19. Ibid., 21–27 December 1817.

20. Matthew Arnold, *Selected Prose,* ed. P.J. Keating (Harmondsworth, Middlesex, 1982), p. 276 (*Culture and Anarchy,* ch. 4). On Arnold and his use of the word 'practical' in relation to the pressure of Utilitarianism, see my *Memory and Writing,* pp. 135, 162–3.

21. Keats, *Letters,* 22 November 1817.

22. Ibid., 27 October 1818.

23. Ibid., 13 March 1818.

24. *Rasselas,* chs IV, XIII.

25. See Alasdair MacIntyre, *After Virtue* (London, 1981), pp. 38–42, cf. pp. 160–3.

26. *The Rambler,* 87.

27. Saul Bellow, *Mr Sammler's Planet* (London, 1970), pp. 3, 63, 236.

28. Boswell, op. cit., p. 1073.

29. Ibid., p. 539.

30. Matthew 10: 16, quoted Jeremy Taylor, *Works,* 10 vols (London, 1861), vol. 4, pp. 570 ff.

31. Mark 14: 6.

32. Taylor, op. cit., p. 575.

33. Ibid., p. 574.

34. Johnson, *Sermons,* p. 80 (Sermon 7).

35. *The Rambler,* 43, 67.

36. Isaac Watts, *Logick,* 9th edn (London, 1761), p. 118.

37. Havelock Ellis, *Selected Essays,* p. 228.

38. *The Rambler,* 185, 29, 137.

39. *Samuel Johnson,* ed. D. Greene, p. 534.

40. *Lives of the Poets,* vol. 1, pp. 202–3.

41. Ibid., p. 203.

42. Boswell, op. cit., p. 1094.

43. South, *Sermons,* 2 vols (London, 1865), vol. 1, pp. 120–1; for Johnson on South, see also Boswell, op. cit., p. 913.

44. Boswell, op. cit., p. 425.

45. South, op. cit., vol. 1, p. 137.

46. Ibid., p. 126.

47. Ibid., p. 123.

48. *Boswell in Holland 1763–1764,* ed. F.A. Pottle (Yale, 1952), p. 350.

49. Ibid., pp. 351–2 (emphasis added).

50. Ibid., p. 339.

51. *In Search of a Wife,* ed. F. Brady and F.A. Pottle (Yale, 1957), p. 167.

52. Wesley, *Journal,* September 1739.
53. Boswell, op. cit., p. 385.
54. South, op. cit., vol. 1, pp. 131, 133.
55. Ibid., p. 129.
56. Burke, *Reflections on the Revolution in France,* p. 120.
57. Boswell, op. cit., pp. 361–2.
58. Ibid., p. 1293.
59. Johnson, *Diaries,* p. 152.
60. Ecclesiastes 9: 10.
61. On Law as an 'over-match' for Johnson, see Boswell, op. cit., pp. 51–2; William Law, *A Serious Call to a Devout and Holy Life* (Glasgow, 1827), pp. 130, 134, 152 (chs IV–V).
62. *The Rambler,* 71.
63. Law, op. cit., p. 167 (ch. VI).
64. George Bull (1634–1710), quoted in *Anglicanism,* ed. P.E. More and F.L. Cross (London, 1935), p. 312.
65. Boswell, op. cit., p. 156.
66. Ibid., p. 750.
67. Foster, op. cit., pp. 96–7.
68. Quoted in J.M. Creed and J.S. Boys Smith (eds), *Religious Thought in the Eighteenth Century* (Cambridge, 1934), p. 271.
69. Boswell, op. cit., p. 1399.
70. *The Autobiography of Richard Baxter,* abridged by J.M. Lloyd Thomas, ed. N.H. Keeble (London, 1974), p. XXIV.
71. Ibid., pp. 105, 113, 106, 115.
72. Boswell, op. cit., p. 1248.
73. *Anglicanism,* p. 325.
74. Boswell, op. cit., p. 982.
75. Ibid., p. 961.
76. Hester Lynch Piozzi, *Anecdotes of Samuel Johnson,* p. 112.
77. *Lives of the Poets,* vol. 1, p. 2.
78. Johnson, *Journey to the Western Islands,* p. 141.
79. Marcus Aurelius, *Meditations,* trans. M. Staniforth (Harmondsworth, Middlesex, 1974), p. 129.
80. Law, op. cit., p. 211.
81. Ibid., pp. 419, 209.
82. *Anglicanism,* p. 41.
83. South, op. cit., vol. 2, p. 90.
84. Gilbert Burnet, op. cit., p. 177.
85. Law, op. cit., pp. 204–5.
86. Boswell, *Tour to the Hebrides,* p. 190; *Life of Johnson,* p. 687.
87. Kierkegaard, *Fear and Trembling,* ed. W. Lowrie (Princeton, 1945), p. 22.
88. Quoted in John Berger, *A Fortunate Man* (London, 1976), p. 143.
89. Law, op. cit., pp. 319–21.

90. Edmund Gibson, *Pastoral Letter,* pp. 46, 52.

91. Johnson, *Sermons,* pp. 140–1 (Sermon 13).

92. Boswell, *Life of Johnson,* p. 737.

93. *The Works of William Cowper,* ed. R. Southey, 15 vols (London, 1836–7), vol. 1, pp. 142–3.

94. Ibid., p. 134.

95. Ibid., vol. 2, pp. 6–7.

96. Boswell, *Life of Johnson,* p. 49.

97. David Hume, *A Treatise of Human Nature,* p. 237.

98. Baxter, op. cit., p. 136.

99. Law, op. cit., pp. 468, 488.

100. Hawkins, op. cit., p. 275.

101. Johnson, *Diaries,* p. 43.

102. *Johnson on Johnson,* ed. John Wain (London, 1976), p. 10.

103. *Anglicanism,* p. 227.

104. Law, op. cit., p. 170.

105. Creed and Boys Smith, op. cit., pp. 268–9.

106. South, op. cit., vol. 1, p. 176.

107. Boswell, *Life of Johnson,* pp. 1189, 1275.

108. Isaac Watts, *The Improvement of the Mind* (1751) (London, 1821), p. 166.

109. South, op. cit., vol. 1, p. 132.

110. Boswell, *Life of Johnson,* p. 427.

111. Saint Augustine, *Confessions,* trans. R.S. Pine-Coffin (Harmondsworth, Middlesex, 1974), p. 80.

112. *Johnson: The Critical Heritage,* p. 88.

113. *Johnson: Selected Prose and Poetry,* p. 79.

114. *The Life and Correspondence of John Foster,* ed. J.E. Ryland (London, 1846), pp. 176–7.

115. *Review* of *A Free Inquiry, Johnson: Selected Prose and Poetry,* p. 374.

116. Johnson, *Sermons,* p. 164 (Sermon 15).

117. Johnson, *Diaries,* pp. 91–2, 133–4, 225.

118. D.H. Lawrence, *The Rainbow,* (Harmondsworth, Middlesex 1981), p. 174 (ch. 5).

119. See I.A. Richards, *Beyond* (New York and London, 1974), pp. 94–6.

120. South, op. cit., vol. 1, p. 122.

121. Johnson, *Sermons,* pp. 305, 307 (Sermon 28).

122. South, op. cit., vol. 1, p. 530.

123. Ibid.

124. Boswell, *Life of Johnson,* pp. 834–5 (emphasis added).

125. Ford Madox Ford, *Parade's End,* p. 496.

Chapter Six

1. Bernard Malamud, *Dubin's Lives* (London, 1979), pp. 317, 298–9.

2. Ibid., pp. 123–4.

3. Ibid., p. 125.

4. Ibid., p. 132.

5. Ibid., p. 158.

6. Ibid., pp. 132–3.

7. Ibid., pp. 150–1.

8. Seneca, *Letters from a Stoic,* trans. R. Campbell (Harmondsworth, Middlesex, 1976), p. 116. (Epistulae Morales ad Lucilium, LXIII).

9. Immanuel Kant, *The Metaphysical Principles of Virtue,* trans. J. Ellington (New York, 1964), p. 83.

10. Boswell, *Journal of a Tour to the Hebrides,* p. 176.

11. Stanley Middleton, *Blind Understanding* (London, 1982), pp. 74–6. This novelist's significantly entitled *Cold Gradations* appeared in 1972.

12. Montaigne, *Essayes,* vol. 3, p. 28 (Book 3, ch. II, 'Of Repentance'); cf. Charles Cotton's translation, 3 vols (London, 1913), vol. 3, p. 25.

13. *Rasselas,* ch. VI.

14. *Johnson: The Critical Heritage,* p. 89.

15. *The Autobiography of Richard Baxter,* p. 111.

16. Boswell, *Life of Johnson,* p. 948.

17. Bernard Mandeville, *The Fable of the Bees,* ed. D. Garman (London, 1934), p. 70.

18. Ibid., p. 52.

19. Ibid, p. 47.

20. Boswell, *Life of Johnson,* p. 948.

21. *Samuel Johnson,* ed. D. Greene, pp. 526–7.

22. See *The Adventurer,* 128, Bruyère and the stonecutter, for a slow demonstration of the necessity to think two thoughts rather than one.

23. *Lives of the Poets,* vol. 1, p. 14.

24. Augustine, *Confessions,* p. 128.

25. Ibid., p. 22.

26. Ibid., p. 230.

27. *Sermons,* p. 131 (Sermon 12).

28. Karl Barth, *Protestant Theology in the Nineteenth Century* (London, 1972), p. 37.

29. *Lives of the Poets,* vol. 2, p. 323.

30. Ibid.

31. *Samuel Johnson,* ed. D. Greene, p. 534.

32. Ibid., pp. 531, 523.

33. *The Rambler,* 17; *The Adventurer,* 120; *The Rambler,* 32.

34. *The Adventurer,* 120.

35. *Essay on Man,* I, 16; *The Rambler,* 32.

36. *Samuel Johnson,* ed. D. Greene, p. 536.

37. Pascal, *Pensées,* trans. A.J. Krailsheimer (Harmondsworth, Middlesex, 1972), pp. 61, 64.

38. *Samuel Johnson,* ed. D. Greene, p. 528 (emphasis added).

39. Ibid., p. 530.
40. *Johnsonian Miscellanies*, ed. G.B. Hill vol. 2, p. 254.
41. *Samuel Johnson*, ed. D. Greene, p. 527 (emphasis added).
42. See G. Wilson Knight, *Laureate of Peace* (London, 1954), pp. 49–51.
43. Ruskin, *The Stones of Venice*, vol. 1, ch. ii, paras xi-xii.
44. *Lives of the Poets*, vol. 2, p. 304.
45. *Samuel Johnson*, ed. D. Greene, p. 529.
46. *The Rambler*, 66; *The Adventurer*, 107.
47. Quoted in Stanley Cavell, *Must We Mean What We Say?* (Cambridge, 1969), p. 176.
48. *The Personal Notebooks of Thomas Hardy*, ed. R.H. Taylor (London, 1978), p. 89.
49. Joseph Butler, *The Analogy of Religion, Natural and Revealed, to the Constitution of Nature* (London, 1898), p.75.
50. Boswell, *Tour to the Hebrides*, pp. 180–1. See also one of Johnson's favourite theologians, Samuel Clarke, in dispute with Leibniz on the idea of the mind as a balance, *The Leibniz–Clarke Correspondence*, ed. H.G. Alexander (Manchester, 1956), pp. 45, 97–8.
51. Butler, op. cit., p. 310.
52. Ibid., p. 144.
53. Ibid., pp. 134–5.
54. *Samuel Johnson*, ed. D. Greene, pp. 538–40.
55. Butler, op. cit., p. 137.
56. Ibid., p. 267.
57. Ibid., p. 335.
58. *The Nichomachean Ethics*, 1139b4 (Book ii).
59. *The Adventurer*, 69.
60. Emphasis added.
61. Butler, op. cit., p. 220.
62. Hume, *Dialogues*, pp. 73–8; the fullest quotation is from p. 75.
63. Boswell, *Life of Johnson*, p. 312.
64. *Samuel Johnson*, ed. D. Greene, p. 535.
65. *Johnson on Shakespeare*, ed. A. Sherbo, 2 vols (Yale, 1968), vol. 2, p. 704.
66. Sir William Cornwallis the younger, *Essayes* (London, 1606), 'Of Adversitie'.
67. *Sermons*, p. 239 (Sermon 23).
68. See *The Leibniz–Clarke Correspondence*, especially pp. 14, 29, 39, 78, 119–20.
69. *Samuel Johnson*, ed. D. Greene, pp. 539–40.
70. Boswell, *Life of Johnson*, p. 948.
71. *Johnson on Shakespeare*, vol. 2, p. 704.
72. Stanley Middleton, *Holiday* (London, 1974), pp. 168–70.
73. *The Adventurer*, 107; *The Idler*, 88; *The Adventurer*, 137.
74. *The Rambler*, 54.
75. *Samuel Johnson*, ed. D. Greene, p. 527.

76. Boswell, *Life of Johnson,* p. 712.
77. See *Sermons,* p. 261, footnote 1; cf. Boswell, *Life of Johnson,* pp. 166–71.
78. *Sermons,* p. 267 (Sermon 25).
79. Boswell, *Life of Johnson,* p. 149.
80. Job 14: 1 chosen by Johnson as text for Sermon 15; Job 1: 22 the text for Sermon 16.
81. *Sermons,* p. 265 (Sermon 25).
82. Ibid., p. 146 (Sermon 13). For an account of the chemistry of Wordsworth's poetry in terms of an analogy with the principles, see my *Memory and Writing,* pp. 95–6.
83. Hester Lynch Piozzi, *Anecdotes of Samuel Johnson,* pp. 68–9.
84. Boswell, *Life of Johnson,* p. 240.
85. *Diaries, Prayers, and Annals,* pp. 66–7.
86. Boswell, *Life of Johnson,* p. 1038.
87. Seneca's dictum is translated by Samuel Daniel: it was taken by Wordsworth as a motto for *The Excursion;* Montaigne's retort is to be found at the end of his 'Apology for Raymond Sebond', *Essayes,* vol. 2, pp. 325–6.
88. *Samuel Johnson,* ed. D. Greene, pp. 533–4.
89. Malamud, *Dubin's Lives,* p. 79.
90. Martin Buber, *Between Man and Man* (London, 1947), pp. 13–14.
91. Boswell, *Life of Johnson,* p. 22.
92. *Samuel Johnson,* ed. D. Greene, p. 420.
93. Bellow, *Mr Sammler's Planet,* p. 147.
94. Tolstoy, *Anna Karenina,* trans. Aylmer Maude (Oxford, 1980), p. 811.
95. *Samuel Johnson,* ed. D. Greene, p. 543.
96. *Rasselas,* ch. XIII.

Index

Aristotle, 21, 109–10, 196, 278

Arnold, Matthew, 1–2, 107, 109, 113, 123–4, 126, 147, 182, 184, 187–8, 191, 193–5, 291

Augustine, 19, 112, 230, 232, 243, 253, 257–8, 263

Aurelius, Marcus, 216–7

Austen, Jane, 58–9, 68

Bacon, Francis, 10, 105

Barth, Karl, 259–60

Bate, Walter Jackson, 9, 18

Baxter, Richard, 55, 172, 212–3, 224, 253–5, 257, 291

Beckett, Samuel, 3, 249, 252

Bellow, Saul, 43, 194, 300

Blake, William, 4, 15, 51, 132, 173

Boerhaave, Dr Herman, 174–8

Boswell, James, 1, 3, 5–6, 10–11, 13, 15–17, 28, 36, 39, 42–3, 45, 47, 49–51, 53, 56–7, 60–5, 69, 73, 76, 79, 81–2, 84, 87, 92, 95, 97–104, 106, 113, 116–9, 121–3, 126, 130–1, 133, 149, 159, 161, 167, 170, 172, 179–80, 193, 195, 199–204, 208–9, 211–3, 216, 221–3, 229–30, 234, 241, 249, 262, 273–4, 290, 295, 299

Buber, Martin, 298

Bunyan, John, 172, 177, 188, 251

Burke, Edmund, 102, 124–6, 150–1, 158, 206–7

Burnet, Bishop Gilbert, 173, 218–9

Butler, Bishop Joseph, 109–10, 126, 158, 273–80, 282, 296, 300

Byron, George Gordon, Lord, 69, 96, 240–1, 297–8

Carlyle, Thomas, 64

Chambers, Catherine, 204–6

Chapone, Hester, 71, 79, 82

Chesterfield, 4th Earl of, 21

Coleridge, Samuel Taylor, 108, 180, 186–7

Congreve, William, 11–12, 14

Conrad, Joseph, 290

Cowley, Abraham, 14, 68, 74, 100, 214

Cowper, William, 65–9, 74, 185, 221–5, 252, 271–2

Defoe, Daniel, 155–60, 176, 180

Dilke, Charles, 185–6, 192

Dodd, William, 239–42

Donne, John, 14, 100

Dryden, John, 14, 16, 19, 25

Eliot, George, 9, 75, 78, 171, 242

Eliot, T.S., 1, 124

Ellis, Havelock, 45–7, 51–2, 55, 71, 79, 82

Ford, Ford Madox, 47, 52–4, 60, 65, 67, 71, 75, 92, 242

Foster, John, 182–9, 192–4, 196, 211, 228, 233

Gibson, Bishop Edmund, 156–7, 220–1

Goethe, J.W. von, 220

Goldsmith, Oliver, 17, 208, 211, 213, 234

Gray, Thomas, 12, 14, 16, 19–20

Hamilton, Gerald, 1

Hardy, Thomas, 93, 190, 251–2, 273

Hawkins, Sir John, 24–6, 32, 37–8, 41–3, 164, 177, 225

Haydon, Benjamin Robert, 130–2, 145–6, 149, 183

Hazlitt, William, 51, 138, 231, 252

Heller, Joseph, 56

Hooker, Richard, 218

Howard, Lord of Effingham, 183–4, 189

Hume, David, 83–92, 94, 101, 116, 134, 138, 140, 142–3, 145, 223–4, 248, 272–3, 281, 285

Hutton, R.H., 179–80, 189–90, 208, 211

James, William, 273

Jenyns, Soame, 199, 236–7, 255–6, 260–1, 263–4, 266, 269–70, 272–3, 276, 279, 281–2, 284–5, 289, 296–7, 301–2

Job, 261, 263–4, 291, 295–6, 301

Johnson, Samuel, *Works*:

The Adventurer, 20, 56, 119, 181, 222, 256–7, 262, 269–71, 279–80, 288, 292, 297

Diaries, Prayers, and Annals, 30, 49, 146, 209, 226, 237–9, 294–5, 301

Dictionary of the English Language, 26, 121–3, 166, 168, 177

The Idler, 21, 167, 190, 233–5, 288, 292–3, 295

Journey to the Western Islands, 97, 157, 159, 216

Life of Dr Herman Boerhaave, 174–6

Life of Savage, 70–3, 75, 118, 176, 182, 200, 231–2

Lives of the Poets, 11, 14, 26, 29, 74, 100, 147–8, 172–5, 194, 200, 214, 256, 260, 267–8

'On the Death of Dr Robert Levet', 16, 18

The Rambler:

Number 2, 32, 82, 117; **4**, 105–6, 145; **6**, 68–9; **7**, 255–6; **8**, 114, 166, 268–70; **11**, 79; **13**, 91, 144, 214–5; **14**, 26–7, 31, 238; **17**, 262, 265; **19**, 102, 106–7, 116; **24**, 7, 105; **25**, 92, 136–7, 139, 145, 172, 178, 257; **28**, 148; **29**, 50, 55, 140–1, 143, 199, 210, 216; **31**, 154; **32**, 76, 111–2, 141, 262–3, 277–9, 299; **38**, 62, 110, 210; **41**, 114–5, 150; **43**, 197; **44**, 60, 217, 219, 228; **47**, 141–2, 155, 245–6, 289, 291; **50**, 73; **54**, 289; **59**, 79–80, 125–6; **63**, 88–9, 113, 133, 180, 235; **64**, 73–4; **66**, 22, 269; **67**, 103–4, 197; **68**, 294; **69**, 46, 288; **71**, 209; **72**, 58; **74**, 50, 70; **79**, 38; **81**, 34–41; **87**, 7, 192, 244–5; **89**, 54, 63, 113; **104**, 190; **108**, 108, 110, 113; **110**, 256; **111**, 138–40; **112**, 161–2; **125**, 125; **127**, 141, 275; **129**, 133, 192–3, 196, 298–9; **134**, 89, 117–9, 129, 131; **135**, 88, 108; **137**, 70, 105–6, 199; **146**, 93–4; **148**, 123; **150**, 146–7; **151**, 55; **154**, 64; **156**, 146; **158**, 146; **160**, 80; **164**, 10; **165**, 193; **166**, 146; **168**, 136; **169**, 87–8; **172**, 143–4; **173**, 215; **175**, 136, 144, 227; **178**, 63; **179**, 13; **180**, 7, 105, 112; **184**, 143–4, 168; **185**, 72, 143, 199, 270; **188**, 57; **189**, 231–2; **194**, 144; **196**, 55, 77–81, 90, 97, 129, 133, 138; **201**, 214; **203**, 152, 207, 230; **207**, 43, 66–7, 232–3, 290–2; **208**, 120–1, 198

Rasselas, 26–7, 56, 91, 102–3, 107,

113, 129, 132ff., 137, 148–71, 174,
181, 188–9, 191, 210–1, 224, 226–7,
232, 241, 247–9, 252, 262, 265, 275,
277, 301–2
*Review of Soame Jenyns's 'A Free
Enquiry into the Nature and Origin
of Evil'*, 34, 86, 199–200, 236, 242,
255, 260–1, 263–6, 269, 276, 279,
281–2, 284–5, 289, 296–7, 301–2
Sermons, 27–8, 32–3, 37, 91,
126–8, 137, 147, 197, 221, 232,
236–7, 239–42, 259, 285, 290–1,
294
The Vanity of Human Wishes, 9,
11, 24, 26, 40, 190–1, 215, 244,
246–7, 252

Kant, Immanuel, 248–9
Keats, John, 2–3, 130, 179–80, 182,
185–196, 200, 207, 211, 215, 233–4
Kierkegaard, Soren, 192, 219, 272

Law, William, 209–10, 217–20, 225,
227, 238–40
Lawrence, D.H., 4–5, 77, 152, 163–4,
237–8, 243–4, 280
Leavis, F.R., 124
Lessing, Doris, 23–4, 27, 181–2
Levet, Dr Robert, 16–9, 21, 24–5, 42,
50–1, 59–60, 71, 92, 174, 251
Locke, John, 138, 172, 174
Luther, Martin, 180, 183, 198–9, 204

Malamud, Bernard, 4–9, 23, 32,
243–8, 250, 252–3, 257, 296, 298
Mandeville, Bernard, 145, 254, 276
Middleton, Stanley, 249–53, 287–8,
290
Mill, John Stuart, 184–6
Milton, John, 15, 47, 74, 104–5, 124,
134–5, 180, 202, 265, 297
Montaigne, Michel de, 4, 111, 150,
243, 252, 296
Mudford, William, 46, 51, 59, 77,
83, 155, 252

Murphy, Arthur, 3

Newton, Sir Isaac, 110, 181, 260,
292, 300
Nietzsche, Friedrich, 75, 92

Pascal, Blaise, 263–4
Percy, Bishop T., 6
Peyton, V.J., 18–9
Pope, Alexander, 147–8, 193–4, 251,
258–70, 272, 278–80, 282

Reid, Thomas, 84, 142
Reynolds, Frances, 5–6, 265–6
Reynolds, Sir Joshua, 6–8, 10–15,
20–1, 42, 61, 64, 71, 77, 81–3, 89,
102
Richardson, Samuel, 204
Rossetti, Dante Gabriel, 54
Rousseau, J.J., 60, 203, 299
Ruskin, John, 267

Sanderson, Bishop Robert, 107, 109,
116, 118, 120, 226
Savage, Richard, 70–3, 75, 118, 176,
178, 181–2, 231–2
Scaliger, J., 121, 178
Seneca, 248, 296
Shakespeare, William, 4, 26, 154,
180, 188, 280–9, 297, 300
Skelton, Philip, 173
Smart, Christopher, 41–2, 136
Smith, Adam, 61–2, 80, 133
Socrates, 3, 105, 188, 210
South, Robert, 19, 201–2, 205–6,
218, 220, 228–9, 238–41
Stephen, Leslie, 83
Swift, Jonathan, 145, 158, 215, 243–4

Taylor, Jeremy, 55, 162, 177, 196–7,
242
Thrale, Mrs Hester Lynch, 21, 29,
38, 44–5, 48–51, 56–7, 59, 61, 73,
80, 83, 101, 114, 125, 214, 226, 238,
268, 294

Tolstoy, Leo, 9, 25, 122–3, 151–2, 301

Tyndale, William, 91

Warburton, Bishop William, 211, 227–8

Watts, Isaac, 172–5, 177, 179, 181, 183, 194, 197, 219, 229

Wesley, John, 204

Wordsworth, William, 46, 79, 94–6, 131, 169–70, 287, 290, 298

Yeats, W.B., 4, 75